The Tobacco
Industry in
Transition

The Tobacco Industry in Transition

Policies for the 1980s

Edited by
William R. Finger
North Carolina Center for
Public Policy Research, Inc.

LexingtonBooks
D.C. Heath and Company
Lexington, Massachusetts
Toronto

Library of Congress Cataloging in Publication Data

Main entry under title:
  The Tobacco industry in transition.

  1. Tobacco manufacture and trade—Government policy—United States.
2. Tobacco manufacture and trade—United States. I. Finger, William R.
II. North Carolina Center for Public Policy Research.
HD9136.T6   338.1'7371'0973   81-47064
 ISBN 0-669-04552-7   AACR2

Published simultaneously in Canada

Printed in the United States of America

International Standard Book Number: 0-669-04552-7

Library of Congress Catalog Card Number: 81-47064

Contents

Acknowledgments

The North Carolina Center for Public Policy Research, Inc., is an independent nonprofit research and educational institution. The Center's purpose is to enrich the dialogue between private citizens and public officials, and its goal is the stimulation of greater interest in public affairs and a better understanding of the profound impact government has each day on the life of every citizen. A nonpartisan organization, the Center was formed in 1977 by a diverse group of private citizens "for the purposes of gathering, analyzing, and disseminating information concerning North Carolina's institutions of government." The North Carolina Center for Public Policy Research, Inc., gratefully acknowledges the assistance of the Ford Foundation, which provided funds to support this study.

The entire staff of the Center participated in the preparation of this book. Those who helped with conceptualization and research included Susan Presti and Robie Patterson. Robert Dalton of the staff wrote two of the chapters in part I. Sallye Branch Teater copyedited the entire manuscript and assisted with production. Jenny Shaia typed each article and disposed of many technical problems. The project was administered by the Center's former executive director, Fred Harwell, who contributed editorially and otherwise from conceptualization through final proofs, by the current executive director, G. Rankin Coble.

In addition, Jennifer Miller, a writer and editor, provided invaluable assistance on many chapter drafts, particularly in parts I (agriculture) and IV (corporate); and Harriet Kestenbaum, a public-health planner, reviewed the voluminous literature on tobacco and health in helping to design part V (health).

Numerous people with busy schedules were willing to take time out to provide information and answer questions. Drs. Charles Pugh and Dale Hoover, both agricultural economists at North Carolina State University in Raleigh, were especially helpful on questions about the tobacco-farm program. Drs. Verner Grise and Robert Miller, both agricultural economists at the U.S. Department of Agriculture, provided the latest data and information on changes in the farm program.

This book would not have been possible, of course, without the cooperation of all of the contributors. Many of them juggled crowded schedules and long-standing commitments to participate in this project. Without their many sacrifices, we could not have produced this book.

Introduction

William R. Finger

Many scientists now feel that some 55 million American smokers voluntarily endanger their health every day by smoking: that it is the nation's number one preventable cause of disease and death. At the same time, policymakers who understand American agriculture believe that the 600,000 American families dependent on income from tobacco crops are the single remaining example of the Jeffersonian ideal, a small-farm yeomanry. How can a government respond to the needs of the tens of millions of Americans dependent on the tobacco economy, nurture a dying small-farm heritage, and build a society based on good health all at the same time?

"I've argued that the two [the smoking issue and the farm issue] should be separated," former U.S. Secretary of Agriculture Robert Bergland says in an interview for this book. "We should take the smoking issue head on and decide if we are going to ban smoking and restrict its use. Then we have to consider not only the production of tobacco, but its importation. We haven't done anything about the health issue if we simply eliminate price supports."

In 1964, the U.S. surgeon general concluded in his landmark report, *Smoking and Health*, that cigarettes are a health hazard. This finding prompted a series of studies and the implementation of many regulations that have permanently altered the western world's perception of tobacco. The most dramatic indication of smoker concern is the rising popularity of low-tar (15 milligrams or less) brands. As late as 1970, low-tar brands commanded less than 5 percent of the market; today their share is almost 50 percent. Besides spending hundreds of millions of dollars to introduce low-tar brands on the domestic market, American manufacturers (as well as leaf-exporting concerns) are investing more and more of their resources and energy in developing the third-world market, where few regulations on tobacco have been implemented and where per capita consumption is increasing.

While health concerns have refocused consumer demand and corporate futures in the last fifteen years, agriculture and international trade changes have transformed the tobacco industry from production through distribution. As late as 1972, only 2 percent of the flue-cured crop was harvested mechanically; today the figure is approaching 50 percent. Mechanization, combined with such changes in the federal farm program as permitting the lease and transfer of allotments, has precipitated a labor displacement of irreversible proportions, a decrease in the number of tobacco farms, and an increase in the size of farms that remain.

Meanwhile, tobacco production is expanding in Africa, Asia, and Latin America and now poses a serious threat to continued American dominance of the world leaf market. Total American exports increased during the last twenty years, but the U.S. share of the world's flue-cured market dropped from 61 percent in 1960 to 27 percent in 1979. Moreover, foreign tobaccos now match American quality but still cost only one-third to one-half as much. In 1980, for example, the federal price-support level on leaf Grade B4F, the "hub" tobacco for British buyers (the United Kingdom is one of America's largest markets), was $1.61 per pound. But British companies could buy a comparable grade from Brazil for $.68 per pound. While leaf buyers worry about the high American price, tobacco farmers, like all American farmers, are beset by inflation, energy costs, fertilizer prices, and a minimum wage on labor. They want the federal price support raised, not lowered.

Transitions have reshaped the tobacco economy swiftly—and in confusing, interrelated ways. *The Tobacco Industry in Transition: Policies for the 1980s* addresses the central policy areas of today's tobacco world: agriculture, farmer alternatives, leaf marketing, manufacturing, health, and politics. Within each of these six parts, a group of experts assesses the transitions. Some report as objective researchers. Others write with passion and prejudice. On controversial subjects—such as health—we include chapters that express opposing positions. For example, both the attorney for The Tobacco Institute and the attorney for the Federal Employees for Non-Smokers' Rights contribute a chapter analyzing the legal implications of the tobacco-health issue.

Although no book could substantially analyze all tobacco issues of importance, this study is designed to provide an interdisciplinary understanding of tobacco in the 1980s. It has been prepared for use by a wide range of readers—from scholars and experts to those with only a casual or limited interest in the subject.

Will future legislation alter the federal tobacco program? Negotiations in Congress might be influenced by issues that range from the sales volume of Seven-Up and Miller beer (both owned by Philip Morris) to the stability of the government of Zimbabwe (a major competitor of the United States on the international leaf market). Will cigarette manufacturing companies be required to label their product "addictive?" The outcome weighs on diverse findings, from prospective studies (which are just beginning) on low-tar smokers to corporate plans to diversify out of tobacco. *The Tobacco Industry in Transition: Policies for the 1980s* attempts to provide a resource for understanding such questions, and perhaps for formulating some answers.

Part I
The Tobacco Program and the Farmer

Title p 1

2 : # Early Efforts to Control the Market—And Why They Failed

Anthony J. Badger

By the 1930s, bright flue-cured tobacco was the most important type of tobacco in the United States. Used on its own in Britain, or blended with other types of leaf in the United States, this tobacco had a distinctive taste that made it an essential ingredient of cigarettes, for which demand had increased dramatically in the years after World War I. By 1929, bright flue-cured crops accounted for more than half the nation's tobacco acreage.

It had first been grown in the Piedmont areas of Virginia and North Carolina, where the poor soil starved the leaf and gave it its characteristic yellow color. In the 1890s, production spread to the coastal plain of eastern North Carolina and South Carolina, and then in the 1920s to Georgia and Florida. By the 1930s, however, the center of flue-cured production was firmly established in North Carolina, which was the largest producer of any type of tobacco and produced almost 70 percent of the flue-cured crop. The eastern counties of the state were the heart of the tobacco region. This "New Belt," centered on a triangle of market towns—Wilson, Kinston, and Greenville—alone grew 40 percent of the crop.

Heavy labor requirements and the high investment costs per acre, because of the need for fertilizer and curing barns, dictated the size of land holdings in the tobacco belt. Since the value of the crop per acre was also relatively high, especially compared with cotton, flue-cured tobacco was always cultivated in small land units, often of no more than four or five acres. A survey in 1928 in the New Belt of North Carolina showed an average cultivated acreage on 230 farms of 27 acres, of which 7 were planted with tobacco. A survey in Pitt County a year later found acreages of tobacco varying from 2 to 25 acres with slightly less than half of the farms cultivating between 4 and 6 acres of tobacco. In the Old and Middle Belts of the North Carolina Piedmont, such small farms were usually operated by their owners, but in the Eastern Belt, they were usually run by tenants. The customary arrangement in the east was for the sharecropper to receive half the proceeds of the crop when the landlord provided the land, seed, wood, and fertilizer, although sometimes, as in the farms surveyed in 1928, the cropper also shared the cost of the fertilizer.

Excerpted from *Prosperity Road: The New Deal, Tobacco, and North Carolina* by Anthony J. Badger. Copyright 1980, The University of North Carolina Press. Reprinted by permission.

3

Most growers were in debt from January onward and they needed year-long credit; their crop was their only security. Banks were reluctant to make such short-term credit available to farmers, who instead had to turn to one of the standard institutions of the tobacco belt—the time merchant. He provided the growers with general supplies and fertilizer on credit, charging not only high rates of interest but also credit prices, which were considerably higher than prices for cash payment. This meant that for the growers the cost of short-term credit, which the banks would not provide, was extremely high. An Agricultural Experiment Station survey in North Carolina in 1926 suggested that merchants charged an interest rate of 25 percent per year, while fertilizer manufacturers charged an even higher rate. About three-quarters of the tenants' annual cash gain had to be used to pay back cash advances from landlords and settle accounts with the time merchants. In the 1930s, banks came to play an increasingly important role in rural areas, but it was still a secondary one.

Tobacco was a perishable crop that needed redrying and storing within weeks of being cured. Since no individual grower could afford the cost of this redrying, he had to sell his tobacco immediately. He could not hold it off the market if the market was glutted and prices were low. Even a decision to hold off the crop until later in the same marketing season could damage the leaf and lower prices. There was a further stimulus to ignore the market situation and sell at once: tobacco was often the grower's only source of income, and he needed ready cash to pay off the debts incurred during the year.

The prices the buyers paid for the tobacco depended on how they graded it. These grades were secret and they varied from company to company, so that the farmer had no means of knowing whether he was receiving a fair price for his tobacco, nor could he concentrate on growing the most profitable grades. Government grading was one solution to this problem. The Warehouse Act of 1916 authorized the government to provide an inspection service that would grade the farmer's tobacco according to standard grades. It was not until 1929 that such a service was introduced, and then it only covered four markets, one of which (Smithfield) was in North Carolina. In the next three years, it was extended to seven more markets in the state, but even then only six million pounds were graded. There was little incentive for the growers to use the service, since they had to pay for it themselves and there was no guarantee that the buyers would take any notice of the government grades.[1]

The buyers' position was strengthened further by the fact that the manufacturers carried stocks-in-hand of two to three years' supply of tobacco, in order to achieve the right blending of grades and the correct aging of the leaf. If in any year the crop was short, pushing prices up, the manufacturers did not have to buy at that higher price. They could afford to wait. The grower could not.

The growers' lack of knowledge and their inability to hold their crops off the markets were compounded by the absence of competition among the buyers. Many in the tobacco belts would have echoed the complaint of Richard Russell, governor of Georgia, that the price paid for tobacco in his state in 1932 forced him to conclude that the manufacturers of tobacco "have as complete a monopoly and combine as this Nation has ever seen." Josephus Daniels, whose hostility to the manufacturers dated back to the days of Duke and the Tobacco Trust, was equally emphatic the following year, in explaining the situation to the Secretary of Agriculture. The tobacco industry, he said, which had once been a monopoly, was still dominated by three American and two foreign companies. "Of course, they do not meet and fix the prices. That would invite prosecution. But there has been no real competition for many years. They have been paying the farmers just enough to encourage them to grow the weed."[2]

Given the structure of the manufacturing industry, therefore, the growers could not look to competition between buyers of their leaf for their salvation from a weak marketing position. The marketing of tobacco by the auction warehouse system also handicapped them. It did have some advantages: it provided a rapid method of sales that gave the growers cash payments immediately, but it also was expensive, duplicated buyers, and was open to abuse. There was no doubt, for example, that the speed of selling led to many mistakes by the buyers. The buyers could average these mistakes out during the day, but for the grower, whose entire year's income might be dependent on the price he received, one such mistake could be disastrous. The grower could reject a bid, turn his tag, and offer his tobacco again, but he had to pay another auction fee with no guarantee of securing a better price.

All these weaknesses—the perishability of the crop, the lack of competition in leaf purchases, the secret grades, the companies' carry-over, and the auction warehouse system—contributed to the growers' basic inability to adjust supply to demand. There was always a chronic tendency to overproduce. Good prices always led to increased production the following year. When prices fell, however, there was not necessarily an equivalent cutback in production. Growers tended to respond to a fall in prices with either a slight curtailment of acreage or even an increase of production in an effort to minimize total losses. The situation was aggravated when poor cotton prices tempted growers to turn to tobacco. Occasionally, as in 1920 and 1931, prices went so low that growers could not finance a large crop the following year. There were then drastic reductions, but they were only temporary. Production leaped again the following year.

Because so much of the flue-cured crop was exported, growers were also affected by the difficulties facing American exports after 1929. The virtual cessation of U.S. lending abroad and the existence of high Republican tariffs made it difficult for foreign nations to buy American goods. Tobacco exports held up better than most. The importance of tobacco as a source of government revenue in Britain, the resistance of consumers to changes in taste or decreases in tobacco use, and the failure of governments to stimulate domestic or colonial tobacco production meant that the United States was still the only source of substantial tobacco exports. Flue-cured exports nevertheless fell by almost 40 percent between 1930 and 1932.[3]

The perennial tendency to overproduce, the decline in foreign markets, and the onset of a general depression had catastrophic consequences for both the tobacco growers and North Carolina between 1929 and 1932. Prices of flue-cured tobacco, which never fell below 20 cents a pound from 1920 to 1927, dropped to 17.3 cents in 1928, to 12 cents in 1930, and plummeted to 8.4 cents in 1931. There was a slight rise to 11.6 cents in 1932, but this was offset by a sharp reduction in acreage that year. Total receipts for the 1932 crop were one-third of those for 1930. In North Carolina, growers of flue-cured tobacco received only $34.9 million in 1932 compared with $93.4 million in 1928. Growers in the east felt the pinch dramatically. Growers in the New Belt who had collected more than $91 million in 1919 and $50 million as recently as 1928 now had to survive on $18.9 million.

Conditions Were Worse than War

Between the end of the war and the advent of the New Deal there were four main efforts to improve the marketing position of the tobacco growers and to raise leaf prices: the Tri-State Growers' Cooperative, Governor O. Max Gardner's "Live at Home" campaign, an attempt to form a cooperative under the auspices of the Federal Farm Board, and an attempt to restrict production by interstate agreement or individual state legislation.

The Tri-State Growers' Cooperative, organized in 1921 and 1922, believed that the tobacco growers could,

> through cooperative action, attain monopoly power and thus set the prices for their leaf. Growers handed their tobacco over to the cooperative, which then graded, redried, and stored the tobacco, which would be pooled according to grade. The crop would then be held off the market until a favorable time for selling. The growers received an advance payment when they delivered their crop and a second payment, depending on the amount of tobacco they held in any particular grade, when the tobacco was sold. They were bound to hand over their entire crop to the cooperative for five years under a legally enforceable "ironclad" contract.

The Tri-State had to contend with the opposition of powerful vested interests—the manufacturers and the warehousemen. There was no evidence of a concerted effort by the manufacturers to break the cooperative, but there was a determined opposition from the warehousemen. Because of the sympathies of the time merchants with the warehousemen and the links between bankers and the tobacco trade, the growers' creditors pressed them to desert the cooperative. Also, the warehousemen could pay the grower immediately, whereas the cooperative fully paid the grower only after all the tobacco had been sold. The cooperative could do little to keep the growers from leaving in the face of these incentives, and by 1926, the Tri-State had failed.

But the basic reason for the cooperative's failure lay in its faulty premise: the belief that farmers could achieve monopoly power through cooperatives and thereby set prices. Such monopoly power was impossible to attain by voluntary methods. Since the cooperative never controlled enough of the crop, it could never guarantee its members a higher price for their tobacco than nonmembers received. In the final analysis, the Tri-State Growers' Cooperative failed because in the mid-1920s North Carolina tobacco growers were not yet ready to cooperate.[4]

Governor O. Max Gardner, a successful textile manufacturer, came into office in 1929 with the intention of capitalizing on a prosperous economy to promote reform. Agricultural economists, extension-service workers, and farm editors had, for many years, preached the virtues of crop diversification to North Carolina farmers, but with little success. The relative absence of livestock and poultry on the state's farms meant that the state had to rely heavily on other states for food and feed. In 1930, for example, the state produced less than one-sixth of the beef and one-third of the milk and butter that it needed.

To lessen this dependence on the staple cash crops, Gardner launched a "Live at Home" promotional and propaganda campaign. This had two main aims. First, by growing their own food and feed, North Carolina farmers would have a subsistence living standard that was not dependent on the fortunes of cotton and tobacco; this program would also cut down the $250 million spent each year on foodstuffs and feed outside the state. Second, it was hoped that if the acreage devoted to staple crops were reduced, the price of cotton and tobacco would rise. What started out in prosperity as a campaign for the more efficient use of resources soon became a desperate struggle to alleviate the effects of depression.[5]

The campaign succeeded to some extent. Gardner recalled that "the power of suggestion is tremendous . . . by appeal and persistent persuasion we persuaded the cotton farmers in North Carolina to reduce their acreage planted in cotton 535,000 acres." One extension official calculated that the acreage in the state in cash crops had been reduced in 1930 and 1931 by 575,342 acres, whereas the acreage in food and feed crops had been increased by 837,841 acres. There can be no calculation of how many farmers may have been able to survive the depression by producing their own food.[6]

Unfortunately, this had no significant effect on the prices of cotton and tobacco. Gardner's wider aim of increasing prices by reducing acreage through diversification could only fail. Subsistence farming appealed only to the small farmer. It had no appeal to the large commercial farmer and landlord, and if they did not cut back their production there could be no effective acreage reduction.

Gardner's remedies for the plight of the tobacco grower were essentially long-term. The low prices in the years before 1933 led the growers to search for more immediate solutions to their problems.

A more promising approach seemed to be the formation of another growers' marketing cooperative, this time under the auspices of the Federal Farm Board, which had been established by the Agricultural Marketing Act of 1929. The board's vice-chairman visited Raleigh in September 1929 and repeatedly stressed that the government could not provide financial assistance to the growers until they organized themselves into a cooperative. His suggestion was enthusiastically endorsed by Clarence Poe, a champion and organizer of the old cooperative and editor of the state's leading farm journal, the *Progressive Farmer*, and Josephus Daniels, editor of the most important newspaper in the tobacco belt, the Raleigh *News and Observer*. It seemed that with the help of the government the growers could avoid the mistakes of the old Tri-State cooperative. Government supervision would control the activities of the organization's officials, while government loans would enable the cooperative to make a much more attractive advance payment to the grower when he delivered his crop. The ironclad contract would be discarded. Growers could simply withdraw from the cooperative at a stated time each year. Also, the cooperative would involve a more compact state- or belt-wide area, rather than attempt to straddle the whole flue-cured area.[7]

In December 1929, five hundred tobacco growers met at North Carolina State College in Raleigh and elected an organization committee to set up the new cooperative. During the next two crops, however, very little was achieved. In February 1931, the organization still had no headquarters and had yet to start a sign-up campaign for the 1931 crop. In May, the organization committee had to admit that it had only managed to sign up 15 million pounds and that the cooperative would not be in operation in 1931. Despite expressions of confidence that enough growers would be signed up by 1932, the failure in May 1931 marked the end of the attempts to form a cooperative under the Federal Farm Board.[8]

The reasons for failure were not hard to find. Despite the conciliatory efforts of supporters of the cooperative, warehousemen and time merchants were still basically hostile. As they controlled the growers' sources of credit, this opposition was bound to be influential. More important was the residual distrust felt by the growers themselves for cooperative marketing.

They were simply unwilling to submit to the discipline involved in belonging to a cooperative. The Craven County agent explained that although the new contract was much more liberal than the old ironclad contract, farmers in his district were refusing to sign it because it was still too much like the old one.

After the Tri-State failed, promoters of a new cooperative faced an insoluble dilemma. A new cooperative could not work and show that it could bring improved prices unless it controlled a large portion of the crop; but growers were unwilling to sign over that large portion of the crop until they could see that cooperative marketing worked.[9]

More and more tobacco spokesmen—from Congressman Lindsay Warren to grower leaders to warehousemen—began to realize that cooperative marketing itself would not bring about higher leaf prices. Whatever else might happen, there would have to be a substantial cutback in production.[10] Such an emphasis on acreage reduction was bound to attract warehousemen, who saw it as a way to deflect the growers' interest in cooperatives while raising tobacco prices—which was in everybody's interest. In March 1931, a committee of leading warehousemen planned a propaganda campaign to secure a 25 to 35 percent cutback in the 1931 crop, and Governor Gardner spoke on the radio in support of its plea. As always, such exhortations failed. As long as an individual grower could finance his crop, he would not voluntarily reduce his own acreage unless he had some guarantee that the other growers would do likewise.

At the same time, there was considerable interest in the cotton situation. In August, the Federal Farm Board had suggested that the solution to cotton overproduction was for the growers to plow under every third row of cotton. Huey Long, governor and senator-elect of Louisiana, had reacted by calling a special session of his legislature to prohibit totally the production of cotton in his state in 1932, provided that states representing three-quarters of the nation's cotton acreage passed similar legislation. Governor Gardner's response was that he would not call a special session in North Carolina to enact the Long plan, but he did suggest a conference of southern governors to formulate a uniform plan and indicated that he would follow any initiative taken by Texas, which planted half the country's cotton acreage.

It was soon clear that Governor Ross Sterling of Texas had no intention of enacting the Long moratorium, but he did call his legislature into session where it was prepared to pass legislation reducing the 1932 cotton acreage by one-third. Mass meetings of cotton growers in North Carolina now called on Gardner to call a special session to enact a similar law. In the tobacco belt, the meetings also called for North Carolina to take the lead and legislate to reduce tobacco acreage. The tobacco growers were supported by Josephus Daniels of the *News and Observer*, who constantly called on

Gardner to follow Texas as far as cotton was concerned, but to take the initiative for tobacco, since North Carolina was far and away the largest producer. There was, the *News and Observer* said, "only one thing that will secure better prices for tobacco—drastic reduction by law." The government could justify such unprecedented action, since the tobacco growers faced a "condition not a theory," an emergency in which "conditions [were] worse than war."[11]

Gardner was concerned by the agitation, but he refused to be moved by the mass meetings, the growers' delegations, and the editorials. His one concession was to call a conference of the governors of the flue-cured tobacco states, but he used that meeting at Charlotte merely to state his total opposition to the idea of trying to reduce tobacco acreage by law. He was also able to show that the governors of Virginia, South Carolina, and Georgia had no intention of acting, even if North Carolina had been prepared to take the lead.[12]

Gardner refused to act, because he was opposed in principle to the idea of compulsory crop control and also because he doubted its practicality. Government had no right to interfere in such areas. He would not "foster any law which will take a North Carolina farmer and make him a criminal to grow anything on his land which he wants to grow." There was no knowing where the power of the state would stop if it controlled planting, for he regarded it as "fundamental that if the State passes a law making it a crime to work that the next and inevitable thing that the State will have to do is to feed the man it denies the right to work." Senator Josiah W. Bailey, who would be in a position of some power when Congress eventually considered crop-control legislation, agreed: "If we control production, we must also control consumption: we might as well go to the logical conclusion and control the number of children in a family." The Constitution had to protect "the unfettered right to sow, to plant, to work, to produce, and to enjoy the fruits of one's labor." Gardner's successor, J.C. Blucher Ehringhaus, who was to play a crucial role in the tobacco growers' later fight for better prices, at the time also agreed with the governor that there was "no power in the State itself to control production."[13]

In addition to having constitutional objections, Gardner could not see how control legislation could be enforced. He remembered the attempts to control production in Kentucky, which had resulted in "night riders, murders, feuds, and total destruction of orderly government." He was satisfied that any crop-control law "would require a million dollars for enforcement and result in infinitely worse conditions than we are now trying to prevent."[14]

Acreage Reduction Accepted

There was very little the tobacco growers could do about their plight, for two main conclusions had emerged from the failure of their various efforts before 1933 to improve their marketing position. First, there had to be some form of acreage reduction to adjust supply to demand; second, voluntary and local efforts to achieve this had failed. The attempts at cooperative marketing had failed, because not enough growers could be persuaded to join; the cooperatives could never control enough of the crop to raise prices. Therefore, by 1933 growers and their leaders appeared to have accepted the theoretical necessity of acreage reduction.

All efforts to translate this principle into practice had failed. Appeals to growers to reduce their tobacco acreage had not succeeded because no grower would voluntarily cut back his own crop unless he had some assurance that other growers would reduce as well. Although the tobacco growers did reduce their acreage in 1932 when they could not finance a larger crop, they still produced as large an acreage as ever in 1933. Compulsory acreage reduction by law clearly did not appeal to key politicians. In any case, no one knew how to enforce such legislation without either vigilante activity or massive and impractical police action. Such action by one state would have been simply quixotic if other states had taken the opportunity to expand their own production. Interstate agreement to avoid this had been impossible to secure. In 1933, therefore, the tobacco growers of North Carolina had little option but to wait for Washington and Franklin Roosevelt's New Deal.

Notes

1. Nannie May Tilley, *The Bright-Tobacco Industry, 1860-1929* (Chapel Hill, N.C.: University of North Carolina Press, 1948); North Carolina Department of Agriculture, *Biennial Report* (Raleigh, N.C., 1930-1932).

2. R. Russell to Josephus Daniels, 29 Oct. 1931, Josephus Daniels Papers; Josephus Daniels to H.A. Wallace, 6 Sept. 1933, Sec. Ag. Papers.

3. Joseph W. Hines, "Development and Trends in the Export Trade in Flue-Cured Tobacco, 1939-50, with Special Emphasis on the Role of the United States Government in Grants and Loans," unpublished Master's Thesis (Chapel Hill, N.C.: University of North Carolina, 1951), pp. 60-70.

4. The most comprehensive examination of the cooperative is John J. Scanlon and J.M. Tinley, *Business Analysis of the Tobacco Growers' Cooperative Association* (Washington, D.C.: U.S. Government Printing Office, 1929); Tilley, *Bright-Tobacco Industry*, pp. 449-486, provides a colorful account of its struggles. It is unlikely that there will be a definitive analysis of the cooperative's failure until scholars have exploited the voluminous papers of the Tri-State Cooperative in the state archives in Raleigh, N.C.

5. David Leroy Corbitt, ed., *Public Papers and Letters of Oliver Max Gardner, Governor of North Carolina, 1929-33* (Raleigh, N.C.: Council of State of North Carolina, 1937), pp. 83-85, 269-274; Joseph L. Morrison,

Governor, *O. Max Gardner: A Power in North Carolina and New Deal Washington* (Chapel Hill, N.C.: University of North Carolina Press, 1971), pp. 75-76, 92. For a similar campaign in Georgia, see Michael S. Holmes, *The New Deal in Georgia, An Administrative History* (Westport, Connecticut: Greenwood Press, 1975), pp. 210-212.

  6. Morrison, *Gardner*, p. 129; *Extension Farm News*, Dec. 1932.

  7. Raleigh *News and Observer*, 8, 15 Sept. 1929.

  8. Ibid., 18 Sept., 1929, 15 Oct. 1930, 6 Feb., 13-14 April 1931; *Progressive Farmer*, 15-31 May 1931.

  9. Raleigh *News and Observer*, 30 Sept., 27 Oct. 1930.

  10. L.C. Warren to J.R. Turnage, 12 Sept. 1930, Warren Papers.

  11. Raleigh *News and Observer*, 25 Sept., 11, 22 Oct. 1931.

  12. Ibid., 13 Nov. 1931.

  13. O.M. Gardner to W. Harris, 7 Oct. 1931; J.C.B. Ehringhaus to Gardner, 19 Sept. 1931, Governor Gardner's Papers. Raleigh *News and Observer*, 2 Sept., 13 Nov. 1931.

  14. O.M. Gardner to R. Powell, 22 Sept. 1931, Governor Gardner's Papers.

2 The Federal Tobacco Program: How It Works and Alternatives for Change

Charles Pugh

Every economic sector requires periodic examination in order to fine-tune its operations, especially one that has been regulated in essentially the same manner for more than forty years. Under the Agricultural Adjustment Act (1938), as amended, the federal government restricts the supply of flue-cured and burley tobacco so as to keep the average price above the open-market level without using direct government subsidies. Although the program has been adjusted during the last four decades by legislative amendment and administrative action, its major features have remained intact.

In recent years, groups within and without the tobacco industry have been questioning the forty-year-old program more vigorously than ever before. Anti-tobacco advocates point to the apparent inconsistency of the federal government having a tobacco program as well as anti-smoking programs. Leaf exporters wonder if the program has priced American tobacco out of the international market, where comparable grades are generally much cheaper. And farmers are complaining about the high cost of leasing quota, a production cost resulting from the tobacco support structure.

The tobacco program could be changed in any of three ways:

1. A particular feature of the current program could be altered without abandoning its general approach. For example, price support levels could be changed upward or downward.
2. Options might be substituted for individual provisions of the current program to achieve the same purposes. For example, pools of surplus tobacco might be financed by loans from private sources or farmer check-off plans instead of by loans from the government.

This chapter is based primarily on "Alternatives regarding Production Controls and Price Supports for Tobacco," by Charles Pugh, the fourth in a series entitled *Tobacco Marketing Policy Alternatives* (1979). This Southern Extension Marketing Publication series was sponsored jointly by the Cooperative Extension Services of Alabama, Arkansas, Florida, Georgia, Kentucky, Louisiana, Mississippi, North Carolina, South Carolina, Oklahoma, Puerto Rico, Tennessee, Texas, and Virginia; by the Science and Education Administration Extension, U.S. Department of Agriculture; and by the Farm Foundation. This chapter also draws on "Provisions of the Tobacco Program," by Charles Pugh and Dale Hoover, *Tar Heel Economist*, October, 1979.

3. Legislative actions could abolish all features of government involvement in the tobacco program at the farm level. This would essentially involve a move to an open-market in producing and marketing tobacco.

This chapter first explains how the present tobacco program functions. It then examines the ramifications of abolishing the entire program, which provides a point of departure for estimating the effects of intermediate alternatives. Finally, it looks at possible adjustments to each of the major features of the program.

The Current Tobacco Program

The overall purpose of the program is to stabilize prices by restricting supply. To accomplish this, the program functions in an interlocking and interdependent way through four central features: a national marketing quota, individual farm quotas based on production history, price supports, and governmental funding of nonrecourse loans. (See appendix 2A at the end of this chapter for an economic interpretation of the supply and demand dynamics involved.) Other miscellaneous features are also important for the program to function properly.

National Marketing Quota

Each year, the U.S. Department of Agriculture (USDA) estimates the amount of tobacco that can sell in domestic and export markets at prices above the year's price-support rate. (This estimate takes into account any existing stocks from previous years.) The USDA uses this estimate to set an annual overall quota level for the country. Since tobacco typically is stored for aging, quotas can be adjusted to align total available supplies with the price-support level. And since tobacco has no close substitutes, restricting supply tends not only to stabilize prices, a function of most government commodity support programs, but also to raise prices.

Quotas must be approved by a two-thirds majority of allotment holders in a referendum every three years. If a quota is not approved, full price supports do not have to be offered. Since the Agricultural Adjustment Act passed in 1938, growers have disapproved quotas only once, in 1939.

Farm Quotas Based on Production History

Quotas are allocated to individual farms according to the production patterns that existed in the 1930s. Because quotas are tied to the land, the entry of new producers is restricted on a permanent basis unless such producers rent or purchase a farm having a quota. Historical assignment of quota has also resulted in tobacco production being essentially "frozen" in certain geographical areas.

When the national marketing quota is announced for a given year, every allotment holder knows that his basic quota will be changed by a certain percentage. Every year since 1965, farmers of flue-cured tobacco have received both a poundage quota and an acreage allotment. (Prior to 1965, quotas were based entirely on acreage.) As a practical matter, farmers are generally able to produce their poundage quota on less than the assigned acreage allotment. To provide farmers some insurance against variable yields, the program allows a quota-holder to carry over underproduced quota or to sell up to 10 percent over his poundage quota; undermarketings and overmarketings are reflected in the effective quota. The right to sell the percentage of tobacco allocated to each farm is represented by a tobacco marketing card issued by the USDA Agricultural Stabilization and Conservation Service (ASCS).

Price-Support Authority

When marketing quotas are in effect, price supports are provided by legislative formula. From the late 1940s through 1959, tobacco was supported at 90 percent of parity. (Parity price generally means equivalent purchasing power for a unit of a product as in a selected base period, which might be maintained by government support of agricultural commodity prices.) Since 1960, the support price has been adjusted annually from the 1959 level according to the moving average of the Parity Index in the three preceding years. The Parity Index is a national indicator of prices paid by all farmers for production items, family living, interest, wage rates, and taxes; thus, it is essentially an index of inflation rates in overall farm costs, not an index of the costs of producing tobacco. Under this formula, the 1980 average support price for flue-cured tobacco was 141.5 cents per pound, compared with 55.5 cents in 1960, whereas burley-tobacco price supports averaged 145.9 cents in 1980, compared with 57.2 cents in 1960.

The USDA determines the grades eligible for price support and loan rates for each grade. This administrative flexibility allows larger increases in price support for the grades in which demand is rising. But, as required by law, the weighted average of all support rates must equal the overall average support for each year's crop.

Commodity Credit Corporation
Nonrecourse Loans

On the auction market, manufacturers and dealers buy tobacco at the
highest bid, provided the bid is at least one cent per pound above the
government support rate for the given grade. Stabilization cooperatives—
one for flue-cured and two for burley—automatically buy the tobacco not
sold at auction at the support rate, using funds advanced by the Commodity
Credit Corporation (CCC), a USDA lending agency. This money provides
the means for implementing the price-support system. The cooperatives,
which have acquired from 2 to 21 percent of a given year's crop during the
last decade, then process, store, and resell the leaf. The proceeds from a
given year's crop are first used to repay principal and interest to the CCC. If
net losses occur from a year's crop, the government bears the loss—hence,
the loans are called *nonrecourse*. If net gains occur, they are distributed to
the farmers. Cumulative losses of principal since the 1930s have amounted
to only 1 percent of the total volume of tobacco loans. Until 1980, CCC
loans were made at an interest rate that was set once a year. Over the course
of a twelve-month period, this rate was at times below the government cost
of borrowing. This has caused critics of the program to label such loans as
government subsidies. In early 1981, the Reagan administration changed
the system of using a single rate for a whole year. Interest rates for new
CCC loans will now be set at prevailing market rates for a given six-month
period.

    Nonrecourse loans from the CCC are also used to support prices of such
commodities as wheat and feed grains. In these cases, however, loans are
provided to individual producers. These individuals receive the gains on all
lots sold above the loan rate, and the government bears the losses from each
individual lot. With tobacco, gains and losses from individual lots are offset
against each other within the cooperatives' total pool. The CCC then bears
a loss only if there is a net deficit by the cooperative.

Other Features

The lease-and-transfer program allows one allotment holder to lease quota
from others in the same county for production on his own farm. The lease is
privately negotiated between the two parties and documented through the
ASCS. Because lease-and-transfer is restricted to the boundaries of a single
county, rents vary from county to county. (See chapters 4 and 6 for a
discussion of lease-and-transfer.)

    In the early 1970s, marketings across tobacco belts flooded some auc-
tion areas. Hence, in 1974, the USDA adopted a market designation plan

to regulate the flow of flue-cured tobacco to the market. Farmers must now designate their choice of sales warehouse within one hundred miles of their county seat in order to be eligible for price supports.

In another example of an administrative response to a marketing problem, the USDA in 1978 created the "four-leaf" or "down-stalk" program for growers of flue-cured tobacco. Stabilization had built up a large inventory of the down-stalk leaves, the lowest grades under the support program. The four-leaf program allows allotment holders to plant additional acreage on which to produce their assigned poundage, if they do not market the four lower leaves.

In addition to its regulatory role in the tobacco program, the federal government is involved in a number of services, such as market news and grading. Inspectors from the Agricultural Marketing Service grade the leaf on the warehouse floor. Grade standards take into account stalk position, color, quality, injury, and other characteristics. Since different support levels are determined for different grades, the grade placed on a given lot of tobacco is prerequisite to the administration of the price-support program.

The USDA assists in a variety of research and education programs related to tobacco. County extension agents, who implement many local education programs, are partially supported by federal funds, along with extension specialists and some researchers at land-grant universities. Tobacco-belt states such as North Carolina also work closely with the USDA on research projects to develop new information on tobacco.

The tobacco program, as just described, could be continued in its current structure. Many legislative and administrative alternatives to the program are also possible. If the current tobacco program were to be changed, the most extreme move would be to abolish it. This approach would essentially establish an open-market policy. The probable consequences of having no supply controls, no price supports, and no other government involvement in tobacco production and marketing will now be examined.

The Open-Market Alternative

The "no tobacco program" alternative would not mean "no tobacco." The major effects of dropping the government's program would be reduction of tobacco prices and redistribution of tobacco income; the size of the crop would not necessarily decrease and might well increase. Under the current program, the quota system controls supply and keeps prices above the open-market level, but in an open market, prices fluctuate to equilibrate supply and demand. For example, if supply increases with no change in demand, prices will decline. Most studies indicate that the demand for tobacco is inelastic. Inelastic demand means that a given percentage increase in quantity results in a larger percentage drop in farm prices; for example, if tobacco quantity increased by 10 percent, farm prices might drop by as much as 20 percent. With no federal program and this scenario, farm income from tobacco would drop.

If the current tobacco program were abolished and no government provisions were adopted to replace it, the following consequences could be expected:

1. Total production would likely fluctuate from year to year but might increase moderately over the long run. Current producers who have been willing to pay substantial quota rents have, in effect, signaled a willingness to expand output. Also, farmers who previously were not allowed to produce because they did not own land with a quota would have freedom to try to produce tobacco.
2. Leaf prices might generally drop by an amount equal to the average lease cost per pound now paid for quota. In addition, prices would probably be very unstable because of variations in production and the lack of assurance of minimum prices.
3. The resale value of many farms now having quotas attached to the land would drop drastically. If the quotas were rendered worthless, the equity position of current allotment holders would be impaired unless there were some program to compensate for the loss of quota value.
4. Incomes would be reduced for persons who have typically received rental income from tobacco quotas.
5. Some geographical shift in production to more efficient areas would occur.
6. The number of tobacco farms would decrease at an accelerated rate. The smaller number of farmers that continue to produce tobacco might expand and mechanize their individual operations, since they would be no longer constrained by quotas. One factor that might slightly limit the degree of enlargement and consolidation of tobacco farms would be the increase in risk perceived if the program were ended. Other farmers might shift from tobacco to less labor-intensive enterprises by attempting to consolidate farms into larger acreages in order to earn a comparable income.
7. With no program, the government would have no obligation to advance loan funds or to absorb losses on price-support operations.
8. The volume of U.S. tobacco exports could increase modestly with lower prices.
9. Reduced tobacco prices at the farm level might result in a small decrease in consumer price for tobacco products. But the farm value of leaf is only 8 percent of the average retail cost of a pack of cigarettes. A one-third reduction in the farm price of raw tobacco would be required

to reduce cigarette costs by one cent per pack. The level of cigarette taxes is a greater determinant of consumer costs than farm-level tobacco prices.

10. Dropping government production controls and price supports would not in itself induce less smoking even though it is the smoking-and-health controversy that has prompted much of the discussion about less government involvement in the farm program for tobacco.

In summary, abolishing the tobacco program would have the following major effects on the tobacco farming economy: a sudden loss in value of tobacco farms; fluctuating and lower tobacco prices; and loss of rental income by persons who had previously held quotas for leasing.

Alternatives to Particular Features

There are many intermediate positions between the current tobacco program and "no tobacco program." The discussion that follows focuses on conceivable options to particular provisions of the present program. Some alternatives mentioned are authorized under existing legislation; others would require new laws or substantial changes in administrative rules. Some alternatives may be practical only through private, cooperative action by the tobacco industry. Since much of the discussion about dropping or modifying the tobacco program questions government involvement, it may be helpful to recognize that government can fulfill a role in three ways: (1) by sanctioning particular actions; (2) by funding specific program activities; and/or (3) by serving as the action agent. Therefore, the various options discussed here can be viewed in terms of both the particular feature of the program and the type of government involvement.

Alternatives to National Marketing Quotas

The capability to control the total supply of tobacco, through the national marketing quota, is the most critical component of the present program. Because demand for tobacco is inelastic, prices are sensitive to even small changes in quantity available. As a result, with a given percentage reduction in quantity available through a lower quota, prices are likely to be increased by a greater percentage. In short, restrictions on supply through quotas raise prices, and hence income for those with tobacco quotas.

Although marketing quotas are currently set by governmental action, other authorities could be empowered to take this action. The two most promising possibilities are marketing orders/agreements or a marketing board. Recommendations on supply level made by nongovernmental bodies that had no enforcement powers, however, would be futile.

Under the Agricultural Marketing Agreement Act of 1937, as amended, tobacco is eligible for marketing orders. The USDA uses a marketing order as a regulatory vehicle with farm commodities. Steps required to put marketing orders into effect include: (1) an initiation of a request to the USDA, typically by an industry group; (2) a written proposed marketing order; (3) a public hearing; (4) a determination of need by the U.S. Secretary of Agriculture; (5) a referendum carried by two-thirds majority of eligible producers voting; and (6) an appointment of an administrative committee by the Secretary.

But federal marketing orders are not commonly used to restrict supply or limit the entry of new producers. Exceptions are orders for cranberries and celery. In the latter case, the authority to control aggregate supply has been sustained in court. If marketing orders were to be a viable alternative for a national tobacco quota, it would be necessary to develop and adopt a specific proposal containing supply-control features. Regulation of flow to market, quality standards, and self-help plans are the most common provisions of marketing orders for other commodities. If such features were applied to a marketing order for tobacco, some indirect limitations on the quantity marketed might be achieved.

While the use of marketing orders for tobacco would plow new ground in the United States, marketing boards already operate in some countries. In the province of Ontario in Canada, a marketing board for tobacco is empowered to establish quotas, allocate quotas to producers, negotiate minimum prices for each grade, and operate cooperative warehouses for sale of the crop. In the various U.S. tobacco-producing states, new legislation would be required to authorize such a marketing board.

Despite the Canadian experience, the ramifications of sanctioning a private U.S. marketing board are difficult to anticipate. Would this approach be more politically acceptable than direct administration of the tobacco program by government agencies? And, without the aid of government as a third party, could the different interests of the various sectors involved in the production and marketing of tobacco and tobacco products reach decisions satisfactory to all parties? It might be difficult, for example, to obtain agreement on how much to limit marketings in order to raise prices and on which parties should be granted production rights. Many of the pro-and-con arguments surrounding the current program might also apply to a tobacco marketing board. However, the removal of a governmental obligation to underwrite the costs of the program might reduce the criticism that it is inconsistent to have a government farm program alongside government efforts to discourage cigarette consumption.

Alternatives to Historical Quotas

The method of assigning farm quotas determines who receives the major program benefits. As with the aggregate quota determination, this function would have to be either performed or sanctioned by government. If the national marketing quota is continued, there are various means by which quotas could be assigned to farms. Historical bases—assigning quotas to those farms having a history of production—have been most often used in commodity programs, but there are some breaks with this precedent. For example, the Agricultural Act of 1977 tied benefits from the feed grains, wheat, and cotton programs to current acreage planted, rather than to historic bases. A cropland set-aside (a minimum acreage kept out of production by farmers for designated crops) is a precondition for commodity loans and target-price payments. Consequently, program benefits go to farmers actually producing the commodity, rather than to those who own farms with a history of production.

Any change in the method of allocating quotas would reduce the value of farms now assigned quotas and hence redistribute tobacco income. Rental income for farms losing quotas would decline and the capital value of such farmland would be reduced. Special financing problems would also be created for those who have recently purchased land with quotas. If undue hardship were created by a new method of assigning quota or by the entry of new producers (who previously did not have a quota to grow), some system of compensation might be devised. Decreases in farm value and losses of rental income might be compensated through public funds or purchases of production rights by producers. Legislation would be required to permit the sale of quotas, but precedent for this alternative does exist in programs for peanuts and for fire-cured, dark air-cured, and sun-cured types of tobacco.

Alternative Price-Support Systems

The periodic debate about possible changes in the price-support system has recently intensified. The price-support formula now guarantees a price for U.S.-produced leaf substantially higher than that for foreign-produced leaf. Consequently, loan stocks have accumulated, especially for flue-cured tobacco, and the U.S. share of world trade has declined.

The philosophy chosen for tobacco in the 1930s and essentially retained to date is that prices and income would be maintained primarily through supply controls, rather than through direct government payments. Hence, achieving a given level of price supports with surplus stocks depends largely on effective supply control. The price-support structure is undergirded by advances of government funds with which cooperatives acquire and hold surplus stocks until the tobacco can be moved into trade channels.

The price-support system itself could be altered by adjusting the price-support formula (its base or escalator provisions) or the distribution of price-supports among grades. Each of the following possible changes would likely require new or amended legislation.

The Formula. The seven ways most often considered to modify the base or escalator provisions are:

1. *A freeze of the support level for some period*: This action would imply that price supports are currently too high, and would not allow changes in the index of farm costs (that is, the Parity Index) to influence price support until after the freeze. Based on recent history, price supports would be held at ten to fifteen cents per pound below the level dictated by the current formula for each year of a freeze. If legislation were enacted to impose a freeze, some action would then be necessary regarding an adjustment formula, to go into effect after the freeze ends.

2. *Replacing the current formula with a mandatory parity level*: Between the late 1940s and 1959, supports were mandatory at 90 percent of parity. But the present formula, even though it is sometimes criticized for making prices too high, has resulted in prices at less than 70 percent of parity. Hence, arriving at an acceptable percentage would be difficult.

3. *Using a general economic indicator, such as the Consumer Price Index, as the escalator, rather than the Parity Index*: Although long-term history shows that agricultural price indices sometimes lag behind changes in the general price level, most economic indicators tend to move at about the same rate.

4. *Moderating the pace of increases in support rates*: Partial rather than full adjustments would be made for inflation; for example, less than a one-for-one adjustment for the percentage change in the Parity Index. Under this method, farmers would have to improve their cost efficiency to maintain net income from tobacco.

5. *Tying support rates to tobacco production costs rather than to general farm costs*: The target price level adopted for agricultural commodities covered by the 1977 Agricultural Act relate to their specific costs, rather than a generalized index of farm cost rates. Use of this approach for tobacco would be subject to several problems, such as determining the cost items to be measured. For example, if quota leases were included in an overall cost indicator, a ratchet effect on support rates could result. Higher rents could force price supports up, which induces further hikes in lease costs as tobacco prices rise. Using tobacco production costs for a base, then, might well adjust supports upward.

6. *Using a "two-price" plan rather than the single formula*: Two-price plans have been used to maintain prices in primary markets while permitting additional quantities to be sold at lower prices in secondary markets. Milk classification plans are based on separating the market for fluid and manufacturing uses. The current peanut program also operates as a two-price plan. The usual notion of a two-price plan for tobacco is to restrict sales domestically and to sell extra production on an export market at a lower price. How this would work is not clear, since export companies appear to be the leaders in the purchase of higher-priced, upstalk flue-cured tobacco.

7. An entirely different approach would be to broaden administrative discretion to allow the overall price supports to be within some legal range. This approach, used now with dairy products, offers latitude for changes as circumstances warrant without requiring lengthy legislative changes.

Distribution of Price Supports among the Grades. The USDA can now make some adjustments to support levels among grades. However, the overall support levels must average out to meet the legal formula. Therefore, if supports are lowered on some grades, increases must be placed on others to meet the statutory average.

Obviously, another alternative is to have no direct price support. To repeat a critical point: restricting total marketings, even without formal price support, can maintain prices above the open-market level. The extent of the price-raising effect depends on how rigidly the quota is set in relation to demand. However, without direct price supports, there is less protection against misjudgments in the appropriate level of quota and against fluctuations in prices for given grades, when demand changes or natural conditions affect a crop's grade distribution.

Alternatives for Financing Price Stabilization

If the Commodity Credit Corporation funding of nonrecourse loans for tobacco were eliminated, the stabilization cooperatives might obtain some funding by borrowing from private sources or by authorizing a marketing order or check-off plan to create a producer reserve. A continued role for cooperatives is possible with adequate financing because of the storable nature of tobacco and the experience and cohesive structure already gained among tobacco cooperatives. But, without being able to borrow government funds, cooperatives might have limitations imposed by the need to avoid losses and by the prospects that interest costs from private sources might be higher than the rate charged for CCC funds.

The probability of the cooperatives succeeding in stabilizing market prices without nonrecourse loans depends largely on continued quota authority and the level at which the national marketing quota is established. For example, if attempts were made to maintain prices at current levels, but with no quotas, production would increase substantially, resulting in large surpluses to be acquired by the cooperative. Without nonrecourse loans from the CCC, cooperatives could go bankrupt if there were losses from such surpluses. If acting without quotas were required, cooperatives could do little more than stabilize prices near the long-term open-market level. On the other hand, if quota authority is retained, downward adjustments in quota can be made as necessary to permit cooperatives to sell their stocks without loss.

If removal of government financing were considered, the means of transition would be important. For example, from 1975-1977, the flue-cured stabilization cooperative acquired about one-fifth of each year's production. How would such surplus stocks be treated if alternative financing became necessary? Any rapid dispersal would depress current market prices. On the other hand, if price-support levels were reduced substantially to assure no loss to cooperatives on future operations, it would be difficult to dispose of current stocks. Therefore, the minimum shock effect of making a transition from government to private financing of cooperatives would occur when surplus stocks were low. Yet, the clamor for dropping government involvement might be greatest when stocks are high. An orderly transition would be critical.

Alternatives to Other Program Features

The *lease-and-transfer* of quota among producers in the same county—the current procedure—is meaningful only when marketing quotas are in effect. If the quota system remains intact, the principal debate is whether to permit lease-and-transfer across county lines. Such an amendment would allow quotas from low-rent counties to be leased into high-rent counties, and vice versa, resulting in a redistribution of income among quota owners and possibly a leveling of lease rates throughout a state. Growers who traditionally have leased quota in low-rent areas object to the prospect of higher lease costs, but quota owners in the same area who lease rather than grow their allotment welcome the opportunity to lease-out to a wider market. Conversely, in high-rent counties, growers seeking larger quotas favor cross-county lease-and-transfer, whereas those who generally lease-out in the same county foresee declining rental income.

Various *tobacco services* currently provided by the federal government could conceivably be funded by other sources. For example, in 1981 the Reagan administration proposed to change the funding mechanism for tobacco graders from a free to a fee system. If a price-stabilization program is maintained, the necessary costs for grading might be assumed by the industry. A government agency might continue to staff the grading service in order to provide the credibility of a third party. If a choice had to be made between losing federally financed grading or other program features, such as supply control and price supports, consideration should be given to the fact that the relative cost to be assumed by private sources for grading would be modest.

Market news information and analysis might be continued, possibly on a reduced scale, by the news media and marketing sectors or by the governments of the tobacco-producing states. In the event of reduced federal support, research and education could be continued at some level by private industry and state governments. Provisions of marketing orders and check-off plans are additional possible means of financing research and education in tobacco production and marketing.

Summary

The current tobacco program encompasses many features—some of greater economic consequence than others, and some more politically vulnerable than others. When there are opportunities to streamline the program—to fine-tune the mechanics involved—the most critical provisions, such as an aggregate marketing quota, need to be of primary concern. But if external pressures force a reduced involvement of government in the tobacco program, those provisions which can be performed by private or collective action within the tobacco industry might be transferred there—not those features which require, at a minimum, the sanction of government policy.

Appendix 2A:
An Economic
Interpretation of the
Current Tobacco
Program

Figure 2A-1 is an economic portrayal of how the current tobacco program operates, using traditional supply-and-demand curve dynamics. It can be explained as follows:

1. *DD* represents an inelastic aggregate demand curve for tobacco at the farm level. Thus, under given conditions of income, population, and consumer taste, a disproportionately lower price would be offered for larger quantities.
2. P_s is the average price support determined by legislative formula for a given year. P_o is the price in the open market.
3. *SS* represents the willingness of present quota holders to supply tobacco at various prices, with this supply curve based on the usual notion that a larger quantity would be supplied at higher prices. (However, the supply curve would be more elastic or flatter, if new producers were allowed to enter production at higher price levels.)
4. Q_o denotes the national marketing quota which is administratively determined at the level expected to sell, at a price at or above the support rate, given the assumed demand conditions. Since the quota sets a specific limit on marketings (subject to tolerances regarding poundage quotas), the industry supply curve becomes vertical at the point of the quota, Q_o.
5. *SS'* represents the kinked supply curve, with its vertical portion intended to intersect the demand curve at or above P_s.
6. The S_r segment of the S_rS' supply curve includes rental (*r*) costs.

The first consequence of the program is to yield a price above the open-market level. Conversely, producers are willing (based on the initial supply curve, *SS*) to furnish the amount of tobacco in the quota (Q_o) at a price below the support rate (as low a price as P_o). But the quota is restricted at a level expected to yield a price, at or above the support rate (P_s).

If demand is misjudged so that prices bid on the market do not exceed the support rate, CCC funds are advanced to acquire excess tobacco. Then, quotas have to be adjusted downward in subsequent years to allow the stabilization cooperatives to move stocks into trade channels and reimburse the CCC, in order to prevent long-term government losses on the non-recourse loans.

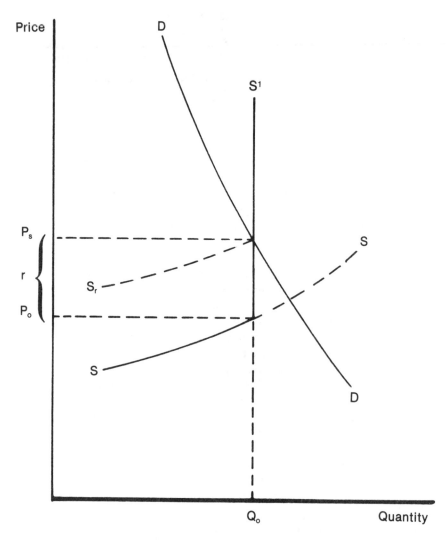

Figure 2A-1. How the Current Tobacco Program Works in Terms of Economics

The price-raising impact of the supply-control program produces a secondary effect. When growers see the profit margins above marginal costs, they bid for additional production rights. Rental rates per pound may be bid up to the point that marginal costs plus rent equal the price of tobacco. (As figure 2A-1 shows, the supply curve, in the relevant range at and below the quota level, shifts upward by the amount of the rent. Rent, r, raises the supply curve from S to S_r.) This higher supply curve indicates the marginal cost, including quota rents disbursed by a grower leasing in essentially all his quota. For others, it represents costs, including the opportunity cost of owned quota.

Under the current program, there are ways of accommodating to a change in demand conditions. Since the level of price support is specified by legal formula in relation to recent farm cost rates, adjustments in the quota level may be used to compensate for changes in demand.

A change in consumer tastes is a traditional economic explanation of a shift in a demand curve. Efforts by private and public groups related to smoking and health purport to affect consumer tastes, not only by enticing people to quit smoking but also by reducing the proportion of people that begin smoking. To whatever extent anti-smoking campaigns shift the aggregate demand curve to the left, tobacco marketing quotas can be adjusted accordingly while maintaining market prices. This conclusion is in sharp contrast to the inclination of some anti-smoking advocates to abolish the tobacco program. What they fail to recognize is that with no program, a supply response above the existing quota levels is possible and smoking material would be available, at the farm level, at a lower price.

Quota adjustments can also be the mechanism that compensates for other causes of change in demand, such as:

1. Population changes (and/or the population size subject to consuming the particular product; for example, smoking-age population).
2. Income changes (in relation to the income elasticity of demand; for example, estimates of the income elasticity of demand for cigarettes in various studies generally range from $+0.1$ to $+0.6$, averaging around $+0.4$).
3. Changes in conditions of international trade, such as changes in tariff structures, national tobacco monopolies, and subsidization of tobacco producers by other countries.
4. Changes in cigarette manufacturing techniques, which affect demand for leaf at the farm level.
5. Changes in taxes that alter the consumer price of cigarettes and affect the derived demand for leaf at the farm level.

3 Landmarks in the Tobacco Program

Charles Pugh

1933

Agricultural Adjustment Act (AAA). This act established the principal of parity prices for tobacco, initially using 1919-1929 as the base period, and the farmer committee system. Administration of the act utilized county and community farmer committees, initially organized by county extension agents and later transferred to a newly formed agency (first named the Agricultural Adjustment Administration, then the Production Marketing Administration, and finally the Agricultural Stabilization and Conservation Service) to administer federal agricultural programs. As the first federal tobacco program, it encouraged growers to reduce 1934 plantings in return for payments. Marketing agreements were negotiated with domestic companies to purchase from the large 1933 crop, which was already planted before the AAA was passed.

1934

Kerr Tobacco Act. This act provided for a tax on growers' sales to compensate growers who adjusted production. Repealed after the 1935 season before the Supreme Court ruled on its validity.

1936

The 1933 Act Ruled Unconstitutional. The Supreme Court ruled the AAA unconstitutional on January 6, 1936.

1936

Soil Conservation and Domestic Allotment Act. Enacted February 29, 1936, it authorized conservation payments from appropriated funds for diverting acreage from soil-depleting crops (including tobacco) to soil-conserving uses. Committees determined bases and normal yields and checked and approved documents in connection with the program.

1938

Agricultural Adjustment Act (AAA). This legislation established tobacco marketing quotas and provided penalties for excess production. The program provided for: (1) advance announcement of national marketing quota by the Secretary of Agriculture; (2) farmer referendum requiring two-thirds vote to approve quotas; (3) apportionment of poundage quotas to states and individual farms; and (4) authorization of parity payments, insofar as funds would permit, for the difference between parity price and market price. This act, as amended, is still in effect today.

1939

Farmers Reject Quotas. In 1938, quotas had not been determined by planting time, which caused excess marketings and some disillusionment with the new system. Farmers then voted in the referendum to reject 1939 quotas, and in 1939 production increased 50 percent over 1938.

1939

Amendments to AAA of 1938. These amendments converted national and state quotas from poundage to individual acreage allotments and changed the base period for flue-cured parity price from 1919-1929 to 1934-1939. After these amendments of August 7, 1939, growers voted through referendum to restore the control program on the 1940 crop. Since then, farmers have never rejected quotas in referenda.

Early 1940s

Administrative Actions Affecting Tobacco Program. These included: (1) a lend-lease program, which helped finance exports to friendly nations, and accounted for 46 percent of flue-cured exports from 1941 to 1945; (2) congressional resolutions permitting quotas to be raised, which led to acreage allotments being boosted 25 percent in 1944 and 10 percent in 1946; (3) the Emergency Price Control Act of 1942, which put price ceilings on flue-cured tobacco.

1946

Flue-Cured Tobacco Cooperative Stabilization Corporation. This corporation was organized to receive tobacco from farmers when prices were not above support level (using nonrecourse loans from the Commodity Credit Corporation to finance its acquisitions), to make provisions for processing and storage, and to offer leaf for resale to domestic and foreign buyers.

1948

Agricultural Act of 1948. This act modernized parity to reflect trends in relative prices of all farm commodities during the preceding ten years.

1949

Agricultural Act of 1949. Flue-cured price supports were made mandatory at 90 percent of parity, when marketing quotas are in effect.

1954

Public Law 83-480. The Agricultural Trade Development and Assistance Act provided for export sales for foreign currencies, long-term credit sales, and barter of surplus commodities such as tobacco.

1956

Soil Bank Act. This act provided for annual payments for retirement of land from tobacco and certain other crops, and long-term payments for commitment of cropland to forestry and other conservation uses.

1957

Variety Discount Program. This program provided supports at only 50 percent of the usual rate for specified varieties.

1960

Change in Method of Price Supports. Congress froze price supports at the 1959 level (55.5 cents per pound for flue-cured, 57.2 cents per pound for burley) and established a formula for future levels based on the moving average of the Parity Index in the three preceding years. This Parity Index incorporates inflation rates in overall farm costs (that is, not just the cost of raising tobacco); consequently, when farm-cost inflation rates are high, the support price rises accordingly. This action replaced the provision passed in 1949 that made flue-cured price supports mandatory at 90 percent of parity. The formula passed in 1960 is still in effect today.

1961-1962

Lease-and-Transfer Program. Public Law 87-200 permitted existing allotment holders (only) to lease allotments from within the same county for production on their own farm. The initial legislation permitted annual lease-and-transfer; later amendments allowed leases up to five years.

1964

Smoking and Health. Released by the surgeon general's advisory committee, this report (similar to a British study) deals with possible health problems related to tobacco.

1965

Acreage-Poundage Program for Flue-Cured Tobacco. This program replaced individual farm acreage allotments with acreage and poundage quotas for each farm. It allows individual growers to sell up to 110 percent of their effective quota in any given year or to accumulate up to 100 percent of excess quota.

1967

Tobacco Growers Services, Inc. Organized as a subsidiary of the stabilization cooperative, this organization engages in tobacco processing and storage to supplement services contracted with others.

1967

Marketing Committee for Flue-Cured Tobacco. This is an ad hoc "industrywide committee" organized with representatives of warehousemen, buyers, and growers from various flue-cured belts. It advises on matters dealing with flow of tobacco to markets.

1968

Loose-Leaf Marketing Extended to All Belts. The "tying" provision was replaced by "loose-leaf" sales. Loose-leaf had been the historical method of marketing in the Georgia-Florida belt.

1971

Restrictions on Cigarette Advertising. Radio and television advertising were banned in January 1971. Other congressional actions included labeling cigarettes with surgeon general's warning.

1971

Burley Program. The burley tobacco program switched from acreage allotments to poundage quotas.

1973

Special Stabilization Pool for Excess Tobacco. The USDA gave the stabilization cooperative authority to buy growers' leaf produced in excess of 110 percent of effective quota at the price-support rate at the beginning of the next marketing year, plus a share in the net proceeds after the special pool was stored, processed, and resold. If producing above his quota, a farmer was essentially borrowing from his quota in future years. (The pool was abolished after 1978 crop.)

1974

Market Designation Plan. Following acute problems of congestion at warehouses in early marketing season, cross-belt hauling, and overtaxing of processing facilities, the plan was adopted through an administrative ruling. Farmers were required to designate in advance a sales warehouse within 100 miles of their county seat as a condition for price supports.

1977

Changes in Grade Standards. Regulations tightened waste tolerance levels and introduced "sand or dirt" factor into lower-stalk grades.

1977-1978

Federal Anti-Smoking Campaign. Secretary of Health, Education, and Welfare proposed a number of federal anti-smoking efforts.

1978

Four-Leaf Program. A program to allow additional planted acreage to growers who would not harvest the four lower leaves on each stalk in an effort to reduce inventories of lower-grade leaf in stabilization cooperative.

1979

Experimental Sales of Burley. Burley that was baled rather than tied (the usual method), permitted for a portion of the crop.

1980

Administrative Action. Price supports dropped on eight low-quality, downstalk grades of flue-cured tobacco.

1980

Growers Petitioned for Reclassification of Imported Leaf. U.S. Tariff Commission has been allowing mechanically threshed leaf to be classified in the "scrap" category. The growers petitioned for the practice to be changed, but the Tariff Commission made only a modest adjustment. Thus import duty levels remained about the same.

1981

Commodity Credit Corporation Loan System Altered. Instead of setting the interest rate once a year for loans to the cooperatives, CCC now adjusts the rate to the prevailing market level twice a year.

The Tobacco Franchise for Whom?

Charles K. Mann

The federal regulations controlling tobacco production and marketing have resulted from political forces as much as from economic factors. At the heart of the tobacco program lies the allotment system, which virtually all analysts recognize as having a central importance. But most have studied the allotment system and, indeed, the entire tobacco program in an economic rather than a political context. This chapter highlights the major political forces that have altered the tobacco program. Specifically, it explains why the allotment system determines, to a large extent, not only where tobacco is grown and who grows it, but also the type of research conducted in the land-grant universities and the type of equipment used to tend and harvest the crop. The chapter then identifies how the system might change in the future, the consequences of such changes, and ways to mitigate the hardships these changes could bring.

In 1933, to halt the disastrous drop in leaf prices, Congress passed a tobacco program that remains virtually intact today. (See chapter 1 for an overview of early efforts to address the volatile market conditions, and chapters 2 and 3 for a full explanation of the federal program.) The program limited the amount of tobacco that could be grown through a national quota system and determined who could grow it by assigning allotments to the land planted in tobacco in the 1930s. The program, which thus controlled the yearly supply of tobacco that reached the market, also included a guaranteed price-support system for farmers. In addition, it required periodic approval of the allotments by a farmer referendum; only the persons who owned allotments were eligible to vote. This system has resulted in some consequences that the original proponents did not anticipate,[1] such as:

1. The right to grow tobacco came to have a high value as the price of tobacco was pushed up far beyond the cost of producing it. The value of a tobacco farm was determined not by the amount or quality of land, but by the allotment assigned to it. Thus the major deterrent to entering tobacco production was not a traditional economic factor such as the cost of land, labor, or equipment but rather a political factor: this high cost of buying the necessary production "right," land with an allotment tied to it.

Professor Dale Hoover of North Carolina State University and Verner Grise of the U.S. Department of Agriculture (USDA) provided comments on drafts of this chapter.

2. The allotment quota system, which was based on acreage, provided a tremendous incentive to increase yields per unit of land. Long before prime farmland became a scarce quantity, the allotment system made tobacco farmers treat it so. Without an allotment system, farmers would have put more of their land into tobacco instead of concentrating on increasing the yield on their allotment acreage. Hence, farm and tobacco industry groups pressed researchers at the land-grant universities and elsewhere for means of obtaining ever higher yields. From an average of 922 pounds per acre in 1939, average yields rose to more than 2,200 pounds per acre by 1964. Tobacco farms today are still valued primarily by how much allotment they have, not how much land.

3. The allotment system froze the spatial distribution of tobacco. In the early 1930s, the tobacco belt was shifting rapidly out of the relatively poor soils of the Virginia and North Carolina Piedmont and into the more fertile and productive coastal plains of North and South Carolina. But the introduction of the allotment system arrested the geographical shifts in production, altering through political means a fundamental principle of economics: production tends to shift to the location of lowest production costs. Although subsequent changes in the system (such as the lease-and-transfer provisions) have permitted allotment to move within counties, the distribution among counties has remained virtually unchanged. The relative shares of the various tobacco belts have been stable since the mid-1930s (see figure 4-1).

Although the tobacco program has remained fundamentally intact since 1933, three important changes have taken place: (1) in 1961, Congress voted to allow lease-and-transfer of allotment within a county; (2) in 1965, the allotment system was changed from an acreage to a poundage base; and (3) in 1968, the "tying" requirement for flue-cured tobacco was eliminated, allowing instead the stacking of "sheets" of the leaf (see chapter 3 for a full chronology of changes in the federal tobacco program.) These alterations in the system may appear minor at a glance, but they have come to reshape the way in which tobacco is grown. Examining just one of the three in some detail shows how the interplay between political and economic forces has reshaped the entire tobacco production economy.

Political Alterations to an Economic System

In the tobacco belts, the sharecropping structure tied labor to the land, in many cases, into the 1960s. But as the allotment system took hold, the technology of tobacco farming began to change. Since the allotment system was based on production per acre, research focused on increasing yields per acre. Although the research led to higher yields, it also resulted in reducing

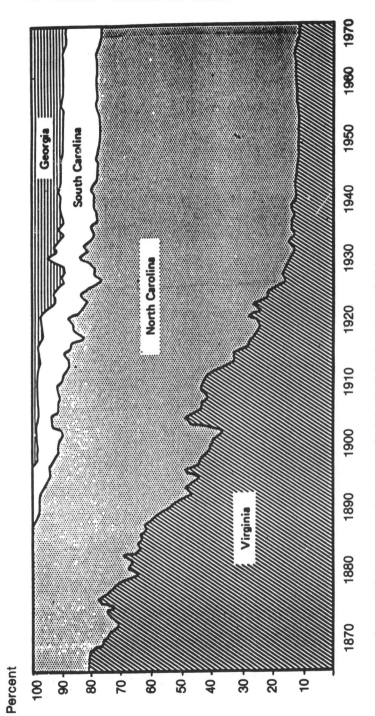

Source: U.S. Department of Agriculture Statistical Bulletin No. 454, pp. 58-64.

Figure 4-1. Changes in Relative Tobacco Production in the Four Major Flue-Cured States

the labor needed at several points in the tobacco-growing cycle. For example, chemicals replaced manpower in removing the sucker leaves and "topping" the plants, important functions during the growth of the crop. By the 1960s, labor requirements were becoming more and more concentrated in the harvest period alone. Providing a share of the crop to farm workers needed only during the short harvest period came to be extremely expensive. Gradually, sharecroppers were being forced from the land. As the "cropper" system declined, assembling large harvest crews needed only for a few weeks during harvest became more and more of a problem for tobacco growers.

While these changes were taking place on tobacco farms, industrial development in the North Carolina Piedmont was expanding. This put great strains on the allotment system which had frozen the southeasterly flow of production in 1933. Potential tobacco field hands, now needed only as seasonal workers, had other job opportunities. The high cost of labor and alternative uses for tobacco land made the right to grow tobacco in the industrializing Piedmont increasingly less valuable. Renting one's allotment was difficult because a farmer had to grow tobacco on the actual farmland to which an allotment was tied. Even if the leasing farmer had the acreage he needed, he could not transfer the allotment to his own farm; that meant extra costs in time, transportation, and shifting equipment and labor from farm to farm.

As industrial development increased, growing numbers of allotments in the Piedmont were going unplanted. The tobacco franchise was becoming essentially worthless. Many Piedmont allotment owners wanted to get out of tobacco production without giving up the income available through an allotment. If a Piedmont farmer could lease his allotment to someone on the coastal plain, he could still receive a good income from his allotment.

But the large coastal-plain farmers were not eager to receive the Piedmont allotments through a lease-and-transfer arrangement. The allotment value—the difference between the output value and the actual production costs (land, labor, capital needed, and so on)—was much higher in the coastal plain than in the Piedmont. The price per pound was about the same for Piedmont and coastal leaf because of the federal price-support system. But the coastal farms had higher yields per acre, resulting in substantially higher output value per acre than the Piedmont. Opening the gates to a flood of cheap allotment from the Piedmont would seriously undermine the capital asset value of the allotments of the coastal-plain farmers.

Although the coastal farmers were careful to protect their allotment values, some of them realized that a limited leasing provision might benefit them as well. The Piedmont farmers, apparently willing to accept a limited leasing arrangement supported by some coastal growers, proceeded to get 75,000 names on a petition asking Congress to allow leasing within a county (but not across county lines). In 1961, such an amendment passed, ushering in a subtle but structural change in the allotment system. Six years later, Congress went a step further, lifting a limitation from the 1961 amendment that prohibited leasing out more than five acres of allotment.

The leasing amendments to the tobacco program allowed the coastal grower to consolidate tobacco acreage into large-scale farm units, thus eliminating a major barrier to mechanizing the tobacco production process. Coinciding with pressures through the political process to remove institutional constraints to mechanization was a strong effort to produce an effective harvester. By 1967, when the forces favoring mechanization succeeded in getting the five-acre transfer restriction removed, a prototype mechanical harvester had been developed, primarily by researchers at North Carolina State University and at R.J. Reynolds Tobacco Company (see chapter 5 for a full discussion of the harvester). The harvester was designed for a forty-acre break-even capacity. Before 1967, the small size of the average allotment, (three to five acres), was a major deterrent to successful marketing of the harvester. And using a mechanical harvester on rented allotments throughout a county was impractical. But the 1961 and 1967 leasing amendments suddenly allowed the consolidation of allotments into farm units much larger than the forty-acre break-even size.

Meanwhile, two other amendments to the program eliminated other significant barriers to mechanization. In 1965, Congress changed the allotment base from an acreage to a poundage system. As long as acreage was the controlling factor, any leaf loss from the harvester represented leaf priced at its market sale value; the early harvesters had a leaf loss as high as 15 percent. On a poundage system, however, the leaf left in the field was not an economic loss.

Another deterrent to mechanization was the requirement that leaf be tied into small bundles—a highly labor-intensive process. In 1968, Congress ended the "tying" provision for flue-cured leaf. Now leaf could be cured in bulk with great labor savings. Bulk barns complemented the harvester in moving toward a mechanized production process. Having one without the other meant that a great deal of labor was still required, but having both eliminated large manpower requirements at the time of peak labor need— the harvest and the curing stages.

By 1968, then, an unlimited allotment acreage could be leased and transferred to a single farm unit within a county; the allotment system was based on pounds instead of acreage; a harvester had been developed under the sponsorship of the tobacco industry; and with the tying provision gone, fewer laborers were needed for curing. Political forces had effectively adjusted the allotment system to permit a major economic transition—from small tobacco farms to large-scale farming, from a labor-intensive system to a mechanized production cycle. With the institutional barriers to mechanization gone, three years later, in 1971, R.J. Reynolds and Harrington Manufacturing Company began marketing the first mechanical harvester. The entire landscape of tobacco production was about to change.

By 1979, just eight years after the harvester hit the market, about 20 percent of the entire flue-cured crop was being harvested mechanically, according to a recent USDA report.[2] Some tobacco analysts, such as the Tobacco Association of the United States, report a substantially higher figure, up to 40 percent in highly productive areas like the coastal plains. Accurate figures on percentage of the crop harvested mechanically, average farm unit size, tobacco farmworkers displaced, and percentage of allotment holders still growing tobacco are difficult to obtain. (For an overview of the current data, see chapter 6.)

The rate of bulk-barn curing has spread even more rapidly, from 8 percent of the acreage in 1972 all the way to 61 percent in 1979, according to the same USDA study. The average size of a flue-cured farm climbed from 9.5 to 13.8 acres, a 45-percent increase. And during this seven-year period, the number of flue-cured operations in the USDA study area (the principal flue-cured areas where three-fourths of the U.S. crop is produced) declined by 28 percent, from 40,500 to 29,000.

As the size of the flue-cured farm increased and the number of farms decreased, technological advances replaced even more sharecroppers, tenants, and seasonal workers. Harvest labor use on flue-cured farms fell from 187 hours per acre in 1972 to 118 hours per acre in 1979. The mechanization and consolidation processes also accelerated another trend: fewer and fewer allotment owners actually grew tobacco. The average allotment size—three to five acres—suggests that the tobacco farmer is the last of the Jeffersonian yeoman farmers; this small-farm image helps sustain political support for the tobacco program. But the reality is quite different from the yeoman ideal. In 1979, each flue-cured farm produced an average of about four quotas, reported the USDA. In other words, three out of every four allotment holders in the USDA study area grew no tobacco.

Post-Mechanization—The Shifts Continue

The political loosening of the rules has accommodated the economic consolidation of the tobacco-farm structure—without damaging the asset value of the allotment. As the mechanization process continues, what further loosening of the rules might occur? Specifically, under what conditions would the influential coastal-plain producers support amendments to permit allotment to flow down out of the Piedmont area?

The key to understanding the economic stake of the large coastal farmers is the ratio between the amount of allotment they own and the amount they lease. If they own a great deal, they wish to keep the value of allotment high to protect the capital asset. If their operations become so large that they begin to lease much more allotment than they own, their attention shifts from the asset value of their own allotment to the cost they must pay to lease. The lease cost could drop drastically if cheaper allotment came in from the Piedmont. As more farms mechanize their harvest and increase in size, the interests of the large coastal farmers will swing steadily toward reducing the cost of leasing allotment rather than protecting the value of the allotment they own. When the ratio of leased to owned allotment on large farms becomes high, the coastal farmers can be expected to support even wider leasing.

As the ratio of leased to owned allotment increases, pressures for cross-county leasing are building inexorably. The tobacco companies probably will resist these pressures because for blending purposes, they like having tobaccos from various agroclimatic conditions. But mechanization will increase pressures for statewide leasing, converting many of its opponents into its proponents. Beltwide leasing (belts usually lie within a region of a state) might represent a compromise position.

There is no question that greater allotment mobility would increase the efficiency of tobacco production, saving from $5.64 to $9.95 million, according to a 1973 study by researchers at North Carolina State University.[3] If the allotments that have been dammed up in the Piedmont since the 1930s were freed, the production would come sluicing down onto the coastal plain. Although cross-country leasing would no doubt increase overall efficiency, the shift would also impose many economic hardships on one-time tobacco communities in the Piedmont. And fewer of the persons benefiting from the federal tobacco program would actually be growing tobacco.

The tobacco program is geared toward benefiting not the tobacco farmer but rather those who own farms on which tobacco happened to have been raised in 1933. These beneficiaries may be farmers, but they are also doctors and lawyers, churches and banks, millworkers and truck drivers, and in many cases, widows. This federal assistance program no doubt helps many people in relatively low-income brackets. However, it would seem a reasonable policy objective—if one is to have a tobacco "farm program"—to include all tobacco farmers in the program, even tobacco-farm laborers.

The tobacco farmer who does not own an allotment benefits very little from the current program. A USDA report put it succinctly, concluding that in the long run, the economic returns to hired and sharecropper labor "were what they would have been without these [flue-cured tobacco] programs."[4] As for tenant farmers, they have not only failed to benefit from the program, but they have also been stripped of their "right" to grow tobacco; the loosening of the leasing provisions often meant that the allotments they once grew were leased out from under them. Those able to bid highest for the allotments are the mechanizers, a group that includes few of today's tenants. The flexibility added to the tobacco program by the amendments described in this chapter, ironically, has already served to push many farmers out of tobacco growing. From 1964 to 1978, the number of persons growing tobacco in North Carolina, according to the state Department of Agriculture, decreased 54 percent, from 87,600 to 39,900.

A Tobacco Franchise for Tobacco Farmers

It is in society's broad interest to ensure that amendments to the tobacco program allow those who wish to continue growing tobacco to stay on the farm, and allow those who wish to find other employment to leave. Although it may be impossible to block continued shifts in production patterns—from the Piedmont to the coastal plains, from small farms to large, consolidated units—at least political forces can prepare for them. For tobacco towns affected by these changes, the federal program should help breathe new life for those who remain. No program narrowly focused on the heirs to the tobacco farms of the 1930s will do these things. Specific programs of economic assistance to stranded communities and to displaced farmers and laborers can buffer the transitions that are ahead. When the inevitable cross-county lease-and-transfer legislation is drafted, it should recognize the devastating side effects that it will bring and should ease the burdens of such action on those vitally affected groups.

Anyone who can demonstrate a history as a tobacco grower should be granted an allotment in relation to that history. There is some precedent in the rice program for vesting allotment rights with an individual and not in land. In Texas and California, the rice allotment belongs to the producer, not to the farm. He may take it where he likes, hence the term *hip-pocket allotment*. It is, after all, the people who face the adjustment hardship, not the land.

To ease the adjustment for those allotment owners wishing to leave and to avoid simply "printing" new allotment, the government could, if necessary, purchase allotment from present owners before parceling it out to tenants. The precedent of government compensation for revocation of such rights should be studied carefully as it could represent an important and potentially costly endeavor. Other allotment programs have been terminated without compensation. Even if those wishing to surrender allotment were compensated, the costs of providing allotment to tenant growers would probably be considerably cheaper than the cost to society of driving them from the farms they are operating, perhaps into the ranks of the unemployed. The program could be financed through general funds or by earmarking a modest share of cigarette tax revenues for the purpose. This process could be repeated periodically, perhaps every five years, to avoid duplicating in the 1980s the "freezing" process that took place in the 1930s.

Owning the asset of the allotment would help the tenant farmers who remain to acquire land on which to grow tobacco. Compared with allotment cost, land cost even today is cheap. Furthermore, owning allotment, a farmer could then lease added allotment from others in order to expand. The program could include special credits for helping with the purchase of farmland. Such an innovation would assure that all persons actually growing tobacco benefit from the program.

As for hired labor, the counties that are likely to experience severe labor displacement can be identified. The tobacco program should be expanded to encompass retraining and other worker-oriented assistance for former tobacco workers who are unemployed because of technology or shifts in production.

Some allotment-exporting communities, such as those within the economic influence of the Raleigh-Durham-Chapel Hill complex, will see allotment migrate out because of competing economic opportunity. Although there may be some individual hardships, leaf tobacco has ceased to be the economic base of these communities, and they probably need no special assistance. However, some exporting counties have few alternative opportunities, and thus they should be provided special rural development assistance under the tobacco program. This is particularly true of tobacco counties fringing the main production areas.

Conclusions

Understanding the tobacco economy means understanding the system of rights under which tobacco is grown and marketed. Rather than focusing exclusively on farm economics to discern major transitions in tobacco production, one must look toward the political process through which the system of rights was devised and continues to be modified. The franchise to grow and market tobacco retains high value. The rules of the allotment system determine how this value changes over time and how it is distributed among individuals and regions. In seeking constructive ways to reconcile efficiency of production with equity toward individuals and communities, one must focus on how changes in the rules of the system affect the distribution of program benefits.

Notes

1. For details on the historical record, see Charles Mann, *Tobacco: The Ants and the Elephants* (Salt Lake City, Utah: Olympus Publishing Company, 1975), p. 53.

2. Verner N. Grise, "Flue-Cured Tobacco Farming: Structural Characteristics, Labor Use, and Mechanization," paper presented at the 29th Tobacco Workers Conference, Lexington, Ky., January 21, 1981, Economics and Statistics Service, USDA. All of the figures in this paragraph and the next are based on this report.

3. Dale M. Hoover and Sophia I. Efstratoglou Todoulos, "Economic Effects on Intercounty Transfer of Flue-Cured Tobacco Quota," Economics Research Report No. 23, North Carolina State University, Department of Economics, March, 1973, p. 70. In commenting on a draft of this chapter, Dr. Hoover wrote: "I think you can approximately double the figures we presented given the amount of inflation that has occurred since 1972/1973."

4. "Effects of Flue-Cured Tobacco Programs on Returns to Land and Labor," Economic Research Service Report No. 379, U.S. Department of Agriculture, 1968, p. iii.

5

Can Tobacco Farmers Adjust to Mechanization? A Look at Allotment Holders in Two North Carolina Counties

Gigi Berardi

In recent years, people from all segments of the political spectrum have called for the preservation of the family farm. Yet the numbers of farms and farmers have been plummeting at an alarming rate in virtually every commodity sector, now even in tobacco. Flue-cured tobacco has always been one of the most labor-intensive crops in the United States and has remained so much longer than almost all other crops.[1] A unique production and marketing system, combined with a farm structure that was stabilized by the Agricultural Adjustment Act of 1938, preserved the tobacco belt as a kind of laboratory, perhaps the best remaining example of the Jeffersonian ideal of an independent yeomanry.[2] But the vast sweep of agricultural mechanization and the escalating pressures common to all farmers, from fertilizer and fuel prices to labor costs and international competition, have begun to transform tobacco farming.

In the last twenty years, two "push" factors—technological innovations and changes in the federal support program—have prompted a dramatic shift in the patterns of tobacco production. And to a lesser degree, the "pull" force of increased industrialization has also caused people to quit farming tobacco. Consequently, a dramatic displacement in the tobacco labor force has begun, a transition that affects every type of tobacco farmer: allotment holders, growers who own land without quotas and have to lease allotments from others, growers who lease land and quota, sharecroppers who farm someone's allotment for a portion of the profits, permanent hired labor, and seasonal workers.

Changes in production technology have had a dramatic impact on the tobacco work force. Chemical controls have virtually eliminated the summer

I wish to thank Professor Dale M. Hoover (Department of Business and Economics) and Professor Michael Schulman (Department of Sociology and Anthropology) at North Carolina State University for their assistance in the design and implementation of this study. Mr. Eugene Naylor (North Carolina State Agricultural Stabilization and Conservation Service office) assisted in obtaining the sampling frame used in the study. In particular, I wish to acknowledge the assistance of Ms. Lisa Bosley in the research design, data collection, and data analysis phases of this project.

47

labor bottleneck when sucker leaves must be removed from the plant. A single machine operator can handle up to twenty acres a day, "topping" the plants and spraying them with a sucker-inhibiting chemical in one pass down the row. Transplanting, although still labor intensive, now requires far fewer hours because of the mechanical transplanters. But the most publicized and perhaps the largest impact on tobacco labor resulted from the introduction of the mechanical harvester and bulk curing barns.

As early as the 1950s, members of the Agricultural Research Service faculty at North Carolina State University (NCSU) had begun to design work on the functional principles needed for a machine that could remove and handle tobacco leaves. The state's land-grant university, NCSU supported this early work through its ongoing federal and state funding received for agricultural research.[3] In the early 1960s, two commercial manufacturing companies attempted to produce a mechanical harvester; they were unsuccessful, primarily because field-harvesting methods had not yet been developed to take advantage of the harvester. (See the discussion of changes in the federal price-support program later in the chapter.)

In the mid-1960s, R.J. Reynolds Tobacco Company, anticipating the need for a harvester in the future, made grants to NCSU to help sustain the research that had begun a decade earlier. Reynolds itself also began design research, utilizing the functional principles developed at NCSU. By 1969, Reynolds—with the close cooperation and assistance of NCSU researchers—had designed, constructed, and field-tested a prototype harvester. In 1970, Reynolds and the Harrington Manufacturing Company announced an agreement for commercial production. Within a few years, mechanical harvesters began appearing in the field.

Although the average tobacco allotment in North Carolina was about three acres at that time, the new harvesters had a break-even capacity of forty to fifty acres. The machine's designers felt that it was impractical to develop a harvester with only a three- to four-acre capacity and that tobacco farming units would move toward larger operational sizes as the harvester became widely available.[4]

In 1975, the U.S. Department of Agriculture (USDA) released the first major study of the harvester's impact.[5] The USDA analyzed data from an area that produced about three-fourths of the flue-cured tobacco in the country, and found that in 1972, 1 percent of the acreage had been harvested mechanically and 8 percent of the crop had been cured in bulk barns. With the technology available in 1972, a farmer could harvest an acre with only 58 hours of labor, a dramatic change from more traditional methods that took up to 257 hours of labor per acre harvested. The USDA then predicted that by 1978, tobacco farmers would harvest 23 to 36 percent mechanically, cure 65 to 80 percent in bulk barns, and reduce the labor needed during the harvest by some 50 percent.[6]

Since the USDA study in 1972, a number of researchers have collected data that support these predictions. Some have found an even more rapid pace of mechanization than the USDA anticipated, especially in the North Carolina belts. In *1980 Tobacco Information*, for example, Rupert Watkins of the North Carolina Agricultural Extension Service reported that 46 percent of North Carolina's crop was harvested mechanically.

These technological innovations took hold in such a short time primarily because of three major changes in the federal tobacco program. First, in 1961 Congress passed Public Law 87-10 which authorized intracounty (that is, within a single county) lease-and-transfer of flue-cured allotments on a limited basis. Subsequent amendments expanded the leasing provision (for example, a 1967 action eliminated the five-acre limit on the amount that could be transferred to a single farm). Intracounty leasing facilitated a consolidation of quotas into larger tobacco management units at central locations. A farmer no longer had to go from one part of a county to another, from farm to farm, to acquire more tobacco quotas. Second, in 1965, federal legislation changed the flue-cured allotment system from an acreage to a poundage basis. A poundage quota eliminated a critical barrier to mechanization: the tobacco harvester's high leaf loss in the field. (Mechanical harvesting can result in up to 15 percent leaf loss.) On a poundage basis, unlike the acreage method, the leaf left in the field was not a loss. Third, in 1968, the "tying" requirement for flue-cured tobacco was eliminated. Marketing flue-cured leaf in loose-leaf "sheets" rather than in tied "hands" required far fewer labor hours and made possible large investments in bulk-curing barns, where loose-leaf sheets (but not tied hands) could be easily stacked.

Although changes in technology and the federal tobacco program were "pushing" people out of tobacco, nonfarm occupations, to some extent, were "pulling" them with the lure of a steady wage. From 1965 to 1977, North Carolina's employment in nonagricultural sectors increased from 1.4 to 2.1 million. But research published in the last four years indicates that people moving into the state accounted for much of this increase, not persons leaving tobacco farms.[7] Some tobacco laborers were losing their old jobs in the fields but failing to find work in the state's newly built factories.

The rapid spread of mechanized tobacco production, facilitated by adjustments to the federal support program, is resulting in increased labor efficiency and decreased per acre production costs for some growers. But those who have not been able to invest in the technology have had to either produce tobacco at relatively higher costs (at a time when costs common to all agricultural sectors were skyrocketing and agricultural labor came under minimum-wage law) or quit tobacco farming completely. Leaving tobacco farming in the largest numbers are sharecroppers, full-time laborers, and seasonal workers. They are not needed, and they can no longer be afforded except in far fewer numbers on the larger, more mechanized farm units.

All types of tobacco farmers have already experienced, or will soon face, some adjustments in employment, income, and possibly location. But persons who own no factor of production other than their own labor face the most severe adjustment problems, which are often exacerbated by age, race, education levels, and lack of vocational training. In 1977, researchers at NCSU reported on the effects of mechanization on harvest workers in eight of the state's coastal counties, an area that produced one-eighth of the nation's flue-cured tobacco. They found that less than 10 percent of the total lost earnings of harvest workers would be replaced by two income-transfer programs: food stamps and Aid to Families with Dependent Children (AFDC).[8]

Allotment Holders: Adjusting to Displacement

Although some income-transfer programs such as food stamps or AFDC have a stigma, others do not. The federal tobacco program, through its lease-and-transfer provisions combined with its other features, effectively functions today as a redistributor of income for allotment holders. Because of such income transfers (and the equity from which it stems), one can assume that allotment holders in general adjust to displacement easier than people who have no land equity. Indeed, a study of displacement among allotment holders (such as the one I have completed) examines minimum-hardship patterns. But it also suggests the degree and form of adjustment that other types of tobacco "farmers" will experience.

In the summer of 1980, I coordinated a study of tobacco allotment holders in Greene and Wayne counties, North Carolina. This research had two primary objectives: (1) to document the socioeconomic characteristics of allotment holders who are no longer producing their quota; and (2) to determine if former tobacco growers who had allotments made the transition out of agriculture successfully, and to record how they replaced to-bacco income.

In this two-county area, located in the coastal plain of North Carolina, 12 percent of the cropland in 1977 was tobacco allotment acreage, 10 percent higher than the state average. In 1979, these two counties produced 6 percent of North Carolina's tobacco; Wayne ranked eighth and Greene thirteenth among the state's counties in total production. Because of this concentration of tobacco production, labor adjustment problems were expected in this area. Cost constraints prevented extending the study into other tobacco-producing counties and sampling other groups such as seasonal and permanent workers.

The North Carolina State Agricultural Stabilization and Conservation Service (ASCS) provided the names of the 4,298 tobacco allotment holders in these counties. A systematic sample of 431 allotment holders was drawn.[9] Sixty-one percent of the sample (261 out of 431) were ineligible: they either were still producing their own quota or owned quota in counties other than Greene and Wayne. Of the remaining 170 allotment holders, 32 percent (54 out of 170) refused to be interviewed. The response rate was thus 68 percent (116 interviews completed out of 170 eligible respondents). The respondents completed a three-page questionnaire that was developed with the assistance of North Carolina State University staff and was pretested to identify unclear or ambiguous questions. A random sampling of the allotment holders who refused to complete the questionnaire determined that no significant differences existed between the eligible nonrespondents and the respondents for the variables tested.

The allotment holders tended to be lifelong residents of their respective county, over sixty years old, and high-school educated. Sixty-nine percent of the respondents were sixty years of age or older; the average age was sixty-three. Two-thirds of the respondents were male, one-third female (most of these women were widowed). The average years lived in the present county of residence was fifty-three, and 98 percent of the respondents planned to continue living in the same county. Two-thirds had completed high school, thus increasing their qualifications for off-farm employment relative to other residents in the area without this level of education. Nevertheless, the older age of the population puts a constraint on their participation in the nonfarm labor force. The nonfarming allotment holders who responded to this survey thus have not migrated nor have they joined the nonfarm labor force at the rates that their educational backgrounds might indicate.

After quitting tobacco farming, these allotment holders either retired (52.8 percent), worked in off-farm employment (30.0 percent), remained a housewife (11.3 percent), or farmed crops other than tobacco (5.9 percent). Most of the off-farm employment was in industry.

It is important to note that although 52.8 percent listed themselves as retired, less than one-third gave "retirement" as the reason they no longer farmed their allotment (table 5-1). Of those who did state "retirement," one out of four were less than 65 years old (primarily 55 to 64) and had some off-farm employment. Retirement age, then, is only one of several factors involved in the decision to stop growing tobacco, despite the age of this population. High production costs, including investment in new technology, were discussed at length by respondents, especially by the elderly persons.

Only 13.7 percent of the respondents had never grown tobacco, and they are grouped in table 5-1 as those who "discontinued" because they

Table 5-1
Distribution of Allotment Holders in Greene and Wayne Counties, by Reasons for Discontinuing Tobacco Production
(percentages)

Reasons	Distribution of Population
Retired	30.5
Health	16.8
Inherited quota	13.7
Labor problems	12.6
Off-farm employment	10.5
Other[a]	15.9
Total	100.0

[a]High cost of machinery, "larger profit to be made from lease and transfer of quota."

inherited a quota. Three-fourths of this 13.7 percent were over 55 years of age, and 80 percent earned more than $20,000 a year. But one must remember that 13.7 percent is barely more than one person out of every eight who is not growing his or her allotment. A common assumption among some critics of the tobacco program is that it benefits primarily those who have never farmed their allotment, insuring from birth a source of income that requires no work. The results in table 5-1 indicate that this is not the case.

Generally, the allotment-holder population has replaced its tobacco earnings by combining income from four sources: lease and transfer of quota, special services (particularly social security), crop and livestock production, and off-farm employment (table 5-2). These income sources are only mutually exclusive in some cases. For example, those dependent on special services most likely would not have off-farm employment. On the other hand, both groups might get some income from crop and livestock production.

Almost all the respondents (95.3 percent) received income from the lease and transfer of their quota, reflecting the extent to which the tobacco

Table 5-2
Replacement of Tobacco Earnings, by Allotment Holders in Greene and Wayne Counties
(percentages)

Income Sources	Population
Lease and transfer of quota	95.3
Special services	56.6
Off-farm employment	31.1
Crop and livestock production	29.2

allotment system now functions as an income-transfer program for allotment holders. In 1979, the average number of pounds leased and transferred out for production was 10,412 (the range was 178 to 64,000). The average payment received was $.44 per pound and thus the rental earnings (based on average price and weight) were $4,581 (the range was $78.32 to $28,160) per year per allotment holder. These earnings constituted a large portion of the yearly household income for allotment holders in Greene and Wayne counties (the average yearly household income ranged from $10,000 to $14,999).

Approximately half (46.7 percent) of the households made less than $10,000 in 1979. Of these households, 29 percent had only one household member, whereas 71 percent had two or more members. Most of these incomes (calculated on a per-household-member basis) would be considerably lower than the 1979 North Carolina state per capita income average of $7,359. The income data for age and occupational classes reflect more hardships among the elderly than among the younger respondents, and lower incomes for housewives and the retired than for those in off-farm jobs and other farm sectors (tables 5-3 and 5-4).

One quarter (26.6 percent) of the allotment holders stopped producing their own quota before 1970. Thus, the decision to lease and transfer quota was made by most allotment holders during the period in the 1970s when mechanization was increasing. Furthermore, the decision is fairly permanent; 98.2 percent had leased and transferred out quota every year since they began transferring their quota. Even so, almost 40 percent said that if they wanted to produce their own quota, they would have the equipment and curing barns to grow tobacco again. Only 10.9 percent (these are younger individuals with off-farm employment) stated that they may want to grow tobacco again.[10]

As table 5-2 shows, 56.6 percent of these persons are supplementing their incomes from special services. But very few of the allotment holders

Table 5-3
Distribution of Allotment Holders in Greene and Wayne Counties, by 1979 Household Income and Age
(percentages)

	Household Income			
Age	Less than $10,000	$10,000-19,999	Greater than $20,000	Total
65+	59.6	29.7	10.7	100.0
64-55	46.0	32.4	21.6	100.0
54-46	30.0	30.0	40.0	100.0
43-34	9.1	18.1	72.8	100.0

Table 5-4
Distribution of Allotment Holders in Greene and Wayne Counties, by 1979
Household Income and Occupation
(percentages)

| | Household Income | | | |
| | Less than | | Greater than | |
Occupation	$10,000	$10,000-19,999	$20,000	Total
Retired	62.8	23.5	13.7	100.0
Off-farm employment	27.2	36.4	36.4	100.0
Housewife	88.9	11.1	0.0	100.0
Farm operator[a]	16.7	33.3	50.0	100.0

[a]Most of these farm operators had off-farm income.

participated in programs other than social security and disability (table 5-5). Income-transfer programs such as food stamps and AFDC were not used at all, although households did qualify.

Those replacing some of their tobacco income by producing other crops (29.2 percent of the population, see table 5-2) were growing primarily corn and soybeans for cash sale and vegetables for home use (table 5-6). Only 21 percent produced vegetables for personal consumption, and only 6 percent or less produced livestock for themselves. Since one-half the households earned less than $10,000 yearly (71 percent of these households had two or more members), and since none of them was participating in the food-stamp program, the nutritional adequacy of the diets of these households might have been in jeopardy.

Off-farm employment was a source of income for 31.1 percent of the sample population no longer growing tobacco (table 5-2). About 40 percent of this group's household income was over $20,000 and only 27.3 percent earned less than $10,000, a sharp contrast to allotment holders who depended more on special services—68.4 percent of whom earned less than $10,000 (table 5-7).

Table 5-5
Distribution of Allotment Holders in Greene and Wayne Counties
Receiving Income from Special Services
(percentages)

Special Services	Population
Social security	55.7
Disability	6.6
Workman's compensation	0.0
Food stamps	0.0
Other (pension, and so on)	6.6

Table 5-6
**Distribution of Allotment Holders in Greene and Wayne Counties
Receiving Income from Crop and Livestock Production**

Crop/Livestock	Cash Sale	Home Use
Peanuts	0.0	1.7
Corn	29.2	5.2
Soybeans	20.7	.9
Vegetables	6.0	20.7
Forest products	5.2	1.7
Poultry	5.2	1.7
Hogs	2.6	3.4
Dairy	0.0	1.7
Other	0.0	2.6

Conclusion

The changing structure of tobacco production in Wayne and Greene counties
suggests ways to view the impact of labor displacement throughout the flue-
cured tobacco belt. First, a subtle but widespread form of labor displacement must be recognized: premature attrition, that is, persons retiring from
tobacco farming before they normally would want to retire. This necessi-
tates some special attention for the elderly. Second, replacement of earnings
for the elderly and for all other displaced tobacco farmers demands careful
attention, particularly the role of off-farm employment, special services,
and lease-and-transfer income. Third, the expectations of younger allotment holders need to be viewed in relationship to the changing tobacco
structure in an era of mechanization. Finally, the impact of labor displacement on those "farmers" without equity in land must be more thoroughly
studied and understood.

    Although most of the respondents in this study could be characterized

Table 5-7
**Distribution of Allotment Holders in Greene and Wayne Counties, by 1979
Household Income and Method of Replacement of Tobacco Earnings**
(percentages)

Replacement of Tobacco Earnings: Income Source[a]	Household Income			
	Less than $10,000	$10,000-19,999	Greater than $20,000	Total
Production of crops and livestock	41.4	34.5	24.1	100.0
Off-farm employment	27.3	33.3	39.4	100.0
Special services	68.4	26.0	5.6	100.0

[a]These income sources are not necessarily mutually exclusive.

as elderly, only one-fourth listed "retirement" as the reason for quitting tobacco farming. Sixty percent of those over 65 years of age and 46 percent of those from age 55 to 64 earned less than $10,000 a year. Tobacco policymakers should note especially that much of this income came from lease and transfer of quota. A change in the tobacco program that affects this source of income would have a severe impact. If the tobacco program is changed so that it no longer functions as an income-transfer program for allotment holders, some other type of income transfer will have to replace it or an additional hardship will be placed on this group of people.

Individuals who can successfully obtain off-farm employment have a substantially higher income than those who must depend on social security or income-transfer payments. Special-service payments are lower than industrial wages (even in North Carolina, which has one of the lowest average industrial wages in the country). Moreover, people are hesitant to utilize income-transfer programs commonly labeled "welfare."

One-third of the population did replace tobacco earnings with off-farm employment. One would expect that individuals who are no longer employed in agriculture in North Carolina could successfully obtain off-farm employment, given the growth rate of industry in the state. During the decade following 1966, only Texas and California gained more manufacturing jobs than North Carolina. Yet who is benefiting from this shift in manufacturing location? As stated earlier and corroborated by these research findings, North Carolina's displaced tobacco farmers may not be able to compete for industrial jobs as well as people moving into the state in pursuit of employment. This is primarily a result of educational and age constraints (particularly true for the population of tobacco allotment holders in Greene and Wayne counties), and the lack of retraining programs for older adults.

The primary objective of this study was to determine the socioeconomic characteristics of allotment holders who are no longer producing their quota. However, information was also obtained from allotment holders who are still producing their quota. These people have a strong commitment to tobacco production, and most are planning to grow tobacco until retirement.[11] But as this study demonstrates, "retirement" can mean quitting tobacco farming long before age sixty-five. As leasing costs increase to one-third and more of the value of tobacco production, the profit margins of tobacco growers (and in particular, small-scale producers who might have higher production costs) are narrowing.[12] This could lead to a greater decline in the number of tobacco growers and an increase in average acreage of tobacco farming units.

In sum, tobacco allotment holders who are no longer producing their own quota have made employment and income adjustments primarily through participating in special services (mainly social security) and leasing and transferring their tobacco quota; fewer than one-third have off-farm employment or other farm income. But it is difficult to draw conclusions as to whether nonfarming allotment holders have successfully made the transition out of agriculture either completely or partially. One-half of the households had yearly incomes of less than $10,000, but no data were obtained to compare income figures before and after allotment holders began to lease and transfer out their quota.

The population of allotment holders sampled in this study had some distinct advantages over other members of the tobacco work force, in terms of replacing tobacco earnings. Allotment holders derived a considerable portion of their income from lease and transfer of their quota, a source not available to those tobacco growers who own no allotment. Furthermore, this particular population did not have the educational constraints (the average number of school years completed was much higher than the state's average) one might expect of the tobacco work force in general.

More research needs to be conducted in the flue-cured tobacco belt on target populations for which adjustment may be particularly difficult, given lower education levels, vocational training, and political power base (for example, for migrant workers).[13] In the same way that concerns have been raised about the adjustment of farm operators to mechanized and modernized tobacco-production technologies (for example, the Ford Foundation and others have suggested programs for training farm operators in mechanical skills and management), so too should concerns be raised about the majority of the tobacco labor force who will no longer be deriving income through employment in tobacco production. Although some adjustment programs, such as special education grants, have been suggested by other researchers, *ex ante facto* research focusing on this group must be expanded.

Researchers and policymakers often assume that those who are displaced from agriculture either participate in federal, state, or private income-transfer programs or find off-farm employment. However, the little research that has been conducted on the adjustment process indicates that changes in employment and location may indeed be difficult, and for some, impossible.[14]

Notes

1. According to the USDA, *Agricultural Statistics 1977*, the 1971-1975 average man-hours per acre required to produce tobacco was 281.0 (compared with 5.1 for corn, 2.9 for wheat, 23.0 for cotton, 42.6 for potatoes, and 161.5 for tomatoes).

2. Throughout the last sixty years, writers have recorded the consequences of labor displacement caused by agriculture mechanization—during the great agricultural depression of 1921-1936, with the arrival of an

automated cotton harvest in the 1950s and 1960s, and following the mechanization of the tomato harvest in California in the late 1960s. Many of these researchers were attempting to explain the unique circumstances of a particular farming sector and then to suggest possible adjustment programs to ameliorate the hardships of labor displacement. Unlike most of this type of research, several studies on the mechanization of the flue-cured tobacco industry have attempted to anticipate this displacement so as to offer some understanding of its effects prior to large-scale mechanization (Grise et al., "Structural Characteristics,"; Hoover and Perkinson, "Flue-Cured Tobacco Harvest"). This chapter represents another effort at exploring policy options prior to full-scale farm displacement.

3. Federal funding of research that is focused on increasing labor efficiency through agricultural mechanization has been the subject of much controversy by academicians (Friedland and Barton, "Destalking") as well as public-interest groups. Recently, California Rural Legal Assistance filed a suit on behalf of nineteen farm workers and a small-farmer organization to contest sixty-nine tax-financed projects at the University of California that benefit large farming operations (Meyerhoff, "Big Farming's").

4. See Suggs, "Mechanical Harvesting."

5. See Grise et al., "Structural Characteristics." The USDA gathered data from four census-of-agricultural subregions: 29 (Ga.), 17 (Coastal Plain, N.C.), 18 (Piedmont, Va.-N.C.), and 16 (Pee Dee-Lumber River).

6. See Grise et al. "Structural Characteristics." The USDA released a follow-up study (Hoff et al., "Mechanization and Labor"), based on the same 1972 data, which projected the most profitable farm structure within this mechanization process. In 1979, the USDA began a new study of the same magnitude as its 1972 survey. A report based on the 1979 data will be released in 1981.

7. See Perkinson, "Migration"; Hoover and Perkinson, "Flue-Cured Tobacco Harvest"; and Long and Hansen, "Selectivity."

8. Research from Legal Services of North Carolina, Pennsylvania State University, State University of New York (Binghamton), and others has shown that monetary and nonmonetary income-transfer programs in North Carolina are vastly underutilized, failing to reach about half of those qualified.

9. The sample size for the survey was calculated using estimates for the population variance of key variables. We assumed that 50 percent of the list would be ineligible and that there would be a 60-percent response rate.

10. This result is interesting from a policy perspective since there has been some discussion of modifying the tobacco program so that allotment holders would be required to produce their own quota periodically.

11. Most of these farmers planned to grow tobacco until retirement (79.5 percent) or were undecided (12.8 percent). Only 7.7 percent were considering leasing and transferring out their quota in the future, and they still planned to farm part-time or full-time until retirement. Slightly more than

two-thirds (69.2 percent) of the growers had no source of income other than farming. Of those who did have other income, the majority of them had jobs in industry. The average size of quota for this group was 24,614 pounds (range: 150 to 330,000), more than twice the quota of allotment holders no longer growing tobacco.

12. As rental rates and thus production costs increase, the price of U.S. flue-cured tobacco also increases. This has resulted in a decrease in the U.S. flue-cured share of the domestic and foreign market. To compete more strongly in the world market, the tobacco program might have to undergo changes that will result in lowered production costs (and perhaps loss of rental income for current tobacco allotment holders). This situation has generated much discussion.

13. Results may show that incomes are higher for former members of the tobacco labor force who have off-farm employment. However, it is also possible that off-farm employment will not be an option for many of these individuals. Migration and participation in income-transfer programs may or may not be viable options. All these hypotheses need to be tested with data collected through surveys, especially longitudinal case studies.

14. See Hamilton, "Social Effects"; and Raper, "Role of Agricultural Technology."

References

Buttel, F.H. "The Political Economy of Agriculture in Advanced Industrial Societies: Some Observations from the United States." Paper presented at the annual meeting of the Canadian Sociology and Anthropology Association. Montreal, June 1980.

Donaldson, G.F., and McInerney, J.P. "Changing Machinery Technology and Agricultural Adjustment." *American Journal of Agricultural Economics* 55, no. 5 (1973):829-839.

Economics, Statistics, and Cooperatives Service. (Prepared by the Development Strategies Project Research Team). "Technological Changes in the Production of Flue-Cured Tobacco: Anticipated Socio-Economic Consequences—An Executive Summary and Annotated Bibliography." Washington, D.C.: U.S. Department of Agriculture, Economics, Statistics, and Cooperatives Service, 1978.

Friedland, W.H., and Barton, A. "Destalking the Wily Tomato: A Case Study in Social Consequences." In *California Agriculture Research.* Davis, Calif.: Univ. of Calif., Department of Applied Behavior Science Research. Monograph No. 15, 1975.

Friedland, W.H., and Kappel, T. "Production or Perish: Changing the Inequities of Agricultural Research Priorities." Santa Cruz, Calif.: Project on Social Impact Assessment and Values, 1979.

Grise, Verner N. et al. "Structural Characteristics of Flue-Cured Tobacco Farms and Prospects for Mechanization." Washington, D.C.: U.S. Department of Agriculture, Economic Research Service. Agricultural Economic Report 277, 1975.

Hamilton, C. Horace. "The Social Effects of Recent Trends in the Mechanization of Agriculture." *Rural Sociology* 4 (1939):3-19.

Hart, John Fraser, and Chestang, Ennis L. "Rural Revolution in East Carolina." *Geographical Review* (1978), pp. 435-458.

Hoff, Frederic L. et al. "Flue-Cured Tobacco—Mechanization and Labor: Impacts of Alternative Production Levels." Washington, D.C.: U.S. Department of Agriculture, Economic Research Service. Agricultural Economic Report 368, 1977.

Hoover, Dale M., and Perkinson, Leon. "Flue-Cured Tobacco Harvest Labor: Its Characteristics and Vulnerability to Mechanization." North Carolina State University, Department of Economics and Business. Economic Research Report 38, June 1977.

Hoover, Dale M., and Pugh, Charles R. "Probable Location of Flue-Cured Tobacco Production under Modified Lease-and-Transfer Programs." Raleigh: North Carolina Agricultural Extension Service. Circular 557, 1973.

Long, Larry H., and Hansen, Kristen A. "Selectivity of Black Return Migration to the South." *Rural Sociology* 42, no. 3 (1977):317-331.

Mahaffey, Doris, and Doty, Mercer M. "Which Way Now? Economic Development and Industrialization in North Carolina." Raleigh, N.C.: North Carolina Center for Public Policy Research, Inc., 1979.

Mann, Charles Kellogg. *Tobacco: The Ants and the Elephants.* Salt Lake City, Utah: Olympus Publishing Company, 1975.

Martin, Philip L., and Johnson, Stanley S. "Tobacco Technology and Agricultural Labor." *American Journal of Agricultural Economics.* 60, no. 4 (1978):655-660.

Meyerhoff, Al. "Big Farming's Angry Harvest." *Newsweek* (March 3, 1980), p. 11.

North Carolina Department of Agriculture. *North Carolina Tobacco Report*, number 235. Raleigh, N.C.: Tobacco Affairs Section, Division of Marketing, North Carolina Department of Agriculture, 1979.

Perkinson, Leon. "Migration Into a North Carolina Rural Area, 1970-74." Economics Information Report No. 57. Raleigh, N.C.: North Carolina State University, Department of Business and Economics, 1979.

Pugh, Charles R. "Provisions of the Tobacco Program, Consequences of Their Elimination and Alternatives." Raleigh, N.C.: North Carolina State University, 1978.

Raper, Arthur. "The Role of Agricultural Technology in Social Change." *Social Forces.* 25 (1946):21-30.

Research and Planning Services. *North Carolina State Government Statistical Abstract*. Raleigh, N.C.: Division of State Budget and Management, 1979.

Sanderson, Dwight. *Research Memorandum on Rural Life in the Depression*, Bulletin 34. New York: Social Science Research Council, 1937.

Schmitz, Andrew and David Seckler. "Mechanized Agriculture and Social Welfare: The Case of the Tomato Harvester." *American Journal of Agricultural Economics*. 52, no. 4:569-577.

Showalter, Ralph. "Tobacco Farm Mechanization Project, Phase II." Raleigh, N.C.: Social Development Corporation, 1973.

Street, James H. *The New Revolution in the Cotton Economy*, pp. 240-251. Chapel Hill: University of North Carolina Press, 1957.

Suggs, C.W. "Mechanical Harvesting of Flue-Cured Tobacco. Part 1, Leaf Removing Device." *Tobacco Science* 16 (1972).

_____ . "Mechanical Harvesting of Flue-Cured Tobacco. Part 5, Factors Affecting Rate of Adoption." *Tobacco Science* 18 (1974).

U.S. Department of Agriculture. *Agricultural Statistics 1976*. Tables 614 and 626. Washington, D.C.: U.S. Department of Agriculture, 1977.

U.S. Senate. "Priorities in Agricultural Research of the U.S. Department of Agriculture: A Summary Report of the Hearings." Washington, D.C.: U.S. Government Printing Office, 1978.

6

Changes in the Structure of the Flue-Cured Tobacco Farm: A Compilation of Available Data Sources

Robert Dalton

In the past decade, flue-cured tobacco farms have changed dramatically. They have become larger and more mechanized, requiring fewer and fewer farmers and relying on more and more leased quota.[1] These four factors—mechanization, farm-unit size, the lease-and-transfer system, and labor displacement—are all closely interrelated and interdependent. As mechanization increases, farms get bigger, more tobacco is leased, and fewer people grow it. Each factor allows and encourages the next, operating in a circular system (figure 6-1). Chapters 2, 4, and 5 discuss the various changes in the tobacco-farm structure in both a political and an economic context. This chapter summarizes the currently available data on the four variables shown in figure 6-1, all of which play a vital role in determining the structure of the flue-cured tobacco farm.

The most wide-ranging and thorough data on this subject have been collected by the U.S. Department of Agriculture (USDA) through surveys of the flue-cured area in 1972 and 1979. The USDA published reports on these data in 1975, 1977, and 1981, documenting a rapid increase in the use of mechanical harvesters and bulk-curing barns and a shift toward larger farm units with decreased overall labor requirements.[2] Other organizations and individuals have also collected these kind of data with similar results.

Size of Farm Management Unit

The size of the flue-cured-tobacco management unit has grown steadily in the last fifteen years. According to U.S. Census of Agriculture data, the flue-cured farm size increased from about 5 acres in 1964 to 8.7 acres in 1969.[3] The 1974 and 1979 Census of Agriculture do not break down the figures by tobacco type.[4] The USDA surveys, however, did gather these data and reported that the flue-cured-tobacco management unit increased from 9.5 acres in 1972 to 13.8 acres in 1979 for the four study regions in its survey (table 6-1).

63

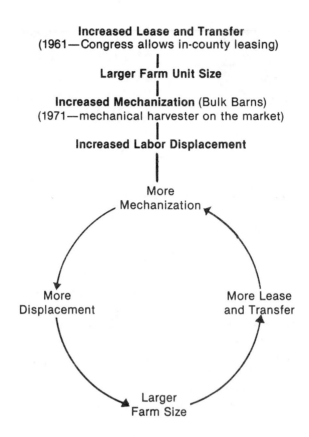

Figure 6-1. Linear Trends Have Evolved into a Circular System

Dr. Charles Pugh of the North Carolina State University Agricultural Extension Service (who has contributed two chapters to this book) calculated a figure similar to the USDA one by using the 1974 Census of Agriculture. Pugh used data from the five-state flue-cured belt of North Carolina, South Carolina, Virginia, Georgia, and Florida, and determined that the average tobacco farm was 9.4 acres in 1974 (for farms selling agricultural products worth $2,500 or more).[5]

The U.S. Census of Agriculture data also confirms the USDA survey for North Carolina flue-cured farms. The average number of acres harvested per farm steadily increased from 5.2 in 1964 to 12.2 in 1978. The

Table 6-1
Flue-Cured-Tobacco Management Units
(Acreage per farm)

Year	Pee Dee-Lumber River North Carolina-South Carolina	Coastal Plain North Carolina	Piedmont North Carolina-Virginia	Georgia	All
1979	13.2	18.8	10.8	11.5	13.8
1972	10.9	11.2	7.7	8.7	9.5

Source: Verner Grise, "Flue-Cured Tobacco Farming: Structural Characteristics, Labor Use, and Mechanization," USDA.

1964 census figures provided these data directly, separating flue-cured from burley farms. For 1969, 1974, and 1978, the figures in table 6-2 were derived by subtracting from the state totals the number of farms and acres in burley-belt counties.

Mechanization

In North Carolina and in all flue-cured areas, the trend is toward greater mechanization of harvest and increased use of bulk-curing barns. (These two aspects of tobacco harvesting go hand-in hand. See chapters 2, 4, and 5 for the context in which they function.) The USDA surveys of 1972 and 1979 indicate the pace of these trends, as shown in table 6-3.

Two other sources, widely recognized among tobacco analysts, make yearly estimates of these data: Rupert Watkins of the North Carolina Agricultural Extension Service and the Tobacco Association of the United States (TAUS). Both Watkins and the TAUS estimate that mechanization has proceeded faster than the USDA survey indicates. The three sources agree on the degree to which bulk barns are being used for curing. Watkins

Table 6-2
Size of North Carolina Flue-Cured-Tobacco Farms
(in thousands)

Year	Acres Produced	Farm Producing	Average per Farm
1964	399.3	76.6	5.2
1969	364.8	54.6	6.7
1974	359.5	37.8	9.5
1978	413.3	33.9	12.2

Source: *U.S. Census of Agriculture* for 1964, 1969, 1974, and 1978, North Carolina section.
Note: Some changes were made during this period which could alter the figures somewhat. For example, in 1969, the collection method changed from direct-interview format to a mail survey; in 1974, farm definition changed to an enterprise with sales of agricultural products worth $1,000 or more, which could inflate the average.

Table 6-3
Pace of Mechanization: All Flue-Cured Belts
(percentages)

Year	Acreage Harvested Mechanically	Acreage Bulk-Cured
1972	1	8
1979	19-33	61
1985 (projected)	35	100

Source: USDA studies described in note 2.

derives his annual estimates by updating the number of mechanical harvesters used in North Carolina with sales figures from the manufacturers. He then multiplies that number by fifty acres per harvester. Watkins selects fifty acres because, as he puts it, it is a "happy medium" among the estimates other researchers use for the capacity per harvester. His methodology for bulk-barn estimates is similar, except he multiplies the number of bulk barns by six acres per barn. The TAUS derives its percentage of the acreage mechanically harvested and bulk cured through a survey of equipment manufacturers, extension agents, agricultural engineers, and tobacco specialists. Table 6-4 summarizes the Watkins and TAUS data.[6]

Lease and Transfer

In 1961, Congress voted to allow lease and transfer of tobacco quota within counties, and in 1967 it removed the limit of five acres that could be leased to any one farm. Lease and transfer is still only permitted within county lines. Both the North Carolina office of the Agricultural Stabilization and Conservation Service and the USDA Economics, Statistics, and Cooperatives Service maintain careful records on quota levels and lease-and-transfer arrangements because they are integral to the operation of the tobacco program.

Since 1966, lease and transfer has been growing in North Carolina, both in raw numbers (pounds of quota and acreage of allotment that are assigned to each farm) and in percentage calculations. From 1966 to 1979, the amount of quota and acreage leased each increased 250 percent, from 80 to 280 million pounds and from 42,200 to 147,600 acres, respectively (table 6-5).[7] Similar trends took place throughout the flue-cured belts (table 6-6).

To understand tables 6-5 and 6-6, one must realize that the total amount of quota significantly affects the poundage and the percentage leased. Since 1962, the figure for pounds of quota leased has increased steadily in North Carolina (until 1976) and in all belts (until 1975). But in recent years, the pattern has been more erratic, primarily because the total quota was

Table 6-4
Pace of Mechanization: Major Flue-Cured Producing States
(percentages)

| | Acreage Harvested Mechanically | | | | | | Acreage Bulk-Cured | | | | | |
| | North Carolina | | Florida | | | | North Carolina | | Florida | | | |
Year	Watkins	TAUS[b]	Alabama[a]	Georgia[a]	South Carolina[a]	Virginia[a]	Watkins	TAUS[b]	Alabama[a]	Georgia[a]	South Carolina[a]	Virginia[a]
1971							3					
1972		1						8				
1973	3	4						14				
1974	10	9					20	20				
1975	18	17					30	30				
1976	25	25					40	40				
1977	36	36	25	35	35	8	52	52	65	50	40	15
1978	38	39	28	39	36	9	58	49	88	63	49	11
1979	46	40	30	40	37	10	62	55	90	75	55	20
1980	50						70					

[a]These estimates are from the Tobacco Association of the United States.
[b]Tobacco Association of the United States.

Table 6-5

Lease and Transfer of North Carolina Flue-Cured Tobacco, 1966-1979

Year	Quota Leased (Millions of Pounds)	Quota Leased[a] (Percentage)	Allotment Leased (Thousands of Acres)	Allotment Leased[b] (Percentage)
1966	79.7	10	42.2	11
1967	97.2	13	51.9	13
1968	125.2	18	67.0	17
1969	127.8	16	67.9	16
1970	146.1	19	78.5	19
1971	167.3	24	89.9	24
1972	187.6	24	100.8	23
1973	210.2	25	111.0	24
1974	243.0	29	128.4	28
1975	n/a	n/a	n/a	n/a
1976	264.6	28	140.6	28
1977	260.3	33	137.8	33
1978	273.5	34	144.3	34
1979	280.0	40	147.6	39

Source: 1966-1979 *Annual Reports/North Carolina,* Agricultural Stabilization and Conservation Service, U.S. Department of Agriculture.

[a]Percentage is based on effective quota.

[b]Percentage is based on effective allotment.

decreasing for North Carolina (from 942.2 million pounds in 1976 to 705.3 million pounds in 1979)[8] and for all belts (from 1,572.3 in 1975 to 1,068.5 in 1979).[9] Even so, the percentage of quota continued to climb until 1980. That year, the total quota for all belts was increased from 1,068.5 million pounds (1979) to 1,187.3 (1980).[10] Hence, even though more pounds were leased in 1980 than in 1979, the portion leased dropped from 45 to 40 percent.

The portion of North Carolina's flue-cured farms leasing in or out grew from 32 percent in 1965 to 85 percent in 1979. The number of farms leasing out increased much more rapidly than those leasing in, which indicates that farms still producing flue-cured tobacco are becoming larger in acreage and fewer in number. By 1979, 60 percent of the flue-cured farms in the state leased out but only 24 percent leased in (table 6-7).

The trends beltwide are similar. Verner Grise of the USDA, reporting on the USDA's 1979 survey results, indicated that a higher percentage of farmers are dependent on leased quota in order to have an economical farm management unit. "Only 16 percent of the farm operators owned the entire tobacco quota that they produced in 1979. The figure was 19 percent in 1972. . . . About 27 percent rented in all their quota in 1979. The remaining 57 percent used some combination of owning, renting, and leasing. . . . Ownership of the entire quota was much more prevalent among operators of the smallest tobacco acreages"[11] (see table 6-8).

Table 6-6
Lease and Transfer of All Flue-Cured Tobacco, 1961-1980

Year	Quota Leased[a] (Millions of Pounds)	Quota Leased[c] (Percentage)	Allotment Leased[e] (Thousands of Acres)	Allotment Leased[d] (Percentage)
1962			23.7	3
1963			33.1	5
1964			41.8	7
1965			54.7	9
1966	138.0	12	80.1	12
1967	167.6	14	97.2	15
1968	214.6	20	122.9	21
1969	230.3	19	131.8	21
1970	255.1	21	146.3	23
1971	289.4	27	166.3	29
1972	322.1	30	182.9	33
1973	363.1	30	192.9	30
1974	416.1	31	234.1	32
1975	474.8	30	251.4	29
1976	464.3	33	246.7	32
1977	448.8	37	241.6	37
1978	464.4	39	245.8	38
1979	477.3[b]	45	267.7[b]	46
1980	479.8[b]	40	268.8[b]	42

[a]From *Tobacco Situation*, quarterly publication of the U.S. Department of Agriculture, No. 169, October 1979.

[b]Telephone interview with Robert Miller, USDA, September 23, 1980.

[c]Percentage is based on effective quota.

[d]Percentage is based on effective allotment.

[e]Figures for 1962 from *Tobacco Situation*, No. 141, September 1972. Figures for 1963-1979 from *Tobacco Situation*, No. 169, October 1979.

Grise reported that an average farm in 1979 produced 4.0 quotas, compared with 3.2 quotas in 1972. In other words, three out of four quota holders did not grow their allotment in 1979. For many years, allotment holders have rented their quota to a local farmer, but this practice has accelerated with the increase in leasing (table 6-9).

Labor Requirements

The amount of labor needed to produce an acre of tobacco has declined dramatically in the last twenty-five years, the period during which labor-saving devices—from weed-control chemicals to the mechanical harvester—have been introduced. Comparing a 1956 study by Pugh at North Carolina State University with a 1977 report issued by the North Carolina Agricultural Extension Service shows the trend among the various stages of tobacco farming and for different farm sizes (see table 6-10).[12] The North

Table 6-7
North Carolina Flue-Cured Tobacco Farms Leasing In or Out

Year	Number of Farms Leasing (in Thousands)			Percentage of Farms with Allotment Leasing		
	In	Out	Total[a]	In	Out	Total
1965	15.9	20.6	36.5	14	18	32
1966	21.4	25.8	47.2	19	23	42
1967	25.0	29.8	54.8	22	26	48
1968	26.2	36.0	61.2	23	31	54
1969	26.2	34.9	61.1	23	30	53
1970	27.9	38.2	66.1	24	33	57
1971	28.7	44.4	73.1	25	39	64
1972	29.7	49.9	79.6	26	43	69
1973	30.8	51.4	82.2	27	45	72
1974	30.6	50.8	81.4	27	44	71
1975	n/a	n/a	n/a	n/a	n/a	n/a
1976	29.3	55.4	84.7	25	48	73
1977	28.9	62.4	91.3	25	54	79
1978	28.7	65.8	94.5	25	57	82
1979	27.4	69.3	96.7	24	60	84

Source: 1965-1979 *Annual Reports/North Carolina,* Agricultural Stabilization and Conservation Service, U.S. Department of Agriculture.

[a]Total may be slightly high owing to possible small overlap of farms leasing in and those leasing out.

Carolina Agricultural Extension Service periodically publishes pamphlets that enable farmers to estimate costs and returns for growing tobacco in North Carolina.

The USDA report of the 1979 survey estimates that the number of flue-cured harvest workers (including family and exchange workers) declined from 325,000 in 1972 to 211,000 in 1979, an average drop of more than 16,000 workers per year. Grise reported:

> The decline occurred because of the adoption of labor-saving harvest technology. . . . Between 1972 and 1979 the greatest harvest labor reduction occurred in the Coastal Plain of North Carolina—the most concentrated production region. Harvest labor use declined by 46 percent in this region from 30.8 million to 16.7 million hours. . . . The number of harvest workers may have declined from 139,000 to 75,000.

> The smallest drop in harvest labor use between 1972 and 1979 was in the Piedmont of North Carolina and Virginia where labor use declined by 16 percent. . . . Because of the rougher topography, operator units have expanded less rapidly and mechanical harvesters have been adopted at a slower rate in this region. Like the Coastal Plain, the Pee Dee-Lumber River and Georgia experienced large reductions in harvest labor use.[13]

Table 6-8
Operators' Tenure for Tobacco Quota, by Flue-Cured-Tobacco Size Group, by Acres of Tobacco Grown (Study Area, 1979 and 1972)

		Acres of tobacco grown				
Tenure	Year	Less than 9.0	9.0-19.9	20.0-34.9	35.0 and over	All
		Percentage of farms				
Own quota	1979	30	3	1	2	16
	1972	27	6	2	16	19
Rent quota	1979	29	30	20	17	27
	1972	27	26	20	4	25
Own and rent	1979	8	18	18	25	14
	1972	10	15	12	21	12
Own and lease	1979	23	20	18	16	21
	1972	21	17	7	4	19
Rent and lease	1979	4	9	14	6	7
	1972	9	13	16	7	10
Own, rent, and lease	1979	6	20	29	34	15
	1972	5	21	36	48	13
Other[a]	1979					
	1972	2	3	7	0	2
Total		100	100	100	100	100

Source: Verner Grise, "Flue-cured Tobacco Farming: Structural Characteristics, Labor Use, and Mechanization," USDA.

[a]Any arrangement that consists of some managed allotment. Managed allotment was included with owned or rented allotment in 1979.

Table 6-9
Flue-Cured-Tobacco Management Units
(individual quotas per farm)

Year	Pee Dee-Lumber River, North Carolina-South Carolina	Coastal Plain, North Carolina	Piedmont North Carolina-Virginia	Georgia	All
1979	4.1	4.5	3.3	4.3	4.0
1972	3.4	2.6	2.5	3.5	3.2

Source: Verner Grise, "Flue-Cured Tobacco Farming: Structural Characteristics, Labor Use, and Mechanization," USDA.

Table 6-10
Estimated Labor Inputs per Acre of Flue-Cured Tobacco
(man-hours)

Operation	1956	Small[a]	1977 Medium[b]	Large[c]
Plant bed	11.0	3.74	2.32	5.87
Land preparation	11.8	5.56	2.86	1.75
Pulling/transplanting	35.0	22.00	16.10	16.20
Growing after transplanting	46.2	13.13	2.87	3.38
Harvesting and curing	145.0	125.00	88.00	59.06
Preparation for market Total	140.0	30.00	15.60	15.60
Assumed yield per acre	1,600.0 lbs.		2,100.00 lbs.	

[a]Small farms—using hand-priming, typing machines, conventional barns, and small tractor and tillage equipment, with 10 acres or less.

[b]Medium farms—using larger tillage equipment, harvesting via racking on priming aid, and bulk barns, with around 25 acres.

[c]Large farms—using large tillage equipment, four-row transplanters, automatic harvester, and bulk barns, with 40 acres or more.

Notes

1. Various systems for harvesting, preparing for curing, and curing flue-cured tobacco exist. The USDA reports cited in note 2 list ten different combinations, including several that could be called partially mechanized systems. This chapter focuses on mechanical harvesters and bulk barns because this combination has the most long-range impact on the tobacco-farm structure in terms of size of farm unit and labor requirements.

2. The following three USDA reports are based on survey data in a four-region area that produces about three-quarters of the nation's flue-cured tobacco. All numbers cited from these studies are based on surveys in this region, not on the entire flue-cured growing area. Verner N. Grise et al., "Structural Characteristics of Flue-Cured Tobacco Farms and Prospects for Mechanization," Agricultural Economic Report 277 (Washington, D.C.: U.S. Department of Agriculture, Economic Research Service), January 1975; Frederic L. Hoff et al., "Flue-Cured Tobacco Mechanization and Labor: Impacts of Alternative Production Levels, Agricultural Economic Report 368 (Washington, D.C.: U.S. Department of Agriculture, Economic Research Service), April 1977; Verner N. Grise, "Flue-Cured Tobacco Farming: Structural Characteristics, Labor Use, and Mechanization," presented at the 29th Tobacco Workers Conference, Lexington, Ky., January 21, 1981, Economics and Statistics Service, USDA. The full report on the 1979 survey data will be published in 1981.

3. *1964 U.S. Census of Agriculture,* vol. 2, chap. 4: Crops, "Horticultural Products, and Forest Products" (Washington, D.C.: U.S. Department of Commerce, Bureau of the Census), pp. 418-419. The 1964 census only shows flue-cured tobacco specifically for North Carolina and Virginia: 91,600 farms harvesting 460,700 acres for an average of 5.03 acres. If one adds farms and acreage for South Carolina, Georgia, and Florida, the average drops to 4.77 acres per farm: 127,800 farms harvesting 610,300 acres. By 1969, the number grew to 8.67 acres per farm with 43,500 farms harvesting 377,400 acres of flue-cured tobacco. *1969 U.S. Census of Agriculture,* vol. 5 Special Reports, part 2: "Tobacco" (Washington, D.C.: U.S. Department of Commerce, Bureau of the Census), p. XVII. The 1969 Census excluded all farms that had agricultural products with less than $2,500 in total value, so the average may be somewhat inflated. The tobacco farms in the sample represent about 72 percent of all tobacco farms. States specifically showing flue-cured tobacco are Alabama, Florida, Georgia, Kentucky, Maryland, Nebraska, North Carolina, South Carolina, Tennessee, Virginia, and Wisconsin.

4. John Blackledge, Agriculture Division, Bureau of the Census, U.S. Department of Commerce. Telephone interviews by author, September 24 and October 1, 1980. The Census Bureau has not classified tobacco by types since it went from a direct interview format to a mail-out/mail-back survey method in 1969. One survey form is used for all states and allows some adjustment to individual states. To recontact people and classify tobacco by types would be too costly for a large-scale operation like the U.S. Census.

5. Charles R. Pugh, "The Structure of Flue-Cured Tobacco Farms," prepared for the Senate Committee on Agriculture, Nutrition, and Family, September 1979, pp. 3-4.

6. Rupert Watkins, extension specialist, North Carolina Agricultural Extension Service, North Carolina State University at Raleigh, N.C. Telephone interviews, September 15 and 22, 1980. Letter from Hugh C. Kiger, executive vice-president, Tobacco Association of the United States, October 8, 1980.

7. The figures for acreage allotment leased refer, at least for North Carolina, to acres leased in. The number of acres leased out tends to be larger than the number of acres leased in because of differing yields per acre. I have chosen to use the figures for leasing in to err on the side of caution.

8. "1976 and 1979 Annual Reports/North Carolina," (Washington, D.C.: U.S. Department of Agriculture, Agricultural Stabilization and Conservation Service).

9. *Tobacco Situation,* no. 169, October 1979, and no. 172, June 1980.

10. *Tobacco Situation,* no. 172, June 1980.

11. Grise, "Flue-Cured Tobacco Farming," pp. 3-4.

12. "Cost of Producing Farm Products in North Carolina," A.E. Information Series 52 (Department of Agricultural Economics, North Carolina State College), December 1956, "Planning for Profit-Field Crops," Circular 519, revised (North Carolina Agricultural Extension Service), November 1977.

13. Grise, "Flue-Cured Tobacco Farming," p. 7.

7

Resources on Tobacco Production and Marketing

Robert Dalton

U.S. Department of Agriculture

Although Congress provides statutory authority for the marketing quota and price-support programs and sets the overall formula for determining the average support price, the U.S. Department of Agriculture (USDA) administers the tobacco program. Various divisions of the USDA determine support rates for individual grades of tobacco, decide which grades will be supported, define the standards for different grades of tobacco, loan funds to the stabilization cooperatives, encourage export sales of tobacco leaf, conduct agricultural and market research, and gather and disseminate tobacco-related information. The following divisions of the USDA are responsible for aspects of the tobacco program (they also work with other commodities). This overview was compiled at the end of 1980 and updated in summer 1981 to reflect the major changes effected by the Reagan administration reorganization announced on June 17, 1981.

Office of the Secretary of Agriculture

Based on work done by the USDA divisions that are listed here, the Secretary makes the final administrative decisions on most aspects of the tobacco program, such as fixing grade standards, setting support prices, determining marketing procedures, and establishing the annual quota. The Secretary traditionally approves the recommendations of the Flue-Cured Tobacco Advisory Committee (this committee was abolished by the Reagan administration) regarding marketing procedures and schedules. The Secretary also advises the President on all aspects of the tobacco program.

Agricultural Stabilization and Conservation Service (ASCS)

The ASCS has the main responsibility of implementing the tobacco program. Through six hundred county offices, the ASCS issues marketing

Portions of "Industry Organizations," the fourth section of this chapter, appeared in *The Flue-Cured Tobacco Farmer* (November 1979) in another form. Permission granted by the publisher. Susan Presti, a staff member at the North Carolina Center for Public Policy Research, and Robie Patterson, a summer intern (1980) at the Center, contributed to this chapter.

cards giving farmers the right to sell tobacco, provides notices of acreage allotments and poundage quotas, mails out ballots for referenda, signs growers up for the four-leaf program (see chapter 2), and documents lease-and-transfer arrangements. The ASCS also has committees at the state, district, county, and community levels that provide a grass-roots vehicle through which farmers can let Washington know of their views. Reorganized during the Carter administration, the ASCS has three main sections.

The *Price Support and Loan Division* decides, within the legally mandated price formula, which grades of tobacco will receive price support and sets the price levels for the individual grades. These decisions are made only after comments are received from growers, tobacco groups, farm organizations, stabilization cooperatives, and other interested parties.

The *Producers' Association Division* deals directly with the stabilization cooperatives and administers the loan agreements between them and the USDA's Commodity Credit Corporation (CCC).

The *Production Adjustment Division* handles the routine details of the tobacco program, dealing directly with individual growers and state and county associations.

Agricultural Marketing Service (AMS): Tobacco Division

The AMS, also called the Grading Service, administers marketing-related matters. Its most important duties are defining the standards for each grade of tobacco and grading the tobacco at 155 market centers in accordance with those grade standards. In these activities, the AMS must work closely with the ASCS, which sets price-support levels for each grade. The AMS also sets the sales schedules for different warehouses under the Flue-Cured Grower Designation plan, whereby the grower designates in the spring the warehouse he will use for selling his tobacco. The Market News Service of the AMS provides daily market information, such as grades sold, quality, prices, and sales volume, to growers, buyers, and other interested people.

The AMS Tobacco Division has two regional offices, one in Raleigh, North Carolina, for flue-cured tobacco, and the other in Lexington, Kentucky, for burley and most other types. Among other functions, the Raleigh regional office does research for the Flue-Cured Tobacco Advisory Committee.

Commodity Credit Corporation

The key financial component in the price-support program, the CCC makes nonrecourse loans to the stabilization cooperatives which in turn use the funds to buy tobacco that is not sold for at least one cent per pound above the support rate. The loans are repaid in future years as the loan stocks are sold. To encourage foreign sales of American agricultural products, including tobacco, the CCC's Export Credit Sales program, begun in 1966, finances sales by private exporters to overseas customers. The financing generally runs from six to thirty-six months.

Foreign Agricultural Service (FAS):
Tobacco, Cotton, and Seeds Division

The FAS goal is to generate long-term demand for U.S. agricultural exports in world markets, and the Tobacco, Cotton, and Seeds Division works to maintain and increase tobacco exports. In its marketing function, this division assists U.S. exporters, not financially, but by trying to insure market access. For example, the division works with foreign government representatives, keeps abreast of tariff changes, engages in international negotiations, develops new markets, and analyzes foreign economic trends in supply, demand, and price. Agricultural attachés in more than a hundred countries provide information to the FAS (and other USDA divisions).

In its market development, the division cooperates closely with such industry groups as the Leaf Tobacco Exporters Association, the Tobacco Association of the United States, the Burley and Dark Leaf Tobacco Exporters Association, and Tobacco Associates. Cooperative projects include organizing trade teams and displays at international trade shows, and bringing foreign buyers to the United States. However, funds for these projects have been sharply cut over the years.

Economic Research Service (ERS)

The Economic Research Service engages in a variety of research projects related to the tobacco industry, often cooperating with such agencies as the Tobacco Division of the AMS and the U.S. Department of Labor. In recent years, the ERS has published reports on supply and demand of tobacco, mechanization and its impact, employment changes in the flue-cured belt, free movement of allotments, and the importance of tobacco to the U.S. economy. The ERS publishes a quarterly report, *Tobacco Situation*, and the *Farm Index Monthly*.

Statistical Reporting Service (SRS)

The Statistical Reporting Service collects data and conducts research, which is supplied to the ERS.

Agricultural Cooperative Service (ACS)

The ACS specializes in various aspects of agricultural cooperatives (farms). The service researches and analyzes cooperative-related data.

Science and Education

On June 17, 1981, the Science and Education Administration (SEA) was reorganized into separate operations as listed below.

Agricultural Research Service (ARS), engages mainly in traditional agricultural research, as well as in other areas such as cigarette design, prevention of mold and insect damage to stored tobacco, and health-related issues. ARS works in close cooperation with state agricultural research efforts when possible. At Oxford, North Carolina, for example, ARS scientists engage in production-methods research at a facility owned by the North Carolina Department of Agriculture. Other sites of tobacco research include Lexington, Kentucky (production, quality, harvesting methods), Athens, Georgia (tobacco and health research), and Beltsville, Maryland (chemical composition of tobacco, and health).

Cooperative State Research Service primarily provides funds for research done by state personnel through grants to land-grant universities, competitive-grant programs, and special-grant programs.

The National Agricultural Library and computerized data services provide technical information services.

Extension Services is probably one of the most widely known of USDA functions. This educational operation is run in very close cooperation with states and counties. In fact, the funding for Extension Services comes from the USDA, states (through land-grant universities), and counties. Extension agents in every tobacco-producing county, supported by extension specialists at the land-grant universities, disseminate information and research on production and marketing of tobacco.

The Science and Educational Management Staff conducts various agricultural research programs and administers educational programs of importance to USDA.

Miscellaneous

One other division of the USDA is occasionally involved with tobacco.

World Agricultural Outlook Board (WAOB) was established in 1977 by the Secretary of Agriculture to improve the quality of USDA's economic intelligence on the world agricultural situation, including tobacco. The key function of the WAOB is to coordinate the USDA information-gathering system with the data from the FAS, ERS, SRS, ACS, ASCS, and Office of General Sales Manager of the CCC. The information provided to the WAOB by these agencies forms the basis of the board's estimates of crop production worldwide, published in a monthly world crop production report. The board also cooperates with the National Oceanic and Atmospheric Administration (NOAA) on global weather forecasts and the possible impact of climate on crop production.

North Carolina Department of Agriculture (NCDA)

The North Carolina Department of Agriculture has relatively little to do with implementing the tobacco price-support program, since the program is primarily a federal operation. While the NCDA concentrates on aiding the state's tobacco growers to raise a healthy and profitable crop, the state's programs inevitably involve the price-support program. The state works with tobacco issues through the following offices.

Office of the Commissioner

The commissioner, who is popularly elected, serves as chief spokesman for North Carolina agriculture, including tobacco. He is charged with carrying out certain regulations which he delegates to the Tobacco Affairs Section, and he advises the U.S. Secretary of Agriculture regarding the tobacco program.

Tobacco Affairs Section of the Marketing Division,
Office of Agri-Business

The section chief reports to the commissioner on policy and program issues and on political matters related to tobacco. This section collects market data, publishes a monthly market bulletin, reports to the Department of Revenue at the end of the market season, oversees warehouse fire insurance for tobacco on the floor, and supervises warehouse commissions and fees. Through the commissioner, this office has input in the federal price-support program. The input is informational and advisory regarding such matters as the level of quota and the loan rates. The section chief served as a consultant to the USDA's Flue-Cured Tobacco Advisory Committee (existed 1967 to 1981), as did designated persons from the departments of agriculture in the other flue-cured-tobacco states of Virginia, South Carolina, Georgia, and Florida.

Division of Research Stations, Office of Agri-Business

The research arm of NCDA, it owns and operates fifteen research stations across the state, six of which have projects on flue-cured tobacco and two of which involve burley tobacco. These stations are also supported by the North Carolina Agricultural Research Service (to be discussed shortly) and Cooperative Research of the Science and Education Administration, USDA (see figure 7-1). Current tobacco research, conducted by North Carolina State University, includes programs on breeding, fertilization, chemical use, weed control, seed-bed and field-preparation methods, irrigation, harvesting methods, curing, and new types of machinery.

*Market News Service of the Marketing Division,
Office of Agri-Business*

The Market News Service has a parallel and cooperative function with the USDA Market News Service. With relation to tobacco, during the selling season, USDA Market News gathers daily information on volume sold, prices, quality of leaf, and so on. The NCDA Market News Service then acquires this information and releases it to North Carolina news outlets and other interested people. The NCDA also provides funds to USDA Market News.

*Crop and Livestock Reporting Service (CLRS) of the
Marketing Division, Office of Agri-Business*

In an information-gathering and dissemination function similar to that of Market News, the CLRS issues official estimates of North Carolina agricultural production. For tobacco, this includes acreage, yield, total production, and cash receipts, by types of tobacco and by county. Throughout the year, the CLRS uses a monthly mail survey of approximately 1,500

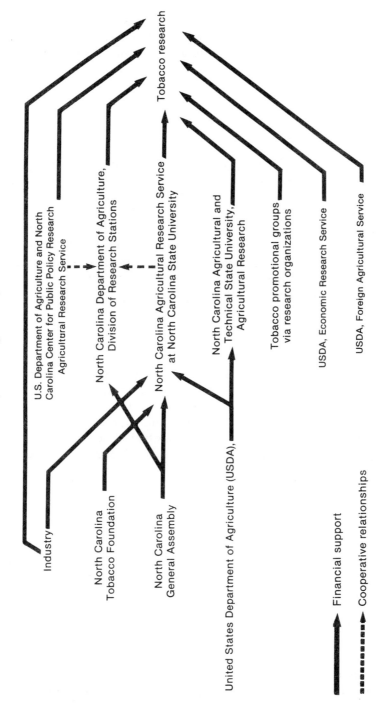

Tobacco research is mainly agricultural research, but includes statistical studies, marketing studies, and so on.

Figure 7-1. Tobacco Research in North Carolina

farmers, it augments this with Market News data during the selling season; and for the January and May reports, it uses USDA data from the Agricultural Stabilization and Conservation Service. All CLRS reports are sent to the USDA Crop Reporting Board, which issues a monthly crop report to news media and interested persons.

Regulatory Functions

Several offices in the NCDA have regulatory operations that affect tobacco. The *Weights and Measures Section of the Consumer Standards Division of the Office of Consumer Services* checks scales at tobacco warehouses, licenses public weightmasters, and checks installations of liquid propane gas units used in bulk curing. The *Pesticide Section of the Pest Control Division* and the *Seed and Fertilizer Division* (both of the Office of Consumer Services) test and approve pesticides and new seeds and fertilizers, respectively. The *Agronomic Services Division of the Office of Agri-Business* provides soil testing and nematode analysis services.

North Carolina Land-Grant Universities

Both North Carolina State University (NCSU) at Raleigh and North Carolina Agricultural and Technical State University (NCA&T) at Greensboro have land-grant status. (In most southern states, two universities—one predominantly black and the other predominantly white—have had land-grant status since the era of racially separate higher-education systems.) The two programs are financially and administratively separate, but they do co operate under one comprehensive research-program statement (see figure 7-1).

Agricultural Research

The research arm of NCSU, *North Carolina Agricultural Research Service (NC-ARS)*, coordinates the bulk of agricultural research for the University of North Carolina system. The NC-ARS, and its tobacco research in particular, are funded primarily by the state, by the Cooperative State Research Service of the USDA, and by grants from the North Carolina Tobacco Foundation and industry groups.

There are currently more than sixty tobacco projects, all which focus on continued production of a high-quality leaf. The studies occur at the NCSU campus in Raleigh and at eight of fifteen outlying research stations.

There is no health research as such (see Division of Research Stations under North Carolina Department of Agriculture). The NC-ARS works closely with the NCDA, especially the Research Station Division, and with Agricultural Research Service of the USDA, which has ongoing projects at the Oxford, North Carolina research station. Also, USDA/ARS personnel carry courtesy appointments to the NCSU faculty. The NC-ARS also works cooperatively with corporations and other private entities.

Almost all of NCA&T's agricultural research money comes from the Cooperative State Research Service, and Agricultural Research Service, USDA. Its one tobacco research project, conducted in cooperation with NC-ARS, is a study of the nature of pesticide residues in soils, plants, water, living organisms, and tobacco smoke. All NCA&T's agricultural research is currently taking place on the Greensboro campus.

Agricultural Extension Service

This is an education and information dissemination service. Until 1977, NCA&T Extension was a satellite of NCSU Extention; since 1977, it has had institutional autonomy and has received funds directly from the USDA Extension Service.

NCSU's extension program is funded by the USDA Extension Service, by state funds through NCSU, and by county-appropriated funds. The Extension Service disseminates the latest production-technology information to tobacco growers, communicates long-range market-demand information, works with the agri-business industry that supplies tobacco growers, and maintains a liaison with the tobacco manufacturers.

NCA&T's extension program is supported primarily by the USDA and by county appropriations. The state contributes to some employees' retirement and other benefits. NCA&T Extension has at least 1 employee in 37 counties, including 23 agricultural technicians, who have direct contact with 30 to 50 farm families, mostly with small farms. There is also one agricultural coordinator on campus who gives support to the technicians in the field.

North Carolina Tobacco Foundation

A fund-raising mechanism to support tobacco research and extension programs at North Carolina State University, this is one of thirteen such foundations serviced by the NCSU Foundations and Development Office. Formed in 1975, it is funded by tobacco growers, warehousemen, manufacturers, and exporters. The foundation grants supplement state legislative appropriations and federal money to support ongoing and special research and extension projects. Annually, the School of Agriculture draws up a budget for approval by the foundation's board of directors.

Industry Organizations

Bright Belt Warehouse Association, Incorporated

This association was chartered June 6, 1945, to serve marketing needs in North Carolina, Virginia, Georgia, and Florida. South Carolina has a separate warehouse association, whose operation is similar to Bright Belt. The corporation has six major objectives:

to promote a more orderly market for the auction sale of flue-cured tobacco

to cooperate with the farmers and their organizations for continued fair and equitable prices for tobacco

to encourage the exportation of tobacco and to work with farmers and farm organizations to attain this goal

to cooperate with farmers in seeing that government authorities have the facts they need to make appropriate decisions, orders, and enactments that will help farmers receive a fair and equitable price for their product

to bring about a better understanding among farmers, warehousemen, tobacco companies, and dealers

to harmonize more completely the total tobacco industry with all others interested in tobacco trade

To accomplish its purposes, Bright Belt has worked to keep a balanced tobacco program with respect to supply and demand; advocated more realistic identification and tariff structure for imported flue-cured leaf; been instrumental in maintaining a realistic price-support program in relation to cost of production; and fully supported the campaign not to harvest the bottom four leaves, realizing that to continue to market less competitive primings poses a threat to the survival of stabilization.

The nonprofit corporation represents 374 flue-cured-tobacco warehouse operators and is located in Raleigh, North Carolina (Post Office Box 12004, Raleigh, North Carolina, 27605).

*Burley and Dark-Leaf Tobacco Export
Association, Incorporated*

Composed of five tobacco-grower cooperatives and three dealer and ware-house associations, this trade organization promotes the sale of burley, Virginia sun-cured, and dark tobaccos in the overseas markets (1100 17th Street Northwest, Suite 306, Washington, D.C., 20036).

Burley Auction Warehouse Association

This association governs sales and practices of warehousemen in Indiana, Kentucky, Ohio, Missouri, West Virginia, Tennessee, North Carolina, and Virginia (Post Office Box 670, Mount Sterling, Kentucky, 40353).

Burley Stabilization Corporation

This is a cooperative of approximately 140,000 burley tobacco growers sell-ing on twenty-five markets of Tennessee, western North Carolina, and Virginia, handling the price-support program on these markets (3919 Holston Drive, Northeast, Knoxville, Tennessee, 37914).

Burley Tobacco Growers Cooperative Association

This cooperative of burley-tobacco farmers in Indiana, Kentucky, Missouri, Ohio, and West Virginia administers the burley price-support program (Post Office Box 860, Lexington, Kentucky, 40501).

Flue-Cured Tobacco Cooperative Stabilization Corporation

Often referred to as Stabilization or the Co-op, this association was organized on June 1, 1946, under the Cooperative Marketing Act of North Carolina and similar acts later passed in the major flue-cured-tobacco states: Virginia, South Carolina, Georgia, and Florida. A cooperative marketing association of flue-cured-tobacco growers, its purpose is to stabilize the tobacco prices on the auction warehouse floor by administering the mandatory federal price-support program for flue-cured tobacco.

Its board of directors consists of ten growers elected by the membership and one appointed public director. Any flue-cured-tobacco grower is eligi-ble for membership; he need only purchase a share of common stock for five dollars. Through its administration of the price-support program, the Co-op assures growers a minimum price for their leaf grown within quota.

Stabilization enters into loan agreements with the Commodity Credit Corporation, (pledging tobacco as collateral) and with industry firms, such as auction warehouse operators, processors, and storers, for the receiving, processing, and storing of the tobacco delivered by the growers to the Co-op.

Any tobacco on the auction floor that was eligible for price support but failed to receive a bid in excess of the support price is turned over to Stabilization. The Co-op has the leaf processed, packed, and stored until it can be sold at an acceptable price.

When Stabilization sells some of its reserves, the money is used to repay the CCC crop loans plus interest. At the end of each fiscal year, any funds that remain in excess of the CCC repayments and other handling costs are passed on in the form of dividends to Co-op members who placed tobacco under loan during that crop year.

Stabilization offices are at 1304 Annapolis Drive (Post Office Box 12300), Raleigh, North Carolina, 27605.

Tobacco Associates, Incorporated (TA)

This is a nonprofit corporation organized in 1947 by tobacco growers with the support of allied groups in the flue-cured tobacco-producing areas, primarily to promote, develop, and expand export markets for U.S. flue-cured leaf. In 1958, the purpose and responsibility were expanded to include domestic promotion, and to represent the tobacco farmers' interest in maintaining and protecting the entire tobacco program.

Tobacco Associates is governed by a twenty-five-member board of directors elected annually from the five flue-cured tobacco-producing states. Seventeen are farmers engaged in the production of flue-cured tobacco, representing farm organizations from Virginia, North Carolina, South Carolina, Georgia, and Florida. Eight members represent warehousemen, export dealers, merchants, bankers, and fertilizer manufacturers in the five-state area.

All members provide financial support for Tobacco Associates: North Carolina and South Carolina tobacco farmers vote in referendum to contribute through an assessment program; Florida, Georgia, and Virginia growers contribute through their respective state tobacco commissions; warehousemen in all states contribute by collecting the assessments or state excise taxes; and leaf export dealers, merchants, bankers, and fertilizer manufacturers make supporting contributions.

Among continuing domestic activities of Tobacco Associates are efforts to maintain and preserve the basic tobacco program; to coordinate state and national farm organizations' fights against legislation that restricts smoking or increases tobacco taxes; to educate the general public as to tobacco's overall economic impact, emphasizing tobacco's unfair tax burden and its surplus balance of trade. In addition, TA contributes to cancer research as well as leaf-quality and advanced-technology research at various universities in the country.

On the foreign scene, TA promotes and advertises foreign cigarettes containing U.S. flue-cured tobacco; works to establish new markets for U.S. flue-cured exports; provides opportunities for officials of foreign cigarette manufacturing companies to visit the United States to study our system of marketing, quality of leaf, and procedures for purchasing U.S. flue-cured leaf; and strongly opposes all tariff and nontariff barriers that restrict U.S. tobacco sales abroad.

Tobacco Associates is located at Suite 912, 1101 17th Street Northwest, Washington, D.C., 20036 and at Suite 102, 1306 Annapolis Drive, Raleigh, North Carolina, 27605.

Tobacco Association of the United States (TAUS)

Founded in 1900 by tobacco firms and businesses providing marketing services to tobacco firms, the TAUS is the oldest tobacco trade association. Its objectives are to foster and promote the growth, sale, distribution, manufacture, and consumption of American-grown tobacco in this country and overseas.

The TAUS consists of more than sixty members engaged in tobacco business and more than sixty associate members who provide various services to the tobacco industry. The association is funded by these members and associates. The TAUS cooperates with other trade associations, growers, government, universities, and farm organizations in efforts to resolve mutual problems and expand the consumption of American tobacco.

Leaf Tobacco Exporters Association (LTEA)

Working closely with the TAUS, even sharing the same executive office in Raleigh, North Carolina (3716 National Drive, Suite 114, Raleigh, North Carolina, 27612), and executive vice president, this association also works to promote export, sale, distribution, and consumption of American-grown leaf tobacco.

Founded in 1941 by firms primarily engaged in the leaf-tobacco-dealer business, LTEA membership consists of forty-five export firms that fund the activities and cooperative work with other trade associations, universities, government, and farm organizations in efforts to protect and promote the market for American leaf tobacco.

Tobacco Growers' Information Committee, Incorporated (TGIC)

This was established in 1958 to serve as spokesman for the entire tobacco industry—growers, warehousemen, domestic companies, and dealers of all types of tobacco. Its purpose is to make available to the public and to the industry important information about the political, marketing, cultural, and production activities of tobacco.

To accomplish this goal, the TGIC maintains a constant flow of information to all segments of the industry and to the public through speeches, personal contact, and all forms of media—radio, television, magazines, and newspapers.

The TGIC is financed by a number of tobacco organizations, including associations of growers, and by general agri-business groups. With the exception of closed business sessions, the annual meeting in October is open to all persons interested in the tobacco industry. Corporate offices are located in Raleigh, North Carolina (Post Office Box 12046, Cameron Village Station, Raleigh, North Carolina, 27605).

Tobacco Institute

It was founded in 1958 by eleven U.S. tobacco-product manufacturers. This nonprofit, noncommercial organization has two aims: to foster public understanding of the smoking-and-health controversy, and to educate the public about the historic role of tobacco and its place in the national economy.

Policy direction is given to the Institute by a board of directors consisting of executives from its member manufacturing companies. Its activities are conducted by a professional staff whose members have backgrounds in government, journalism, law, education, statistics, agriculture, business, and other fields.

Four staff members travel nearly all the time, appearing on radio and television talk shows, at conventions, at local civic clubs, anywhere they can spread the word about tobacco. It is supported by the principal U.S. tobacco manufacturers. Its offices are at 1875 I Street, Northwest, Washington, D.C., 20006.

Tobacco Tax Council

Established in 1949, this council provides statistical and educational service to anyone interested in taxation of tobacco products. Its purposes are:

to secure and record information, data, and statistics concerning all aspects of federal, state, and local excise taxes on tobacco and tobacco products

to furnish that information to growers, processors, manufacturers, wholesale distributors, retailers, public officials, and the general public

to conduct research studies in the field of excise taxes on tobacco or tobacco products

to support equal treatment by all government agencies in relation to tobacco taxation

to help assure, through government policy, that the tobacco industry will not be subjected to disproportionate tax burdens compared to other industries.

Executive and research departments are headquartered at 5407 Patterson Avenue (Post Office Box 8269), Richmond, Virginia, 23226.

Part II
Alternatives for Tobacco Farmers

8

Vegetable and Fruit Crops: Viable Alternatives for Tobacco Farmers

Frank Adams

Hundreds of North Carolina's family farmers are quietly searching for profitable alternatives to tobacco, a crop many of them learned about at the knees of fathers or grandfathers, and a crop that is as much a way of life as a source of income. That way of life and of producing income has changed dramatically in recent decades. Tobacco operations have increased in size, requiring large capital investments. Bulk-curing barns and mechanical harvesters are transforming tobacco production from a labor-intensive to a capital-intensive enterprise (see chapters 4 and 5 for a full discussion of this transformation).

As a result, fewer farmers today can afford to grow tobacco than in years past. In 1972, according to the U.S. Department of Agriculture (USDA), there were about 40,500 flue-cured operations in the major growing regions of Virginia, North Carolina, South Carolina, and Georgia; by 1979, the number had fallen to 29,000, a 28 percent decline in seven years.[1]

The director of the North Carolina Agricultural Extension Service, T.C. Blalock, sums it up: "Tobacco farmers are either going big and mechanized or they are leasing [their allotments]. . . . Thousands of farmers who used to be full time have now taken a job in industry." This is especially true for tobacco farmers who do not have the capital to invest in mechanized systems, small allotment holders who can make more money leasing than growing, and sharecroppers who have had the allotments they used to grow leased away to large-scale operations.

A farmer with a small tobacco operation seems to have three options. He can (1) continue to borrow money and invest in the tobacco operation, hoping to be one of the shrinking number of survivors; (2) take an off-farm job (and perhaps grow a little corn, hay, or other pasture crop part-time); or (3) try to change to other crops and remain on the farm. This chapter addresses prospects and problems of the third option.

Tobacco farmers have grown accustomed to guaranteed market outlets and sales price levels, both of which are assured through the federal support system. Coping with new crop systems can be a difficult challenge for a tobacco farmer, especially at the marketing end. "Yes, there are alternatives

Others who contributed to this chapter are Donna Dyer, a planner and economist; Mark Harland, a marketing specialist; and Hope Shand, a community educator and researcher.

to tobacco," says J.E. Legate, dean of North Carolina State University's School of Agriculture. But he adds, "No other crop *for which we have a stable market* can provide the per-acre return that is realized from tobacco" (emphasis added).

For those who determine agricultural policy in tobacco-belt states, the quest for suitable substitutes to tobacco and a regular market for those substitutes looms large in economic and political importance. Finding ways to keep people on their farms and out of unemployment lines and cities lowers the monetary and social costs of displacement. Keeping people on farms relieves the pressure that industrial recruiters face to provide jobs in rural areas for farmers forced off their land. Most important, alternative crops and new market mechanisms can help farmers continue what they want to do and know how to do: farm.

A Lack of Government Support

Displaced tobacco farmers cannot make a transition to soybeans, corn, wheat, or some other grain. All these crops require large acreage units for profit. In 1979, soybeans netted about $72 per acre in North Carolina; wheat, $63; corn, $106; and even fresh market corn, $250 (table 8-1). Meanwhile, the state's flue-cured tobacco crop brought about $1,200 profit per acre.

Various fruit and vegetable crops, however, are viable alternatives for tobacco farmers. Strawberries, for example, netted over $3,000 an acre in North Carolina in 1979. Trellis tomatoes, peaches, and apples also topped the per-acre return of flue-cured tobacco; blueberries, cucumbers, and sweet potatoes were not far behind (see table 8-1). Moreover, all of these crops can be grown on small acreage units, similar to the old-style, three-to-five-acre tobacco farm.

To switch to these crops, tobacco farmers need a great deal of technical advice and support. They face large, sometimes insurmountable hurdles. Many of them have large investments in modern curing and harvesting equipment, and some lack the practical skills needed for growing unfamiliar crops. And the biggest constraint is the lack of a guaranteed market.

If strawberries, trellis tomatoes, apples, and other high-income-yielding crops had guaranteed markets and sales prices, many now-reluctant farmers might see their way clear to diversifying their operations into vegetables or fruits. In a state like North Carolina, the agricultural support systems are geared to those crops—like tobacco—where federal programs are already functioning, rather than to crops for which backup systems have yet to be developed. Research in Washington, D.C., and in field stations, farm bulletins and surveys, and extension projects all have the funding and momentum of the tobacco program behind them. Alternative crops do not

Table 8-1
Ranking of Crops according to Net Return per Acre in North Carolina

Crops	Net Return per Acre
1. Tomatoes (mountains; trellis)	$3,454.46
2. Strawberries (fresh market)	3,008.00
3. Apples	1,974.65
4. Peaches (fresh market)	1,960.00
5. Strawberries (pick your own)	1,278.00
6. Tobacco (flue cured)	1,198.02
7. Blueberries (fresh market)	1,142.37
8. Cucumbers (fresh market)	799.19
9. Watermelons	775.15
10. Sweet potatoes	653.05
11. Okra (fresh market)	466.96
12. Cabbage	437.96
13. Summer squash (fresh market)	339.04
14. Snap beans (fresh market)	330.24
15. Pole beans	301.16
16. White potatoes	260.84
17. Sweet corn (fresh market)	249.89
18. Peanuts	223.18
19. Alfalfa hay	171.00
20. Tomatoes (processing; hand harvested)	157.42
21. Snap beans (processing)	144.39
22. Cotton	130.44
23. Green pepper (fresh market)	125.00
24. Red clover/orchard grass hay	117.68
25. Okra (processing)	116.74
26. Cucumbers (processing)	107.41
27. Corn (no till)	106.34
28. Corn	101.71
29. Tall fescue hay	101.22
30. Wheat and soybeans double cropped	98.30
31. Grapes	97.52
32. Soybeans	72.45
33. Wheat	62.77
34. Milo	39.61
35. Barley	30.92
36. Oats	0.51
37. Coastal bermuda hay	−98.50

Source: Crop budgets prepared by the Agricultural Extension Service at North Carolina State University, updated with current market data in January 1980, by Mark Epp, coordinator of training and research, Frank Porter Graham Center, Wadesboro, North Carolina.

receive the same research or attention from the governmental support systems, such as the land-grant universities and the farmer loan agencies, that tobacco gets.

The North Carolina Agricultural Extension Service, for example, has assisted in seeking alternative crops for tobacco farmers in only isolated instances. In the western counties, the Extension Service did assist in expanding the trellis-tomato industry, which has helped some burley tobacco farmers. But it has not mounted any type of intensive effort to help tobacco farmers throughout the state adapt their operations to other crops. Its research efforts also have been limited. In 1978, when the governor's office expressed concern regarding possible modification or loss of the tobacco program, the state extension office at North Carolina State University made a study of alternative gross farm incomes that might be generated in case of some catastrophic drop in tobacco income. The study put far greater hopes in beef cattle, poultry, swine, dairying, and horticulture than in a minor category called "agronomy" (new crops).[2] And any initiatives toward finding new ways to adapt tobacco farms to fruit and vegetable operations do not appear likely. "We have not done any overall study since that report," says Extension Director Blalock.

The experiences of Phil Wood, a tobacco farmer in Fuquay-Varina, North Carolina, illustrate another limitation of government support for alternatives to tobacco. In 1980, Wood grew fifty-five acres of flue-cured tobacco, but even a farm that big was not enough. "Expenses were so high that I had to start borrowing for the winter," Wood says. "I just broke even, didn't make a thing." For the 1981 season, Wood wanted to grow twenty acres of peppers and forty acres of cotton, but he ran into another kind of money problem. Farmers borrow large sums each year to get their crop in the ground, and Wood went to the usual lending source, Production Credit Association. But Production Credit, which was willing to lend Wood money to grow tobacco, would not take a risk on peppers or cotton. "I'm in a trap right now," Wood said in January 1981, still deciding what to plant in the spring. "Production Credit won't loan me money so I can diversify and Farmers Home [Association] won't loan me any money unless Production Credit refuses [to give] me [money]." Since Production Credit is willing to loan Wood money for tobacco, he is stuck. "I can't diversify now because funds aren't available to me."

How to Survive the Constraints to Switching

In Wadesboro, North Carolina, a private, nonprofit research farm is working to provide models for small farmers to continue living and working on the land. A project of the forty-five-year-old National Sharecroppers Fund, the Frank Porter Graham Center has been training small farmers and conducting crop and livestock experimentation for almost ten years. The bottom line for any commodity tested at the Graham Center is profits: the central concern is what the net income yield per acre will be. The farm's staff also closely examine possible constraints farmers face in growing particular crops, especially on three-to-five-acre operations—the size of a small tobacco farm. The Graham Center has found that most of the crops listed in table 8-1 can be grown profitably on a small farm operation. Moreover, few carry with them technical or investment problems that cannot be overcome. Some possible constraints and ways to overcome them are as follows.

Irrigation. Vegetables and berry crops require more water than tobacco, and irrigation would be necessary during especially dry years. Graham Center staff member Mark Epp says the cost of an irrigation system is not insurmountable to small farmers. An irrigation system for a ten-to-fifteen acre vegetable operation can be installed for $10,000 to $15,000, says Epp, by digging a pond on the farm. Also, the Farmers Home Administration will loan money for irrigation systems. "Though it's expensive, it's no more expensive than a lot of machinery and energy used in grains and tobacco," Epp explains.

Start-up time. Farmers interested in orchards as a livelihood are often deterred by the long wait for fruit trees to mature. Peach trees require a three-year start-up time; apple trees need five years before producing the first crop. The Graham Center suggests planting row crops, such as sweet potatoes, sorghum cane, peanuts, or watermelons between the rows of young trees while they are maturing, thus alleviating an income dormancy during this period.

Machinery and labor. Many tobacco farmers have sizable investments in curing barns and other equipment associated exclusively with tobacco, and they naturally fear the loss of their investments if they switch to alternative crops. In addition, one initial reason for purchasing tobacco-production technology was probably the farmer's difficulty in finding and affording seasonal labor. So, another obstacle to growing crops other than tobacco is the farmer's fear of a renewed, increased need for hand labor.

Farmers who own one-row planting and tilling equipment require little capital investment when starting alternative-crop farming, aside from irrigation costs already mentioned. The tobacco transplanter can be used to set out sweet potatoes or tomato plants, and bulk-curing barns might be used for sweet-potato curing or peanut drying. Farmers might have to sell their automatic tobacco harvesters since only one-row machinery transfers to vegetable crops, but many smaller tobacco farmers have not yet invested in that costly piece of machinery.

Labor used to produce flue-cured tobacco averaged about 172 hours per acre in 1979, with more than two-thirds of that labor used to harvest and prepare the tobacco for market, according to the USDA. Most crops studied at the Graham Center to date require a similar amount of labor for production and harvest. And, if some alternative crops do require more hand labor than tobacco, the savings in capital costs and increasing fuel bills may soften that particular blow.

Energy. Tobacco is an energy-intensive crop, particularly as the harvest and curing becomes more mechanized. Flue-cured tobacco accounts for more than 60 percent of North Carolina's energy uses in agriculture. Approximately 316 gallons of fuel are needed per acre, on the average.[3] Nationally, tobacco grows on only 0.03 percent of the available cropland, but consumes only 15 percent less energy than what is used to raise all the vegetables in the United States. Many farm chemicals are oil based, and one USDA study found a higher percentage of tobacco acres sprayed with insecticides than any other major crop.[4] Alternative crops tested at the Graham Center pose no greater pest or disease threat than tobacco and historically have required less fuel and oil-based chemicals.

Soil and climate. There is nothing unique about the soil that supports the successful growth of tobacco. Tobacco can be raised on a great variety of soils in all climates from southern Canada to tropical areas. Tobacco production was frozen in its present location by the federal tobacco program enacted in 1938 (see chapter 4 for a discussion of this "freezing"). Most crops tested at the Graham Center would grow well in all the major tobacco belts.

In sum, then, other than the cost of irrigation for berries and some vegetable crops, changing over to any of the alternatives as profitable as tobacco does not present multiple hurdles. The crops would not require additional machinery or labor; would probably use less fuel and pesticides; and would not be adversely affected by the soil and climate conditions of the region. But alternative crops grown widely would require a dependable and accessible market, plus additional organizational means for distribution.

Marketing: The Biggest Deterrent

The key deterrent to tobacco farmers interested in growing alternative crops is the lack of a stable market and distribution system. Only tobacco has a guaranteed market. Warehouses are located in dozens of hamlets, and, because of the support-price and quota system, tobacco prices do not fluctuate according to supply and demand. Prices for most other crops do fluctuate, rendering growers' incomes uncertain from year to year.

It is ironic that North Carolina, with its bountiful fields and many miles of as yet undeveloped land, imports more than three-fourths of the vegetables its residents consume. In the central Piedmont alone, there are more than two million consumers who, conceivably, could buy local produce if farmers chose to grow it and if it were made accessible. But because of established marketing and distribution systems, getting large quantities of locally grown vegetables into consumers' grocery bags is no easy enterprise.

If enough vegetable farmers pool their individual harvests into an adequate quantity, it is possible to make the links to established bulk buyers—jobbers, wholesalers, and processors—who sell in large population centers and through supermarket chains. One such cooperative effort under way may handily serve Piedmont vegetable growers someday, and, if successful, will serve as a much needed marketing model for farmers in other areas.

In the Piedmont, where small-size tobacco operations are steadily dwindling in number, a group of farmers have been working to establish the Piedmont Vegetable Marketing Cooperative, Incorporated. The co-op has its roots among a small group of Chatham County farmers who quickly discovered that a key step toward obtaining start-up capital from traditional lending institutions is a USDA feasibility study. The USDA ascertains the need for a marketing co-op, ensures that a sufficient number of farmers wish to take part, and finds the probable buyers for the co-op's supply of produce. In 1978, the farmers wrote the USDA requesting a feasibility study, which the USDA does for free. Two USDA agricultural economists surveyed 131 farmers in 6 Piedmont counties to learn about their current crop production and their interest in a vegetable co-op warehouse in their area. During this time, the North Carolina Land Trustees, a nonprofit group based in Durham, was providing technical assistance to the co-op and holding meetings in the six counties to generate interest in the idea.

The economists found that 66 percent of those surveyed farmed full time, raising tobacco, soybeans, hogs, beef, and vegetables. They planted a total of 815 acres in vegetables, an average of about 6 acres each. See table 8-2 for a description of the types of vegetables grown and their yields. Twenty-two farmers sold their vegetables on consignment, and four sold on contract. Fifteen relied on door-to-door sales. The economists multiplied the farmer's reported yields by the 1978 North Carolina average seasonal price and determined their total gross revenue was $858,857.97 (see table 8-2). Nearly all the 131 farmers told the economists that if a market were established, they would be willing to expand their vegetable production.

The feasibility study sought to determine the demand for home-grown produce, the prices farmers could expect, the location of the markets, and any requisite quality standards. In gathering data, the USDA contacted operators of packing sheds, wholesale shippers, processors, retailers, and operators of a few consumer food cooperatives. Each was questioned about grading and packing preferences, minimum volume requirements, contractual arrangements, and pricing patterns. The USDA report suggested three marketing strategies for the Piedmont vegetable growers: (1) that the farmers form a cooperative initially based on sweet potatoes, cucumbers, and green peppers; (2) that the co-op find a warehouse where produce could be assembled, cleaned, graded, and packed on a large-scale basis; and (3) that the co-op hire a full-time manager.

With this blueprint in mind, the fledgling Piedmont co-op set out to gather the membership and raise the equity necessary to lease warehouse space, to furnish it with loading docks and refrigerated storage, and to hire

Table 8-2

Types of Vegetables Grown, Yield, and Prices Received for Growers Surveyed

Crop	Unit	Acres Harvested	Yield per Acre	Price per Unit	Total Yield	Total Revenue
Cabbage	Pounds	36.65	18,000	$ .08	659,700	$ 52,776.00
Cucumbers	Bushels	155.40	188	3.07	29,215	89,690.64
Okra	Pounds	15.20	9,800	.20	148,960	29,792.00
Peppers	Bushels	57.50	338	6.09	19,435	118,359.15
Pole beans	Bushels	29.90	225	6.00	6,728	40,365.00
Snap beans	Pounds	37.15	3,000	.07	111,450	7,801.50
Summer squash	Bushels	23.50	225	7.00	5,288	37,012.50
Sweet corn	Crates	135.45	187	3.50	29,329	88,652.03
Sweet potatoes	Bushels	86.20	337	3.50	29,049	101,672.90
White potatoes	Pounds	25.30	15,000	.11	379,500	41,745.00
Tomatoes	Pounds	30.80	22,500	.15	693,000	103,950.00
Watermelons	Pounds	64.95	16,875	.04	1,096,031	43,841.25
Cantaloupes	Pounds	68.80	6,000	.25	412,800	103,200.00
Total[a]		766.80				858,857.97

Source: Preliminary Report, U.S. Department of Agriculture Economics, Statistics, and Cooperatives Service, Washington, D.C. 20250, "Vegetable Growers Cooperative, Piedmont Area of North Carolina," n.d.

[a]The figure for total acres harvested does not take into account that growers allocated 48.2 acres to the production of crops such as grapes, peas, collards, and so on. The total acreage of all vegetables harvested thus becomes 815 acres.

a manager. On July 15, 1980, farmers from six Piedmont counties voted to create a co-op for shipping green peas, cucumbers, summer squash, okra, and sweet potatoes to local markets and to Washington and Baltimore. In September, the co-op formally organized and incorporated itself with about fifty members. Next came the critical step: generating the start-up capital.

To be a member, a farmer has to buy one share (thirty dollars) in the co-op. The feasibility study indicated that at least 650 acres of produce were needed as commitment from members before the co-op's success could be assured. Lending institutions look closely at the portion of start-up capital invested by the co-op members. The co-op board decided that for the project to be on solid footing, the members would have to contribute 30 to 50 percent of the start-up capital needed. Inflation, grant applications, and other factors will affect the amount of the investment needed; the board thinks each member may have to invest up to $300 per acre for each acre of vegetables he plans to sell through the warehouse. If this equity could be raised from members, the rest of the financing necessary—some $150,000 to $200,000—could be secured more easily.

Farmers sometimes can get low-interest loans from Production Credit or Farmers Home Administration for investing in a co-op, but many farmers, especially after a poor 1980 crop, have had difficulty making an investment commitment. Consequently, the co-op did not reach its goal of a 650-acre commitment from members in time for the 1981 season. "It's a chicken and egg problem," says Arnie Katz, a Land Trustees staff member who works with the co-op. "There's no doubt several hundred farmers would join in a year once they saw it going." Katz has talked to many tobacco farmers who either want to diversify or leave tobacco altogether. An uncertain market is a severe initial deterrent. The Piedmont co-op's board of directors is continuing efforts to build interest—and equity—in its venture, and is coordinating a smaller, pilot operation during the 1981 marketing season.

Conclusion

These private endeavors to rearrange economic relations on a small scale provide policymakers with valuable practical examples of how new economic institutions can be forged for the benefit of family farmers. The Graham Center's work reaffirms the viability of small farms; the efforts of farmers to establish their own marketing mechanism show that the will to continue their traditional way of making a living is as strong as ever. The problems enterprising small farmers face—and the farmers' reluctance to put their money and efforts into new ventures before they see some strong assurance of success—should point the way toward redirected governmental efforts, both in the administration of state-level agriculture programs and at the land-grant university centers such as North Carolina State University. Meaningful policies could result from public discussion about why family farmers are searching for alternatives to tobacco. Solid research and technical assistance are needed on ways to improve marketing and distribution systems for small farmers' potentially valuable contribution: food crops.

For many years tobacco farmers generally had an edge over other kinds of farmers because of their guaranteed market and support program. But small operators lack the capital to keep up with intensive mechanization trends. Tobacco farmers have to find new ways to survive on the land or join the hundreds of thousands who must search for nonfarm employment. Tobacco farmers who wish to grow alternative crops, such as vegetables, have some advantages from the start: they can transfer much of their equipment to the revamped operations; in most cases, they will save on energy costs; they may receive even better profits from many of the alternative crops; and they can stay on the farm. In marketing their produce, though, they will need assistance, and that is the challenge that private and public interests must meet, cooperatively.

Notes

1. Verner N. Grise, "Flue-Cured Tobacco Farming: Structural Characteristics, Labor Use, and Mechanization," paper presented at the 29th Tobacco Workers Conference, Lexington, Ky., January 21, 1981, Economics and Statistics Service, USDA.

2. Letter from T.C. Blalock, director of the Agricultural Extension Service, to W.D. Lewis, agricultural policy advisor to North Carolina Governor James Hunt, July 7, 1978. The pertinent parts of the letter follow:

> In view of the apprehension from the Governor's office regarding the possible modification or loss of the tobacco support program, I have asked our commodity-oriented departments to estimate the additional annual gross cash farm income that might be generated through accelerated efforts on the part of producers and processors working with the Agricultural Extension Service if a substantial drop in tobacco income were to occur. A summary of these estimates is attached. . . . By commodity categories, our estimates for increased annual gross farm income under accelerated effort look like this:

Commodity category	Present estimated annual gross farm income	Future estimated annual gross farm income
Christmas trees	$ 5,400,000	$ 21,000,000
Beef cattle	94,600,000	253,900,000
Horses	110,000,000	300,000,000
Dairying	171,130,000	214,378,932
Horticulture	246,200,000	432,900,000
Poultry	606,205,000	893,471,743
Swine	314,000,000	450,000,000
Agronomy (new crops)	671,000	2,240,000

> Yield increases could result in even more dramatic income increases. . . . These estimates are not considered additive because they were developed independently and do not reflect competition for the same resources of production. However, if all this expansion could occur under the most favorable circumstances, even so we could not replace all the income normally resulting from tobacco production. This optimistic pattern of increased production of alternatives to tobacco would require about as much land as required for tobacco. Depending upon the degree of mechanization adopted, the alternatives to tobacco could require almost as much labor as for tobacco. Some of these categories would require substantial amounts of investment capital.

3. 1979 Tobacco Information, North Carolina State University Extension Service, p. 62.

4. William Lockeretz, ed., *Agriculture and Energy* (New York: Academic Press, 1977), p. 704.

Industrial Growth: An Alternative for North Carolina's Tobacco Farmers

J. Barlow Herget

The middle-aged man squirms uncomfortably in his seat, explaining why he wants a job in one of the new electronic industries that has located in the Research Triangle area of North Carolina during the last three years. He has the hands of a farmer and looks awkward in his three-piece knit suit. He has applied for a computer operator's job, a skill he acquired as a state employee several years back. He is explaining a five-year gap in his work record between 1972-1977. "I decided to go back to farming," he says. "I farmed tobacco and some other crops. I didn't have an allotment so I rented about fifteen acres. I quit because I got tired of working for nothing."

This time it is the wife of a Johnston County, North Carolina, farmer. Her husband tills fifty-five acres of tobacco, thirteen of which he owns. Her name is Peggy Williams, age thirty-seven, neat and soft-spoken and mother of three children. She now has a job as a traffic clerk with Data General Corporation, a manufacturer of small computers that located research-and-development and manufacturing operations in North Carolina during the 1970s. "We had a bad year in 1979, and I had to go to work," says Mrs. Williams matter-of-factly. "I have worked part-time for the state at Motor Vehicles during registration time and for Hudson Belk's some. I have been farming tobacco since I was a girl. I've seen it go from mule and plow to automatic harvester and bulk barns. This is my first full-time job and it has really helped out, especially the medical and dental insurance. It's hard to tell what our children will do. My daughter wants to farm, but she's hoping to get on over here [at Data General]." Mrs. Williams pauses and then shakes her head. "Farming is getting so there's so much expense to it."

It doesn't take a Ph.D. in history to know that the stories of the ex-farmer and Mrs. Williams have been repeated time and again across North Carolina and other southern states. Both people are part of the exodus from farm to factory that has taken place in every agricultural region in the country as one crop after another has become mechanized. And now, the flight from farm to factory has become particularly apparent among to-bacco growers.

In North Carolina, the small farm gave way to agri-business during the 1970s, and even tobacco, the last major cash crop still grown on small farms, was affected by the shift. Recent figures for the declining tobacco-farmer population illustrate a trend that has been developing for a decade. In 1978, only 52,000 people were growing tobacco in North Carolina out of a total labor force of more than 2.6 million. In 1979, there were only 46,000, a 12 percent decline in 1 year. Where have these people gone? Where can they find new jobs and incomes?

Scientific research may pinpoint the answer to the first question. A careful observer would probably find that the stories of Mrs. Williams and the ex-farmer reflect what has happened to most of those tobacco farmers who are younger and continue to work. One study of two North Carolina counties (see chapter 5), for instance, showed that of those allotment holders who recently quit tobacco farming, 53 percent retired and 17 percent either turned to other types of farming or remained housewives. The remaining 30 percent, mostly those still of working age, found jobs in local industries. Industrial expansion, then, offers an essential alternative for those who now either cannot or will not continue to farm tobacco.

Attracting new industry to North Carolina was a major part of Governor Jim Hunt's first administration (1977-1981) and of his successful 1980 campaign for reelection. The present chief executive's interest in industrialization has deep roots in North Carolina politics, going back at least as far as the policies of Governor Luther Hodges (1954-1961). Almost every governor since Hodges has worked hard at attracting new industry, and Hodges's salesmanship paid off. Perhaps the capstone of his effort was the establishment of the Research Triangle Park between Raleigh, Durham, and Chapel Hill as a center for high technology and research jobs. The park has become a model for economic developers across the country and has given the Triangle area the distinction of having the highest number of Ph.D.s per capita in the nation.

Like Hodges, Hunt has been guided by two principal goals: first, to diversify the state's industrial base, long dominated by textiles, apparel, and furniture; and, second, to attract new industries that would raise the state's low manufacturing wage. In addition to these traditional development objectives, Hunt has emphasized a third dimension: "balanced growth," a geographic distribution plan for new industrial expansion that encompasses the preservation of the state's dispersed population centers, and the avoidance of the urban blight that has scarred some other fast-growth regions. Thus, "balanced growth" has come to signify not only the familiar effort to balance wages and industry sectors, but also the new effort to maintain a geographic balance in industrialization.

Although these may sound like apple pie and motherhood policies, they have proved politically volatile on more than one occasion. For example, Hunt's call to diversify the industrial base offended some supporters in the textile and furniture business. The description of certain sectors of the state as low-wage areas did not sit well with others. And some spokesmen for the state's politically powerful larger cities saw an anti-urban bias in the call for geographic balance in industrial growth.

Yet in 1977, when Hunt took office, the logic of these policies was persuasive. The "big three"—textiles, apparel, and furniture, all of which are low paying—still accounted for almost 56 percent of the state's factory jobs. Historically, this concentration has caused the state's average industrial wage to remain at forty-ninth or fiftieth (alternating with Mississippi) nationwide. (Standing alone, this statistic might be misleading. It does not, for example, take into account the differences in cost of living among states. But it nevertheless has remained a burr under the blanket of successive administrations in Raleigh.)

Moreover, these industries are all tied to the consumer goods market and thus often are vulnerable to boom and bust cycles. The state economy had a habit of catching a cold when the national economy sneezed. Industrial diversification was part of the cure for such violent economic swings, particularly when a new industry involved research and technology. At the same time, diversification was expected to boost the state's low average industrial wage and provide alternatives for workers turning from the farm to the factory for a livelihood.

But just what kinds of jobs are becoming available to tobacco farmers? How successful has industrial diversification been? What kinds of new jobs has this new growth provided? Where have these jobs located, and why? Is the credit due to political leadership, labor supply, good roads, adequate water, sound business habits, low unionization rates, low construction costs, or some other factors? (I recall one instance when an Exxon official gave credit to a persistent wife of one of his vice presidents who was a Tarheel—a native of North Carolina—and wanted to move home.) Has there, indeed, been balanced growth in North Carolina? And what alternative does this growth offer to the state's tobacco economy?

North Carolina, like most sunbelt states, benefited during the 1970s from the general growth of the South. Population figures stabilized, but in North Carolina, rose dramatically. By 1980, demographers were expecting the state to surpass Massachusetts as the tenth largest in the union with more than 5.6 million people. And this growth was not in the farm sectors. "What used to be called Tobacco Road in some quarters is now hailed as the dawning Sunbelt," noted North Carolina Secretary of Commerce D.M. (Lauch) Faircloth in an essay in *The New York Times*, January 1978.

In July 1980, the North Carolina Department of Commerce (DOC) reported that during the 1970s more than $11 billion in investment capital for new and expanding industry was committed in the state.[1] The number of jobs projected to flow from this investment totaled 246,770. Although many of these jobs remained in the labor-intensive "big three" industries, the trend in capital investment appeared to be outside these traditional sectors. In 1970, companies in North Carolina that expanded their local operations accounted for about 65 percent of the capital announced for the state's industrial projects; most of this expansion was in the traditional sectors. In 1977, by contrast, more than 50 percent of the announced capital investment for industrial projects was committed to new facilities (not expansion of existing physical plants), most of which came from newcomer companies outside the "big three" sectors. In 1978, such new growth rose to almost 75 percent of the announced capital investment; in 1979, it was 55 percent.[2]

Although this projected investment was made both by companies new to North Carolina and by those already in the state, it was often for jobs in high-paying sectors such as tobacco manufacturing or oil refining. In 1978, for example, the year Philip Morris announced its decision to build a major facility in Cabarrus County, tobacco manufacturing led the list of industrial sectors in the amount of investment capital committed to North Carolina. And in 1979, when a multimillion-dollar oil refinery was announced for Brunswick County on the coast, petroleum interests projected the state's highest investment figures. (On May 14, 1981, the Brunswick Energy Company announced the cancellation of its plan to build the refinery due to increased production costs, from $400 million in 1979 to $1 billion in 1981, and a declining demand for petroleum products.) Jobs in both sectors pay high wages.

New jobs created by industrial growth tended to be in higher wage sectors. The "big three" continued to account for large numbers of the new jobs—in 1979, 35 percent of all jobs in new and expanded industry. But in both 1978 and 1979, machinery manufacturers committed more new positions than any other sector. Electrical machinery, chemicals, transportation equipment, tobacco, and fabricated-metals manufacturers also brought in substantial numbers of new jobs.

These new corporate citizens were familiar to *Fortune 500* readers: IBM, Exxon, Philip Morris, Miller Brewing, Eaton, Clark Equipment, General Electric, Squibb, Data General, and Crown Petroleum. A case study could be made of growth in the Triangle area of Raleigh, Durham, and Chapel Hill. Using the Research Triangle Park and the attractions of Duke University, the University of North Carolina, and North Carolina State University as lures, industry hunters brought a steady and diverse group of new companies to the area. IBM located in the Triangle area in the 1960s and now has about four thousand employees there. Pharmaceutical companies such as Burroughs-Wellcome, Bristol Myers, and Cutter Laboratories have put operations nearby, and other medical-related businesses such as Squibb and Ajinomoto of Japan have found a home near Raleigh.

The geographic-dispersion aspect of balanced growth has also had an impact on recent industrialization in North Carolina. Historically, the crescent stretching through the Piedmont—from Raleigh to Durham across

Greensboro and Winston-Salem to Charlotte—has been a well-defined corridor for industrial growth. This strip remains the industrial heartland of the state, but during the 1970s industries also invested in the smaller communities outside this corridor. Although the largest share of investment dollars went into the Piedmont, substantial investment also went into eastern North Carolina counties—Brunswick, Columbus, Robeson, Nash, Martin, Beaufort, Johnston, Wilson, Wayne, Lenoir, and Halifax—as well as into the western counties of Buncombe, Burke, McDowell, and Rutherford. Even in the Piedmont, development often occurred on the fringes of urban concentrations rather than within metropolitan areas, which explains why 70 percent of the announced industrial investments during the last decade took place outside the state's major cities.[3]

Thus, the state's growth in recent years has been diverse and in industrial sectors that include high-paying companies, a type of growth that offers alternatives to tobacco farmers. Although many of the *Fortune 500* companies relocate professionals from other parts of the country—particularly such high-technology concerns as IBM, the new research facilities often spawn manufacturing operations that draw on local workers. Data General, for example, first located a research and development facility in the Triangle area and then built a manufacturing operation in nearby Johnston County, in the eastern part of the state still known to many as "tobacco road." Such facilities offer displaced tobacco farmers a place to go as do traditional sector jobs. But the percentage of factory jobs in textiles, apparel, and furniture, although still substantial, has declined annually and now accounts for slightly more than 50 percent of the state's industrial work force.

The record, then, shows that industrial growth during the 1970s had the effect of creating an alternative job market for tobacco growers at a time when the farming of this important crop began to depend less on manpower and more on machines. Whether the state's policy to encourage industrial growth represents a response to the displacement of tobacco farmers or mere coincidence is difficult to know, especially in a state where support for tobacco is vital politically as well as economically. North Carolina does not—and perhaps should not—have a stated policy of converting tobacco farms to factory sites. But in its search for balanced growth, the state has promoted the location of new factories in rural counties with the clear intention of creating new jobs in areas previously dependent on tobacco farming for economic survival.

Notes

1. North Carolina Department of Commerce (DOC), "Research Report," vol. 3, no. 2 (1980).

2. North Carolina DOC, Annual Report for Economic Development, 1979.

3. North Carolina DOC, "Research Report," vol. 3, no. 2 (1980).

10 Tobacco for Protein: A Revolutionary Upheaval?

Bruce Siceloff

Biologists, nutritionists, and agricultural authorities are convinced that tobacco can and eventually will be cultivated and marketed as a source of protein. But until more agronomic and economic research is done, no one is prepared to say how soon that will happen, or on how large a scale.

From the breeding laboratory to the field to the processing plant, tobacco grown for protein will be a new crop altogether—a distant cousin of burley and flue-cured smoking leaf. If it is ever grown on a commercial scale in North Carolina, even the most enthusiastic observers predict it will be only as an alternative, coexisting with the traditional tobacco crops rather than supplanting them.

Since the early 1970s, scientists in several laboratories—including the U.S. Department of Agriculture (USDA) Tobacco Research Laboratory near Oxford, North Carolina—have worked to find ways both to extract protein from tobacco leaves and to utilize the tobacco pulp once the protein has been removed. Begun in the aftermath of the 1964 surgeon general's report, the USDA research initially focused on developing a "safe" cigarette by removing the harmful components of the leaf. But the Oxford scientists soon discovered that the process they had developed, called homogenized leaf-curing, also was ideal for removing the high-quality protein that earlier researchers had found to be abundant in tobacco leaves. So they shifted their interest to the nutritional prospects of tobacco.

A leading spokesman for the protein potential has been Dr. Donald W. De Jong, who directed the USDA protein research until 1979, when he left the Oxford laboratory for a private-industry research job. De Jong sees the American research in this field in a global context. "There's a lot of interest in tobacco protein overseas. Groups in France and Italy are now working on it. They're even shorter on protein than we are. It'll take off eventually, I'm sure—perhaps when pressures [for protein] get a little tighter."

But De Jong also realizes that the new use of the product would have to fit into the local agricultural economies. He doubts that the high-technology feats of the protein-extraction plant will ever push flue-cured tobacco out of the field it has dominated for a century. "I envision it as a dual system," says De Jong. "You'd have farmers growing leaves pretty much the traditional way, and you'd have another, parallel system that would put more emphasis on protein production. Farmers could opt to go along with either one."

109

State Officials Cautious

North Carolina officials agree with De Jong about the potential value of tobacco for the nutritional needs of a hungry planet. "I am convinced, in the long run, whether from tobacco or other sources, that leaf protein is going to become a diet source for animals and humans," says Dr. Thurston Mann, tobacco research chief for the North Carolina State University (NCSU) Agricultural Research Service.

Even so, North Carolina farm leaders are not pushing for further study that would answer crucial questions about its viability as a commercial crop. They seem to fear some of the answers, already suggested by preliminary study, that further research would likely reveal. In particular, while discovering new protein uses for tobacco, scientists also may succeed in developing a new, inexpensive form of smoking tobacco. Researchers are confident that deproteinized tobacco—the green, mushy pulp that remains after protein has been extracted from the leaves—can be processed into a mild smoking leaf that could cut into the portion of flue-cured leaf blended into every cigarette.

The flue-cured tobacco grown in five southeastern states, prized for its high nicotine content and aroma, makes up about 45 percent of the tobacco used in American-made cigarettes. Flue-cured tobacco's share in the cigarette blend has declined in recent years, because of the rise in cheap imports and changes in cigarette manufacturing practices, and it could be expected to drop even more with the introduction of an inexpensive filler tobacco.

USDA scientists now believe that tobacco grown almost anywhere—and varieties exist from the equator to Siberia—can be deproteinized and then processed into a mild, low-tar filler that is somewhat less flavorful than flue-cured but also less costly to produce. If a satisfying tobacco aroma could be developed in processing plants anywhere in the country, and if this deproteinized leaf became acceptable to cigarette manufacturers on a wide scale, it could threaten the Virginia-to-Florida flue-cured belt's multibillion-dollar monopoly on flavor.

"It could cause a revolutionary upheaval in North Carolina," says John H. Cyrus, North Carolina Department of Agriculture tobacco affairs chief. "I doubt you could prevent it from being grown all over the country. That would mean the elimination of the [federal] tobacco program, the tobacco auction system, and so on."

Although cautious about the protein potentials of tobacco, state officials also realize they cannot afford to ignore the implications of recent research. "We're looking into the feasibility of it. If it's going to happen, we want to be in on the ground floor," Cyrus says. "Maybe we can get a jump on the rest of the country. We don't want to stand idly by and let someone out in California take the rug from under us and run with it."

In the summer of 1980, the North Carolina Farm Bureau, the largest and most influential farm advocacy group in the state, quietly started a protein-extraction pilot plant near Wilson, North Carolina. "We want to be as sure as possible that this stuff does not become a direct competitor with flue-cured tobacco," says John W. Sledge, president of the North Carolina Farm Bureau. Like Cyrus, Sledge seems to understand the importance of being "in on the ground floor." But thus far, Farm Bureau officials have refused to release details on their protein project, saying only that they will delay public discussion until they can report some results. A clue to the direction of their efforts may lie in Sledge's suggestion that deproteinized tobacco be marketed as animal fodder or fuel for methanol production.

Their caution is not surprising, when one considers the many political and economic threats to the existing tobacco-farm system and the fervor with which state officials defend tobacco. But what if De Jong and other researchers are right? What if tobacco could become a source of protein for a hungry world?

Promises and Problems of Tobacco Protein

A high-quality protein called Fraction-I and other useful proteins are abundant in the leaves of all green plants. In 1947, a team of California scientists first identified the enzymatic reaction that isolates Fraction-I in tobacco. Dr. Samuel G. Wildman, a recently retired biologist from the University of California at Los Angeles (UCLA), was part of that team and has been a pioneer in tobacco-protein research for the last three decades. Scientists recently have learned to extract protein from a variety of plants including alfalfa, spinach, cotton, rice, wheat, tomatoes, and corn. But only from tobacco have they learned to extract Fraction-I easily and in an unadulterated, crystalline form.

A single acre of tobacco grown for protein purposes, Wildman reports, could yield:

1,188 pounds of insoluble proteins that could be added to bread and other solid foods or used like soybean extracts

1,166 pounds of several water-soluble, tasteless, and odorless proteins known collectively as Fraction-II, which could become an additive to beverages, soups, and snack foods or could replace soybeans as a major source of animal feed, thus freeing more soy protein for people of developing nations

286 pounds of pure, crystalline Fraction-I protein, which far exceeds soy protein in nutritional quality and has potential medical uses.

Of the nine amino acids considered essential to the human diet, Fraction-I has concentrations of eight that are equal to or greater than the minimum set by the United Nations Food and Agricultural Organization. For all nine amino acids, soy protein has less than half the levels of Fraction-I. In a test to measure what is called the protein efficiency ratio, rats that were fed Fraction-I gained 22 percent more weight in four weeks than did rats fed milk protein, which was the yardstick for the test. And soy protein tested about 20 percent below milk protein.

Although Fraction-I probably would be too expensive for ordinary food use, its purity and high digestibility may give it valuable medical applications. Wildman believes, for example, that it could be added to the liquid diets of patients with pancreatitis, gastrointestinal tumors, and other diseases involving maldigestion and malabsorption. It might be fed to infants who are allergic to cow's milk and who cannot get human milk. And patients with aggravated kidney disease, who must severely limit sodium and potassium consumption and must undergo frequent hemodialysis to wash these salts from their blood, might need dialysis less frequently if mineral-free Fraction-I were made an important part of their diets.

To get such protein yields, farmers would grow and handle tobacco more like a silage crop than like traditional smoking tobacco. They would sow seeds directly into the field, up to 150,000 plants per acre, and harvest the crop with a mower in about 6 weeks, when, according to Wildman, the leaves of the 18- to 20-inch-tall plants have their peak protein content. The cut plants would sprout new stalks and leaves, allowing up to six successive harvests in a growing season of six to eight months. Wildman projects that a single acre of such a "close-grown" crop could produce up to sixty-six tons of tobacco per year. This harvest would measure 6.6 to 13.0 tons of dried leaf, depending on moisture content, compared with a conventional dried-leaf crop in North Carolina of about 1.0 ton. The 6.6 tons from a close-grown crop would produce 2,640 pounds of protein—almost 4 times the protein gained from 1 acre of soybeans, according to Wildman.

Tobacco growers would have to make a major adjustment in traditional planting and harvesting methods for a close-grown crop. Flue-cured and burley tobaccos are sown in seedbeds during winter and transplanted to the field in the spring, about 6,000 seedlings per acre (in contrast to Wildman's 150,000 seeds directly planted). Farmers harvest about four leaves per plant each week, moving up the stalk as the leaves mature. Then the flue-cured is scorched in a curing barn until it turns golden and sweet; burley is air-cured in unheated barns.

Some agronomists doubt that Wildman's projections for protein yields could be realized in North Carolina. They point out that his estimates depend on a growing season longer than the state's average of five and one-half months, and they warn that direct seeding of tobacco—as opposed to the traditional transplanting—would bring new weed, disease, and pest problems that would limit protein yields. Also, the widely used flue-cured and burley strains have been bred so that much of the leaf protein breaks down quickly as the plant matures (protein is not desirable in cigarette smoke because it burns poorly and has the bitter odor of burnt feathers).

But no plant has been more thoroughly studied and manipulated in the breeding laboratory than tobacco, and protein researchers are confident that plant geneticists can develop new strains that will produce more protein and release it more readily than do the breeds that have been tested by Wildman in California and De Jong in North Carolina. If the researchers are right, Wildman's projection of more than a ton of protein per acre could prove to be low rather than high.

USDA researchers have paid attention to the concerns of farm leaders that a market must be found for the tobacco pulp remaining after the protein extraction. At Oxford in the 1970s, De Jong developed a process called homogenized leaf-curing (HLC) in his quest for a safer cigarette. In the HLC process, immature, green leaves are washed, chopped, and ground into a semi-liquid slurry that is pressed into a sheet with the juices squeezed out of it. De Jong extracted leaf proteins from this liquid. Researchers hope that by chemically manipulating the juices squeezed out of it, they can learn to neutralize the tobacco components that turn into carcinogens in cigarette smoke.

The deproteinized leaf comes out as a green mush that is dried and pressed into sheets much like wood chips made into particle board. It is low in tar and nicotine. It does not have a pleasant smell at first, but it acquires one. "After three years on the shelf it has a good aroma and a nice color," says Dr. T.C. Tso, a USDA researcher in Beltsville, Maryland.

De Jong believes deproteinized smoking tobacco could be produced more cheaply than conventional leaf since the close-grown, multiple-harvest method would produce greater yields per acre while requiring far less labor since it could be mechanized from seed to processing plants. "The tobacco companies told us informally that they could use a material that was bland, that had some nicotine in it, provided it did not have an objectionable odor that had to be masked," De Jong says. "They could add the flavoring to it—that would be no problem."

Developing deproteinized tobacco as a cigarette-filler product could be the key to making the close-grown crop commercially viable. But North Carolina tobacco leaders, viewing this possibility as too much of a threat to current flue-cured and burley production, have instead advocated less lucrative uses such as methanol production or animal fodder.

Further Research Needs

Tobacco protein could be used for food and medical purposes only after years of testing by the U.S. Food and Drug Administration (FDA) to ensure safety. "We need to do a lot of research with the protein, to feed it to animals and even, down the road, feed it to humans," says Dr. James F. Chaplin, director of the USDA laboratory at Oxford. "[We need] to try to extract protein on a commercial basis, on a large scale." More study is needed, too, to find the best ways to grow and market this new crop and to perfect the smoking quality of the deproteinized tobacco.

Work at Oxford, stalled for more than a year after De Jong's departure in 1979, cranked up again early in 1981 under his newly appointed successor, Dr. Denise Blume. Blume said she was resuming study of protein extraction and development of a "safer" cigarette, but that the Oxford laboratory would need to find outside funding before it could set up a pilot plant for protein extraction in summer 1981. USDA researchers hope further study can improve the smoking quality of deproteinized leaf. Farm leaders in North Carolina, however, do not seem to share their hope.

NCSU researchers, for example, who frequently work with Oxford scientists, are waiting for Blume to take the lead in protein study. "Right now, we're committed to the continued production of a quality [traditional tobacco] product as a smoking material," says Mann, the NCSU tobacco research chief. And, even in spring 1981, the North Carolina Farm Bureau would make no comment about progress at its pilot extraction plant near Wilson.

Echoing the concerns of Farm Bureau President Sledge, North Carolina Department of Agriculture tobacco affairs chief Cyrus, and other farm leaders who want to protect flue-cured tobacco's dominant position in the industry, Chaplin downplays De Jong and Tso's insistence that deproteinized leaf can be developed as a smoking material. "We want to develop protein use in a way that dovetails into the existing tobacco industry. We've about come to the conclusion that it's going to be really difficult to use tobacco both for smoking and for protein," Chaplin says. Chaplin's laboratory, occasionally threatened with termination of funding by the antismoking lobby in Washington, owes its continued existence in part to the good will of North Carolina's congressional delegation, which tends to respond on tobacco matters to such groups as the Farm Bureau.

Conclusion

Most tobacco policymakers, farm researchers, and farm leaders seem hesitant to embrace the advantages that tobacco-for-protein may offer. The long-term opportunities for the crop seem unlimited in a world already scarred with famine. Yet no one is pursuing the research needs aggressively; no one is advocating that North Carolina become a leader in experimenting with this crop. With few exceptions, such as the UCLA findings and some USDA work, research seems to be motivated by fear more than by a sense of opportunity.

To the powerful anti-smoking lobby, protein offers an alternative for tobacco that is unassailable. To champions of tobacco, protein extraction could represent an important marketing option that complements—not replaces—the existing tobacco crop. Farms could remain small: a single acre could probably produce nearly four times as much protein as an acre of soybeans. And the federal tobacco program could probably be amended to accommodate the tobacco-for-protein crop.

Research needs to be done, certainly, to ensure that this alternative is a viable commercial enterprise. But what scientists have already demonstrated—in the laboratory and in the field—should assure even policymakers with very different views that harvesting tobacco for protein might well be an alternative for the flue-cured-tobacco farmer, an alternative as attractive to the most strident anti-smoking voices as it is to the most provincial pro-tobacco spokesmen.

Part III
World Leaf Sales Expand—But U.S. Share Shrinks

11 Tobacco's Global Economy: Is North Carolina Losing?

Joseph A. Kinney

As the 1980s unfold, the world marketplace offers a myriad of challenges and opportunities for the North Carolina tobacco farmer. At home, tobacco sales continue to erode, owing in part to declining per capita consumption and in part to wider use of less expensive foreign tobaccos combined with more efficient technologies used in manufacturing cigarettes. Abroad, the prospects are mixed. The United States continues to lead the world in leaf exports, and its total export sales (in all tobaccos) are increasing, from 259,091 metric tons in 1975 to 358,000 metric tons in 1980 (for the marketing year ending June 30, 1980). But as the world market grows, the U.S. share of that market is decreasing, from as high as 61 percent in 1960 to 29 percent in 1979. Whether exports will continue to provide U.S. tobacco producers a source of market strength depends on a variety of economic and political factors.

The Domestic Situation

Some review of the domestic situation is necessary in order to place the international situation in its proper context. Per capita use of tobacco in the United States has continued to slip by 1 or 2 percent per year. In 1979, the average American smoked, chewed, or sniffed less tobacco than in any year since 1898. From a high of 1.43 billion pounds in 1965, domestic tobacco consumption dropped to an estimated 1.25 billion pounds in 1979. This translates into a reduction of per capita cigarette consumption from 4,345 in 1963 to 3,967 in 1978.

Several interrelated factors have played important roles in the reduction of demand from domestic sources for U.S. tobacco. A series of government steps on the health front, most notably the 1964 surgeon general's report on smoking and health, helped prompt the decline. Increased tobacco taxes have also served to discourage consumption. Meanwhile, domestic cigarette manufacturers have adopted technologies that reduce tobacco waste in the manufacturing process. Likewise, the drive for low-tar, low-nicotine brands has led to less tobacco being used in cigarettes. Finally, and perhaps most significant, domestic manufacturers have increased the percentage of foreign tobacco in U.S. cigarettes from 11 percent in 1965 to 30 percent in 1980.

119

Tobacco: A World Economy

The United States has flourished in the world tobacco marketplace since the colonial days. Our tobacco exports date back more than 350 years, to a small farm in Jamestown, Virginia, owned by the legendary John Rolfe. Virginia, Britain's fifth attempt to establish a colony in the New World, was close to failure. The first shipment of Rolfe's tobacco, a few hundred pounds, went to England in 1613. It was well received and the demand increased. By 1617, exports totaled ten tons. By the close of the colonial era, Virginia, Maryland, and the Carolinas were exporting 100 million pounds a year, a small fraction of today's exports but the principal export commodity in those early days of the nation.

Today, tobacco is produced in at least a hundred countries and is imported or produced by virtually every nation. China and the United States are the dominant producing nations; China, however, is not a significant exporter and is not expected to be for the remainder of this decade. India, Brazil, Turkey, Japan, Bulgaria, South Korea, Canada, Greece, and Italy, in addition to the tobacco giants of China and the United States, produced at least 100,000 metric tons in 1978 (see table 11-1).

Only a small percentage of the tobacco that is produced actually enters international markets. The United States still dominates world exports with nearly three times the volume of runner-up Brazil. India, Bulgaria, Turkey, Senegal, Greece, South Korea, and Italy follow in order of importance (see table 11-2). This order is not likely to change in the early years of the 1980s. In some cases, tobacco from a number of countries is exported to a central

Table 11-1
Major Tobacco-Producing Nations
(in metric tons)

	1976	1977	1978
China[a]	980,000	975,000	975,000
United States	944,776	869,251	910,861
India	380,000	414,200	430,000
Brazil	253,024	310,000	329,000
Turkey	260,200	245,232	290,300
Japan	165,220	173,249	172,600
Bulgaria	145,000	118,000	170,000
South Korea	108,408	144,532	138,494
Canada	89,641	104,275	114,747
Greece	126,630	118,938	113,470
Italy	108,600	109,706	107,840

Source: U.S. Department of Agriculture.
Note: Table includes nations that produced 100,000 or more metric tons in 1978.
[a]Excludes Taiwan.

Table 11-2
Major Tobacco (Unmanufactured) Exporting Nations
(in metric tons)

	1975	1976	1977
United States	259,091	266,310	290,130
Brazil	101,196	106,648	108,111
India	78,203	79,600	75,000
Bulgaria	71,200	70,200	68,300
Turkey	65,639	75,153	61,835
Senegal	75,000	80,000	60,000
Greece	50,733	55,677	53,144
South Korea	44,258	42,133	48,549
Italy	58,860	53,598	40,536

Source: U.S. Department of Agriculture.

Note: Table includes nations that exported more than 40,000 metric tons in 1977.

point, blended, and then reexported. This phenomenon, long a practice in countries such as the United Kingdom, is beginning to occur in the United States, which may help the U.S. tobacco industry as world competition increases.

China, Japan, and Canada are leading producers of tobacco but relatively insignificant exporters. On the other hand, Senegal, an Africa nation with large tobacco-producing potential, joins the ranks of the leading exporters even though its output as yet is relatively small. Other African nations, principally Zimbabwe (Rhodesia) and Malawi, are likely to follow Senegal's lead. Zimbabwe, a quality flue-cured producing nation restrained for sixteen years by United Nations trade sanctions, will probably surpass Senegal in 1980 exports, and could emerge as a world leader by the late 1980s.

Clearly, these African nations, along with Thailand and some nations in Latin America, are learning what the United States has long known—that tobacco is a labor-intensive cash crop with significant foreign-exchange earning potential. The international agencies charged with encouraging economic development in financially weak countries have also realized the value of tobacco to developing economies. The World Bank, for example, has funded broad agricultural development schemes that included tobacco for a number of countries, including Malawi.

Ironically, some of the leading producers are also leading importers, including the United States, Japan, and Italy. This phenomenon is not unique to tobacco; other commodities, particularly rice, follow the same pattern. Japan, for example, exports low-quality rice but imports high-quality rice. In India, the situation is just the opposite. The Indians export high-quality rice to earn foreign exchange to buy lower-quality rice in large volumes for domestic consumption. Traditionally, U.S. tobacco manufacturers have imported low-quality tobacco to use as a filler because it is much cheaper than the lowest American grades. The U.S. exports have been primarily the highest grades because the quality of the American leaf was not available in necessary quantities in other countries.

Perhaps the dominant characteristic of leading importing nations is that they are wealthy (see table 11-3). With the exception of the United States, Japan, and Egypt, the primary importing nations are European. Worldwide imports have been shifting gradually, away from the high-priced U.S. tobacco to third-world-produced tobacco. The nine-member European Economic Community (EEC) aided this trend by the Treaty of Rome in 1958, and further enhanced it in 1975 at the Lomé Convention by reducing tariffs and other export barriers to developing nations.

The United States is losing some of its share of the world tobacco market to other countries, but worldwide tobacco demand continues to ease upward. Therefore, as total world exports of manufactured tobacco have continued to grow, so have total U.S. tobacco exports (see table 11-4). Since 1955, flue-cured exports have remained at approximately the same level and burley exports have increased (see tables 11-5 and 11-6).

In the next decade, there will be some shifts in the location of tobacco markets. The advanced, developed countries will likely see a plateau in their imports and perhaps a slight decline. This leveling off of imports is primarily a result of the reduced per capita cigarette consumption which appears to be stabilizing. The causes for this reduction are similar to the factors affecting the U.S. decline, which were discussed at the beginning of this chapter. Meanwhile, consumption in the developing nations, which here-

Table 11-3
Major Tobacco (Unmanufactured) Importing Nations
(in metric tons)

	1975	1976	1977
Federal Republic of Germany	179,046	167,256	171,902
United Kingdom	142,637	144,491	142,292
United States	172,889	158,352	139,048
Japan	95,989	94,193	85,980
Netherlands	65,800	57,400	62,000
Italy	58,860	53,598	40,536
Spain	36,885	38,522	40,463
Belgium, Luxembourg	39,426	41,387	39,285
France	74,887	83,000	39,135
Switzerland	27,435	26,176	30,867
Egypt	25,888	22,966	29,038

Source: U.S. Department of Agriculture.

Note: Table includes nations that imported more than 29,000 metric tons in 1977.

Table 11-4
Exports of Unmanufactured Tobacco (Flue-Cured and Burley)
(in million pounds)

Year	World Total	United States	United States as Percentage of Total
1955-1959	730	441	60
1960-1964	846	439	52
1966	817	469	57
1967	847	473	56
1968	908	487	54
1969	972	482	50
1970	922	409	44
1971	959	378	39
1972	1,221	479	39
1973	1,298	477	37
1974	1,497	502	34
1975	1,430	453	32
1976	1,456	447	31
1977	1,520	491	32
1978	1,612	546	34
1979	1,619	453	28

Source: U.S. Department of Agriculture.

tofore has been minimal, is increasing at about 2 percent per year. And this rise is expected to continue consonant with economic growth, increased exposure to western culture (including cigarette advertising), and disinterest in health-and-smoking regulations. Per capita consumption in most third-world countries is very low, an estimated one cigarette per day. Hence, a doubling to just two cigarettes per day could bring a dramatic increase in demand for U.S. tobacco and for tobacco generally. If per capita consumption worldwide approaches the U.S. level of almost eleven per day, the world tobacco market will be booming indeed. The central question then becomes: which countries' tobacco will fill that market?

Zimbabwe: Tobacco Giant

Most tobacco experts believe that the outcome of the political changes in Zimbabwe will have significant impact on the world marketplace for tobacco. In 1965, the year that Rhodesia declared independence from the United Kingdom, it ranked second only to the United States in export of tobacco. At that time, Rhodesia accounted for nearly one-third of free-world flue-cured-tobacco exports, supplying tobacco to sixty-seven countries, often in direct competition with the United States. Rhodesia exported 120,000 tons of tobacco, the majority of which went to the United Kingdom and West Germany.

Table 11-5
Exports of Unmanufactured Tobacco, Flue-Cured
(in million pounds)

Year	World Total	United States	United States as Percentage of Total
Average:			
1955-1959	683	413	60
1960-1964	772	397	52
1966	710	423	60
1967	750	427	57
1968	800	444	56
1969	845	430	51
1970	797	368	46
1971	831	342	41
1972	1,046	425	41
1973	1,088	418	38
1974	1,232	441	36
1975	1,199	391	33
1976	1,198	379	32
1977	1,229	412	34
1978	1,299	455	35
1979	1,306	371	28

Source: U.S. Department of Agriculture.

But in 1966, responding to international protest over white-majority rule, the United Nations (U.N.) imposed trade sanctions over Rhodesia, which included an embargo on tobacco exports. As a consequence, tobacco production in 1968 dropped to 60,000 tons from a record high of 138,000 tons in 1964.

U.N. sanctions did not totally stop Rhodesia from exporting, however. The country gradually increased its production from the low levels in 1968 as buyers found ways of circumventing the sanctions, such as routing tobacco through South Africa. By 1976, production had climbed to an estimated 85,000 tons, 95 percent of which found its way into the world marketplace. Then, in 1979, when a new black-majority government took control of the country (and changed its name to Zimbabwe), the tobacco embargo was lifted. With an open export market available in 1980, tobacco trade experts anticipated Zimbabwe production to increase rapidly.

The Rhodesia Tobacco Association has expressed some concern about its ability to continue to increase tobacco production for two reasons. First, a new draft procedure for the military has reduced the number of workers available to harvest the tobacco crop. Second, the rail and road system out of the landlocked country has not been stabilized. But there appears to be a reasonably smooth transition of governments with minimal political and economic disruption. Furthermore, the new government has announced

Table 11-6
Exports of Unmanufactured Tobacco, Burley
(in million pounds)

Year	World Total	United States	United States as Percentage of Total
Average:			
1955-1959	47	28	60
1960-1964	74	42	57
1966	107	46	43
1967	97	46	47
1968	108	43	40
1969	127	52	41
1970	125	41	33
1971	128	36	28
1972	175	54	31
1973	210	59	28
1974	265	61	23
1975	231	62	27
1976	258	68	26
1977	291	79	29
1978	313	91	29
1979	313	82	26

Source: U.S. Department of Agriculture.

that it would make available some $30 million to purchase and hold middle grades out of the market for up to two years—a financial boost to producers. Unless there are unforeseen changes, tobacco production could reach 180,000 tons within five years, with exports exceeding 160,000 tons.

Unquestionably, tobacco represents a commodity with a high cash return. Zimbabwe leaf is currently considered second in quality only to that of the United States, yet it is roughly half the price of American tobacco. By the late 1980s, Zimbabwe could be challenging the United States for the world's leading export position.

The Role of the Federal Government

Historically, the U.S. government has supported tobacco export interests in a number of ways: providing market information, sponsoring market development efforts, negotiating favorable tariff and trade agreements, and financing loan and credit programs. For a variety of reasons, including the growing power of anti-tobacco forces, policies supporting exports have begun to shift. Nonetheless, the federal government remains a positive force for tobacco exports to both developed and developing countries.

The U.S. government provides the best market information in the world, a valuable tool for tobacco exporters. But its market development programs have been greatly reduced. In the early 1960s, the United States provided nearly a million dollars annually for market development efforts. But after the 1964 surgeon general's report, spending slowed to a trickle. The current effort, funded at only $20,000 to $30,000 a year, supports American trade teams going abroad and potential importers coming to the United States.

In 1978, the federal government won some hard-fought concessions for tobacco during the Multi-Lateral Trade Negotiations (MTN), especially the agreement by the EEC to reduce its duty on U.S. tobacco by one-third. Thus, U.S. tobacco bound for the European market will be priced more competitively with other exporters. Although this agreement will not lead to a sharp increase in U.S. exports, it will slow the constant erosion of the U.S. share of the European market. Some experts believe that the gain could be worth $200 to $300 million a year to tobacco export earnings.

The government continues to finance tobacco exports under direct-lending and credit-guarantee programs, but to a much lesser degree than in the past. The most important example of lessening federal support is the reduction of tobacco exports under the Public Law (PL) 83-480 "Food for Peace" program. In 1954, Congress passed the PL 83-480 program to help poor nations receive U.S. food and to bolster the foreign exchange position of developing countries by allowing the importing country to purchase an American product with its own currency through favorable repayment terms (twenty to forty years, at low interest rates) rather than with dollars. (In recent years, though, repayment has been required in dollars.) Tobacco was included in this program to encourage other U.S. farm products "market entry" into the developing countries. Tobacco exports under PL 83-480 were as high as $62 million as recently as fiscal year 1978, despite several efforts made in Congress to exclude tobacco from the program. Finally, in 1978, Congress mandated that food commodities be accorded highest priority under PL 83-480. As a consequence, very little tobacco in recent years has been shipped under this program.

The Price-Support Program

It is difficult to ascertain the role of the price-support program in U.S. tobacco exports. To the extent that the program has caused prices to rise above the market price, it has discouraged growth for exports. As table 11-4 shows, the United States has experienced an overall increase in exports along with a steady decline in market share. But most experts do not believe that the United States could "buy back" any significant portion of its historical share of the market by lowering support levels.

Today, U.S. tobacco is the highest priced leaf on the world market. In 1975, the average import prices in the United Kingdom were (per kilogram):

United States, $3.55; Malawi, $2.47; and Tanzania, $2.49. But U.S. tobacco prices were highest in 1965 as well on the same market: United States, $2.27; Malawi, $1.26; Rhodesia, $1.26; and Tanzania, $.99. And during this decade, tobacco exports have not declined significantly (although import levels have been erratic). Clearly, price relationships between the United States and other principal exporting nations have remained relatively the same. Given this situation, it is safe to say that importers would have shifted to less expensive markets earlier if price were the sole consideration. The fact is, price is merely one of the factors in a decision to import. The primary consideration is leaf quality, but security of supply, packaging, shipping, amount of chemical in the leaf [West Germany has strongly urged U.S. growers to use less MH (maleic hydrazide)—a sucker-control agent—by threatening not to buy American leaf with high MH residue], blending practices, and other factors are also important to many importing countries.

It is reasonably clear that the United States would not make sharp gains in the world market by lowering price through a change in the support program. Major adjustments in the price-support program would likely only reduce the number of farmers in states like North Carolina, with only marginal impact on the supply and export volume. This is true not only because of relative price relationships, but also because the fixed cost of producing tobacco is higher for the United States than for our principal exporters.

Health

As a result of the 1964 surgeon general's report, concerns about the relationship of tobacco to health have caused per capita consumption of tobacco to decrease, first in the United States and now in many countries, especially in Europe and Japan. Most developed nations have adopted anti-smoking health programs and have tried to discourage consumption by increasing taxes, restraining advertising, and limiting locations where consumers can smoke. (See chapter 27 for a table on smoking regulation in thirty-two countries.)

It is generally agreed that by 1980 most adults in developed countries had heard evidence concerning smoking and health. Experts believe that persons have reacted in varying degrees, depending on what kind of smoker they are: marginal, experimenter, or hard-core. The marginals probably have already quit because of health concerns and the increased cost of cigarettes. Experimenters are new to smoking and have not yet developed a prolonged habit. Teenagers are the main experimenters in developed countries; women might also be considered experimenters, especially in the United

States. Cigarette manufacturers have made a concerted effort to produce brands with lower tar and nicotine levels. These brands might offer a long-term option to experimenters unless studies on the so-called less hazardous cigarette show significant health dangers. (See chapter 22 for a discussion of less hazardous cigarettes.) Finally, the hard-core smoker is not likely to cease his or her habit unless even more significant evidence about smoking and health is produced. Even then, hard-core smokers might turn to low-tar brands.

The evidence seems to indicate that per capita consumption is leveling in developed countries. The marginals have already quit. The hard-cores have not been affected by health concerns or have shifted to a lower-tar brand. And, as experimenters continue to join the smoking population, an increasing percentage of them may remain smokers if there is a low-tar option. The health studies have had all the impact they are going to have in developed countries.

At the same time, evidence indicates that people in developing countries do not associate smoking with health problems. This is true even in health-conscious China, where cigarettes have become a major status symbol. Few developing countries are likely to begin significant anti-smoking campaigns in the near future. Decision makers in developing nations simply have more pressing problems. Moreover, health officials in developing nations who encourage such campaigns have been viewed as ethnocentric and paternalistic. Consumption of tobacco, then, is likely to increase in developing countries, even if exposure to health studies expands.

Hence, it seems safe to conclude that tobacco exports from North Carolina and the United States are not likely to be further reduced by health concerns. If dramatic new evidence concerning the link between smoking and health does emerge, accompanied by wide publicity, then exports could be affected.

Conclusion

Is the United States losing its share of the world tobacco marketplace? From controlling 61 percent of the world's exports in 1960, the United States now has only 29 percent of the market. Nonetheless, the aggregate amount of tobacco that the United States, and hence North Carolina, is sending to the world marketplace continues to increase. This has occurred basically because the driving forces of demand—population and affluence—are on the increase, especially in the developing countries. Because many nations are devoting more acres to tobacco production, and are increasing yields, the United States faces much stronger worldwide competition than ever before. But since the pie is getting steadily larger, the United States manages to continue increasing total tobacco exports (see table 11-4).

In addition, the demand for U.S. tobacco is reasonably price inelastic. That is, importers purchase U.S. tobacco with only marginal regard for price. They come to the United States for superior-quality leaf, packaging, security of supply, and stable transportation, all of which are unlikely to change in the near future. Also, the impact of health issues may have leveled off in developed countries and is unlikely to be a force any time soon in developing nations. If gradual growth in the world economy continues, there is sufficient reason to believe that the United States will remain in its dominant role as the world's leading tobacco exporter at least for the remainder of this decade.

4210
7110
4220
7130
Global; U.S.

12 Open Trade and Modernized Tobacco Program: The Keys to an Expanded U.S. Flue-Cured World Market

Hugh C. Kiger

International trade is vital to the U.S. tobacco economy. The United States is at once the world's largest exporter and third largest importer of tobacco. In 1979, U.S. tobacco and tobacco products exported totaled $2.15 billion, and U.S. duty-paid imports of leaf and products amounted to $463.4 million—a favorable difference of $1.69 billion.

The 1979 figures indicate a healthy balance of trade for U.S. tobacco, but recent trends suggest a diminishing world position and the possibility of a less prosperous future. In the last five years, imports of flue-cured and burley tobacco have increased sharply. These imports have begun to supplant the use of U.S.-grown tobacco by domestic buyers and thus have increased the share of American leaf that must be exported. In 1979, more than 50 percent of the U.S. flue-cured crop was exported in the form of leaf and manufactured products.

The decreasing domestic use of U.S. flue-cured tobacco makes an expanding world market even more important now than in the past, for the U.S. share of world tobacco trade is also declining sharply. From 1966 to 1979, the U.S. share of world trade in flue-cured tobacco fell from 60 percent to about 28 percent. During that same thirteen-year period, flue-cured exports by competing countries tripled. Moreover, the United States Department of Agriculture (USDA) recently projected further declines in the U.S. share of world production and exports—assuming that the present tobacco program and policies continue without change (see figure 12-1).

In order to help increase the volume of U.S. flue-cured exports and the U.S. share of world flue-cured tobacco trade, U.S. tobacco exporters feel that two types of changes need to be made in the country's tobacco program and policies: (1) the tobacco program needs to be modified to make U.S. flue-cured prices more competitive on the world market; and (2) freer trade must be encouraged to ensure that the United States gains a more substantial share of the world market so that tobacco exports will continue to contribute to a favorable balance of payments. The exports market provides the United States the best potential for increasing production and income from

131

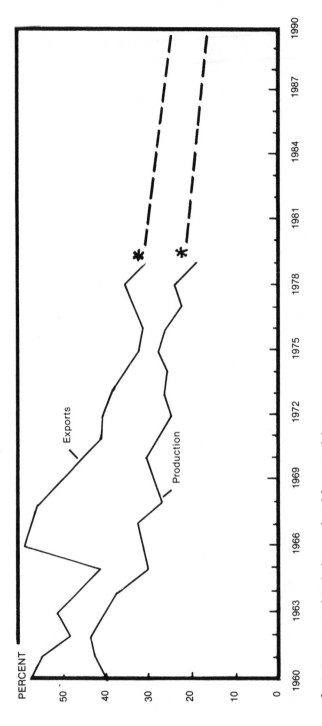

a U.S. Department of Agriculture projected from actual data.

Figure 12-1. Flue-Cured Tobacco: U.S. Share of World Production and Exports

tobacco. Any future increase in U.S. flue-cured production will depend on the ability of the United States to expand foreign sales of leaf and products.

Domestic Background

In the last twenty years, the U.S. tobacco economy has grown more dependent on exports than ever before. A wide range of factors is responsible for this, including a leveling off in U.S. cigarette consumption, a shift to lower tar and nicotine cigarettes (which use less tobacco), a disparity in price between American and foreign leaf, and higher U.S. taxes on cigarettes.

From 1973 to 1979, domestic use of U.S. flue-cured leaf dropped from 703 million pounds to 563 million pounds—a decline of 140 million pounds in just six years (see table 12-1). Twenty years ago, U.S. flue-cured leaf accounted for more than half the content of U.S. cigarettes, but by 1979 that portion had dropped to 38.6 percent. And during the same period, the portion of the average American cigarette made up of imported leaf increased from 10.2 to 27.2 percent (see table 12-2). In the past, American cigarette companies imported primarily oriental tobacco, a type of leaf not grown in the United States. But large quantities of flue-cured and burley have also been imported in recent years, mostly because of price. In 1979, for example, when U.S. flue-cured exports were valued at about $2.30 per pound,

Table 12-1
Production and Disappearance of Flue-Cured Tobacco, 1973-1979
(millions of pounds)

Marketing Year	Production[a]	Total[c]	Disappearance (Tobacco Used)[b] Domestic	Exports
1973	1,159	1,301	703	598
1974	1,245	1,200	652	548
1975	1,415	1,193	671	522
1976	1,316	1,148	634	514
1977	1,124	1,147	608	539
1978	1,204	1,185	584	599
1979	974	1,084	563	520

Note: Figures are based on farm sales weight, which is about 10 percent above dry weight normally reported in trade statistics.

[a]Data in this column represent sales on the auction floor. Source: ESCS and FAS, USDA.

[b]The difference in production and total disappearance data from year to year is because: (1) much U.S. tobacco is not exported during the year it is produced; and (2) U.S. manufacturers normally age tobacco two years or more prior to use in cigarettes.

[c]Figures have been rounded off, so the sum of "domestic" and "exports" columns may not equal the amount in the "total" column.

Table 12-2

Estimated Leaf Used for United States Cigarettes by Kinds of Tobacco,
1950-1979

Year	Flue-Cured	Unstemmed (Processing Weight)		Imported	Total
		Burley	Maryland		
(millions of pounds)					
Average:					
1950-1954	651	373	22	73	1,119
1955-1959	622	371	19	92	1,104
1960-1964	661	404	16	123	1,204
1965-1969	594	426	21	150	1,191
1970	548	400	27	163	1,138
1971	532	386	24	165	1,107
1972	555	411	16	193	1,175
1973	588	433	14	196	1,231
1974	558	418	13	213	1,202
1975	548	420	25	231	1,224
1976	566	421	22	237	1,246
1977	525	405	16	242	1,188
1978	514	410	19	284	1,227
1979	494	416	22	348	1,280
(percentage)					
Average:					
1950-1954	58.2	33.3	2.0	6.5	100.0
1955-1959	56.3	33.6	1.7	8.3	100.0
1960-1964	54.9	33.6	1.3	10.2	100.0
1965-1969	49.9	35.8	1.8	12.6	100.0
1970	48.2	35.1	2.4	14.3	100.0
1971	48.1	34.8	2.2	14.9	100.0
1972	47.2	35.0	1.4	16.4	100.0
1973	47.8	35.2	1.1	15.9	100.0
1974	46.5	34.8	1.0	17.7	100.0
1975	44.8	34.3	2.0	18.9	100.0
1976	45.4	33.8	1.8	19.0	100.0
1977	44.1	34.2	1.3	20.4	100.0
1978[a]	42.0	33.4	1.5	23.1	100.0
1979	38.6	32.5	1.7	27.2	100.0

Source: *Tobacco Situation,* September 1980, USDA.
[a]Subject to revision.

imported flue-cured tobacco averaged about 90 cents per pound. Even after
U.S. import duties, the foreign flue-cured leaf cost manufacturers substantially less than comparable-quality U.S. flue-cured leaf (see figure 12-2).

While U.S. leaf used in American cigarettes declined, some 60 million
pounds of U.S. flue-cured leaf moved overseas in the form of exported
cigarettes. If this amount is subtracted from the total domestic use (563
million pounds), it shows that only 503 million pounds of U.S. flue-cured

U.S. ¢ per lb.

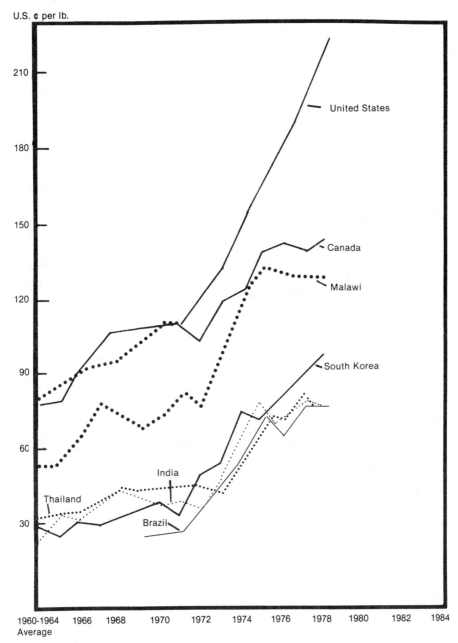

Figure 12-2. Flue-Cured Tobacco: Average Estimated Export Prices, by Major Producers

tobacco were consumed by smokers in the United States in 1979, an 18 percent decline in only five years.

According to most estimates, U.S. cigarette consumption will remain stable or decline slightly during the next several years. Unless there are changes in the tobacco program, it appears that the share of U.S. flue-cured leaf used in U.S. cigarettes will continue to decline in the period ahead.

Farm-Program Problems

Many of the problems of the U.S. flue-cured-tobacco program are related to production and marketing issues (see part I of this book). The program as now operated has had some adverse impact on production, marketing, trade, and the United States' ability to compete with foreign-grown tobacco, especially lower-quality tobacco.

The United States has not shared in the growing world market for flue-cured tobacco. Since 1960, world flue-cured production outside this country increased by about 2.3 billion pounds. But during this time, U.S. production decreased 250 million pounds, from 1.2 billion to 950 million. Moreover, competitive suppliers have produced tobacco at a faster rate than the world increase. Brazil, for example, increased production by 98.3 percent from the 1972-1976 period to 1979. During the same span, U.S. production decreased 22 percent (see table 12-3).

Table 12-3
Flue-Cured Tobacco: World Production in Selected Countries, 1972-1979
(in thousand metric tons)

Country	Average 1972-1976	1977	1978	1979[a]	Percentage Change 1972-1976 to 1979
Mainland China	582	585	590	580	− .4
United States	557	512	558	431	− 22.0
Brazil	117	165	179	232	+ 98.3
India	123	95	164	137	+ 9.2
Canada	99	104	113	81	− 18.2
Republic of Korea	76	92	92	80	+ 5.0
Japan	91	102	100	87	− 3.0
Rhodesia (Zimbabwe)	78	80	83	110	+ 40.0
Thailand	28	48	46	46	+ 64.0
Other	362	460	440	457	+ 20.2
Total	2,113	2,238	2,365	2,241	+ 6.1

Source: USDA, FAS Commodity Programs.

Note: Production on farm-sales-weight basis, which is about 10 percent above dry weight normally reported in trade statistics.

[a]Preliminary figures; estimates only.

Because of this declining share of the market, the United States has reduced quotas to farmers. This in turn has caused allotment values to increase substantially, so that many producers have been paying more than a third of their estimated gross income for the privilege of producing tobacco. More than 40 percent of all flue-cured tobacco is now grown under lease arrangements; the portion under lease reaches almost 60 percent in Georgia and nearly 70 percent in Florida. In recent years, lease rates in some areas have reached 50 to 70 cents per pound. Under this system, the primary benefits of price-support increases have accrued to the allotment holder rather than to the grower. But U.S. farm commodity programs are normally designed to benefit the persons who actually grow the agricultural products. The president of Tobacco Associates addressed these leasing trends at the group's 1978 annual meeting:

> Let me issue this word of warning and I know full well the merits of both sides of this question: Some states have already crossed over the median 50 percent of allotments being leased. Once this is done on a national basis, many think that the acreage-poundage and price-support program will collapse from within and no coalition of the industry, congressional delegations, or farm organizations can save it.

The high price of U.S. flue-cured leaf is to a large extent the result of the domestic tobacco program. Under this program, support prices are based on the Parity Index, a national indicator of prices paid by all farmers for production items, family living, interest, wage rates, and taxes. (It is essentially an index of inflation rates in overall farm costs, not in tobacco costs.) Under this formula, the 1979 average support price for flue-cured leaf was $1.29 per pound compared with 55.5 cents in 1960, and burley price supports averaged $1.33 in 1979 compared with 57.2 cents in 1960. By 1979, the support prices and market prices were well above actual production costs (that is, excluding lease costs) which enabled farmers to pay 50 to 60 cents per pound to lease quotas and still make a profit.

Because of provisions of the current price-support program, it has also been necessary to price bottom-of-the-stalk leaves at levels that are not competitive in the world market. Consequently, by the end of 1980, about 150 million pounds of "down-stalk" tobacco from the last several years remained in loan stocks. (If buyers do not purchase tobacco on the open market above the minimum price-support level, farmers can sell their tobacco to the Flue-Cured Tobacco Cooperative Stabilization Corporation, which buys the crop with federally guaranteed loan funds. For more background on this system, see part I of this book, particularly chapter 2.) This "down-stalk" is now priced substantially above its market value, and there is little demand for it (at its current price) on the domestic or foreign market.

In a 1979 issue of the *Georgia Tobacco Farmer*, Fred Bond, general manager of the Flue-Cured Tobacco Cooperative Stabilization Corporation, explained it this way: "Loan rates have been established at levels above the true market value due to statutory requirements built into the price support formula, [and] foreign-grown tobacco with comparable quality is available at a much lower rate."

Public debate over the tobacco program often polarizes the issue: abolishing the program on the one hand or keeping it intact, without modification, on the other. But many people working with tobacco see an option in-between—improving and updating the current program. (See chapter 2 for a full discussion of alternatives to different parts of the program.) Certainly the tobacco program needs to allow farmers to cover their costs of production and make a reasonable profit. But it also must allow the United States to compete in the world leaf market and to expand exports. Changes in the program should accommodate the needs of both the farmers and the leaf exporters.

American Exports Declining

U.S. flue-cured exports in 1978 were about 599 million pounds. The USDA estimates U.S. flue-cured exports in 1980 to be nearly 100 million pounds less than they were in 1978. Some of this decline was a result of the quality and size of the 1979 and 1980 crops; however, increased competition at relatively attractive prices was also a big factor. Unless this country can become more competitive on the world market, the declining trend in the U.S. share of world flue-cured trade is expected to continue (see figure 12-1).

The United Kingdom, West Germany, and Japan—our three major markets—account for more than one-half of our total exports of flue-cured tobacco. But we face problems in each of these markets.

Until recently, the United Kingdom (U.K.) was the major market for U.S. tobacco. But U.K. manufacturers have sharply reduced their purchases of U.S. tobacco, from 165 million pounds in 1968 to 52 million pounds in 1977. According to U.K. officials, the primary reasons for this decline were the availability of competing quality leaf, the decline in quality of U.S. flue-cured, and the high price of the U.S. leaf. (See chapter 13 for information on the declining purchases of American leaf by Imperial Tobacco Limited.)

Over the last twenty-five years, West Germany has generally ranked second as a market for U.S. tobacco. But the share of U.S. flue-cured leaf in West German tobacco products has also been declining. In 1978, total West German use of flue-cured leaf was up about 2.2 million pounds (from the previous year), but use of U.S. flue-cured tobacco was down by 1.7 million pounds, despite the weakness of the dollar in relation to the German mark. The "1979 Annual Tobacco Report" from the U.S. Consulate in West Germany warned of even greater declines in the future:

> If . . . the share of U.S. leaf in the German market is to be sustained, it appears imperative that American tobacco growers continue their efforts to improve the quality of their tobacco, produce an adequate supply of export grades and keep the cost of their tobacco down.

Since 1977, Japan has imported more U.S. flue-cured leaf than any other country. From 1978-1980, the value of our flue-cured tobacco exports to Japan averaged about $250 million annually, more than 25 percent of the total value of U.S. flue-cured exports. But since 1979, for the first time in twenty-five years, the United States has faced problems in the Japanese market as well. Like other countries, Japan has expressed concern over the price and quality of U.S. flue-cured leaf. Japan now has a surplus of its own tobacco and has recently increased its cigarette prices, which adversely affect consumption. Moreover, the best-selling Japanese brands (with low tar and nicotine content) contain less U.S. flue-cured leaf than brands that once were the most popular.

During the 1950s, Western Europe (including the United Kingdom and West Germany) provided the market for about 75 percent of U.S. tobacco exports. This share has declined since that time and now accounts for only about 52 percent of U.S. tobacco exports. There are problems relating to U.S. quality and price in these markets; however, some of the decline of Western Europe as a market for U.S. tobacco is a result of the protectionist tobacco policies of the European Economic Community (EEC). These policies include duty-free status for associated states, preferential duty for many developing countries, an excise-tax system that discriminates against nonmembers, provisions for subsidies and surplus disposal, and a safeguard clause that can be used to limit imports. Faced with these problems in the EEC, the United States will be fortunate to maintain its current export level to Western Europe during the 1980s.

The Soviet Union and Eastern Europe countries purchase only about $10 million of U.S. tobacco annually. In 1979, Poland was a major market, importing more than six million pounds. Trade prospects with this region should improve if all these countries are granted Most-Favored Nations (MFN) tariff rates by the United States. (The United States can grant MFN to some countries unilaterally. By the end of 1980, it had done so for Yugoslavia, Poland, and Rumania. MFN tariff rates are discussed in more detail later.) Extended credit and/or credit guarantees would also help expand tobacco trade to these countries.

About fifty years ago, China ranked second to the United Kingdom as an outlet for U.S. tobacco. But from the late 1940s to the late 1970s, official trade between the United States and the People's Republic of China (PRC) stopped. Today, the PRC is a major producer of tobacco, and as relations between the United States and the PRC continue opening, there are prospects for tobacco trade. In 1980, the two largest American cigarette manufacturers, R.J. Reynolds and Philip Morris, signed agreements with China that allow them to operate there. In November 1980, Philip Morris started manufacturing in Canton; in 1981, Reynolds is scheduled to produce some two million dollars' worth of one of its brands in China's Fujian Province. Over the long term, U.S. sales of tobacco to the PRC could be sizable, especially if that country develops its oil and mineral resources and improves its economy.

Prospects for Growth in the Eighties

Although world cigarette output has slowed down in recent years, it is still increasing. From 1960-1975, world cigarette output increased about 3.2 percent annually; during the last five years, it increased 2.2 percent annually. The USDA estimates that in 1979 world cigarette output increased by only 1.8 percent, about the same as the 1978 level, and that utilization stabilized or fell in the United Kingdom, the United States, France, Italy, Portugal, and the Soviet Union.

During the 1980s, world cigarette output should increase at about 1 to 2 percent annually, which means that additional flue-cured leaf will be needed in the world market, especially in some of the developing countries. Substantial growth in demand can be expected in the upper- and middle-income developing countries, particularly in those which export oil. Developing countries with rapidly growing economies in East Asia, the Middle East, and North Africa offer good market potential for U.S. tobacco. The developing countries that do not produce oil and are in poor economic condition have little capacity to import tobacco commercially during the 1980s.

But the extent to which the United States participates in the growing world market will be determined, to no small extent, by the direction this country takes in modifying its current tobacco program and trade policy. The price of U.S. flue-cured leaf is now about double that of such competitors as Brazil, South Korea, India, and Thailand (see figure 12-2). And many competing countries have taken steps to improve the quality of their tobacco as well, thus eliminating one of the last major differences between their tobacco and that of the United States.

The United States can increase its share in the world market for flue-cured tobacco if it follows a policy that results in adequate supplies of good-quality leaf at competitive prices. This farm policy should be accompanied by a trade policy that recognizes the importance of two-way trade and access to foreign markets.

General Agreement on Tariffs and Trade and Improved Market Access

For almost fifty years, the United States has had a trade policy that is as free from barriers as possible. During this period, U.S. tobacco achieved its dominance in a world trade that was generally characterized by open competition. Still the world's leading tobacco trader, the United States has more to gain from trade policies that are as free as possible—and more to lose from protectionism—than any other country. Yet, in recent years, as U.S. tobacco imports have increased, some tobacco officials have proposed that the United States adopt a protectionist policy and unilaterally take steps to restrict tobacco imports. Such action is contrary to both the General Agreement on Tariffs and Trade (GATT) and U.S. trade policy.

In the 1930s, when the world was suffering from an intense economic depression, many governments attempted to take shelter behind various kinds of protective trade barriers. It became evident during World War II that these restrictions might become permanently fastened on the world unless resolute attempts were made to dismantle and outlaw them. Today, the GATT is the major result of the efforts made in this direction.

The GATT entered into force on January 1, 1948. The starting point lies in the Atlantic Charter and in the Lend-Lease Agreements in which the wartime allies bound themselves together to seek a world trading system based on nondiscrimination and aimed at higher standards of living, to be achieved through fair, full, and free exchange of goods and services. Headquartered in Geneva, Switzerland, the GATT is administered by a secretariat under a director general. Its membership has increased from its original 23 nations to 102 countries, which today are responsible for more than four-fifths of world trade. Basically, the GATT provides three things: (1) a set of negotiated tariff concessions; (2) a set of written general rules designed in large measure to make these concessions meaningful; and (3) a forum for contracting parties to hear complaints, make decisions, and make arrangements for further negotiations.

The GATT, a multilateral trade treaty embodying reciprocal rights and obligations, provides a framework within which negotiations can be held for the reduction of tariffs and other barriers to trade, and furnishes a structure for embodying the results of such negotiations in a legal instrument. It contains, in essence, three fundamental principles: (1) that trade should be conducted on the basis of nondiscrimination; (2) that protection shall be afforded to domestic industries exclusively through the customs tariff and not through other commercial measures; and (3) that the concept of consultation, aimed at avoiding damage to the trading interests of contracting parties (members), shall be inherent in all agreements.

During the GATT's first twenty-five years, six major trade negotiations took place under its auspices: in 1947 (Geneva); in 1949 (Annecy, France); in 1951 (Torquay, England); in 1956 (Geneva); 1960-1961 (Geneva, the Dillon Round); and in 1979 (Geneva, the Tokyo Round). As a result of these negotiations, the levels of world tariffs have been reduced to the point that they are not now a major obstacle to trade. Thus, the GATT has contributed greatly to the spectacular growth of world trade since 1948.

In its tobacco trade policy, the United States has favored an open international trading system. U.S. tobacco has been protected through a customs tariff with essentially no nontariff barriers. Most countries are extended the MFN tariff rate on tobacco by the United States. However, some centrally planned economies, such as the Soviet Union, East Germany, and Bulgaria, are subject to the U.S. tariff rate on tobacco established by the Tariff Act of 1930. The U.S. tariff rate on unstemmed flue-cured leaf subject to the Tariff Act of 1930 is 35 cents per pound compared with the current MFN rate of 12.75 cents per pound.

All GATT member countries should be treated equally when measures are applied affecting exports or imports, according to the GATT rule known as the MFN clause. No member country should receive better treatment than any other. (Exceptions to this include preference systems that existed at the time GATT was drafted, preferences created when countries formed or joined customs unions and free trade areas, and preferences approved for developing nations.) As a member of the GATT, the United States adheres to this principle. Consequently, it applies the same (MFN) duty to products from all members of GATT. The United States does not apply one level of duty on tobacco imported from Brazil and another to tobacco imported from Japan.

U.S. tariff rates on tobacco are the result of agreements that have been negotiated with trading partners, beginning with the Tariff Act of 1930. Over the years, officials from grower associations and all other segments of U.S. tobacco economy, as well as members of Congress and key officials of government, have either participated in or influenced the negotiating process and the resulting trade agreements. The tariff rates were not forced on the United States by its trading partners, but were agreed to by U.S. representatives. Thus, U.S. tariff rates on tobacco are bound under the GATT. The United States could not unilaterally restrict trade in a manner that is contrary to these trade agreements, unless fully warranted under provisions of Section 22 of the Agricultural Adjustment Act or the Trade Act of 1974. These acts provide for relief from injury caused by import competition if imports are a substantial cause of serious injury to the tobacco program or tobacco economy.

In the Tokyo Round, real progress was made in modernizing the GATT. The mechanisms for settling disputes were improved, and steps were taken to bring the developing countries into the disciplines of the agreement. Prior to the Tokyo Round, negotiating sessions under the auspices of the GATT had dealt primarily with tariff reductions. However, in recent years, as tariffs have been progressively reduced, many nations have adopted nontariff measures to restrict trade. Some of the major nontariff measures include customs valuation methods (should duty on whiskey, for example, be based on volume per bottle or proof?), unilateral government procurement patterns, import-licensing regulations, imposition of product standards and—perhaps most important—subsidies and countervailing duties (that is, quid pro quo arrangements). In many countries, such nontariff measures have replaced tariffs as primary obstacles to trade. The new codes, which establish ground rules for such vital areas as the nontariff barriers, are designed for modern economic reality and should substantially benefit U.S. trade. If vigorously enforced, these new codes will effectively diffuse the protectionist measures contained in the nontariff barriers to trade.

At the Tokyo Round, the U.S. delegation pushed hard to achieve better market access for U.S. tobacco, and the trade package negotiated contains some major concessions. For example, the tariff on U.S. tobacco (and tobacco from other nonmember developing countries) going to the EEC was reduced by about one-third on January 1, 1981. This gives better access to the key European market where nearly half of the U.S. tobacco exports have gone in recent years. The Tokyo Round also yielded other concessions from such trading partners as Australia and New Zealand. No substantial concession on tobacco imports was required of the United States in connection with the benefits the country obtained from the negotiations. (The U.S. did agree to reduce its duty on stemmed cigarette leaf from 45 cents per pound to 20 cents per pound over an eight-year period beginning January 1, 1980, in order to put the duty on stemmed and unstemmed on the same basis.)

A good-quality product that is competitively priced cannot be sold on foreign markets if it is denied access to the market because of artificial trade barriers. If the United States hopes to expand exports in the period ahead, all segments of U.S. tobacco economy should support trade legislation and policies designed to reduce tariff and nontariff barriers with trading partners on a *reciprocal* basis. Trade is a two-way street—to export, one must import.

Conclusion

What is the outlook for exports of U.S. flue-cured tobacco during the decade of the 1980s? Will the U.S. share of the domestic and foreign market for flue-cured tobacco continue to decline or will it increase? A policy that moves us in the direction of tight supplies of high-quality leaf, disproportionately high prices (noncompetitive), and protectionism will result in decreased exports, decreased domestic use, lower farm income, a reduction in our balance of payments, and increases in production and trade by competitive suppliers. But a policy that encourages production of adequate supplies of good-quality tobacco at competitive prices and better access to foreign markets will result in expanded exports, increased domestic use, higher farm income, and an increase in our balance of payments.

Farm leaders in the tobacco areas, in cooperation with economists in agricultural universities and state and federal departments of agriculture, should be able to develop policies that will improve the U.S. tobacco program and, consequently, the outlook for tobacco exports. At the same time, trade negotiators should continue to work toward better trade access for U.S. tobacco—including lower tobacco tariffs and removal of nontariff barriers.

If all sectors of the American tobacco economy are aggressive and innovative in their trade approach, it should be possible for the United States to secure a larger share of the world tobacco market. If peace and prosperity prevail and if the United States makes the necessary changes in its tobacco program and policies, I believe that the value of our tobacco exports (leaf and products) could reach $4 billion by the end of this decade—almost double the $2.15 billion of 1979. If the United States makes the right decisions relative to production and trade policies, it could double the volume of tobacco exports before the year 2000.

13

American Leaf Exports on Decline: Imperial Tobacco Limited Closes Its Last American Primary-Processing Plant

John Campbell

Historically, tobacco manufacturers in the United Kingdom (U.K.) have ranked high as quantity purchasers of U.S. flue-cured tobacco. In fact, for much of this century Imperial Tobacco Limited (ITL), the largest cigarette manufacturer in the United Kingdom, bought more American leaf than any other export buyer in the world. But in recent years, the United Kingdom has been using far less American tobacco. From 1973 to 1977, exports of U.S. flue-cured leaf to the United Kingdom declined 46 percent.[1] In 1977, ITL purchased approximately 30 million pounds less than its average yearly purchase in the five-year period, 1966-1970, a drop of more than 80 percent.[2] Since 1977, ITL purchases have remained at this greatly reduced level.

As ITL spokesmen have explained publicly,[3] a primary reason for this dramatic decline is that ITL no longer profits by paying the high price for American leaf. The amount of good-quality U.S. tobacco carefully handled and graded, which ITL requires, diminishes each year. And the demand for the limited amount of such quality leaf has forced prices up to unrealistic levels. For example, from 1973 to 1977, the U.S. support price on flue-cured Grade B4F (which might be regarded as the "hub" grade of the U.K. market) increased 52 percent, from 83 to 126 cents per pound. As prices rose and supply of the necessary quality diminished, ITL was not able to be as selective in its leaf-grade standards to obtain its required amounts of tobacco.

ITL foresaw problems with U.S. supply long before such patterns developed. Consequently, in the early 1960s, ITL began reducing staff and closing processing plants in the United States in order to get overheads in line with the decreasing amounts of its American purchases. And in the 1970s, the pace of such reductions accelerated. In 1980, when the level of purchases no longer warranted a large capital investment, ITL sold its last remaining leaf-processing plant, located in Wilson, North Carolina. After nearly eighty years in the United States, during which ITL had owned and operated as many as twenty leaf-processing plants at one time, the British company now purchases its American leaf through a single U.S. dealer, who processes the tobacco for ITL and exports it to the United Kingdom.

The U.S. Advantage Wanes

Because health concerns are growing, and low-tar brands are gaining a greater share of the market (among other factors), foreign cigarette manufacturers are no longer so dependent on a small number of grades for production. In the past, many U.K. brands depended to a great extent on a few high-quality U.S. grades. But today, cigarette manufacturers, including those in the United Kingdom, are attempting to produce blends made up from varying qualities of leaf purchased in all parts of the world. These blends must satisfy the smoker's taste at the cheapest possible price. The emphasis on price during the last few years has been heightened by severe inflation, problems of cash flow within manufacturing organizations, preferential duties on leaf from different countries, changing consumer requirements, needs to cut manufacturing costs, high taxes on tobacco products, intense competition, and many other factors.[4]

At the same time, both at home and abroad, research techniques have been developed to allow the fuller utilization of the purchased leaf with as little waste as possible.[5] Considerable advances have been made in developing mechanical techniques to change the physical properties of the tobacco so that less leaf is required to produce a single cigarette.[6] Research efforts have also resulted in ways to replace high-cost leaf with cheaper, lower-quality leaf in some instances.

It is widely recognized that U.S. flue-cured tobacco is superior to leaf grown in most other countries in terms of manufacturing quality, aroma, and nicotine content. But its cost has reached such a high level that U.K. manufacturers have been forced by economic factors to use as little U.S. tobacco as possible in their products.[7] From 1973 to 1977, the average support price of U.S. flue-cured tobacco increased 48 percent, from 76.6 cents per pound to 113.8 cents per pound. At the same time, as noted earlier, support on the hub Grade B4F increased 52 percent. Because of the U.S. support-price formula, the prices on the top grades tend to increase faster than those on the medium and lower grades. In 1980, B4F was supported at $1.61 per pound, an increase of 11 percent over 1979, compared with the overall average increase of 9.4 percent in support prices. The higher prices on the top grades are necessary to protect the grower, but ultimately the same growers suffer in the international market. In 1980, the United Kingdom could purchase leaf equivalent to a B4F grade from Brazil at 68 cents per pound, almost two and one-half times cheaper than the U.S. prices. Based on current projections of support prices, therefore, the future of U.S. flue-cured exports is not promising.[8]

While U.S. tobacco prices rose in the 1970s, foreign cigarette manufacturers successfully developed alternative sources of flue-cured tobacco in Brazil, South Korea, Thailand, India, and other countries where production costs are lower and leaf quality is steadily improving to match that of the United States. Many of these new sources now have superior systems for leaf grading and sale, including the removal of foreign matter, suckers, stalk, and sand which are unwanted because sales are based on weight. Also, other countries have acquired the necessary technology for high-standard packaging of tobacco for export. Finally, tariff concessions—even duty-free status—have often been given to developing nations, notably by the European Economic Community. These reduced tariffs have had the effect of encouraging increased production within, and exports from, these countries.

International purchasers who have the ability to buy leaf throughout the world look chiefly for two things: *quality* and *value for money*. As the buyers' choices among other countries increased, the U.S. share of world flue-cured-tobacco trade dropped, from 61 percent in 1960 to 27 percent in 1979.[9]

What Is Good Quality?

In international tobacco circles, the reputation of the quality of U.S. leaf is declining. The characteristics of "quality" are somewhat different for the buyer on the warehouse floor, the primary processor in the country of origin, and the tobacco manufacturer. Persons buying tobacco for export must be concerned about quality at each of these stages in the marketing and manufacturing process.

In the warehouse, subjective "looks" are still important. To meet export demands, a buyer generally picks leaves from the top half of the plant, which have a higher nicotine content, richer flavor, and stronger concentration of aroma than the lower leaves. He likes tobacco with clean color, grainy texture indicating ripeness, good body, and a fair degree of blemish; he does not like molds, excess moisture, or foreign matter.

The primary processor is more concerned with threshing and drying specifications which must be met prior to packaging for export. He looks for uniformity of plant position, color, and texture in the purchased leaf. He wants to obtain the highest yield of lamina (the leaf minus the midrib, or stem) since the lamina is valued higher than the midrib. The particle size of the strips (lamina, after threshing) relates to subsequent cigarette quality. The strips/stem ratio, together with moisture content, are carefully measured for proper packing.

The foreign tobacco manufacturer, beset by health requirements[10] and concerned with flavor and taste, looks at the chemistry of the threshed product in detail, especially the nicotine and sugar content, the level of tar and the tar/nicotine ratio, and pesticide residues. Filling value, a volume measurement of the level of cut rag (that is, the finely cut strips) in a cigarette, together with high shatter resistance (how firmly the cut rag remains packed) are important cost-related qualities. These factors must be measured accurately because the tobaccos that make up the blend have to be mixed so that the tar, nicotine, and other chemical figures printed on the cigarette package are met. And finally, the aroma must be highly desirable so that the consumer is encouraged to purchase the brand.

As the cigarette manufacturing process changes to meet new health requirements, to produce a higher percentage of low-tar brands, and to respond to other transitions within the industry, the relative importance of the quality characteristics just explained—and of others of a more technical nature—is also changing. And as some qualities of the leaf improve to meet manufacturers' needs, other qualities tend to suffer. Growers must, therefore, understand the demands for quality of the manufacturers and attempt to meet the quality standards as they change.

Though flue-cured tobaccos look fairly similar regardless of country of origin, their intrinsic qualities are not the same because of different growing methods and the climatic and soil conditions under which they are cultivated. The U.S. leaf has traditionally been considered supreme by cigarette manufacturers because of its balanced chemical content, flavor, and aroma. In the past, most other countries have produced lower grades of tobacco that have generally been used as filler. All quality levels have a price/usability ratio.

International tobacco price analysis is a complex subject that has received insufficient attention from government and private-sector researchers.[11] Yet increasingly, international buyers are equating the value of each particular country and grade per unit of quality with new formulas for brands of cigarettes that are both popular and profitable. The key to the future is the relationship of price to the quality of the tobacco—for all grades. The country of origin is no longer the primary concern.[12]

In many ways, the United States is a perfect country for growing tobacco. The climate is ideal (from Maryland to Florida) and there is plenty of land and good soils to increase poundage. Unlike many developing countries, the United States does not yet face competition between food and tobacco producers over prime farmland. The growers are extremely knowledgeable and are backed up with outstanding agricultural extension services and an abundance of research and technical know-how. Advanced mechanization—the means of producing "labor-cheap" crops—is readily available. Finally, leaf supplies have a certain level of dependability year to year and the government is stable.

Despite these many assets, since 1970 the United States has exported vastly reduced amounts of flue-cured tobacco to the United Kingdom, traditionally, a leading buyer of American leaf. Imperial Tobacco Limited's decision in the spring of 1980 to close its final American processing facility dramatized this trend. ITL apparently has chosen to stake more of its future on the tobacco of other countries rather than on U.S. leaf. The closing of this ITL facility, in many ways, should be a signal of alarm to the whole U.S. tobacco industry.

Unless the current tobacco support program is completely overhauled, the U.S. market could suffer even greater losses. The federal program must be changed so as to enable those farmers who wish to continue growing tobacco to increase production and at the same time maintain competitive prices in the world market. The solution lies in the hands of the people producing and marketing the crop and the policymakers and farm advocates involved in setting policy. It is in the foremost interest of these people to safeguard their export markets. Their will to produce, to change, and to achieve according to the dictates of the marketplace is vital.

Notes

1. Tobacco Advisory Council, "Factors Affecting U.K. Requirements of U.S. Tobacco," London, England, April 28, 1978.

2. R.A. Garrett, Chairman, Imperial Tobacco Limited, Public Statement, October 3, 1977.

3. Ibid.

4. John Campbell, "Are We Pricing Ourselves Out of the Export Market (with Particular Reference to Flue-Cured Tobacco)?" Paper presented at 27th Tobacco Workers' Conference, 1977.

5. Robert H. Miller, "The Domestic Tobacco Market—A Look Ahead through the 1980s," *Tobacco Situation* 171 (1980):31-38.

6. Ibid.

7. Tobacco Advisory Council, "Factors."

8. Ibid.

9. Samuel Smith, Foreign Agricultural Service, USDA, "U.S. Flue-Cured Tobacco Competition in the Southern Hemisphere." Paper presented at the South Carolina tobacco warehouse meeting, May 13, 1980.

10. See part V of this book for compendium of health requirements in thirty-two countries, many of which have stronger restrictions than the United States.

11. USDA, Foreign Agricultural Service, "World Tobacco Prices Assume Greater Importance in Trade," *Tobacco* FT (Foreign Agricultural Circular) 6, 1976.

12. Campbell, "Are We Pricing?"

151-156

[1979]

14 Making the Third-World Marlboro Country

Albert Huebner

Transnational tobacco companies are looking to a vast new market of cigarette smokers in the third world to compensate for the leveling off of their other, established markets. In America, fewer people are smoking but they are smoking more, creating an $18 billion cigarette market—up from $10.1 billion in 1968—that is the largest ever. The rest of the world market, most of it in Europe and the largest nations in Asia, is more than five times as large, representing $100 billion in worldwide sales—approximately one-fourth the size of the bloated world-arms budget. But the tobacco giants are not happy with their balance sheets. Growth in the United States has averaged only about 1 percent annually over the past five years. The European market is becoming equally stagnant as Britain, France, Sweden, and Russia intensify their anti-smoking campaigns.

By contrast, the developing nations offer a market capable of most lucrative exploitation. The potential smokers comprise more than half the world's population. Governments in those nations are unlikely to spend scarce funds on anti-smoking campaigns and will be reluctant to give up increasing tax revenue from cigarette sales. And because direct evidence of the health hazards is not yet visible in their countries, inhabitants of the third world are as likely to succumb to the subtle but powerful call of cigarette advertising as were millions of Americans in the decades before the first surgeon general's report in 1964.

Lured by this hot new market, transnational tobacco companies have been vigorously stepping up their sales campaigns in the third world. According to *Forbes*, U.S. cigarette exports have nearly tripled during the last decade, although some of this increase went to Europe and Japan. Philip Morris, first of the U.S. companies into the foreign market, has been increasing its overseas cigarettes sales at a spectacular 18 percent a year over the last decade. R.J. Reynolds got a later start, but its foreign earnings soared from $52 million to $82 million last year. British-based Rothmans International reported last year that "healthy gains in exports" to developing countries "helped profits to rise 30 percent."

This chapter appeared originally as "Making the Third World Marlboro Country," by Albert Huebner, June 16, 1979. Copyright 1979 *Nation* magazine, The Nation Magazine, The Nation Associates, Inc. Reprinted by permission.

Dr. Mumtaz Ahmad of the Pakistan Tobacco Company, a subsidiary of British-American Tobacco (BAT), reports that sales have been increasing by 8 percent annually in his country. He predicts that starting in 1978, this figure will rise to 10 percent. Similar growth is sweeping other third-world countries; overall, according to the United Nations Food and Agriculture Organization, cigarette consumption in the developing world is growing at 5 percent a year. This means that consumption of cigarettes is rising in regions of the world least able to afford the many woes that accompany addiction to tobacco.

Philip Morris is selling cigarettes in more than 160 countries and British-American Tobacco, the world's largest cigarette maker, distributes some 300 brands in 180 countries. In Brazil, for example, BAT controls 83 percent of a market that is already large and growing faster than any other in the western world. Philip Morris and Reynolds, trying to catch up, have poured millions into buying local companies and establishing brands. They are still losing money in Brazil, but according to Hugh Cullman, president of Philip Morris International, "The carrot there is definitely worth the effort."

Signs of this invasion by the tobacco transnationals are ominously present in other Latin American countries. A 1975 survey by the Pan American Health Organization showed that 45 percent of the men in eight urban areas smoked cigarettes; by contrast, barely 39 percent of the males in the United States were still smoking then. As economic conditions improve among some segments of the population, so exploitation of this market will further enrich the tobacco companies.

At the heart of this penetration into the third world is what has been at the core of making the United States the highest per capita consumer of cigarettes in the world: salesmanship. "We're a marketing organization," says Philip Morris's Cullman. "Our success is related to our ability to market and merchandise, using consistent and integrated themes aimed at the growth segments of the markets." What is marketed, as we well know, is not just a product but the symbol of a way of life. Erik Eckholm, senior researcher at Worldwatch Institute in Washington, notes: "Simple tubes of tobacco have come to represent modernity, savoir-faire, and in the minds of children, who for decades have plunked down nickels for candy cigarettes and bubble-gum cigars, adulthood." He adds that "a street waif in Cairo is as apt to beg for a cigarette as for coins."

A report by Dr. Martin Fishbein to the Federal Trade Commission proves the effectiveness with which cigarette advertisements create appeal for the poisons they push. One survey among young Americans showed that this advertising reinforced "the image of the teen-age smoker as young, attractive, healthy, and sexy." Another found that smokers of each sex see the female smoker as "sexually open, sophisticated, sociable, flirtatious, good-looking, and a career woman."

The tobacco merchandisers have found that implanting images in the third world is a process remarkably similar to that in their domestic markets. When Philip Morris made its initial assault on the cigarette market overseas, Marlboro, its major brand, logically led the way. The "Marlboro country" theme needed little modification, thanks largely to the global popularity of western movies. *Dun's Review*, in an article appropriately titled "P.M.'s Foreign Invasion," reported that "P.M. soon realized that the [Marlboro] cowboy was a winner, attracting smokers right across Europe and as far afield as Lebanon and Kuwait."

Other standard themes are attracting smokers even further afield. The French brand, Gauloise, stresses two ideas in its African marketing: it is a "virile cigarette," this cited as an important quality "considering the male pride of the African," and it is a "high-status" cigarette. In Niger, a beauty pageant selects "Miss Gitanes," the name being that of a brand sold by the tobacco company that created the pageant. Elsewhere, sports competitions are sponsored and publicized by the tobacco transnationals, which make effective use of testimonials from local athletes.

In 1977, R.J. Reynolds launched in the United States a new campaign at an estimated $50 million for its new cigarette, Real—this in a national market that is stagnant. It should come as no surprise, then, that the tobacco giants are spending vast sums in the developing world, where the potential for growth is almost incalculable. In Malaysia, for example, the two leading companies spent approximately one pound per adult male for advertising in 1976, although per capita gross national product is only 400 pounds. In Kenya, where British-American Tobacco operates without any competition, it is the country's fourth largest media advertiser, and also spends heavily on sports sponsorship and competitions in schools.

The goal is nothing less than to make virtually every man and woman, and a considerable number of children, smokers. That goal is being appreciably aided by the general absence of advertising restrictions and health warnings on cigarette packs. If developing nations follow the example of industrialized countries, policy toward tobacco will not change until its effects begin to show in the mortality tables.

To insure that this example *is* followed, the tobacco giants use some powerful weapons. They can produce copious figures demonstrating how much tax they have collected for a government—one invariably in desperate need of revenue. Their persuasion is further strengthened by recruitment of the highest in the land to the cause of smoking. BAT, for example, has among the directors of its third-world subsidiaries former Cabinet members, central bank governors, and members of ruling families.

If third-world governments have been seduced into passively accepting the tobacco transnationals, western governments, the United States among them, have played an active role in the invasion. In 1933, the U.S. Agricultural Adjustment Act classified tobacco as a "basic agricultural commodity," thus defining the crop as a necessity to the farm and general economy. That paved the way for support payments and for export under lend-lease during World War II.

Whatever the legitimacy of government subsidies may have been for both domestic and exported tobacco, it steadily eroded as study after study reached the conclusions about the hazards of smoking that culminated in the first surgeon general's report. Yet the United States still spends more than $60 million a year for tobacco subsidies, in addition to tying up about $650 million in price-stabilization loans. The most contemptible participation by the U.S. government in support of the foreign invasion is through the "Food for Peace" program. Although allegedly created to aid needy countries, its underlying goals have been to dump agricultural surpluses, develop commercial markets, and provide indirect economic aid to friendly governments. Consistent with these objectives, if not with the program's altruistic title, tobacco valued at hundreds of millions of dollars has been shipped to third-world countries.

The standard argument for continuing the government support of tobacco is that cutting it off would bring economic hardship to tobacco farmers and seasonal workers. Leaving aside the human misery created in this country by a wide range of cigarette-related disease and the expansion of that misery into other parts of the world, it is not clear how the value of the entire $2.3 billion tobacco crop in the United States can justify the direct health costs of smoking, estimated by the American Cancer Society at $15 billion. It certainly is not clear how government subsidies can be justified. And ironically, some of this money goes for mechanization that will squeeze out small farmers and eliminate the need for many of the seasonal workers.

The United States is not alone in its hypocritical support of tobacco colonization. Even as many countries in Europe intensify anti-smoking programs at home, the European Economic Community (EEC) pays a large subsidy to tobacco farmers. According to Eckholm, "In 1975, EEC tobacco growers . . . received $206 million in 'premiums' from the community," and to keep Italy's exports competitive outside the European Community, "the EEC provides a subsidy of about 10 cents for each pound of tobacco sold."

China, the largest tobacco-producing country in the world, follows a distressingly similar path. Eckholm describes the participation of the Chinese government monopoly at a recent Philippine trade fair, displaying brands "with names like Peony, Golden Orchid and Golden Deer; and Sailing Boat herb cigarettes, which, the Chinese salesmen pointed out, have a reputation for 'allaying asthma and relieving cough.'"

China's attitude toward smoking is unique among major powers. Despite strong emphasis on improving the health of its people, it has had no anti-smoking campaigns. In fact, until very recently, information about the hazards of smoking has been systematically excluded from the Chinese press. Finally, last August (1978), an article in the *Kwangming Daily* by two of the country's most distinguished doctors set before the public for the first time the facts about the contribution of cigarettes to bronchitis, emphysema, throat and lung cancer, hypertension, and heart disease. The article placed the blame for China's lax attitude toward the use of tobacco on "the pernicious influence of the Gang of Four."

Even the United Nations has not consistently resisted the rapid spread of cigarettes to the underdeveloped world. One agency, the World Health Organization (WHO), has declared that control of smoking could do more to improve health and prolong life than any other single action in the whole field of preventive medicine. It greatly fears that increased use of tobacco in developing countries may reverse gains in public health that it has been supporting. But WHO has to contend with the Food and Agriculture Organization (FAO) and the United Nations Development Program, both of which have been actively promoting tobacco as a cash crop in many underdevelped countries.

The conflict comes down to a trade-off between health and economic growth. Fears about consequences to health are more likely to be realized, however, than any hopes for genuine economic development. The wave of mechanization sweeping U.S. tobacco farms will quickly be brought to areas of cultivation in the third world. There, as here, reduced demand for labor and increased need of capital are likely to eliminate both jobs and small farmers.

As for health in the third world, there is a more immediate cost than that due to the effects of increased smoking. According to the FAO, 10.9 million acres of scarce arable land were given over to tobacco in 1976, 69 percent of this in underdeveloped countries. The tobacco industry rejects the charge that this is a colossal waste of acreage badly needed to feed the hungry, claiming that its operations provide the technical advice, marketing assistance, and cash necessary to boost food production. Sir Richard Dobson, then-chairman of BAT, said in 1976: "I believe it is safe to say that more food is produced because of the presence of tobacco than would be grown in its absence."

This argument holds only if the tobacco produced is exported to provide a net gain in earnings that can be used to increase food production. But worldwide trends in smoking mean that an increasing proportion of tobacco grown in third-world countries is smoked within their borders. Tobacco-exporting nations such as Zambia and Sri Lanka are already finding that the cost of tobacco is greater than the revenue it produces when the price paid for domestic smoking is taken into account.

If economic progress through tobacco cultivation is unlikely, the health hazards of increased smoking are not. Smoking is virtually unrivaled as a cause of disease in developed countries. The young will be the most tragically victimized in the third world. Concern over the effect of cigarette smoking during pregnancy has risen sharply in the past few years. Women who smoke during the last two trimesters of pregnancy have babies with significantly lower birth weights than nonsmoking mothers, increasing the child's risk of disease and death. These greater risks are aggravated by the poverty and poor maternal nutrition that are widespread in many of the third-world countries targeted by the tobacco giants.

The special victimization of the young is particularly offensive in light of another corporate invasion of the third world. People in many industrial nations were outraged a few years ago when reports began appearing that several multinational corporations were irresponsibly and deceitfully marketing infant formulas in underdeveloped nations of Asia, Africa, and Latin America. The tactics used ranged from the usual advertising emphasis on status and sophistication to sending employees, dressed in white uniforms, to visit mothers in maternity wards and, later, in their homes. The goal was to convince the women to abandon breast-feeding in favor of the bottle.

The campaign has had tragic consequences. According to an article in *Science*, "Illnesses . . . are more common among the bottle-fed infants, to such an extent that their mortality rate is much higher than that of babies that are exclusively breast-fed." Derrick Jelliffe, professor of pediatrics and public health at the University of California at Los Angeles and former director of the Caribbean Food and Nutrition Institute in Jamaica, has estimated that about 10 million cases of malnutrition and severe diarrhea in developing countries can be attributed to improper bottle feeding.

The governments of underdeveloped countries are in a poor position to resist such incursions, precisely because their nations are underdeveloped. Unemployment, inadequate revenue, the need for investment capital, and lack of technical information make them easy prey. Just as the infant-formula companies have been made the focus of a large and still growing campaign against exporting dangerous bottle-feeding practices, the tobacco companies must be made the focus of any campaign against export of smoking to poor countries. It is certain to benefit people of both the developing and the developed worlds.

Part IV
Corporate Diversification and International Expansion

6318
4420
U.S.

15

Diversification and International Expansion: The Future of the American Tobacco Manufacturing Industry with Corporate Profiles of the "Big Six"

James Overton

Since the turn of the century, cigarette manufacturers have captured the attention of American consumers to an extent few other goods producers have achieved. From the past age of "Reach for a Lucky Instead of a Sweet" to the era of "Winston Tastes Good Like a Cigarette Should" to the broad appeal today of the rugged Marlboro man, a handful of cigarette companies have virtually written the book on how to establish and maintain a strong market for their product.

During the first half-century of cigarette promotion in the United States, the formula for success was a relatively simple one: the "Big Six" manufacturers concentrated on inducing hundreds of millions of Americans to light up. R.J. Reynolds, Philip Morris (PM), Ligget and Myers, American Tobacco, Brown and Williamson, and Lorillard each promoted a few reliable brands, such as Lucky Strike, Pall Mall, Camel, and Chesterfield. They succeeded in achieving loyal followings for particular brands which, in essence, differed little from those of their competitors. Creative promotion schemes, including catchy slogans, baseball cards, coupons, and other lures, enabled the companies to corner their exclusive segments of the growing market.

Tobacco manufacturers today continue their traditions of intense competition and clever advertising. It is still true, too, that a small number of firms dominate the U.S. cigarette market. Yet, the nature of the six companies has changed profoundly in the last thirty years. As concern about the health effects of smoking swept the country in the 1950s and 1960s, the Big Six discovered that the benign age of baseball-card promotion schemes was over. Sales growth rates slowed, and the market stagnated. The companies began to look toward new frontiers for profits. With varying degrees of aggressiveness, luck, and skill—and amid the

159

general trend toward diversification among American corporations in the 1960s—the cigarette companies used their considerable assets to acquire new companies and new products, even as they continued the battle to snare large segments of the domestic tobacco market.

Several of the companies also intensified their efforts to sell cigarettes internationally, first in Europe, and more recently in the developing nations of the third world. Philip Morris and R.J. Reynolds especially have targeted the third world as a pivotal area for further growth in their cigarette businesses and are working diligently to nail down a large share of this rapidly growing market.

No longer the simple promoters of several well-known brands, U.S. tobacco manufacturers today must be examined with special attention to the three major thrusts of their corporate programs: domestic cigarette operations, a spate of diversified product lines, and the potentially lucrative international cigarette market.

Domestic Scene

In the last decades of the nineteenth century, James Buchanan "Buck" Duke of Durham County, North Carolina, made himself the unquestioned leader of the American tobacco industry. Duke assembled and presided over the American Tobacco Company which had a hammerlock on all but a tiny fraction of the U.S. cigarette market (and most other tobacco enterprises). In 1902, Duke broadened his sphere of power beyond the United States by merging with the major British tobacco companies, who had already grouped themselves into the Imperial Tobacco Company. American Tobacco and Imperial formed the British-American Tobacco Company (BAT) with Buck Duke at its helm. BAT held a virtual worldwide monopoly on tobacco, controlling the industry not only in the United States but also throughout the British Empire, which was still intact around the globe. (See chapter 18 for more detail on this era.)

In 1911, during America's trust-busting era, the U.S. Supreme Court dissolved Duke's holdings into a handful of smaller companies. Within several years, three of them—American Tobacco, R.J. Reynolds, and Liggett and Myers—dominated the rapidly growing market for pre-rolled cigarettes. American Tobacco led the field until 1918, when Reynolds wrested away the top sales spot. American resurged as the industry leader in the 1930s, an era when three other manufacturers—Lorillard, Brown and Williamson, and Philip Morris—emerged as serious contenders in the cigarette sweepstakes, transforming the Big Three into the Big Six. Reynolds managed to regain the top position, ahead of American, in 1958, and has reigned supreme since that time, though Philip Morris now threatens to dethrone Reynolds within the next five years (see table 15-1).

Table 15-1
Distribution of the Domestic Cigarette Market of the Big Six
(percentages)

Year	Reynolds	Philip Morris	Brown and Williamson	American Brands	Lorillard	Liggett and Myers	Others
1911		n/a		37.1	15.3	27.8	19.8
1913	0.2	n/a	n/a	35.3	22.1	34.1	9.3
1925	41.6	0.5	n/a	21.2	1.9	26.6	8.2
1930	28.6	0.4	0.2	37.6	6.9	25.0	1.5
1939	23.7	7.1	10.6	23.5	5.8	21.6	7.8
1940	21.7	9.6	7.8	29.5	5.4	20.6	5.4
1949	26.3	9.2	5.9	31.3	5.0	20.2	2.1
1955	25.8	8.5	10.5	32.9	6.1	15.6	
1960	32.1	9.4	10.4	26.1	10.6	11.3	
1965	32.6	10.5	13.3	25.7	9.2	8.7	
1970	31.8	16.8	16.9	19.3	8.7	6.5	
1971	31.8	18.2	16.8	17.8	9.2	6.2	
1972	31.4	20.0	17.3	16.8	8.9	5.6	
1973	31.3	21.8	17.6	15.7	8.4	5.1	
1974	31.5	23.0	17.5	15.0	8.2	4.7	
1975	32.5	23.8	17.0	14.2	7.9	4.4	
1976	33.2	25.2	16.5	13.4	7.8	3.9	
1977	33.1	26.7	15.8	12.3	8.7	3.6	
1978	32.9	27.9	15.3	11.6	9.0	3.2	
1979	32.7	29.0	14.5	11.5	9.6	2.7	
1980[a]	32.8	30.8	13.7	10.7	9.8	2.2	

Source: Richard Tennant, *The American Cigarette Industry* (figures for 1911-1949) and *Business Week's* Annual Survey of Cigarette Industry (figures for 1955-1980).
[a]Estimate.

Until the early 1950s, cigarette sales grew steadily in the United States, with only a few brands to choose from. Because consumers tended to stick to one brand throughout their smoking careers, advertising and marketing strategies were aimed simply at snaring new smokers and keeping them. Nonfiltered cigarettes were the rage, and there was little need for product innovation.

Cigarette promotion became more complicated in the fifties, though. In 1954, *Reader's Digest* published a series of articles about the health hazards of tobacco. And a decade later, cigarette manufacturers found themselves even more in the hot seat when the U.S. surgeon general, in the highly publicized smoking and health report, concluded that "cigarette smoking is a health hazard of sufficient importance in the United States to warrant remedial action." Filter cigarettes, such as Winston and Viceroy, which were presumed to be less hazardous to the smoker's health, surged in popularity; filtered menthol brands also began to flourish. Those firms which responded well to the changing market, by developing and promoting the filter and menthol brands, not only survived this transition in marketing variables but actually prospered in the process. Reynolds, Brown and Williamson, Lorillard, and Philip Morris all enjoyed a substantial boost in sales in the 1950s, while American Tobacco and Liggett and Myers both fell into a tailspin.

As large numbers of new brands began appearing in the 1960s, the advertising strategy of the industry changed. No longer could companies afford to focus only on winning the loyalties of new smokers. While the new brands usurped the traditional favored position of nonfilters, they were also undermining smokers' brand-loyalties in general.

More important, the furor over health hazards was hurting sales; many smokers were quitting and the number of new smokers was declining. Consequently, advertising became less a matter of attracting new smokers and more a matter of snagging established smokers from competing brands. A cigarette-manufacturing executive explained the new advertising strategy to *Business Week* in 1969, saying that advertising efforts result mainly in share swapping in a market that is growing only with the population. Even if a company can grab some business at one end, "Someone else is pulling it away from you at the other," said the executive.

The intensely competitive nature of cigarette promotion in this era led to some pretty drastic reactions. In 1969, for instance, one tobacco executive, according to *Business Week,* said that his company "boosted the nicotine" of most of its brands. If cigarette advertising were to be totally banned, perhaps the "need for a smoke," as the executive put it, would keep people hooked.

The rising swell of anti-smoking fervor led in 1971 to a ban on cigarette advertising from radio and television. The industry fought the ban diligently, and after it was instituted, many observers quickly rang the death knell for the industry. Anti-smoking advocates felt that the ban would cut off the industry's main inducement avenue to nonsmokers and result in a steady decline in the number of smokers.

But the effects of the ban were not nearly so catastrophic. The networks were less compelled to run a plethora of anti-smoking spots to refute the cigarette ads, so, indirectly, some pressure was actually taken off the industry. Also, not having to buy television advertising saved the companies hundreds of millions of dollars. Industry experts believed the ban would not immediately damage their business. "The experience of cigarette manufacturers in other countries shows that dropping television commercials does not hurt consumption at all," noted *Barron's.*

After the ad-ban began, attention to the cigarette problem waned, and, ironically, sales in the early 1970s once again grew at a moderate but steady pace. The industry helped this growth along with another major marketing innovation—the low-tar, low-nicotine cigarette. What the filters did for the

1950s, the low tars did for the 1970s. Although low-tar cigarettes had been around since the fifties, they had never attracted much attention. In the 1970s, however, smokers concerned about their health but not wanting to kick the habit turned to the low-tar brands in rapidly increasing numbers. By 1979, the low-tar, low-nicotine cigarette market accounted for close to 50 percent of cigarette sales in the United States. Philip Morris's Merit ranked ninth among all brands in 1979; its sales grew more than 25 percent in that year alone. Kent, Vantage, Winston Light, and other low-tar brands have also jumped upward in the charts (see table 15-2).

The popularity of the low-tar brands gave the industry new life, both in sales and in earnings. *Consumer Reports,* in 1976, explained why:

> The average weight of the tobacco content in Now [a low-tar brand] was only 64 percent of that in Winston. Smokers tend to smoke more cigarettes when the cigarettes are low in nicotine, which is an addicting agent. That of course, means more unit sales. And when the tar and nicotine content is reduced . . . such cigarettes cost less to produce.

Although low-tar-and-nicotine sales did boost the cigarette industry in the 1970s, they carry no promise of a long-range growth pattern. Introducing new brands costs staggering sums. Reynolds plunked down $40 million for its "all natural" Real cigarette only to watch it languish on retailers' shelves across the country, and Brown and Williamson is likely to spend $150 million on its new Barclay brand. More important, perhaps, the companies are battling over a market that by 1979 had a growth rate, according to *Business Week* calculations, of less than 1 percent. The size of the domestic pie is not expanding. It can only be sliced in different ways, producing what *Business Week* terms the "cannibalization of the marketplace." During the 1970s, for example, total U.S. cigarette sales increased by *84 billion* units, but Philip Morris boosted its sales *88 billion* units over the same period, largely with its popular Marlboro brand. This marketing coup enabled Philip Morris to win smokers away from the other five competitors, even in a relatively stagnant market.

But even in a leveling market, cigarettes still generate healthy income for all of the Big Six except Liggett and Myers. Demand for cigarettes is inelastic (that is, sales do not decrease rapidly as prices rise), so the manufacturers can pass on increased production costs to consumers without sizable sales losses. And, even though per capita consumption for Americans (who are over eighteen years old) has fallen in the last few years to a still-high level of 3,924 per person, the adult population should increase by more than 18 million people by 1990. If per capita consumption stays constant or even continues to fall slightly, this population increase would result in a sales increase of up to 80 billion extra units by 1990.

Table 15-2
Top-Twenty Cigarette Brands in the United States
(percentage of U.S. market)

Name	Company	Major Type^b	1971	1972	1973	1974	1975	1976	1977	1978	1979	1980
1. Marlboro	Philip Morris	Filter	11.0	12.6	14.2	15.2	15.4	15.6	16.4	16.8	17.1	17.8
2. Winston	R.J. Reynolds	Filter	15.2	15.4	15.2	15.2	15.5	15.2	14.7	14.2	13.4	13.3
3. Kool	Brown and Williamson	Menthol	8.2	9.1	9.7	10.2	10.5	10.0	10.0	10.1	9.4	8.9
4. Salem	R.J. Reynolds	Menthol	8.3	8.6	8.4	8.7	8.5	8.7	9.0	9.1	8.8	8.9
5. Pall Mall	American Brands	Unfiltered	10.1	9.7	8.9	8.4	7.8	7.3	6.6	6.2	5.6	5.2
6. Benson and Hedges	Philip Morris	100 mm filter	3.0	3.4	3.9	4.1	4.3	4.4	4.1	4.5	4.6	4.6
7. Camel	R.J. Reynolds	Unfiltered	5.8	5.4	5.1	4.9	4.6	4.4	4.1	4.3	4.3	4.3
8. Merit	Philip Morris	Low tar		[a]				1.3	2.4	2.9	3.7	4.3
9. Vantage	R.J. Reynolds	Low tar			1.4	1.5	1.9	2.4	2.9	3.1	3.4	3.9
10. Kent^c	Lorillard	Low tar	5.5	5.4	5.1	5.0	4.5	4.5	5.1	5.1	3.2	3.3
11. Carlton	American Brands	Low tar					0.8	1.1	1.3	1.5	2.5	2.5
12. Virginia Slims	Philip Morris	100 mm (for women)	1.0	1.1	1.2	1.3	1.4	1.5	1.6	1.6	1.7	2.3
13. Newport	Lorillard	Menthol							1.2	1.4	1.6	1.9
14. Golden Lights^c	Lorillard	Low tar									2.2	1.9
15. Raleigh	Brown and Williamson	Filter	3.0	3.0	2.8	2.6	2.4	2.0	2.1	2.2	1.9	1.8
16. True	Lorillard	Low tar	1.5	1.6	1.4	1.4	1.6	1.4	1.8	1.9	1.9	1.8
17. Viceroy	Brown and Williamson	Filter	3.6	3.5	3.2	3.0	2.7	2.2	2.1	2.0	1.9	1.8
18. Tareyton	American Brands	Filter	3.7	3.5	3.3	3.2	2.7	2.6	2.2	2.2	2.0	1.7
19. Parliament	Philip Morris	Filter	1.7	1.5	1.6	1.7	1.6	1.5	1.4	1.3	1.3	1.2
20. Bel-Air	Brown and Williamson	Menthol	1.7	1.7	1.7	1.7	1.6	1.4	1.5	1.4	1.2	1.2

Source: *Business Week* annual cigarette survey.

^a A blank does not mean that the cigarettes were not for sale in that year. It simply means that the figures were unavailable.

^b The category "Major Type" refers to the cigarette category in which the brand receives the majority of its sales. However, it should be noted that many of these brands now come in multiple forms; for instance, there are Winston 100s and Winston Lights (low tar). For a detailed breakdown on sales of each brand by type, see John Maxwell's annual cigarette survey, published in *Tobacco Reporter.*

^c Golden Lights were originally included in the figures for Kent's annual sales. This accounts for the seemingly large drop in sales Kent experienced between 1978 and 1979.

Diversification

Long wedded to a single product line, the Big Six cigarette companies in the United States initially resisted a corporate transition to diversification. Indeed, the corporate charters of Lorillard and American Tobacco expressly forbade expansion into nontobacco lines. And there was fear among some industry executives that diversification attempts could appear as a turning away from cigarettes at a time when health studies were already raising many questions about them.

A wide range of factors broke the companies of their total cigarette dependence and boosted them onto the path blazed by such conglomerates as Gulf and Western, AT&T, and others. In the 1960s, the tobacco companies had more money than they knew how to spend. While sales stagnated and there was little need to invest in new production facilities, cigarettes continued to return over twenty cents on every sales dollar. Moreover, prices climbed, netting an increase in revenues and earnings for the companies.

The firms had accumulated little long-term debt, and they had a marvelous asset—their tobacco stocks—to use as collateral for borrowing power to supplement their large cash reserves. Converting this cash into a flood of acquisitions made good business sense.

Although the industry had plenty of cash and collateral, it did not have the full confidence of the stock market. Wall Street is obsessed with ''growth'' stocks, stocks that consistently show sales and earnings growth rates far above the overall economy's average growth rate. Investment analysts saw the cigarette industry as stagnating. Between 1964 and 1969, even though profits were climbing, cigarette stock prices fell from fifteen-times-earnings per share to about ten-times-earnings per share—a steep industrywide decline. The trends in price-to-earnings ratios reflect the degree of confidence with which analysts view an industry's performance. The message from Wall Street to the tobacco companies was clear: expand into other product lines.

From cigarettes, the companies turned first to natural product-cousins, food and liquor. The corporate parents of such products usually had low price-to-earnings ratios, as did the cigarette industry, and therefore were relatively inexpensive to acquire. Many such firms also had substantially higher sales growth rates than cigarettes. In the 1970s, candy and snack sales were climbing about 4 percent annually, liquor sales were rising 6 to 8 percent, and pet-food sales were skyrocketing at a 14-percent annual rate. More important, these product lines utilized the same basic skill required for cigarettes: a deft marketing touch, the ability to create new products and sell them to consumers. In the late 1960s, diversification fever swept the tobacco industry.

By 1970, though, cigarettes were still the mainstay for all of the Big Six except Liggett and Myers, which reaped only 50 percent of its 1970 revenues from tobacco. In fact, the diversification fever had not translated into instant successes in the hands of the dynamite marketers. The cigarette firms were having to grapple with the particular problems of each product in a wide variety of lines. If the payoff came at all, it would only be in the long term.

In the meantime, the cigarette companies were themselves vulnerable to takeover bids because of their low price-to-earnings figures. Tiny Loews Corporation swallowed Lorillard in 1968, and even R.J. Reynolds was rumored to have suitors eyeing its operations. As *Business Week* commented in 1969:

> Indeed, as diversifiers, the cigarette companies have a long way to go, analysts of the industry feel, and tobacco for most of them will still be king for some time to come. They [the analysts] reason that cancer talk and fears of TV advertising bans and other restrictions have so deflated the price-earnings multiples of tobacco stocks that some companies are more often in a position to be acquired . . . than to do the acquiring.

But the television ban in 1971 provided just the spark the industry needed to diversify further. The advertising budgets formerly devoted to the media—running into the hundreds of millions of dollars—could be channeled into new acquisitions. All six firms did just that. Most continued to focus on consumer-oriented goods, but there were a few surprises. For instance, American Brands bought Franklin National Life Insurance Company, and R.J. Reynolds branched off into oil and shipping concerns.

The results of this diversification have been as varied as the fortunes of the companies' cigarette sales. The corporate profiles that conclude this chapter detail the role of diversification for each of the Big Six. American Brands (American Tobacco, after diversification, changed its corporate name), though slumping in the cigarette business, has prospered in non-tobacco lines. While remaining the industry leader, Reynolds continues to experience problems with its oil and shipping divisions; it has now turned back toward marketing-oriented goods, picking up Del Monte Foods in 1978. Philip Morris has matched its Marlboro triumph with the success of its Miller beer subsidiary, and hopes to do the same with Seven-Up. By blending together strong divisions in three different consumer commodities, PM has been one of the great business successes of the 1970s.

In the next decade, look for further diversification among the major firms. Despite the increasing advertising costs for new brands, cigarette sales still generate significant cash flows which can be channeled into new purchases. It is safe to assume that the Big Six (or, in the case of Lorillard and Liggett, their parent corporations) will pump even more money into their currently productive nontobacco divisions and will keep their eyes peeled for other fast-growing companies that could benefit from the touch of some marketing pros.

International Scene

Several of the major firms have another option available for investing the cash generated by domestic cigarette sales: a booming international cigarette market. Although the overseas market is not new to the U.S. industry, intense efforts to corner it are. American cigarettes have been exported for decades, particularly to European nations. Since World War II, when many Europeans learned to prefer the rich blends and flavor-enhancing additives of U.S. cigarettes over their own brands, export sales have been climbing. U.S. firms quickly became interested in taking advantage of this European fascination with their product, particularly as domestic sales stagnated, but they have had to contend with complex international marketing barriers.

All but a few European countries have state-owned tobacco monopolies which own the tobacco manufacturing facilities and run the retailing and distribution systems. Foreign cigarette firms have to market their brands through these state monopolies. For many years, U.S. firms attempted with little success to sell their cigarettes through the state-owned distribution systems. European tariffs on foreign-produced cigarettes remained high, and the monopolies promoted their own brands far more heavily than they did the foreign products.

To overcome these obstacles, Philip Morris devised a fresh approach and negotiated a series of contracts with the European monopolies. Initially, PM provided technical assistance, allowing the monopolies to continue producing and selling the brands themselves. Then, the company began acquiring and constructing manufacturing facilities abroad. Soon PM was producing cigarettes in the Netherlands, Belgium, Britain, West Germany, and Spain at minimal marketing costs since it turned over its cigarettes to the state monopolies for distribution.

The monopolies receive a high share of the income from Philip Morris sales, reducing the company's royalties below its domestic profit margin. But because of this income, the monopolies have a stronger incentive to promote the Philip Morris brands than to push their own. Meanwhile, Philip Morris has applied its deft marketing touch to the European situation, usually promoting the popular Marlboro along with a single local brand, such as Sweden's Bond Street. And the Marlboro man has proved as enticing a figure in Europe as in the United States. In 1970, Philip Morris had minimal European sales, but by 1980 the company controlled almost 10 percent of this market, ranking alongside Rothmans (South African) and BAT Industries, the two giants of the international market.

Other domestic firms have attempted to follow Philip Morris's lead, negotiating their own license agreements and acquiring overseas production capacity. The effort has proved to be too great for Liggett and Lorillard, which both sold their overseas business in the late 1970s, and for American Brands. By the terms of the 1911 trust dissolution decree, BAT Industries has overseas rights to most of American Brand's cigarettes; to gain access to foreign sales, American bought Britain's Gallaher Limited in 1968, but Gallaher has little market penetration outside Britain. Brown and Williamson markets its popular brands, such as Kool, through its parent, BAT Industries.

Besides Philip Morris, then, only Reynolds is pursuing the international market—but with some difficulty. Winston once had the popular advantage abroad that Marlboro now enjoys, providing Reynolds a solid base. But the company did not begin signing licensing arrangements until the early 1970s, thus achieving slower growth than Philip Morris. Reynolds also made early mistakes that hurt sales: it developed costly excess production capacity in West Germany, did not quickly target local brands such as Philip Morris's Bond Street, and had to revamp its entire Swedish distribution system at great expense. Although it now has numerous licensing arrangements and production facilities overseas, Reynolds's sales have not grown to rival those of Philip Morris, BAT Industries, or Rothmans. But Reynolds has at least established itself as a formidable competitor for future international growth.

Having cut their teeth in Europe, Philip Morris and R.J. Reynolds are now hungrily eyeing the rapidly expanding worldwide market. In 1979, 4.2 trillion cigarettes worth almost $100 billion were sold worldwide, an all-time high. Over the last decade, while sales inched upward at a 4-percent rate in the United States, they increased 33 percent in Africa and 24 percent in Latin America. The United Nations had predicted a 5-percent annual growth rate in the developing nations, more than enough to generate continued high growth for Philip Morris and Reynolds, particularly if they can buy or take business away from smaller firms. The latest coup for the two largest U.S. cigarette manufacturers was the signing of production agreements with the People's Republic of China. In November 1980, Philip Morris began manufacturing in Canton; in 1981, Reynolds is scheduled to produce some two million dollars' worth of one of its brands in the Fujian Province.

Several strong incentives have led third-world nations to boost the cigarette industry within their borders. They receive large quantities of tobacco from various foreign-aid programs. They see tobacco as a potentially lucrative cash crop for exportation purposes, and a growing domestic market as an incentive to production. The promise of high tax revenues from cigarette sales holds great appeal to cash-strapped countries. Finally, the major tobacco companies have spent millions on advertising and public relations in third-world nations, increasing their acceptability to the foreign consumer.

The U.S. companies are patterning their advertising pitch in developing nations after their earlier domestic experience; advertising is directed at the youth and at the newly emerging middle classes who aspire to western symbols of success. In most developing countries, the push to develop new consumers is not being offset by anti-smoking policies or regulations.

Prospects appear favorable for a continuing boom in overseas cigarette sales. For both Philip Morris and R.J. Reynolds, these international sales should bring steady growth to their cigarette operations. Also, the contacts and marketing network established through this expansion should reap substantial benefits for the other consumer-oriented products of the two tobacco giants. R.J. Reynolds's Del Monte Foods and Philip Morris's Miller beer and Seven-Up may prove equally attractive to third-world tastes, and further boost the firms' corporate growth.

In the near future, Philip Morris will probably enjoy a solid edge in the booming overseas cigarette craze. It already sells three times as many cigarettes outside the United States as does R.J. Reynolds, and recently engineered a major coup that places them in a position to move further ahead of R.J. Reynolds on the international scene. In April 1981, R.J. Reynolds began negotiations for a joint venture with the Rothmans International branch of Rothmans World Tobacco Group, the world's fifth largest tobacco company, controlled by South African entrepreneur A.E. Rupert. Reynolds also indicated an interest in purchasing Rothmans International outright at some future point, but Rupert broke off the negotiations the next month. Several days later, on the morning of R.J. Reynolds's annual stockholders meeting, Board Chairman J. Paul Sticht received a telegram from Rupert that revealed why Rupert had stopped the discussions so suddenly: he was selling a quarter of Rothmans International to Philip Morris.

"Philip Morris has less to gain from the $350 million Rothmans deal than Reynolds stands to lose," analyzed *Fortune*. Though Philip Morris will be able to boost its international sales substantially, the main impact of the deal will be to thwart Reynolds's advancement on the international scene. With Reynolds on the defensive, Philip Morris seems certain to expand its international sales lead and take off after the big target at the top of the charts: BAT Industries.

R.J. Reynolds

R.J. Reynolds Industries has a lot to be proud of these days. Its cigarette business remains the front-runner in the industry, as it has for 22 years, nailing down 32.6 percent of the available market in 1979 with sales of 200 billion cigarettes. The company owns the world's largest container-shipping firm, Sea-Land Service, Incorporated; a crude-oil and natural-gas developer and explorer, Aminoil USA; a packaging-products concern, RJR Archer; and food and beverage divisions in Del Monte and RJR Foods, Ltd. And the company's international cigarette sales have risen steadily in recent years. The 39th largest corporation in the country, Reynolds's 1979 revenues totaled $8.9 billion (a 33.2-percent increase from 1978), netting $551 million in earnings (a 24.7-percent increase from 1978). (See table 15-3.)

Despite such wealth and high rank in the corporate world, R.J. Reynolds seems to have a bit of a chip on its shoulder. "People don't understand us," Chairman of the Board and Chief Executive Officer J. Paul Sticht told *Forbes* in 1980, complaining that Wall Street was focusing more attention on competitor Philip Morris. Indeed, Philip Morris's dazzling performance has Wall Street investors speculating that the company may

Table 15-3
R.J. Reynolds Data
(percentages)

Product Division	1972	1973	1974	1975	1976	1977	1978	1979
Distribution of Gross Revenues								
Domestic tobacco[b]	63	60	48	48	44	42	44	35
International tobacco	9	11	16	19	20	21	23	20
Foods and beverages	5	4	4	4	4	4	4	22[a]
Transportation	19	16	15	17	16	15	16	14
Energy	3	3	10	9	13	15	10	7
Packaging	3	3	3	3	3	3	3	2
Distribution of Net Earnings								
Domestic tobacco[b]	81	81	59	68	68	72	69	64
International tobacco	6	7	4	6	8	11	13	13
Foods and beverages	1	2	1	3	3	3	2	11[a]
Transportation	7	3	22	13	15	10	12	5
Energy	3	4	13	9	4	2	2	6
Packaging	2	3	1	1	2	2	2	1

Source: Annual reports.

[a]The jump from 1978 reflects the acquisition of Del Monte Foods.

[b]The percentages for cigarette revenues are based on figures that include the excise taxes paid to state and federal governments. Many financial analysts omit these figures from their calculations of a company's revenues because they tend to reflect an artificially high rate of revenues; in general, the excise taxes paid to state and federal governments account for as much as 25 percent of revenues. If these excise tax figures are removed from the statement of revenues, then the percentage of sales contributed from cigarettes to each company appears even lower—and the high rate of earnings generated by cigarette sales appears all the more impressive. This point should be noted for the earnings and revenues table with each corporate profile.

surpass Reynolds in domestic cigarette sales as early as 1983. "We have no intention of relinquishing our position of leadership in 1983 or any other year in the foreseeable future," says William Hobbs, Reynolds's executive vice-president.

Hobbs stands in a long Reynolds tradition of meeting challengers in the cigarette industry. In the 1870s, Richard Joshua Reynolds entered the business by bartering his father's chewing tobacco for such goods as cowhides and a gold watch. After several years of experience in the family's southwestern Virginia business, he opened in 1875 his "Little Red Factory" in Winston, North Carolina, and began churning out chewing tobacco. The business prospered, was incorporated as R.J. Reynolds Tobacco Company in 1890, and soon became one of Winston's most highly respected corporate citizens.

At the end of the nineteenth century, Reynolds needed expansion capital for his outfit and began selling shares of stock, two-thirds of which the Duke Tobacco Trust soon gobbled up. Reynolds bitterly resented Duke's domination and retained a fierce independence even while functioning as a subsidiary of the American Tobacco Company. When the 1911 Supreme Court decision granted Reynolds his freedom from Buck Duke, he once again took charge of his small chewing-tobacco concern.

R.J. Reynolds disliked cigarettes, but his antipathy toward Buck Duke was even stronger. And he desired more speedy growth for his company than chewing tobacco could provide alone. So in 1909 he introduced Red Kamel cigarettes, which did not sell well but had the potential for a catchy name, one that Reynolds liked. Four years later, he launched an imaginative promotion campaign for Camels that made the brand an instant success and soon propelled the company to the top of the cigarette business. This achievement gave Reynolds the satisfaction of beating his old rival, Buck Duke; Reynolds died in 1918 as the king of the tobacco industry.

American Tobacco reasserted itself in the 1930s with the popular Lucky Strike brand and overtook Reynolds, holding the lead for two decades. In the early 1950s, the health scare generated by *Reader's Digest* led to the booming market for filter cigarettes, and Reynolds responded with Winston. The brand's advertising slogan—"Winston Tastes Good like a Cigarette Should"—prompted a wave of criticism about its poor grammar, which only served to boost its sales further. Adding Winston to Camel, a leading U.S. brand in the 1950s, pushed Reynolds ahead of American Tobacco in 1958. The company then added Salem, which took the menthol market by storm and ultimately became the third-highest-selling cigarette in the country. Finally, in 1966, Winston bested American Tobacco's Pall Mall for first place in individual brand sales. R.J. Reynolds's domination of the domestic market was complete.

During this time, the company's management was already looking at new frontiers and, in 1956, amended its corporate charter to permit investments in nontobacco enterprises. The official corporate history explains why: "First, having captured one-third of the U.S. cigarette market, the company could see a point of diminishing returns for growth potential. Second, significant cash was being generated which could be invested advantageously elsewhere."

The company began diversifying very cautiously. First it separated its foil-products division, which had previously only produced materials for Reynolds cigarettes, into subsidiary Archer Aluminum (now RJR Archer), which began selling to other businesses. Reynolds expanded this subsidiary in 1967 when it bought Filmco, which produces stretch-and-shrink films for wrapping fresh meat and vegetables; the divisions have continued as a small but steady part of Reynolds since.

In 1963 Reynolds bought Hawaiian Punch, its first nontobacco acquisition, and two years later, Penick and Ford, which produced Vermont Maid Syrups and My-T-Fine desserts. Next came ethnic food companies—Chun King (Chinese) and Patio Foods (Mexican). Reynolds officials appeared confident that their marketing prowess with cigarettes could translate easily to food products.

After developing a base in food products, however, Reynolds moved completely out of its traditional marketing strength. Prospects seemed favorable for rapid expansion in the shipping field, and in 1969, Reynolds paid about $200 million for Sea-Land Service, Incorporated, the largest containerized-freight shipping operation in the world. Reynolds then moved to acquire Sea-Land's top competitor, U.S. Lines, but in 1970 the U.S. Justice Department blocked the purchase with an anti-trust suit. The same year, continuing its bold diversification drive and seeking an oil source for Sea-Land's fleet of ships, Reynolds plunked down $55 million for Aminoil (the American Independent Oil Company), an oil producer operating in the Persian Gulf (in the divided zone between Kuwait, Iran, and Saudi Arabia). Part of the Iranian Consortium, Aminoil was seeking new business around the globe.

By 1970, R.J. Reynolds Tobacco Company no longer seemed a proper name for such a diversified conglomerate. So the directors approved a name change to R.J. Reynolds Industries and announced that they were no longer just the "tobacco people." But all was not well in Winston-Salem, North Carolina, Reynolds's home base. None of the food subsidiaries had a nationally leading brand name, making the promotion job tougher and cutting into profits significantly. A major dock strike in 1971 crippled Sea-Land, and the blocked purchase of U.S. Lines thwarted the company's long-range plans. Aminoil did not produce stellar earnings figures either. And Reynolds's share of the domestic cigarette sales market slipped slightly, from 31.8 percent in 1970 to 31.5 percent in 1974.

These woes prompted some mutinous grousings from Reynolds's largest block of stockholders, the Reynolds family. As quoted in *Forbes,* one family member snapped, "Look, these guys are the world's best at marketing and selling tobacco products, but what do they know about ships or oil?" The new debt taken on by the company—$100 million in debentures in 1971—also alarmed the stockholders. Concern soon spread throughout the financial community. In 1974, *Dun's Review* noted; "When Reynolds bought McLean Industries [Sea-Land] and followed with Aminoil, many an analyst began to wonder what they were smoking in Winston-Salem."

In 1973, a new management team took over. New board chairman Colin Stokes had almost forty years of experience in the company tobacco business. But the real power quickly fell into the hands of Paul Sticht, a seasoned marketing executive who had taken an early retirement from the presidency of Federated Department Stores before Reynolds pressed him into service as its new president. Sticht brought in marketing executives from outside the company, exercised much more centralized control over the divisions, and pumped huge amounts of tobacco capital into the other subsidiaries. He also spearheaded an aggressive campaign to take the company's position to American financial analysts through a series of presentations on the company's operations; this move contrasted sharply with Reynolds's renowned "tight-lipped, close-to-the-vest attitude." When Stokes retired in 1979, Sticht replaced him as chairman. For the first time in Reynolds history, the top management officers included no one who had risen through the ranks of the cigarette business.

Although Sticht has brought new life to much of Reynolds's business, he has not eliminated all doubts about the company's future. Domestic cigarette sales have brightened somewhat, increasing from 31.5 percent of the market in 1974 to 32.6 percent in 1979. Reynolds cornered 43 percent of total low-tar cigarette sales in 1979, up from 38 percent in 1978; since low-tar cigarettes are the fastest-growing segment of the industry, Reynolds should be able to ward off further decline. Even so, Winston and Salem, the firm's two top sellers, have continued to slide, and Philip Morris's Merit has edged out Reynolds's Vantage for first place in low-tar sales. The company was also very embarrassed when its $40 million campaign to promote Real, the "natural cigarette, " fizzled, never netting more than 0.5 percent of the total sales market. And every year, Philip Morris gets closer to taking the number-one spot in total domestic sales away from Reynolds. Still, according to *Business Week,* Reynolds's tobacco sales yield more than $200 million annually for investments in other fields. In fact, the corporation pumped $1.18 billion into capital investments from 1975 to 1979 and expects to spend $2 billion more between 1979 and 1982, most of which goes to the struggling subsidiaries.

In other product lines, questions center on Aminoil and Sea-Land. Aminoil produced huge earnings during the oil crisis of 1974, but most of that went to the Kuwait government in royalties and other payments. In 1977, Kuwait nationalized its Aminoil holdings, eventually offering Reynolds $55 million in reparations, a figure far from satisfactory to the company. Already concerned about its strong dependence on Kuwait, in 1976 Reynolds had paid Burmah Oil a whopping $522 million—the largest cash transaction in U.S. history—for its U.S. holdings. In need of new supplies of oil after the Kuwaiti move, Reynolds then pumped $550 million into Aminoil between 1976 and 1979 to try to boost its performance. But in 1979, Aminoil suffered another loss when it lost its Iranian interests. That year, revenues fell 11 percent, down to $628 million, but earnings rose 28 percent to $66 million as the firm scored on new well explorations. Then in 1980, Aminoil announced the discovery of a large potential reserve of high-quality crude oil in Montana, which could bolster its future profits. Aminoil is now the twenty-eighth largest oil producer in the United States, and the business will require at least $700 million more in capital by 1982. Despite Aminoil's recently improved performance, investment analysts are still leery of Reynolds's ability to handle the oil business.

Sea-Land also remains a question mark. Paul Sticht pumped over $600 million into Sea-Land in the second half of the 1970s, and may invest $600 million more by 1982. Meanwhile, freight rates have not climbed sharply enough to offset vessel and terminal operating expenses. Consequently, though revenues climbed 11 percent to $1.22 billion in 1979, earnings nose-dived by 50 percent from $119 million (1978) to $58 million (1979). In 1980, the company sold eight of its transport ships to the U.S. Navy. These oil-burning ships were too expensive to operate commercially (even Aminoil could not provide fuel for them cheaply enough), and the Navy needed new ships for transporting troops and supplies in emergency situations. Congress has approved a payment of $285 million for these ships, a handsome price that will relieve Reynolds of an expensive burden on a troubled division.

Reynold's food operations, in contrast, have promising futures. In 1979, Reynolds paid $618 million for Del Monte, a canned-fruit and vegetable producer. In its 1979 annual report, Reynolds explained the move: "Del Monte brings to RJR the strengths of an international production and marketing network, a broad expanse of product lines and an unequalled reputation for quality and brand recognition." Sticht has dispatched several Reynolds executives to the Del Monte chain of command and is now slowly merging Del Monte's operations with those of RJR Foods, Ltd. In 1980, the company marketed food products in more than sixty countries. With the inclusion of Del Monte, revenues from food-products sales increased sevenfold, from $281 million in 1978 to $1.96

billion in 1979, and earnings jumped from $19 million to $128 million in that fiscal year.

The final major sphere of Reynolds's operations is its international cigarette sales, which have received significant attention from Sticht. "When we entered the international market, we made some mistakes," says Sticht. "We concentrated on exporting our domestic brands and we learned too late that we were, in effect, imposing American tastes on smokers with different preferences. As a result, the acceptance of our brands among international smokers was limited, and we missed major portions of the market." Philip Morris, which entered the international market ahead of Reynolds, bested Reynolds in total volume of cigarette sales as early as 1972, and has expanded its lead ever since.

Sticht has revamped overseas operations, consolidating all operations in the R.J. Reynolds Tobacco International division, a separate subsidiary also headquartered in Winston-Salem. He organized an International Advisory Board in 1974 that includes executives from Britain, West Germany, Japan, and other countries, and concentrated on establishing overseas manufacturing facilities and entering into license agreements with foreign producers. By 1980, the company had manufacturing plants in West Germany, Switzerland, Spain, Canada, Brazil, Ecuador, West Malaysia, Puerto Rico, and Curacao; and licensing agreements in Austria, Bulgaria, East Germany, Finland, Greece, Mexico, New Zealand, the Philippines, Peru, Spain, Yugoslavia, Portugal, and Andorra. Reynolds markets cigarettes in more than 140 countries and territories, including China, where it sells Winston and More. Since 1975, sales have grown at an annual rate of 18 percent. In 1979, revenues increased 19 percent, to $1.85 billion; and earnings also jumped 19 percent, to $144 million. Reynolds will devote more than $200 million in capital expenditures to the foreign market by 1982.

In 1980, Sticht surprised the financial community when he announced a ten-year, $1 billion capital investment program for upgrading and expanding its domestic cigarette manufacturing facilities. Although the company hopes to recharge its stagnant domestic sales, much of the expansion will serve to promote growth in cigarette sales in the third world. The company has also announced plans to invest $1.6 billion in its nontobacco lines by 1982. Much of that money will go to Sea-Land and Aminoil. Sticht recently described the corporation's priorities to *Forbes* as a consumer, packaged-goods company, but with "tobacco being our largest activity followed by food, with strategic investments in oil and shipping."

Despite Sticht's attempts to shore up existing operations and expand overseas, R.J. Reynolds's nonmarketing-oriented product lines continually produce ambivalent financial results. It has not yet trumped Philip Morris's vigorous play to surpass it in domestic cigarette sales and also lost the bidding war for Rothmans International in spring 1981. Even with this crushing setback, the drive to expand international cigarette operations could be the key to a more stable financial future for Reynolds—and to an increased acceptance by Wall Street observers.

Philip Morris

Life for Philip Morris executives must be quite satisfying these days. The company closed the 1970s with accolades from across the U.S. financial community. From being the fourth largest cigarette manufacturer and the seventh largest beer producer at the beginning of the decade, Philip Morris has bolted to second place in both fields and is seriously challenging front-runners R.J. Reynolds and Anheuser-Busch. Revenues climbed more than 450 percent in the 1970s, from $1.5 billion to $8.3 billion; operating income took a dramatic jump from $203 million to $1.2 billion (see table 15-4). *Fortune* magazine, in recognition of this achievement, proclaimed Philip Morris one of the "ten most impressive business triumphs of the decade."

At the core of this success is the company's most highly touted asset: marketing wizardry. The spearhead of the company's rise, former chairman Joseph F. Cullman III (who retired in 1978), came to Philip Morris after years of marketing experience at Canada's Benson and Hedges, which Philip Morris acquired in 1954. Cullman surrounded himself with a cadre of marketing-wise pros and set out to conquer the worlds of cigarettes and beer. In 1977, Cullman explained why his team has been successful: "Our

Table 15-4
Philip Morris Data
(percentages)

Product Division	1972	1973	1974	1975	1976	1977	1978	1979
			Distribution of Gross Revenues					
Domestic tobacco	(85)[a]	(79)[a]	50	47	46	41	37	33.5
International tobacco			27	27	24	26	27	30.5
Beer	10	11	13	18	23	26	28	27
Other	10	10	10	8	7	7	8	9
			Distribution of Net Earnings					
Domestic tobacco	(97)[a]	(97)[a]	76	72	65	61	59	61
International tobacco			18	19	18	19	19	21
Beer	(0)	(-1)	2	6	12	14	16	16
Other	3	4	4	3	5	6	6	2

Source: Annual reports.

[a]The 1972 and 1973 figures represent the total from domestic and international tobacco. Further breakdowns were not available for these years.

senior management are all market-oriented. We've all stayed close to the marketplace. So we respond quickly to market trends, but we don't over-react. We haven't had any losers in a long time.''

This analysis especially applies to the company's domestic cigarette line, which stretches back to 1847 when London merchant Philip Morris began using cigarette hand-rollers to produce popular brands like Cambridge, Oxford Blues, and Ovals. The company incorporated in the United States in 1919 and imported several of its popular English brands, but it achieved only minor sales. However, in the Depression-torn 1930s, the company astutely introduced several economy-priced cigarettes that boosted it into the ranks of the top six cigarette manufacturers. Encouraged by this success, it began producing cigarettes in the United States in 1934. As late as 1960, however, Philip Morris ranked last among the Big Six, garnering only 9 percent of the market.

But then came the Marlboro man. From the ninth biggest seller on the market in 1960, Marlboro vaulted to third place by 1970 and finally inched ahead of Winston for the top spot in 1976. The romantic figure of the Marlboro man, a rugged, masculine character in an outdoors setting, was a particularly potent image after the television and radio advertising ban of 1971. His proud image translated to print far more effectively than the famous "Winston Tastes Good like a Cigarette Should" jingle.

PM did not rely exclusively on Marlboro for sales growth, however. The company's 100-millimeter brands—Virginia Slims and Benson and Hedges —performed well in the late 1960s. Then in 1976, PM entered the low-tar field with Merit; a phenomenal 7.4 billion Merits sold in that first year alone. In just three years, Merit edged ahead of Reynolds's Vantage for first place in low-tar cigarette sales. By 1979, in fact, Philip Morris had in its sphere the best-selling cigarette, domestically and internationally (Marlboro), the number-one low tar (Merit), the largest selling 100-millimeter brand (Benson and Hedges), and the highest sales of any cigarette brand designed especially for women (Virginia Slims). It managed this feat by taking sales away from its competitors. During the 1970s, while the company was growing at a phenomenal rate, the other top five had an aggregate decrease in sales.

In achieving these gains, Philip Morris has been more opportunist than innovator. It has generally not introduced brands in new fields without first checking a competitor's performance. Once a market is clearly established, Philip Morris jumps in with an aggressive marketing strategy, skipping the traditional cautious testing period preferred by most other companies. The company has often been accused of merely following Reynolds's lead in brand introduction. But PM has done so effectively, as in the case of besting Vantage with Merit, and clearly is threatening Reynolds's twenty-two-year reign at the top of the cigarette world. In 1979 alone, the gap between the two closed from 30.2 billion cigarettes sold to 17.8 billion.

Outgunning the rest of the industry is not the only reason Philip Morris has drawn Wall Street's praise. The company has also made some deft diversification moves, reinvesting more of its earnings in the 1950s and 1960s than did its competitors and thus sacrificing higher dividends in favor of rapid expansion. In fact, Philip Morris effectively initiated the cigarette industry's diversification syndrome in 1957 when it acquired Milprint Industries, a packaging manufacturer, and shortly followed with the acquisition of a chemical company, Polymer Industries. The company further diversified in the 1960s with American Safety Razor, Burma Shave, and Clark Gum. In 1968 it stunned Wall Street by buying 53 percent of a minor beer distributor, Miller. Later investments included Mission Viejo Company (land development), and Armstrong Products (chemicals).

Philip Morris executives admit that none of these purchases initially set the world on fire. By 1972, tobacco still accounted for 85 percent of its revenues, and the company had little strength to offer aside from the Marlboro man. So Cullman streamlined operations. He abandoned several stagnating lines and dispatched experienced Philip Morris officers to the other divisions. One key move was his naming of executive vice-president John A. Murphy to head up Miller beer in 1971. In 1974 Murphy introduced Miller Lite with an aggressive advertising strategy that capitalized on the low-calorie craze sweeping the country. In the process, Miller caught the rather conservative beer industry by surprise, zooming from seventh place to the heels of top-ranking Anheuser-Busch. After spending huge sums to boost the business, Philip Morris has started reaping sizable profits from Miller ($181 million in 1979 on sales of $2.2 billion) and prospects appear good for continued growth and prosperity.

As one last addition before his retirement in 1978, Cullman picked up the Seven-Up soft-drink company for a whopping $520 million. Like Miller in 1968, Seven-Up is a weak performer in its market, garnering only 7 percent of sales compared to Coca-Cola's 34 percent and Pepsi's 22 percent in 1979. Philip Morris is showing signs of marketing Seven-Up much as it did Miller; Murphy is now in charge of both. Most observers are confident that Philip Morris's marketing prowess will pay off in rapid sales increases; the company has already sunk millions of dollars into its Seven-Up division and created a national advertising campaign that employs noted sports figures to promote the product. But the company is up against tough competition; Coca-Cola and Pepsi are practiced marketers themselves, and are more prepared for a challenge than were Miller's competitors. Seven-Up's success could hinge on whether the company can introduce a new, high-sales cola product to complement Seven-Up.

The other divisions of the company, Mission Viejo and Philip Morris Industrial (which includes Armstrong Products), produce small but steady business (5.1 percent of revenues and 3.4 percent of earnings in 1979). But the company's strength remains vested in marketing cigarettes, beer, and soft drinks. However, none of these three enjoys rapid sales growth on an industrywide basis. Philip Morris mostly has spirited business away from its competitors in beer and tobacco and hopes to do the same with soft drinks. Eventually there will be a ceiling on how much business it can secure, and to sustain its corporate expansion it will need a brisk business in a high-sales market—like the international cigarette field.

Philip Morris was the first U.S. firm to concentrate heavily on the foreign cigarette market. Its innovative leasing arrangements with state-owned tobacco monopolies in Europe and its early decision to invest in foreign manufacturing facilities secured a strong base for increased sales, and the Marlboro man attracted foreign smokers as effectively as he did Americans. Philip Morris took first place in international sales from R.J. Reynolds in 1972 and has steadily increased its lead since then. The company snared 6 percent of the 4.2 trillion-unit international sales market in 1979—a whopping 250 billion cigarettes that year. It achieved over 15 percent of the market in more than twenty countries and over 30 percent in Italy, Switzerland, and Austria. Overall, the company markets more than 160 brands in about 170 countries and territories; its far-flung operations include 27 manufacturing and marketing affiliates, 36 licensees, and a string of regional export-sales organizations. As current licensing arrangements expire, Philip Morris will rely more heavily on locating manufacturing facilities in countries with rapidly expanding markets.

The booming international cigarette market has filled the company's coffers handsomely. Revenues on international sales increased from $424 million in 1970 to $2.5 billion in 1979; profits jumped from $54 million to $260 million. In 1979 alone, revenues and income rose 42.5 percent and 38.2 percent, respectively. And in 1981 Philip Morris added another bright asset by acquiring a one-quarter interest in the Rothmans International branch of the Rothmans World Tobacco Group; eventually, this purchase could lead to Philip Morris's acquiring all of Rothmans International. In this one acquisition, Philip Morris not only added to its potential for sales growth; it also put the brakes on the expansion aims of the top American competitor, R.J. Reynolds, which had previously been courting Rothmans.

Expansion in the developing global cigarette market still requires large amounts of capital. Well over half of Philip Morris's expenditures on tobacco go to the international market. But with the anticipated steady growth in third-world cigarette sales, these investments should reap Philip Morris substantial earnings and continued growth. Current board chairman George Weissman, who succeeded Joseph Cullman, was the architect of the company's international growth in the 1960s and 1970s, and can be expected to continue his lucrative expansion work for many years to come.

The growth of the international cigarette business also bodes well for the future of the company's other major product lines. Worldwide marketing arrangements already established through cigarette sales should prove valuable for Miller beer and Seven-Up, particularly for the latter. Fruit drinks have proved more successful than colas in the foreign sector, so Seven-Up has a good chance for sustained growth overseas.

After a decade of truly phenomenal growth, with an experienced core of marketing pros for top executives, and with good positions in three consumer-oriented markets, Philip Morris will likely continue its stellar performance. Of all the major cigarette manufacturers, this company exhibits the most confidence—and the best prospects for growth—in its tobacco operations. In fact, in 1980 the company had almost completed a major new production facility in Cabarrus County, North Carolina, to further expand its domestic production capacity. Philip Morris USA president Shepard Pollock sums up the company's outlook: "Five years from now, we as a corporation, as Philip Morris, Inc., will still make most of our money in tobacco. We'll still be mostly a cigarette company, and we'll still be damn proud of it."

Brown and Williamson[a]

Brown and Williamson, the third largest cigarette manufacturer in the United States, is the quietest member of the industry. The company shuns publicity, issuing neither sales figures not annual reports, and receives little attention from Wall Street and the financial journals. Less than flashy, never vying with the two top domestic performers, Brown and Williamson exists in the shadow of its corporate parent—BAT Industries, Incorporated, headquartered in London, England.

BAT Industries (formerly British-American Tobacco) is the forty-ninth largest company in the world and the largest tobacco-products company, generating more than $16 billion from sales in 1979, with $542.6 million profits. BAT Industries spans the globe, promoting its paper products, retail stores, cosmetics, and its primary commodity—the golden leaf. BAT handles more than five hundred brands internationally (including overseas sales of many U.S. brands and exclusive rights to Lorillard's brands). In 1975, it was selling more cigarettes than R.J. Reynolds and American Tobacco combined. In 1976, the company produced almost 20 percent of all cigarettes sold in the free world.

British-American Tobacco grew out of a 1902 agreement between the American Tobacco Company trust and Britain's Imperial Tobacco Company; it operated as the sole exporting agency for both companies outside the United States and Great Britain. The 1911 Supreme Court dissolution of the American Tobacco Company monopoly cut BAT free of its U.S. part-

---

[a]As a subsidiary of BAT Industries, Brown and Williamson is not required to publish an annual report; therefore, there are no publicly available figures on the percentage of revenues and earnings by product line, as are included with the other corporate profiles.

ner (which had owned two-thirds of the stock), leaving BAT without any stake in the U.S. tobacco market.

Initially, avoiding the wrath of U.S. anti-trust sentiment, BAT steered clear of the rapidly growing market in the United States. Then, in 1927, it decided the time had come to compete with the Big Three on their own turf; BAT bought Brown and Williamson Company, a small snuff-and-plug firm founded in Winston-Salem, North Carolina, by merchants Robert Williamson and George Brown.

Brown and Williamson slowly entered the cigarette competition in the 1930s. It achieved modest sales with economy brands during the Depression and also scored with Kool, which became the leading menthol brand during the 1940s. The company responded well to the filter-cigarette boom during the 1950s and 1960s, with Viceroy and Kool supplementing its predominantly nonfilter sales of Raleigh. Brown and Williamson's market share grew steadily, rising from 9.4 percent in 1954 to 13.3 percent in 1965 to a high of about 17 percent in 1975. Like American Brands, Brown and Williamson stuck to its several top performers—Viceroy, Kool, Raleigh, and Bel-Air—and promoted them with an effective marketing strategy centered on coupons offered with each pack. Kool outstripped Reynolds's Salem for top position in the menthol market and by 1980 ranked as the third best-selling brand in the country.

Despite the success of Kool, overall unit sales have been on a decline, from 103 billion in 1974 to 88 billion in 1979. Its new-brand introductions have not produced significant sales, and until 1980 Brown and Williamson had not even introduced a low-tar brand that effectively competed with the successful introductions of its major competitors. Both Fact and Arctic Lights have failed to generate significant sales. A look at Brown and Williamson's executive ranks even indicates a sense of floundering; in the last four years, it has had three presidents, three vice-presidents in charge of brand management, and two marketing vice-presidents.

But the latest marketing vice-president, Scott A. Wallace, has unleashed a new campaign to revive Brown and Williamson's sales picture: ultra-low-tar Barclay cigarettes. Wallace adopted an innovative slogan; he claims Barclay cigarettes are "99 percent tar free," and offers smokers a free carton for testing. (Most companies offer free packs, but none has ever offered free cartons.) Brown and Williamson has pumped tens of millions of dollars into advertising Barclays. The total budget for the brand introduction could run as high as $150 million; the previous high figure in the industry for an introduction is $60 million. Industry observers remain skeptical of the brand's chances for success. Wallace maintains the promotion campaign has already proved "a great success," but selling cigarettes is more difficult than giving them away. Other recent ultra-low-tar entries, such as Philip Morris's Cambridge, have been unable to attract much business away from ultra-low-tar sales leaders Carlton (American Brands) and Now (R.J. Reynolds).

Brown and Williamson remained undiversified longer than its principal competitors, primarily because parent BAT feared the Securities and Exchange Commission's distaste for foreign acquisitions of U.S. businesses. But in 1969, Brown and Williamson bought processor and packer Vita Foods Products, Aleutian King Crabs, Incorporated, and Sea Pass Corporation. Later, Brown and Williamson, following BAT's overall interest in retail trade, purchased Gimbel Brothers and Saks Fifth Avenue department stores and the Kohl Corporation, a large midwestern grocery chain. BAT has reorganized its holdings under Batus (British-American Tobacco—U.S.) Industries, with Brown and Williamson set up as a division.

Brown and Williamson's future does not look exciting unless Barclay achieves high sales rates. Its dependence on high-tar brands such as Kool and Viceroy for the bulk of its sales bodes ill for succeeding in a market that is rapidly turning to low-tar cigarettes. Long-popular brands such as Kool, though, will help BAT's drive to nail down a sizable chunk of the third-world cigarette market. Brown and Williamson seems destined to plod along quietly, racking up high sales through Kool, Viceroy, and Raleigh, and aiding BAT's attempt to conquer even more of the international market.

American Brands

"We have the determination," declared Robert Heimann, chairman of the board of American Brands, at the firm's annual meeting. That confidence typified Heimann's recently ended reign at American Brands; in eleven years, he managed to turn an ailing tobacco giant into a flourishing diversified corporation involved in everything from Titleist golf balls to Jim Beam whiskey to Master Lock padlocks (see table 15-5). In the process, he

Table 15-5
American Brands Data
(percentages)

Product Division	1969	1970	1971	1972	1973	1974	1975	1976	1977	1978	1979
Distribution of Gross Revenues											
Domestic tobacco	46.1	38.5	35.3	32.4	31.1	27.9	25.9	25.9	23.1	20.8	19.7
International tobacco	40.2	38.4	37.0	38.9	38.3	38.8	38.6	37.1	40.4	42.0	42.1
Other	19.7	23.1	27.7	28.7	30.6	33.3	35.5	37.0	36.5	37.2	38.2
Distribution of Net Earnings											
Domestic tobacco	65.2	67.3	61.3	57.2	51.5	50.9	52.5	54.7	54.2	48.2	41.1
International tobacco	19.1	18.4	16.8	20.8	23.0	20.0	17.3	12.2	12.3	17.4	17.5
Other	15.7	14.3	21.9	22.0	25.5	29.1	31.2	33.1	33.5	34.4	41.4

Source: Annual reports.

produced an admirable record of earnings: from 1969 (when he became president) to 1978, American Brands's dividend rate grew at twice the Dow Jones Industrial average.

This new diversified look provides a sharp contrast to the early days of American Brands. Once known as American Tobacco, the company was the corporate parent for the vast tobacco trust James B. Duke assembled in the 1890s. Even after the Supreme Court busted the trust in 1911, American Tobacco remained the industry powerhouse through the 1950s, primarily because of the sustained success of Pall Mall and Lucky Strike.

But American Tobacco adapted slowly to the changing market conditions prompted in large part by the anti-smoking fervor of the 1950s. The company did not develop a filter brand to compete with front-runners Viceroy and Winston. In 1958, R.J. Reynolds slipped ahead of American for first place in cigarette sales, and American lapsed into a steady decline.

By 1964, though still a billion-dollar domestic cigarette company, American Tobacco was relying chiefly on nonfilter cigarettes for sales. But the days of prosperity for nonfilters had already passed. The company had accumulated little debt, maintained a good cash flow, and built up considerable borrowing power, but it had not diversified into other product lines and had no significant overseas operations. By late 1960s, American was often compared to Lorillard as an ideal candidate for takeover by another corporation.

Company executives realized that something was wrong and in 1964 seriously reevaluated their aims. In 1975, at the annual stockholders' meeting, Heimann recalled that turning point:

> It was about that time that the old American Tobacco Company stopped living in the past and started to map out a future. We had three things to do: First, update our cigarette business to increase our filter sales and thus cushion the effect of the nonfilter decline. Second, use our cash flow to acquire some meaningful diversification, broadening the earnings base and thereby increasing the stability and quality of our earnings. Third, find a way to build up our business abroad.

Then-chairman Robert Walker started moving toward the future by barraging the market with a scatter-shot introduction of new brands. Overly dependent on old-time sales leader Pall Mall, "Brand-a-Month" Walker quickly introduced such forgettable names as Montclair, Waterford, Sweet Caporals, and Bull Durham. The company did have some success with 100-millimeter versions of Pall Mall, Tareyton, and Silva Thins, a new cigarette for women. The company promoted Tareyton heavily with its "Us Tareyton Smokers Would Rather Fight than Switch" campaign, but American continued to slump.

One of Walker's lasting entries was Carlton, which the company bills as "the first truly low-tar cigarette." Walker printed the low tar and nicotine contents on the package in an attempt to cut into sales of Lorillard's low-tar Kent. The brand did not take off immediately, but the company—and particularly Robert Heimann, who moved up to the presidency in 1969—did not abandon it. After sixteen years (Carlton was introduced in 1964), that faith has paid off. In 1980, Carlton was the eleventh top-selling and the fastest growing cigarette on the market. Produced in four styles ranging from 0.05 to 5 milligrams of tar, the cigarette got a boost from a 1978 National Institutes of Health study that called Carlton a safer smoke than other brands. It took off from there.

Still, Carlton's surge has not slowed American's cigarette sales decline. The company's market share dropped from 14.2 percent in 1975 to 11.6 percent in 1979. Although that in itself is not a catastrophic slump, it was a further slide from American's former number-one ranking where its market share was 32.9 percent as late as 1955. And, since almost 50 percent of the company's cigarette sales still come from the dwindling nonfilter sector, American shows few signs of effectively braking its decline as a tobacco power.

Diversification has produced more positive results, however. The company remained exclusively a tobacco concern until 1966, long after its competitors had branched out. Walker approached the broadening of the company with the same thunderous style he took to the proliferation of brand names. Despite the sales decline, American's cigarette sales still generated enough cash to fund a dash to diversifying. In just seven years, Walker took over Sunshine Biscuits (snack foods), James B. Beam Distilling Company, Swingline (staplers), Acme Visible Records (information systems), Master Lock, Duff-Mott (applesauce), and Andrew Jergens (personal-care products). In the midst of this purchasing spree, one company official announced, "The name 'American Tobacco' doesn't quite fit a company that markets cookies and bourbons and applesauce." So, on July 1, 1969, American Tobacco became American Brands.

Robert Heimann slowed the acquisition drive when he assumed full command upon Walker's death in 1973. Heimann's first purchase that year was the $110 million Acushnet Company (golf and rubber products). Six years passed before Heimann moved again. This time he pulled off a celebrated coup by acquiring the Franklin Life Insurance Company, an outfit with $15 billion in policies that boosted American Brands's income by $100 million in its first year.

Heimann likes to term the fruits of this diversification drive "American Nontobacco." At the 1980 annual stockholders' meeting, he summed up the remarkable achievements of American Brands:

We have added the equivalent of one and a half American Tobacco companies. Although domestic tobacco profits have increased since 1965—from

$152 million to $282 million—our diversification profits have increased even faster—from scratch in 1965 to $396 million last year. So our business base is bigger, our income is bigger, our income growth is bigger and your dividend increases are not only bigger but more frequent.

A single acquisition satisfied another major corporate need facing the company: international tobacco expansion. American Tobacco was bumped out of the international market by the 1911 Supreme Court decision; British-American Tobacco got the rights to foreign sales of most of American's brands. But in 1968, American secured 76 percent ownership of Britain's second largest cigarette seller, Gallaher Limited, and assumed full ownership in 1975. Gallaher grew steadily through most of the 1970s—in 1977 alone sales increased 3 percent while the British market shrank 6 percent. But its share of the British market slipped from 29 percent in 1977 to 28 percent in 1979. And, like its corporate parent, it continues to rely on a heavy concentration of high-tar brands. Gallaher is trying to expand into the European market and has already established subsidiaries in Ireland and the Netherlands, but it has not made a strong move into the third world as have BAT Industries, Philip Morris, and R.J. Reynolds. Meanwhile, also like its parent, Gallaher diversified widely, netting approximately 25 percent of its operating income from optical services, engineering, wholesaling, and retailing.

The conglomerate that has resulted from American's widespread diversification would at first glance seem to be a management nightmare: a slew of businesses spread across thirteen divisions, consisting of what Heimann calculates to be "some forty-odd profit centers." Nevertheless, most of the divisions and products relate to cigarette manufacturers' traditional strength: consumer-oriented products requiring heavy marketing. Heimann has effectively blended the disparate product lines into a financially sound whole: dividends jumped from $2.80 in 1978 to $5.50 in 1980, and the Franklin Life acquisition boosted the stock's value from $48.50 to $80.00 in eighteen months.

Having revitalized American Brands's flagging fortunes and brought Franklin Life Insurance into the fold, Heimann again surprised the company by taking an early retirement in 1980. He chose executive president Edward W. Whittemore to succeed him as chairman, and named Virginius B. Lougee III president. Can this new management team continue Heimann's record of success? Prospects appear good. Whittemore understands American Brands thoroughly, having risen through the ranks from Wilson Jones business supplies and Swingline staplers. Lougee is a longtime southern tobacco man. Together they should be able to continue Heimann's policy of using tobacco's cash flow to fund a careful diversification program.

But what role will cigarette sales—particularly in the domestic sector—play in the company's future? The company sank about $1.8 *billion* into diversification from 1965 to 1980; very little money was invested back into cigarette production. According to *Barron's,* only 10 percent of American -Brands's 1977 capital expenditures went to domestic tobacco operations. In 1979, 40 percent of capital expenditures went into tobacco, but most of that funded Gallaher's production modernization program. The company has introduced few new brands and seems more enamored with its smaller nontobacco subsidiaries than with its domestic cigarette operations. "Like a two-pack-a-day man," *Barron's* notes, "American has been kicking the cigarette habit for years, turning to the healthier lines of consumer goods, food and life insurance."

It seems logical to look for further decline in American's cigarette sales and to expect tobacco to serve mainly as the cash producer for the slow and steady diversification program Whittemore and Lougee have inherited from Heimann. American Brands is indeed no longer American Tobacco.

Lorillard

The merger fervor that infected the cigarette industry in the 1960s had a reverse effect in one instance, and a corporate David swallowed one of the Big Six. In the 1960s, Lorillard, the nation's oldest tobacco company, did not respond to the changing market and remained heavily committed to its nonfilter lines. It started diversifying late (until 1962, the corporate charter forbade branching beyond tobacco) and, when it did, had dismal results with a small cat-food company and a candy manufacturer. By 1968, Lorillard was overly extended in nonfilters and its new lines were flagging. It was ripe for a takeover.

Enter one of Wall Street's most controversial wheeler-dealers, Laurence Tisch. Tisch and his brother Preston had begun with hotels and theaters, speculated astutely on the stock market, and then engaged in several hostile takeovers in the course of building their company to a $137-million-a-year business. Picking off the $567-million-a-year Lorillard officially pushed the tiny but feisty company, Loews Theaters, into the big time and gave Tisch the assets he needed to expand even further. He displayed his hopeful outlook by changing the business's name from Loews Theaters to the Loews Corporation in 1969, emphasizing the conglomerate nature of his venture.

Although Tisch was moving on the crest of the nouveau conglomerate era, his first major purchase carried a great deal of tradition. The nation's oldest tobacco company, Lorillard traces its origin all the way back to 1760, when twenty-two-year-old French immigrant Pierre Lorillard opened a "manufactory" in New York City to produce pipe tobacco and snuff. The firm continued as a family business well into the nineteenth century, adding cigars to its product line and becoming a major producer of plug tobacco.

In 1899, however, the firm succumbed to the power of the Duke Tobacco Trust, becoming part of Duke's Continental Company. When the Duke Trust was dissolved in 1911, Lorillard emerged as an independent company—but it bore little resemblance to the original P. Lorillard Company. The new firm received little of Duke's plug interests; its major product lines became smoking tobacco, snuff, and little cigars. It did receive 15 precent of Duke's cigarette concerns, but most of the brands involved less-popular Turkish tobacco blends instead of the burley blends of the brand leaders like Pall Mall. Lorillard's sales dropped from 15 percent of the market in 1911 to only 1.9 percent in 1925. In 1926, Lorillard introduced the burley-blended Old Gold brand, which upped its sales somewhat, but the company languished at or near the bottom of the Big Six throughout the middle of the century.

Its sales expanded somewhat in the 1950s, largely on the strength of its Kent brand; in 1960, it garnered more than 10 percent of the cigarette market for the first time since the 1910s. But the company could not sustain the momentum, as its competitors innovated faster and marketed more cleverly than the Bix Six's oldest firm. From 1960 to 1969, the company actually lost sales, from 49.8 billion units sold in 1960 to 46.5 billion in 1969. Even with declining sales, however, Lorillard combined increased revenues from price hikes, reduced advertising costs, and the high income-to-sales ratio of the industry to produce a steady flow of cash.

And a barrel of cash was just what Laurence Tisch wanted. Tisch used Lorillard to augment Loews's expansion capital by revaluing Lorillard's assets (netting a healthy tax savings), cutting leaf inventories to the bone, and dumping Lorillard's candy subsidiary for $50 million. Tisch plowed all this new cash into a flurry of stock speculation and a series of unsuccessful acquisition attempts; Goodrich, Radio Corporation of America (RCA), Franklin National Bank, Gimbel Brothers department stores, and the Talcott National Corporation all survived his onslaught.

Though obviously more concerned with the stock market and new mergers, Tisch did not abandon Lorillard. With characteristic brashness, Tisch cleaned house in the Lorillard executive suites, replacing the old-time executives with a hand-picked set of new officers. Key among them was new president Curtis Judge, a former Reynolds vice-president who had handled domestic sales and advertising. A seasoned marketer in several industries, Judge had much of the brashness of his new boss. Once at the helm, he revamped the run-down operation. He got Tisch to sink $75 million into sorely needed capital improvements in the shoddy cigarette manufacturing facilities and streamlined the brand-management system and the advertising strategies.

Not all his new ventures proved successful. In the early 1970s, Lorillard introduced such forgettable names as Zack, Maverick, and Redford. But Judge did score in one of the company's long-standing strong fields: the low-tar market.

Lorillard's Kent, a popular brand introduced in the 1950s, had slumped by the 1970s. Judge reduced its tar content from 16 to 12 milligrams (placing it in the low-tar category), brought out Kent Golden Lights in the 6 to 9 milligram very-low-tar field, and reduced True from 11 to 5 milligrams (the ultra-low-tar entry). Having thus thoroughly segmented and attacked the entire spectrum of the low-tar market, Judge defied the traditional practices of frontrunners Philip Morris and R.J. Reynolds by promoting the new low-tar brands with a flood of comparative advertising, "factually" demonstrating the superiority of Lorillard's brands with tar levels and survey results.

The innovation proved highly successful. Since 1976, Lorillard's sales have increased by 25 percent, ten times the growth rate of the entire industry. Lorillard is about to overtake American Brands for fourth position in the cigarette sweepstakes and has cast eyes hungrily on the third spot now occupied by Brown and Williamson. Low-tar cigarettes now account for more than 80 perent of the company's sales (48 percent of the entire industry). In 1979, Lorillard nailed down a healthy 17 percent of the low-tar market, third place behind industry giants Reynolds and Philip Morris.

More important (from Tisch's point of view), Lorillard remains a vital cash factory for the Loews Corporation. Cigarette earnings jumped 59 percent from 1977 to 1979, to a level of $950 million. The cash flow enabled Tisch to make another major acquisition. In 1974, after failing to take over RCA and others, Loews found a target that could not escape: ailing insurance giant CNA Financial Corporation. Beset by financial woes and the near insolvency of its Continental Casualty subsidiary, CNA finally gave in to the merger after prolonged and heated opposition. Once again Tisch cleaned house, bringing in an outside president—former Allstate executive vice-president Edward J. Noha. And in 1979, Tisch followed this method of picking up undervalued companies in stagnating industries by latching onto Bulova Watch Company.

With the acquisition of CNA, Tisch relegated Lorillard to the status of junior partner in Loews's corporate structure, producing only 23 percent of revenues and 22 percent of incomes in 1979. (In 1973, Lorillard produced 76 percent of Loews's revenues and 55 percent of its earnings. See table 15-6.) And in 1977, Tisch sold off Lorillard's international interests—including licensing agreements and all brand-name rights—to BAT Industries for $141 million (an after-tax gain of some $50 million). Though the company intends to continue its efforts in the domestic cigarette market, this move takes it completely out of the international growth arena now being pursued so eagerly by Philip Morris and R.J. Reynolds.

Table 15-6
Lorillard (Loews Corporation) Data
(percentages)

Product Division	1971	1972	1973	1974	1975[a]	1976	1977	1978	1979
	Distribution of Gross Revenues								
Cigarettes	71	69	76	77	22	22	23	24	23
Insurance	0	0	0	0	65	67	66	64	62
Other	29	31	24	23	13	11	11	12	15[b]
	Distribution of Net Earnings								
Cigarettes	50	50	55	59	21[a]	29	25	22	22
Insurance	0	0	0	0	34	27	26	40	39
Other	50	50	45	41	45	44	49	38	39[b]

Source: Annual reports.

[a]After the purchase of CNA Financial Corporation by the Loews Corporation in 1974, cigarettes (which were the major Lorillard product) dropped to a much smaller portion of the Loews's portfolio.

[b]Much of Loews Corporation's income results from income on investments, which generate only a minimal amount of revenue in the balance sheets but which contribute heavily to the earnings figures marked "other."

No longer the nation's most eager diversifier, Laurence Tisch seems content, for the time being, with his insurance business and cigarette money-maker. Indications are, though, that he is still on the lookout for attractive acquisition opportunities. Lorillard is not likely to rival Philip Morris or R.J. Reynolds for first place in the cigarette sweepstakes, but it should continue to generate the steady cash Tisch needs to wheel and deal in the U.S. financial community.

Liggett and Myers

Among all corporations, Liggett and Myers Tobacco Company has to rate as one of the great business failures of the post-World War II era. From a strong position as one of the industry's Big Three (with American Tobacco and R.J. Reynolds) in 1946, Liggett and Myers fell to last place among the Big Six producers in 1962 and has steadily declined since then, netting a dismal 2.7 percent of industry sales in 1979. New brand introductions in the 100-millimeter and low-tar markets have been busts, and the company has not even developed a strong filter entry.

Liggett and Myers's lineage in tobacco dates back to a small snuff manufacturing shop opened in Belleville, Illinois, in 1822. The business shifted to St. Louis, Missouri, in 1833 and was taken over by the founder's grandson, John E. Liggett, in 1849. Liggett took on partner George S. Myers in 1873. In addition to its snuff manufacturing, the company became the largest plug-chewing tobacco producer in the world by 1885. Naturally, such a healthy business attracted the attention of trust-builder James B. Duke. After vigorously resisting takeover attempts for several years, Liggett and Myers finally withered under Duke's pressure in 1899 and became part of the American Tobacco Company.

After the Supreme Court dissolved the trust in 1911, Liggett and Myers emerged as one of the country's three leading tobacco firms: it was handed a third of the trust's chewing-plug business, a sizable chunk of snuff production, and a variety of cigarette brands, including Fatima, American Beauty, and Home Run. The company soon augmented its cigarette business with a new entry, Chesterfield, and settled into third place in the cigarette sweepstakes, where it remained for forty years.

However, like the 1950s front-runner American Tobacco, Liggett and Myers reacted sluggishly to the changing market conditions of the post-war era. Sales of nonfilter Chesterfield dropped as filter brands became more popular. The L&M brand did pick up some filter sales for awhile, as did Lark after it was introduced in 1962. But the company developed no strong product in any segment of the cigarette market. It lacked an effective menthol brand; Chesterfield slumped out of the top ten brands; and L&M's rise stuck at eighth place and then declined. Other companies had already staked out the turf in new market segments, leaving Liggett and Myers on the outside looking in. Eve cigarettes could not compete with Virginia Slims, and Decade did not make a dent in the flourishing low-tar market when introduced. The company's innovations—such as Adam, a 100-millimeter cigarette aimed at men, and Eagle 20's, "a quality cigarette at economy prices"—created scarcely a ripple of enthusiasm.

Consequently, Liggett and Myers's sales have plummeted. From unit sales of 51.2 billion in 1960, the company fell to 16.5 billion in 1979. Despite continued price increases, sales have dropped so rapidly that total revenues from cigarettes have decreased as well. Even international sales, the growth bonanza for Reynolds and Philip Morris, increased so little during the 1970s that Liggett and Myers finally sold its overseas business—the rights to its brands and tobacco inventories held for the export market—to Phillip Morris for $108 million in 1978.

In spite of its other woes, Liggett and Myers proved a skilled diversifier, thanks mainly to the efforts of Milton E. Harrington. In July 1964, when Harrington took over as chief executive, the company was totally undiversified and was well into its decline. Harrington's efforts could not shore up the domestic or international cigarette trade but his diversification program did net some results (see table 15-7).

Harrington stayed on the company's home turf, investing in marketing-heavy product lines, especially pet foods and liquor. In 1964, Liggett and Myers picked up Allen Products, which produces Alpo dog food. Alpo has since climbed to the top of the rapidly growing dog-food business and has

Table 15-7
Liggett and Myers (The Liggett Group) Data
(percentages)

Product Division	1971	1972	1973	1974	1975	1976	1977	1978	1979
			Distribution of Gross Revenues						
Cigarettes			45	43	42	40	39	32	27
Chewing and smoking tobacco			5	6	6	7	7	6	6
Spirits and wines			19	21	20	19	21	24	24
Pet foods			22	21	21	20	19	19	19
Other			9	9	11	14	14	19	24
			Distribution of Net Earnings						
Cigarettes			42	35	28	25	31	15	15
Chewing and smoking tobacco			7	10	13	15	31	20	13
Spirits and wines			36	33	31	33	63	48	33
Pet foods			6	10	15	13	−48	12	13
Other			9	12	13	14	22	5	26

Source: Annual reports.

proved a steady profit-maker. In 1969, Harrington added two other pet-food concerns, Liv-A-Snaps and Perk Foods. Liquor offered the other major avenue of diversification. In 1966, Harrington snagged the Paddington Corporation and Carillon Importers, Limited. Paddington has an exclusive contract to import J&B Scotch (produced by Britain's Grand Metropolitan Limited—Grand Met), the most popular brand of scotch in the United States. Carillon Importers, another solid performer, imports a variety of spirits—most notably, Grand Marnier liqueur. Encouraged by these additions, Harrington moved again in 1969, picking up distiller and importer Austin, Nichols, and Company, which markets Wild Turkey bourbon. Finally, Liggett and Myers added a host of smaller operations during the late 1960s, including National Oats Company (popcorn and oats), Brite Industries (watch bands), and Earl Grissmer Company, (home-care products).

In five short years, Liggett and Myers had the most highly diversified corporation of the Big Six. Nontobacco operations provided 46 percent of revenues and 53 percent of operating income as early as 1970. These figures continued to rise as cigarette sales waned and diversification continued, reaching 65 percent and 71 percent, respectively, in 1979. The company then added the nation's largest bottling company (Atlantic Soft Drink) and a sporting-goods company, Diversified Products, which had a record year in 1979.

Just how decreasingly important tobacco was to the company's overall operation was made clear in 1974. That year, Raymond Mulligan, head of Allen Products, became the first nontobacco man to head one of the Big Six, and Liggett and Myers changed its name to the Liggett Group. In the company's annual report, Mulligan declared, "It is a new name with an old aim: 'better products to make the good life better.' "

By 1979, cigarettes had become the company's albatross. The Liggett Group announced plans to sell its domestic tobacco operations to North Carolina construction-magnate Dolph Overton. But after investigating the finances needed to revive Liggett's tobacco trade, Overton got cold feet and the deal dissolved. The financial disclosure information made public during the negotiations laid bare Liggett's vital statistics to any interested suitors. A year later, another came knocking.

In March 1980, Grand Metropolitan Limited offered $50 a share ($415 million) to buy the 90.5 percent of the Ligget Group that it did not already own. Originally a hotel chain, Grand Met has branched out into other leisure, food, and drink areas, particularly liquor. For some time, Grand Met had sought to buy some of Liggett's liquor interests but years of discussions produced no sale. So Grand Met simply swallowed the entire company instead.

Liggett furiously resisted the takeover bid, filing numerous court actions against the purchase and encouraging its stockholders to resist Grand Met. Ultimately, Standard Brands entered the bidding as a white knight that might save Liggett from foreign control. However, Grand Met raised its bid to $69 a share, Standard Brands dropped out of the picture, and the court suits produced no results; Liggett became part of Grand Met in May 1980. What will happen to Liggett and Myers tobacco?

Grand Met's managing director, Sidney Grimstead, has tactfully stated in *The Wall Street Journal* that although the company might eventually change the makeup of Liggett Group, "we aren't under any pressure to sell off anything." London financial analyst Michael Gearing, however, has predicted that Grand Met will probably not get involved in cigarettes since it does not know that market. If Grand Met sells off Liggett's tobacco lines, it might well recoup much of the Liggett purchase price and be left with "the bits they really want," as Gearing puts it.

Odds are that Liggett and Myers will not remain in the Liggett Group subsidiary for long. But purchase by any of the other Big Six firms could prompt anti-trust charges. Also, none of Liggett's brands ranks particularly high at present; by 1980, flagship brand L&M no longer was in the top-twenty sellers. One former Liggett executive predicted in 1979 that it would cost at least $300 million over three years to revive Liggett and Myers's failing fortunes. That is a sizable chunk of money to pump into an outfit that generated only $291 million in sales and $18 million in operating income in 1979. So, unless a foreign firm wants to enter the lagging U.S. cigarette industry, Liggett and Myers could be dissolved piecemeal, with separate sales of its tobacco inventories, machinery, and other assets. And then the Big Six would be the Big Five.

References

General

Business Week, annual surveys of cigarette industry, 1947-1980.
"Cigarette Companies Ignite Spark to 'Tar Wars,' " Raleigh *News and Observer*, April 27, 1980, p. 2B.
"Embattled Tobacco's New Strategy," *Fortune*, January 1963, p. 100.
Huebner, Albert, "Making the Third World Marlboro Country," *The Nation*, June 16, 1979, p. 717.
Sobol, Robert, *They Satisfy.*
Thomas, Dan. L., "Turning a New Leaf," *Barron's*, September 1, 1969, p. 3.
"Tobacco Smoke Signals," *Financial World*, May 21, 1969, p. 17.

American Brands

"American Brands Branches Out," *Financial World*, December 9, 1970, p. 10.
"American Brands," *Forbes*, November 15, 1971, p. 73.
"American Brands Stockholders Meeting," *Wall Street Transcript*, May 12, 1980, p. 37881.
"American Brands," *Wall Street Transcript*, May 12, 1975, p. 40, 263.
"American Tobacco Bucks Industry Down-Trend," *Financial World*, November 4, 1964, p. 5.
"Diversification Aids American Brands," *Financial World*, November 26, 1969, p. 5.
Grant, James, "On Nobody's Hit Parade," *Barron's*, December 11, 1978, p. 9.

Brown and Williamson

"Dobson Looks beyond Britain," *Business Week*, April 13, 1974, p. 91.
"King-Size and Unfiltered," *Forbes,* June 15, 1972, p. 36.
Louis, Arthur M., "The $150 Million Cigarette," *Fortune*, November 17, 1980, p. 121.
"You Can't Win 'Em All," *Forbes*, February 15, 1976, p. 52.

Liggett and Myers

"Grand Met Wins Bidding War," *Wall Street Journal*, May 15, 1980, p. 6.
"L&M Industry Laggard," *Financial World,* May 25, 1966, p. 28.

"L&M Looks Afield," *Financial World*, July 3, 1968, p. 14.
"Liggett & Myers," *Tobacco Reporter*, January, 1967, p. 24.
"Tar Wars," *The New York Times*, April 15, 1980, p. D1.
"The Palladium Perplex," *Forbes*, November 27, 1978, p. 36.
"Why Grand Met Wants Liggett," *Wall Street Journal*, April 17, 1980, p. 24.
"Why L&M Looks Inviting to Suitors," *Business Week*, April 14, 1973, p. 28.

Lorillard

Buck, Charles G., "How the Tisches Run Their Little Store," *Fortune*, May, 1971, p. 158.
"How Loews's Loan Management Tattered Profits at CNA," *Business Week*, November 1, 1976, p. 64.
"Loews: A Lot More than Theatres," *Financial World,* April 15, 1970, p. 10.
"Loews Steps Up Its Fight for CNA," *Business Week,* June 8, 1974, p. 25.
Schuyton, Peter J., "Lorillard Serves Big in the Low-Tar Derby," *Fortune*, August 14, 1978, p. 124.
"The Deflation of Larry Tisch," *Forbes*, August 15, 1973, p. 32.
"What Loews Will Get Out of CNA," *Business Week*, November 9, 1974, p. 152.
"Why Larry Tisch Is Cautious," *Forbes*, June 11, 1974, p. 93.

Philip Morris

"Business Triumphs of the Seventies," *Fortune*, December 31, 1979, p. 30.
"Diversification Pushed," *Financial World*, June 16, 1965, p. 14.
Gibson, Paul, "The George Weissman Road Show," *Forbes*, November 10, 1980, p. 179.
"Joseph F. Cullman III," *Financial World*, March 15, 1977, p. 30.
"PM's Foreign Invasion," *Dun's Review*, November, 1976, p. 83.
"Philip Morris: The Hot Hand in Cigarettes," *Business Week*, December 6, 1976, p. 60.
"Philip Morris," *Wall Street Transcipt*, December 25, 1978, p. 52889.
"Philip Morris' Year of Decision," *Forbes*, July 10, 1978, p. 29.
"Top Hand in Marlboro Country," *Fortune*, August 14, 1978, p. 15.
"Why Philip Morris Thrives," *Business Week*, January 27, 1973, p. 48.

R.J. Reynolds

"A Fresh Start at Reynolds," *Business Week*, May 5, 1973, p. 63.

Barnfather, Maurice, "Tar Wars?," *Forbes*, November 10, 1980, p. 190.

"When Marketing Takes Over at R.J. Reynolds," *Business Week*, November 13, 1978, p. 82.

"Reynolds Discontinuing Real 'Natural' Cigarettes," *The New York Times*, June 24, 1980, p. D1.

"R.J. Reynolds Presentation to N.Y. Society of Security Analysts," *Wall Street Transcipt*, July 7, 1975, p. 40779.

"R.J. Reynolds Stops a Slide in Market Shares," *Business Week*, January 26, 1976, p. 92.

"R.J. Reynolds: The Deft Diversifier," *Dun's Review*, December, 1974, p. 50.

16 R.J. Reynolds Industries: A Hundred Years of Progress in North Carolina

J. Paul Sticht

R.J. Reynolds (RJR) Industries operates worldwide in several lines of business, but our foundation is in agriculture and we have a deep, traditional commitment to the producers of our raw materials and the regions where they are produced. We began business over a century ago as a one-product tobacco company. A brief look at the history of R.J. Reynolds Tobacco Company offers insight into some of the changes that have taken place in the manufacturing and marketing of tobacco products.

After starting the company in 1875 with a line of plug-chewing tobacco, Richard Joshua Reynolds in 1907 introduced Prince Albert smoking tobacco, which still remains the best-selling smoking tobacco in America. It was in 1913, however, that Reynolds assumed full leadership in the manufacturing and marketing structure of the tobacco industry. He introduced Camel, the first blended, nationally marketed cigarette.

Camel remained Reynold's flagship brand for almost five decades and today still ranks seventh among all cigarettes sold. This is particularly impressive, since the domestic cigarette market has expanded drastically over the last few years, and there are now almost 190 brands available to consumers. Winston, introduced in 1954, led the dramatic growth of filter cigarettes and within ten years became the best-selling cigarette in America. Today it ranks second. Salem, the first filter-tipped menthol cigarette, made its debut in 1956. It, too, was an immediate success and is today the third-ranked brand in the country. Innovation—being first to meet emerging consumer demand with quality products—has been the cornerstone of Reynolds Tobacco's rise to the top of the U.S. tobacco industry.

As the U.S. tobacco industry enters the 1980s, we are viewing what is basically a stable, mature domestic market. We feel that there will be some years of no growth or declining growth, and overall we foresee modest growth during the decade. Some observers of the industry feel that this situation has come about solely because of the smoking-and-health controversy. This is a contributing factor, though not the only one. Smoking, like many social customs, has a long history of moving in and out of controversies and moving in concert with broad social tides.

We subscribe to the tobacco industry's position on the smoking-and-health controversy. It is still just that, a controversy. Despite the fact that millions of dollars have been spent on research, no element as found in cigarette smoke has been shown to be the cause of any human disease. We continue investing millions of dollars to support the scientists engaged in the research. They pursue their work without restriction and publish the results of their work as they deem appropriate. In addition to grants made through the Council for Tobacco Research, we have a major program of grants that support independent basic biomedical research. This research, being conducted in major medical facilities throughout the nation, seeks to uncover the causes of disease.

One characteristic of a successful tobacco industry is its capacity to generate large amounts of cash flow. As a publicly held corporation, it was incumbent upon R.J. Reynolds to invest this money in the most productive manner. This is the basis for the diversification program.

Diversification began in the 1950s when the company's Archer Aluminum Division started making packaging products for customers other than Reynolds Tobacco. During the 1960s, Reynolds Tobacco continued to diversify by acquiring companies in foods, snacks, and fruit-juice beverages. Archer became a separate subsidiary company in 1967 (named RJR Archer in 1970), and all food interests were unified in 1967 to form R.J. Reynolds Foods, the nucleus of what became RJR Foods, Incorporated.

Sea-Land Services, Incorporated, a containerized-shipping company, joined the RJR family in 1969. Our diversification into the energy business began with the acquisition of American Independent Oil Company (Aminoil) in 1970. Also in 1970, RJR implemented a reorganization of its corporate structure to provide coordinated services and more efficient control. Out of this reorganization came R.J. Reynolds Industries, Incorporated, the new parent corporation of the RJR organization.

In 1976, R.J. Reynolds Tobacco International, Incorporated was created to direct the corporation's growing worldwide tobacco operation. Also in 1976, RJR acquired the American holdings of Burmah Oil and Gas Company and it became a part of our energy subsidiary, Aminoil USA, Incorporated. In early 1979, R.J. Reynolds Industries continued its diversification program by merging with Del Monte Corporation.

As the 1980s begin, we view ourselves primarily as a company engaged in the manufacture and marketing of consumer packaged goods with significant interests in transportation and energy. Any future diversification can be expected to be compatible with this mix of businesses.

Over the years, R.J. Reynolds has felt a special commitment to the quality of life in our heartland region. Testifying to this commitment is an unparalleled record of corporate support for education and cultural institutions in North Carolina. At the heart of this commitment is a sensitivity to the changing aspirations and solid achievements of the North Carolinians whose lives have been so closely bound up with RJR for over a century, our fellow employees, our shareholders, tobacco-farm families, and our neighbors across the state.

17

A Future of Great Promise—for Tobacco and for Philip Morris

George Weissman

For the last 133 years, Philip Morris has been a tobacco company. It is a tobacco company today and will remain a tobacco company, in very basic terms, for a great many years to come. The company has changed over the last two decades, becoming first an international company and then a diversified company, doing business in several different industries. But the foundation for this change has been, simply, quality cigarettes from America.

We became an international company because, soon after World War II, we saw an opportunity to meet the growing demand for American-blend cigarettes around the world. American GIs had introduced people in many countries to the flavor and quality of American cigarettes.

As our sales and profits grew during the fifties and sixties—a piece of good fortune shared by other members of our industry—we began to look for ways to achieve greater balance in our business, first with further geographic expansion into the international cigarette business and then with expansion into other consumer-product areas, particularly those which had some things in common with tobacco.

Our international business has grown over the last two decades so that we now market more than 160 different brands in more than 170 countries and territories. We have 31 manufacturing and marketing affiliates, 34 licensees, and a variety of regional export organizations. We are the world's largest exporter of cigarettes with more than a 40 percent share of the U.S. cigarette export market. In fact, 19 percent of Philip Morris's total U.S. production is exported.

In the early seventies, we acquired the Miller Brewing Company, which has since become the world's second largest brewing company. In the late seventies, we entered the U.S. and international soft-drink business by acquiring the Seven-Up Company. To make the picture complete, let me note that our Philip Morris Industrial and Mission Viejo Company subsidiaries are active in the fields of packaging and paper, and land development, respectively. Their combined revenues, however, amounted in 1979 to less than 5 percent of the Philip Morris total. These new businesses met our standard that required we stick with things we know—things we had learned in the tobacco industry:

Cigarettes, beer, and soft drinks are uniformly large, consistently profitable, historically recession-resistant industries.

All three are agriculturally based consumer products, low priced (with high visibility and turnover), widely used, and enjoyed both in the United States and around the world.

Their sales are responsive to product innovation and to imaginative advertising, merchandising, and packaging.

More than any other single factor, these similarities have determined the direction of our expansion and diversification. Because skills and experience acquired in one of the three industries can be transferred to the other two, we have been able to use the talents of existing management to enter new fields. Over the years and right up to the present, Philip Morris's cigarette business has grown so steadily and profitably that we have been able to look outside the industry for ways to put our assets to work.

I should also add that our expansion and diversification were greatly assisted by the fact that we own large and growing inventories of high-quality U.S.-grown tobacco against which we could borrow when we had to. Tobacco was and is regarded by banks as a premier asset, one whose value is so assured and dependable that it truly can be characterized as "good as gold."

Although Philip Morris's new businesses have received a great deal of attention in the media lately, the fact is that our diversification has not changed the basic nature of the company. Tobacco continues to be far and away our dominant business. In 1979, following a decade in which Philip Morris's after-tax earnings had grown at a compounded annual rate of more than 24 percent, tobacco still accounted for 64 percent of total revenues and 82 percent of operating profits.

Perhaps an even more significant statistic is the recent growth record of our tobacco business, especially as reckoned in the inflation-free constant of units, or numbers of cigarettes sold. In 1969, Philip Morris sold 150 billion cigarettes worldwide. In 1979, worldwide unit sales were 400 billion—more than two and a half times greater. This works out to a compounded annual growth rate of 12.4 percent over the last decade. But that is the record of the past. In business, our focus and emphasis need always to be on the future.

In the United States, the cigarette market has matured. The post-World War II baby boom reached its high point in 1957. The numbers of men and women moving into adulthood—and thus into smoking age—have begun to trend downward. Outside the United States, the picture is very different. The current growth rate overseas is about 3 percent a year—more than 100 billion cigarettes. We expect this trend to continue.

Although the U.S. market for cigarettes will continue to be large and stable, future tobacco growth will come chiefly from international sales, that is, overseas sales of American-made cigarettes, and export sales of American tobacco. Philip Morris last year exported more than 40 billion cigarette units, more than our entire company output in 1952. We also caused the export of more than 144.6 million pounds of tobacco, to meet the needs of our affiliates and licensees.

These international sales significantly influence the U.S. balance of trade. In 1979, foreign sales of American-grown tobacco and American-made tobacco products generated a net trade surplus of $1.7 billion—money coming into the United States, not going out. And for the entire decade of the seventies, the tobacco trade surplus exceeded $10 billion.

Our worldwide presence and leadership as a cigarette company have greatly increased the demand for the cigarettes we make in the United States, and thus have increased the number of people employed in manufacturing these cigarettes. In North Carolina, for instance, we are building a cigarette-manufacturing plant that ultimately will employ 2,500 people. (In addition, we are already contributing to this state's economy with our Miller Brewing facilities at Eden and Reidsville. At capacity, they employ more than 1,900 people and have an annual economic impact of nearly $145 million.) Obviously, then, foreign sales are important to the country as well as to the grower and manufacturer.

Because of the partnership we feel with the grower, we have acted to support America's position as a producer of quality leaf. In the last four years, we have made major grants in the field of tobacco agricultural research and extension to North Carolina State University, the University of Kentucky College of Agriculture, Virginia Polytechnic Institute, and the University of Tennessee. The broad purpose of the grant program is to improve and promote the efficient production of quality U.S. tobacco in the United States. We believe that the increased resources made available through these programs to further tobacco science and technology will help insure a prosperous future for tobacco farmers and the industry in general.

At Philip Morris we believe that the future of tobacco is great, so long as there is a constant striving for higher-quality tobacco and greater efficiency throughout our industry—from grower through manufacturer. Both are necessary if we are to make the most of the vast opportunity inherent in the growing international market.

As for whether the smoking-and-health controversy could undercut our encouraging prospects overseas, I do not think so. Through direct manufacturing, affiliated companies, licensing, and exporting, Philip Morris today is doing business in more than 170 countries and territories. Our sales are growing at twice the rate of the international market as a whole. Yet in many of those countries, we face strictures much more severe than anything known here.

In the long run, though criticism of our product may not die down and from time to time may even flare up, I believe it will continue to take second place to a truth that has been observable for nearly four hundred years: people enjoy smoking. They find it a pleasure, a comfort, a means of improving the human condition. Tens of millions of men and women around the world feel that way. Their tastes in cigarettes may change, of course. More and more consumers throughout the world are choosing "lighter" cigarettes, just as they are in the United States; and American-blend cigarettes appear to be an increasingly important part of this growing segment. Facts like those create confidence in the future. In my opinion, few industries as large and long-established as ours have future prospects as good as ours.

That is why, in the last ten years, Philip Morris has opened both a large new tobacco operations center for manufacturing and a research center in Richmond, Virginia; has begun construction of an administration and technical center there; has begun construction of a major new plant in Cabarrus County, North Carolina; has upgraded and expanded our tobacco facilities in countries outside the United States; and is constructing new manufacturing facilities in the Netherlands and in West Germany (Munich and West Berlin). In these projects, the shareholders of Philip Morris have invested a sum exceeding $1 billion. Over the next five years, we plan to invest $3.5 billion in capital projects, roughly half of which will be for tobacco.

My message, in short, is that we see a future of great promise, of great achievement, for tobacco and for Philip Morris. We are also putting our money where our faith is. And in business that is what counts.

18 World Tobacco: A Portrait of Corporate Power

Frederick F. Clairmonte

The world tobacco economy is largely dominated by a number of transnational tobacco conglomerates (TTCs), whose global sales exceeded $56 billion in 1979. Tobacco manufacturing in the developed and underdeveloped capitalist economies is dominated by seven giant TTCs: British-American Tobacco Company (BAT); Imperial Tobacco Company (ITC); R.J. Reynolds (RJR); Philip Morris (PM); the South-African-controlled Rupert Rembrandt/Rothmans group; American Brands; and Gulf and Western (see table 18-1).

These corporations (except for Gulf and Western, which is one of the world's leading cigar producers) produce more than 39 percent of the world's cigarettes—about 58 percent if centrally planned economies (CPEs) such as the Soviet Union, East Germany, and Bulgaria are excluded, and more than 80 percent if both the CPEs and the state monopolies (France, Japan, Italy, and so on) are excluded. In recent years, TTC brands have also begun to make great inroads into the state monopoly markets, and to a

Table 18-1
The Seven Major Tobacco Conglomerates: 1979
(in billions of dollars)

Corporation	Sales	Employees
British-American Tobacco Industries (United Kingdom)	16.0	153,000
R.J. Reynolds (United States)	8.9	79,487
Philip Morris (United States)	8.3	65,000
Imperial Group (United Kingdom)	8.0	101,200
Rembrandt/Rothmans (S. Africa/United Kingdom)	6.2[a]	n/a
Gulf and Western (United States)	5.3	102,160
American Brands (United States)	3.8	54,690
Totals	$56.5	555,537

Source: Annual reports and trade sources.
[a]Estimate.

This chapter is based, in part, on *Marketing and Distribution of Tobacco,* published by the United Nations Conference on Trade and Development (UNCTAD) (TD/B/C.1/205, Geneva, 1978). Dr. Clairmonte wishes to thank his colleague John Cavanagh of Princeton University for his comments. Definitions of economic terms appear in an appendix at the end of this chapter.

lesser extent, into the CPEs (these sales are not reflected in the figures just given). TTC penetration into CPEs (including China) via exports, brand licensing, and common production arrangements represents a significant pattern which should lead to an even greater share of the market.

The tobacco industry is one of the most highly concentrated of all manufacturing industries, both worldwide and in the United States. By four major indicators—sales, total assets, net capital assets, and profits—the U.S. tobacco industry ranks second only to the automobile industry in degree of concentration. R.J. Reynolds, Philip Morris, and Brown and Williamson (a wholly-owned BAT affiliate) control 77 percent of the market. With American Brands thrown in, this figure climbs to 88 percent (see table 18-2).

Origins

In 1890, James Buchanan Duke (1857-1925) engineered the fusion of the five large tobacco manufacturing companies in the United States into the American Tobacco Company (ATC). Incorporated as a New Jersey holding company with Buck Duke as chairman of the board,[1] the ATC at its birth controlled 89 percent of the U.S. cigarette market, a proportion that remained about the same up to 1910 (see figure 18-1). It also took over other tobacco markets, increasing its share of smoking, fine-cut, and plug tobacco, and little cigars, from as low as 7 percent to 76, 78, 85, and 91 percent, respectively, and gaining control of 75 to 80 percent of domestically manufactured leaf. (The large cigar market, because of its still pervasive craft nature, remained too fragmented for ATC to control.)

Table 18-2
U.S. Estimated Cigarette Output: 1979
(in billions of cigarettes)

	Domestic	Foreign	Total	Percent of United States market[c]
R.J. Reynolds	199.3	28.0	227.3	32.8
Philip Morris	176.1	40.0	216.1	30.8
Brown and Williamson	87.9	18.4	106.3	13.7
American Brands	71.0	1.6	72.6	10.7
Lorillard[a]	59.6		59.6	9.8
Liggett Group[b]	16.9		16.9	2.2

Source: *Tobacco Reporter,* March 1980, and *Business Week,* December 15, 1980.
[a]A division of the Loews Corporation.
[b]Partially owned by the Rupert/Rembrandt Group.
[c]Percentages in this column are for 1980.

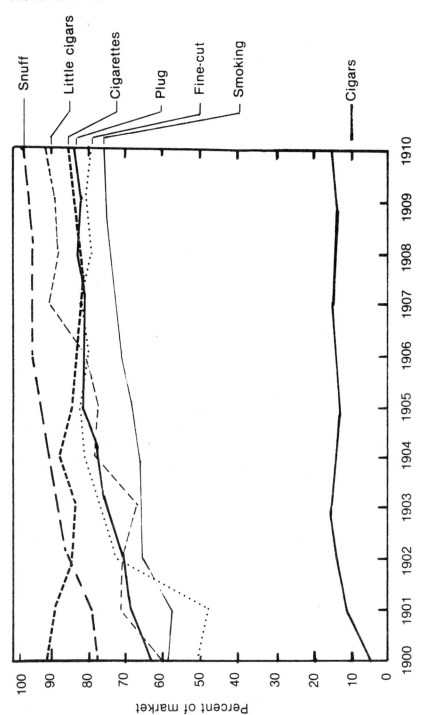

Snuff

Little cigars

Cigarettes

Plug

Fine-cut

Smoking

Cigars

Percent of market

100 90 80 70 60 50 40 30 20 10 0

1900 1901 1902 1903 1904 1905 1906 1907 1908 1909 1910

Source: *Report of the U.S. Commissioner of Corporations on the Tobacco Industry*, Vol. 3, Washington, 1915.

Figure 18-1. American Tobacco Company Market Shares, 1900-1910

The American Tobacco Company soon matched its domestic dominance with a series of stunning expansions abroad. Manufacturing plants sprung up in Australia (1894), Canada (1895), Japan (1899), and West Germany (1901). As a result of the Spanish-American War (1898), the ATC gained hegemony over the market in Cuba, Puerto Rico, and the Philippines. But establishing these market beachheads was merely a prelude to the greatest invasion of all: entry into the United Kingdom, then the nation with the world's highest standard of living and the country that controlled access to the inner recesses of the British Empire.

During the 1890s, British tobacco magnates (notably Lord Wilkes) began making plans to resist Duke's expected onslaught, and finally welded thirteen independent tobacco companies into the Imperial Tobacco Company in response to the threat he posed. But the battle that might have occurred between ITC and ATC was avoided by a corporate "treaty" out of which the British-American Tobacco Company was formed on September 27, 1902. The tobacco market had been divided in "a deal with British manufacturers covering the world," as Buck Duke, the chairman of the new BAT board, put it. Duke had fully grasped the marketing implications of vertical integration pioneered by Standard Oil: "If John D. Rockefeller can do what he is doing in oil, why should I not do it in tobacco?"[2] Indeed, Standard Oil provided the technical, inspirational, and managerial blueprint for the buildup of the ATC, and its leadership graced the membership of the ATC board of directors.

In 1911, during the trust-busting era, the U.S. Supreme Court broke up the portion of the worldwide tobacco monopoly operating in the United States. But the court-ordered divestiture could not quell ATC's predatory marketing practices nor drastically alter corporate destinies. Although no single tobacco conglomerate has ever controlled the market quite like the ATC once did, the model for today's TTCs was created during the trust-building period. Brief descriptions of how five of the major tobacco companies have recently grown into transnational conglomerates will be presented here. (For a more detailed history of the major American tobacco companies, see chapter 15.)

Selected TTC Profiles

R.J. Reynolds

In 1970, a new holding company, R.J. Reynolds Industries, was spawned, with the Reynolds Tobacco Company becoming a fully owned subsidiary. The new holding company was not, as a company report explained, "a sign of decreasing interest in our tobacco enterprises. Rather, it is a sign that our diverse subsidiary interests have matured to the stage where they stand as fully-fledged members along with tobacco." Adopting "an unrestricted approach towards diversification, Reynolds moved into entirely new areas, shipping and petroleum on the theory that it made sense, when appropriate, to apply cash to any strong well-established business."[3] It would be difficult, in the world of corporate literature, to unearth a more concise rationale of conglomerate annexationism.

The unfolding of successive phases of R.J. Reynolds tobacco-market penetration can be traced to the early 1960s when Reynolds acquired Haus Neuerburg,[4] one of the leading cigarette producers in the Federal Republic of Germany. Systematic acquisition of foreign enterprises led to the setting up of R.J. Reynolds (Europe) as a subsidiary for operating within the framework of the European Economic Community (EEC) and the European Free Trade Association (EFTA), as well as for managing corporate interests in Africa and the Middle East. In 1972, with the further growth of international operations, a new market reorganization resulted in the emergence of the Geneva-based R.J. Reynolds Tobacco International S.A., with regional extensions in Hong Kong, Rio de Janeiro, and Beirut. In 1970, the Macdonald Tobacco Company of Canada (with 22 percent of the Canadian market) became the exclusive Canadian distributor of R.J. Reynolds's cigarettes, and in 1974, it became a wholly owned subsidiary. In short order, Reynolds also bought out the Simon Cigar Company, Canada's second biggest cigar manufacturer. (With the acquisition of Macdonald's, Canada's cigarette industry is now dominated by three non-Canadian TTCs: Imasco, a joint holding company of BAT and Imperial; R.J. Reynolds; and Rothmans.) Finally, a greater stress on centralization of decision making resulted in a new subsidiary—R.J. Reynolds Tobacco Company International, Incorporated, headquartered in Winston-Salem, North Carolina, the decisional power center of Reynolds Industries.

The Reynolds breakthrough in the oligopolistic food industry has been even more stunning, with annual sales of its food subsidiary jumping from $30 million in the mid-sixties to $1,962 million in 1979. However, corporate strategy dictated further aggrandizement of an already large agri-business concern. "What the R.J.R. food company needs, Reynolds executives believe, is not only new blood in the management tasks but some new products that can probably best be bought from outside—and which would give the operation the 'critical mass' to come up against bigger competitors like Pillsbury in the national markets," wrote *Business Week* in 1977.[5]

That "critical mass" has been satisfied—momentarily—by the annexation of Del Monte (one of the world's agri-business leviathans and a hegemonic force in the world banana economy) for $618 million in February 1979.[6] Del Monte and its own subsidiaries produce and market more than 250 canned, dried, snack, and frozen foods for the world's major consumer markets. This food subsidiary of Reynolds also operates its own refrigerated vessels to ship its bananas from Central America to U.S. and Japanese ports; engages in dry and refrigerated trucking and warehouse operations; manages several hundred cafeterias; and provides vending, building maintenance, and security services to a range of institutional clients.

To smash into the world shipping market, an overall market that tops $100 billion yearly, Reynolds acquired the world's largest containerized-freight operation, the Sea-Land Service (innovator of this revolutionary mode of transportation) for $530 million. After acquiring Sea-Land, it bought out the American Independent Oil Company (Aminoil) in a move apparently geared to meet the full fuel demands of its new fleet. Aminoil's main source of fuel oil, thus far, has been the divided zone between Kuwait, Saudi Arabia, and Iran, where it participated in the Iranian consortium. Onshore and offshore explorations are also underway on the Atlantic and Pacific coasts, Gulf of Alaska, Gulf of Mexico, North Sea, and off Paraguay, Guatemala, Spain, and Indonesia.[7]

Philip Morris

In 1979, Philip Morris could rightly boast about its success as a conglomerate. It controlled 29 percent of the U.S. cigarette market, 6 percent of international tobacco sales, 21 percent of U.S. beer consumption, and 7 percent of the U.S. soft-drink market.[8] Philip Morris has also expanded its market in Europe, the Middle East, and Africa, relying primarily on annexation of national cigarette companies, plant expansion, and licensing agreements through which a TTC sells or licenses its brands to a state monopoly or CPE. In Eastern Europe and China, TTC licensing policies have become a multimillion-dollar market. Consumer attraction for TTC brands in the CPEs is immense, owing to emulation of capitalist modes of consumption and the tourist industry. The PM brand produced in Moscow now accounts for 1.4 percent of quality cigarette markets in the Soviet Union; in Italy, where a state tobacco monopoly exists, the TTCs have carved out over a third of the market, with PM's share of that being almost three quarters. PM has set up manufacturing subsidiaries and entered into licensing agreements where tariff barriers precluded United States exports. PM's Marlboro brand has now acquired an important foothold in the socialist countries of Eastern Europe. In Bulgaria, for example, both PM and Reynolds receive royalties of 50 to 55 cents per 1,000 cigarettes, a yield of some $2 million per year.

The PM industrial division embraces food, packaging materials, chemicals, paper, and other industrial products. Its principal companies are: Milprint, Incorporated, a packaging company whose products are used for snack foods, candy, coffee, processed meat, and dry processed goods; Nicolet Paper Company, a maker of technical and specialty paper; Polymer Industries, Incorporated, a manufacturer of specialty adhesive and textile chemicals; the Wikalin Polymer Chemie BmbH in the Federal Republic of Germany; and the Koch Label Company, a specialized printer. And PM has entered the land-development business, acquiring, for example, the Mission Viejo Company in southern California, a real-estate and home-building corporation.

The staggering growth of PM's national and international cigarette business has been matched by its equally weighty conglomerate extensions into beer and beverages. When Philip Morris annexed Miller Brewing Company in 1970, there were 92 beer producers in the United States; by 1979, there were only 41. From a seventh-place ranking in 1972, Miller jumped to second (after Anheuser-Busch) in the industry by the onset of the 1980s. And in the nonalcoholic-beverage field, Philip Morris shattered all its previous takeover records by purchasing the Seven-Up Company for $520 million. Philip Morris now joins such global conglomerates as Pepsi-Cola and Coca-Cola as a leader of the soft-drink trade.

Gulf and Western

Consolidated Cigar, owned by Gulf and Western, controls about one-third of the U.S. cigar market and sells its Spanish, Dutch, and American cigars in some 100 countries, making it one of the world's leading cigar corporations. Although a power in the cigar market, Consolidated Cigar is but a ripple in the corporate ocean of Gulf and Western, which exemplifies par excellence the growth of conglomerate power over the last twenty years. From 1958 to 1979, its overall sales rocketed from $8.4 *million* to more than $5 *billion,* and its labor force grew from a mere 500 workers to more than 100,000. By 1979, this giant ranked fifty-second on the *Fortune* 500 list.

Gulf and Western structures its multimillion-dollar corporation into major product groups: (1) leisure time; (2) financial services; (3) consumer and agricultural products; (4) apparel products; (5) paper and building products; (6) automotive replacement parts; (7) manufacturing; and (8) natural resources. An inventory of only one product category discloses the ubiquity of Gulf and Western. The leisure group, for example, includes Paramount Pictures; the Madison Square Garden Corporation; Paramount Television; Cinema International Corporation (which is the international marketing arm of Paramount, Universal, and Metro-Goldwyn-Mayer); Paramount's Famous Music Corporation (which publishes and promotes songs and sheet music); Famous Players Limited (which operates about 235 theaters with nearly 400 screens in Canada and some 35 theaters with more than 60 screens in France); and Simon and Schuster, one of the world's leading publishers. The scale of Gulf and Western's diversification is clearly delineated in plantation agriculture (notably sugar) where it is one of the biggest corporate landowners in the Americas. In the Dominican Republic alone, its landholdings encompass 11 percent of the arable area.

The British Duo

With total 1979 sales exceeding 7.2 billion pounds,[9] the British-American Tobacco Company remains the world's tobacco giant and third largest British industrial corporation (after British Petroleum and Unilever). From BAT's beginning in 1902, it has had certain common interlocks with the Imperial Tobacco Company, primarily through joint ownership in several corporate bodies. (As late as 1960, the ITC held about 28 percent of BAT's ordinary stock.) In 1972, a formal spheres-of-influence agreement between BAT and ITC was alleged to have been terminated, but even then, in the words of BAT's chairman, BAT and ITC intended by "all legal means, to arrange our affairs so that we don't compete with each other with identical brands in the same market." And the two companies continue to engage in intimate corporate relations, including joint ownership roles in Imasco in Canada, the Molins Machine Company, and Mardon's Packaging International.

As with other tobacco conglomerates, the Imperial Tobacco Company (with more than 60 percent of the U.K. cigarette market) is swiftly diversifying into food and beverages. One of its largest annexations, the U.K. Courage Brewing group in 1972, was a decisive step into retailing as well as brewing and wholesaling. Its six manufacturing divisions include poultry, poultry breeding and eggs, frozen foods, fish, potato chips, and other varied product lines. The 1978 takeover of the J.B. Eastwood eggs and poultry group (38 million pounds) gives ITC a third of the U.K. broiler-chicken market and leadership in the egg and turkey markets. The ITC's latest coup was its purchase of Howard Johnson (one of the biggest U.S. restaurant and motel chains) for $630 million cash.

Mechanisms of Corporate Power

Conglomeration

With such oligopolistic structures, no single index can describe the pervasive influence of these TTCs on market behavior, nor can any conventional economic measure really define their reach. The TTC's commodity-product boundaries have become blurred because they represent such a broad range of markets. Tobacco-industry conglomerates now straddle most of the modern industrial spectrum and have tentacles reaching into transportation, services, and plantation agriculture. A sample list of "member" industries reveals the staggering ubiquity of tobacco conglomeration: pulp and paper, paperboard, folding cartons, book matches, alcoholic and distilled beverages, department stores and supermarkets, cosmetics, toiletries, insurance and financial services, pipeline construction, refinery and chemical construction, oil and gas drilling equipment, automotive and aviation spare parts, public-safety control systems, industrial-process control systems, metalworking presses, molded plastics, iron and steel castings, heat-transfer components, construction and building products, dog food, raw and refined cane sugar, transportation and distribution of bananas, citrus fruits and vegetables, mining enterprising (covering titanium, chrome, iron ore, uranium, coal, gold, platinum, asbestos, manganese, fluorspar, and zinc), petroleum exploration, oil refining and marketing, breweries, food industry, optical goods and services, real estate, residential construction, cinema films, television, entertainment, records, textiles and apparel, watchmaking, and proprietary drugs. There are others even now, and, ineluctably, the product range of annexations seems likely to continue expanding in the future.

Cross-Subsidization

In the last twenty years, these summits of conglomeration within the cigarette industry have utilized cross-subsidization to an unprecedented degree. They have deployed masses of capital from one profit center to another to acquire essentially unfettered control over other industries. "When the system becomes global," write Barnett and Müller, "the parent company can shift profits through transfer pricing, 'profit loan swaps' and other accounting miracles on a world-wide scale, cross-subsidizing its various operations with the profits of others."[10] Centralization and concentration of capital are therefore not adventitious but endemic to the system. Thus, at a certain point in time the profit centers, as they are corporately designated, fuse to become mutually self-reinforcing. Survival of an oligopolistic conglomerate is thus predicated on management's unwavering commitment to infinite expansion exemplified in ever-larger market shares.

As with many other corporate financial transactions, cross-subsidization is carried out in the closed boardrooms of highly secretive conglomerates and is thus extremely difficult to pinpoint. Even so, one can gain a full appreciation of the impact of cross-subsidization by viewing the results of Philip Morris's takeover of the Miller Brewing Company in 1970.[11]

Employing the traditional marketing muscle of the cigarette industry, and with net profits two and a half times the brewing industry's leader, the Philip Morris approach called for slicing up the U.S. beer market into demand segments, generating new products and packages specifically for these segments, and then, as a Philip Morris spokesman put it, "spending with abandon to produce them." In 1979 alone, PM allocated more than $1.3 billion to Miller plant expansion, almost six times the original acquisition price of $227 million. The bulk of these investments flowed from tobacco profits. In other words, every smoker who purchased a Philip Morris brand was subsidizing the market aggrandizement of Miller beer through cross-subsidization. In 1976, *Business Week* predicted what this process could mean: "This is bound to create such overcapacity plus heated competition that the numbers of brewers could be reduced from 49 today to 15 by 1980, putting almost 90 percent of the market into the hands of five companies."[12]

Appropriation of Technology

Another keystone of the arch of the TTCs, and subsequently the world tobacco-manufacturing oligopoly, was the dazzling technical stride between 1881 and 1905, with the inevitable drop in the labor force. In one day, the first Bonsack machine could produce as many cigarettes as could 488 skilled workers. In the 1870s, labor costs were around 96 cents per thousand cigarettes; by the mid-nineties, the figure had shriveled to 8 cents. In the early 1890s, ATC acquired a controlling interest in the Bonsack Machine Company, the first in an impressive series of conquests of other leading tobacco-engineering firms. But the technological distance traversed can best be glimpsed in the development of the Molins cigarette machines. A corporation partially owned by BAT and ITC, Molins produces almost all of the world's packaging and automatic machinery for manufacturing cigarettes. By 1976, the Mark-9 Molins machine was producing more than 5,000 cigarettes per minute (see table 18-3).

Accordingly, the technological pacesetters of the industry have generated ever-larger economies of scale, directly contributing to boosting capital concentration. In the United States, for example, capital invested in tobacco manufacturing per production worker in 1972 was $108,300. This figure amounted to more than twice the average of all manufacturing industry, outpaced only by the petroleum industry.

The industry's highly capital-intensive nature is epitomized by the striking productivity advances in Sweden. The Swedish experience illustrates the worldwide pattern—a growing reliance on fewer workers to produce more cigarettes (see table 18-4).

Table 18-3
Cigarettes: Trends in Machine Output, 1881-1976

Manufacturer	Year	Model	Output per Minute (number)
Bonsack	1881	Original	200
Bonsack	1899	Revised	500
Molins	1927	Mark 1	1,000
Molins	1951	Mark 5	1,250
Molins	1955	Mark 6	1,600
Molins	1972	Mark 8	3,000
Molins	1976	Mark 9	5,000

Source: Trade sources.

Finance Capital

In addition to its technological underpinnings, the irrepressible annexation-ist momentum of the tobacco conglomerates was made possible by global working relations between financial institutions and the tobacco industry. TTCs cannot be viewed as entities wholly separate from the larger banks, particularly the seven huge New York banks, the British "Big Four," and the major European financial institutions. The chairman of Bankers Trust and the senior executive vice-president of Citibank sit on Philip Morris's board of directors. Archie Davis, former chairman of the board of Wacho-via Bank and Trust Company, is a member of R.J. Reynolds's international advisory board, as are the chairmen of the Deutsche Bank, Banca Commer-ciale Italiana, and Mitsubishi. BAT's chairman is a director of the West-minister Bank. Edmund L. de Rothschild is an institutional shareholder and

Table 18-4
Sweden: Labor Force and Productivity in the Cigarette Industry, 1916-1976

Year	Number of Workers in Cigarette Production		Output per Worker (1,000 Pieces)	
		Index (1916 = 100)		Index (1916 = 100)
1916	641	100	1,098	100
1940	464	72	4,640	423
1950	448	70	8,672	790
1960	447	70	14,181	1,292
1970	395	62	22,722	2,069
1976	481	75	23,447	2,135

Source: Trade sources.

a member of the board of directors of Rothmans International, and in 1976, he joined the board of the Rembrandt/Rothmans's combine.

This welding of industrial and finance capital gives the TTCs massive financial leverage, allowing R.J. Reynolds, for example, to acquire two corporations worth well over $1 billion in a very short time span. As an executive officer of the Dresdner Bank describes the process: "It is banks who are in the best position to decide the question of mergers."

Recognition of this interdependence does not imply that the banks control the conglomerates in their managerial and marketing operations. In 1973, U.S. Congressman Wright Patman explained how finance capital provided the stimulus for conglomeration.

> One of the favorite pastimes of concentrated financial power is promoting concentration in non-financial industries. There is substantial evidence that the major commercial banks have been actively fueling the corporate merger movement. A 1971 congressional report for example, found that the major banks financed acquisitions, furnished key financial personnel to conglomerates, and were even willing to clean stock from their trust departments to aid in takeover bids. Thus Gulf and Western, one of the most aggressive conglomerates of the 1950s and 1960s (92 acquisitions involving almost a billion dollars in eleven years) expanded hand in glove with Chase Manhattan. Friendly representatives of Chase made funds available and provided advice that assisted Gulf and Western in its acquisitions. In return, in addition to the customary business charges for Gulf and Western's accounts and loans, Chase secured banking business generated by the newly developing conglomerate that formerly had gone to other banks, and was recipient of advance inside information on proposed future acquisitions.[13]

In 1971, banks held more than 25 percent of Philip Morris's equity shares, and three—Chase Manhattan, Citibank, and Morgan—held 13 percent. Bank holdings made up more than 18 percent of R.J. Reynolds's outstanding equity shares, and the Wachovia Bank and Trust Company had about 7 percent.[14] The imperatives of expansion make self-financing an unsound economic proposition, especially for TTCs. Successful production of cigarettes requires tobacco aged two to three years; consequently, a sizable proportion of the TTCs' tangible assets is tied up in inventories.

Intracorporate interlocks between the giant transnational banks and industrial conglomerates are a familiar trait of the corporate landscape. In the 1960s, about four-fifths of U.S. manufacturing operations in Latin America were financed by domestic capital. For the TTCs during this period, 90 percent of their aggregate investments in Latin America were financed by domestic capital siphoned through the transnational banking structure. Sri Lanka, perhaps, offers the extreme example of how transnational banks affect a country's development. Indeed, BAT's Sri Lanka enclave operations and the power that they wield bear comparison with that of the United Fruit Company in Honduras.[15]

Advertising and the Payoff Complex

Another central pillar of the TTCs' edifice and a formidable barrier to entry is advertising and its corollary, the "payoff complex." The momentum of cross-subsidization is inseparable from these equally arresting changes in the realm of communications ideology. Consequently, TTCs are in control of three vital, interacting components of market power: industrial technology; finance capital; and the hypersophisticated technology of consumer manipulation vulgarized under the designation of marketing techniques. Global advertising costs of the TTCs were $1.8 billion in 1976, and are now well over $2 billion a year and rising rapidly. Moreover, official pronouncements on advertising outlays are at best highly misleading if not wholly mendacious, in view of "transfer pricing" techniques (see appendix at the end of the chapter for an explanation of this term). The sheer magnitude of advertising muscle demanded can be gauged by the fact that the cost of launching a new brand is around $80 to $100 million.

In the struggle for ever-larger market shares, TTCs have drawn not only on mass advertising's ideological encroachment but also on global corporate payoffs involving tens of millions of dollars. The U.S. Securities and Exchange Commission (SEC) and other federal agencies have uncovered dubious tax deductions, rebates, and payments to domestic and foreign politicians as a component of advertising and corporate practice. The payoffs of R.J. Reynolds alone over five years (1970-1975) exceeded $19 million in illegal rebates (by its shipping subsidiary) to shippers, consignees, and forwarding agents. Its tobacco subsidiaries made another $5.4 million in questionable payments as a marketing booster. Reynolds also acknowledged using $190,000 in corporate funds to promote U.S. congressional and presidential candidates between 1968 and 1973. The total of these questionable payments amounted to more than $24.5 million.[16]

Philip Morris has also relied on corporate payoffs.[17] In its 1976 10-K report to the SEC, Philip Morris indicated that "questionable payments" of $2.4 million were made by the parent company and its subsidiaries from 1971 to 1975. Also, the director of a Philip Morris subsidiary declared that his company made payoffs in a Latin American state to all major political parties and particularly to the party in power. The corporate rationale, in the view of the director, was that "such payoffs are necessary for corporate survival and profitability," and "that payoffs were essential to get favorable legislation enacted."[18]

Future Prospects

As the global capitalist economy enters a decade of mounting uncertainty, the TTCs are formulating strategies for further corporate aggrandizement.

Given the decelerated tempo of tobacco consumption in the United States (which has dropped about 11 percent since 1963 and is expected to continue to fall at about 2 percent yearly), the TTCs are launching international assaults of unprecedented intensity. In the case of R.J. Reynolds, for example, domestic tobacco sales grew by 35 percent between 1975 and 1979, while international sales soared 93 percent.[19] Likewise, Philip Morris chalked up a 31-percent annual growth rate in its 1979 West German market barrage. And the TTCs are now attempting to gain some control of China's massive market. Such onslaughts will be stepped up not only in the developed countries but also in the third world.

Competition for larger market shares will continue to figure at the top of the corporate agenda, but at the same time, corporate collusion may become even more conspicuous. Portents of these changes can be seen in the 1980 collective corporate promotion of containerized shipping by the top United Kingdom TTCs, as well as in the collective counteroffensives against regulatory agencies in the United States and elsewhere by the phalanx of TTC power. In this constellation of collusion, the remaining smaller tobacco corporations will be either driven into bankruptcy or simply annexed by the TTCs. And the drive toward conglomeration with the blazing of new marketing vistas for nontobacco products will become even more pronounced in the 1980s.

Evolution of the political economy of tobacco is, of course, not unique. Its historic trends, global dominance by a handful of transnational conglomerates, and relegation of peripheral economies to a dubious, dependent relationship under TTC hegemony are common to a majority of the twenty-five-odd commodities that dominate nonpetroleum exports from the underdeveloped capitalist countries. Likewise, the TTCs are not unique, but typical, in: (1) effectively creating barriers to new entrants; (2) actively not competing in price with each other; (3) generating massive surplus cash flows; (4) cross-subsidizing to boost new product lines; and (5) building up mutual self-reinforcing relations with other transnational conglomerate corporations. In the remaining decades of our century, the TTCs will represent the ultimate stage in the development of oligopolistic capitalism.

Notes

1. The holding company: "Any company, incorporated or unincorporated, which is in a position to control, or materially to influence, the management of one or more other companies by virtue, in part at least, of its ownership of securities in the other company or companies." See T.C. Bonbright and G.C. Means, *The Holding Company: Its Public Significance and Its Regulation,* reprint (New York: Kelley, 1969), p.10. The state of

New Jersey was the birthplace of the modern holding company when, in 1888, it added to its stock corporation law provisions for a corporation articled in the state to include in its charter the specific power to hold stocks in other corporations. The impact of this legislative innovation on the dynamics of capital accumulation was that it entailed economic consequences that have "seldom been equalled in the entire history of business legislation." Ibid., p. 337.

2. Quoted in his obituary in *The New York Times,* October 11, 1925.

3. R.J. Reynolds, *Our 100th Anniversary, 1875-1975* (Winston-Salem, 1975). For the unfolding of this development see Reavis Cox, *Competition in the American Tobacco Industry,* 1911-1932 (N.Y.: Columbia University Press, 1933), and N.M. Tilley, *"History of the R.J. Reynolds Tobacco Co.,"* unpublished (Commerce, Texas, 1976).

4. The name has been changed to R.J. Reynolds GmbH.

5. *Business Week,* January 17, 1977. At that time, a committee had been galvanized to examine potentially appropriate takeover candidates.

6. UNCTAD, *Marketing and Distribution System for Bananas,* TD/B/C.1/162, 1977. With financial leverage that is immensely greater than United Brands and Castle and Cooke, it has the clout to become, in quick order, the hegemonic force in the world banana economy.

7. In one year (1974), petroleum earnings jumped from 10 to 31 percent of total Reynolds sales.

8. Presentation to the Los Angeles Society of Financial Analysts, by Ross Millhiser, vice-chairman of the board of Philip Morris, New York, March 13, 1980, p. 6.

9. See British-American Tobacco Company's annual report, London, 1979.

10. R.J. Barnet and R.E. Müller, *Global Reach: The Power of the Multinational Corporations* (New York: Simon and Schuster, 1974), pp. 255-256.

11. U.S. Senate, Hearings before the Subcommittee on Antitrust and Monopoly of the Committee on the Judiciary, U.S. Senate, 95th Congress, 2nd session, on acquisitions and mergers by conglomerates of unrelated businesses, May 21-September 21, 1978, (Washington, D.C.: U.S. Government Printing Office, 1978), pp. 57-123.

12. *Business Week,* November 8, 1976. The five are Anheuser-Busch, Miller, Schlitz, Pabst, and Coors.

13. "Other People's Money," *The New Republic,* February 17, 1973.

14. The strategems deployed by banks to conceal the amplitude of corporate holdings from regulators have been done through a maze of multiple nominees. A pioneer U.S. Senate Committee report commented that "the consequence of this continuing use of nominees in ownership reports to Federal regulators is a massive cover-up of the extent to which holdings of

stock have become concentrated in the hands of very few institutional investors, especially banks." *Disclosures of Corporate Ownership,* prepared by the U.S. Congress, House Banking and Currency Subcommittee on Intergovernmental Relations, and Budgeting, Management, and Expenditures, 93rd Congress, 2nd session, March 4, 1974 (Washington, D.C.: U.S. Government Printing Office, 1974), p. 5.

15. Father Tissa Balasuriya, "Our Multinationals," *Ceylon Daily News,* March 25, 1976. Also Balasuriya, "Ceylon Tobacco Co.," *Logos* 15, no. 1 (1976). In 1968, a former United Fruit Company chairman articulated: "There remains the question of the political impact of a large world corporation in a country such as Honduras. The United Fruit Company, for example, last year provided 11.2 percent of the country's taxes, 6 percent of its foreign exchange and 6.98 percent of its gross national product. It would be foolish to pretend that the company is without influence in Honduras." Chairman H. Cornuelle, "The Enormous Future: An Outline to the Challenge of the Multinational Corporation," *United Fruit Company Annual Report 1968.* He goes on: "Among the most important reasons for the internationalization of the multinational corporation is to increase its utility in the developing world of Latin America, Asia and Africa. Its role in the development process becomes more urgently clear every day, as we witness the limitations and handicaps of local governments. . . . Even if local governments were strong and assistance to them plentiful, the fact is that the enormous complexities of the development process require abilities and attributes which are as natural to the multinational corporation as they are unnatural to government." This last utterance is at once the implicit and explicit justification of transnational hegemonism and the internationalization of capital.

16. *Wall Street Journal,* September 13, 1976.

17. UNCTAD, *Marketing and Distribution of Tobacco,* TD/B/C.1/205, 1978, p. 24.

18. Ibid.

19. R.J. Reynolds, 10-K report, December 31, 1979.

Appendix 18A: Definitions

Conglomerate A corporation generally consisting of a holding company and a group of subsidiaries engaged in unrelated economic activities. Expansion of conglomerates takes place through mergers and take-overs. Such diversification allows the conglomerate to survive periods of losses in certain product lines by profits earned in other divisions.

Cross-Subsidization A familiar practice of conglomerates whereby profits from one product line are used to subsidize the price of another below the level of long-term total costs. This is an ideal marketing device to enhance market shares in a given sector by underpricing competitors.

Oligopoly Defines a market structure characterized by dominance of a handful of firms, whose corporate and pricing policies are coordinated via such mechanisms as pricing policies that deviate from those which might prevail under more competitive conditions; various collusive practices; and a multiplicity of effective barriers against other firms aspiring to enter the sector.

Transfer Pricing This technique refers to prices assigned by transnational corporations (TNCs) to the transfer of goods, services, technology, or loans between their related enterprises in various countries. By shifting figures on their subsidiaries' accounts, TNCs can avoid the pitfalls of certain countries' high corporate tax rates, government price controls, currency devaluations, and other government actions that attempt to regulate TNCs.

Transnational Corporation (TNC) Any corporation (industrial, agricultural, trading, or any combination of these) whose corporate subsidiaries or economic transactions straddle more than one country. These corporations range in size from sales of a few million dollars to Exxon's 1979 global sales of $84 billion.

221-228

19 Labor Displacement in Tobacco Manufacturing: Some Policy Considerations

Elizabeth Tornquist

A steady decline in the number of tobacco manufacturing jobs during the last decade has thrown people out of work and reduced the presence of the industry in towns like Petersburg and Richmond, Virginia, Louisville, Kentucky, and Durham, North Carolina. In North Carolina, the nation's leading tobacco manufacturing state, the number of workers declined from 31,850 in 1965 to 25,100 in 1979, a 21-percent decline in 14 years.[1] The reduced work force has resulted from three types of corporate actions—attrition, gradual layoffs, and plant closings. The declines could accelerate in the future as the prospering companies depend to a greater degree on mechanization and those with a declining share of the market have to reduce their work forces to make fewer cigarettes.

Whether through attrition, a series of layoffs, or plant closings, tobacco manufacturing workers face a future of diminishing opportunities. Some mechanisms exist that can help in the plant-closing situation. The Bakery, Confectionary, and Tobacco Workers International Union (BC&TWIU) represents tobacco workers in several places where layoffs and plant closings have occurred. The standard BC&TWIU contract provides that a six-month notice be given to workers prior to a plant closing and that severance pay be given (usually, one week's pay for each year of service). In addition, some companies have taken the initiative of notifying workers and the community about layoffs and have provided various kinds of assistance to displaced workers, both through liberal severance arrangements and through help to employees in finding new work.

But relying on union contracts or on a company's initiatives may not result in adequate economic planning for communities where tobacco plants are located. Union contracts do not require notices for layoffs, and companies that are not unionized are not obligated to give any kind of notice. Providing job retraining programs or other aids to displaced workers may be beyond the range of options for a declining company. And if tobacco workers suddenly become unemployed with no assistance from the company, they will have to turn to the public sector for help.

In the auto, steel, and rubber industries, large-scale layoffs attract publicity and at least the possibility of governmental assistance. But layoffs in cigarette manufacturing have been and will continue to be more gradual

221

and hence less visible. This is especially true in the Sunbelt where most cigarette plants are located and where economic developers focus on expanding sectors, such as microelectronics, instead of industries with a declining work force, like tobacco manufacturing. Consequently, current public policies address economic displacement in a limited and fragmented way.

"We Had Built Beyond Our Needs"

Both industry leaders and other companies are using fewer workers now than in recent years. Philip Morris and R.J. Reynolds, while expanding their operations, are relying on more sophisticated technology, not on ever larger work forces. In the early decades of this century, the cigarette-rolling Bonsack machine displaced large numbers of workers. Many plants built in that era are today considered obsolete, and another wave of automation is sweeping through the industry. The oldest Reynolds facilities in operation, for example, use machines capable of producing about 2,000 cigarettes a minute; rollers in its newest plants turn out some 4,000 to 5,000 a minute; and machines now on the drawing board will produce some 8,000 cigarettes a minute, nearly twice as much output per machine as the best Reynolds model now in use. In September 1980, Edward Horrigan, Jr., chairman and president of R.J. Reynolds's Tobacco Division, announced a ten-year, $1 billion capital improvement plan. He said that Reynolds expects to retain all of its current full-time workers, but that the newer machines will gradually reduce the number of employees needed: "As we move to more sophisticated equipment over the years, attrition will take care of that."[2]

Companies that have not kept pace with the leaders—from third-place Brown and Williamson to last-place Liggett and Myers—have contributed to the industrywide worker decline in a more serious way than through attrition. In the early 1970s, Brown and Williamson's share of the domestic market was increasing faster than the industry rate, and it launched an expansion and capital improvement program with a new facility in Macon, Georgia. Company vice-president Carroll Teague, in testimony before a U.S. Senate committee hearing on plant closings, described what happened next:

> Then came the downturn. In 1973, our rate of growth declined. By 1975, our market share was decreasing at an accelerating rate. . . . We had built beyond our needs. We had two multi-floor plants that were some forty years old. . . . We had one single-floor, ultra-modern operation with unparalleled production capabilities. . . . Macon [Georgia] had to become Brown and Williamson's primary manufacturing facility. Louisville [Kentucky] operations would have to be phased out, Petersburg's [Virginia] reduced.[3]

The way in which Brown and Williamson closed its Louisville plant and reduced its Petersburg work force is considered a model by many. "I've never heard of a company in the United States providing better benefits and protections for its workers in a plant closing situation," said Ross Eisenbrey, legislative counsel to Representative William Ford (Democrat, Michigan). Ford is the principal sponsor of the National Employment Priorities Act which addresses plant-closing issues. In his testimony before the Senate committee, Teague described how the company's planning for closure was guided by the principles of advance notification and gradual reduction of work force. The company's union contract provided for eighteen months of advance notice for plant closure, and Brown and Williamson reduced its work force over a three-year period rather than laying off everyone at once. The closure settlement negotiated with the unions included severance pay that went up to fifty-six weeks of pay for a worker with thirty years of service, and life and medical insurance continuation for up to six months after a worker leaves the company. Workers were also assisted in moving to Macon, if they chose to do so; if they stayed in Louisville, they were given an option to participate in a profit-sharing arrangement during the year of severance. Finally, the company provided a number of programs to assist workers in finding new jobs, including the following:

mailings to companies throughout the state, announcing the closure and the availability of the company's workers

contracting with the state and local boards of education to conduct high-school classroom training, leading to the high-school equivalency degree

retraining some groups of workers, such as the highly skilled making and packing machine adjusters, for new jobs

working with the union to get the Kentucky State Unemployment Compensation Commission to revise its rules to allow employees receiving severance benefits as a result of a plant closing to receive unemployment benefits as well.

The Brown and Williamson initiatives, however, are the exception, not the rule. A cigarette company with a declining volume of trade usually presents an optimistic viewpoint of the company's future in order to retain smoker loyalty rather than admitting difficulties so that workers can plan ahead. Consequently, when layoffs come, they are usually sudden and unexpected. The most dramatic example of this pattern is the Liggett and Myers experience.

"It's No Secret They Want Out"

In 1970, with its share of the U.S. cigarette market in a sharp decline, Liggett and Myers closed one of its two major manufacturing facilities, the plant in Richmond, Virginia. Some 250 of the Richmond employees were transferred to the company's Durham, North Carolina, operation, and the other 850 received one week's pay for each year of work as severance compensation. Nine years later, 410 of Liggett and Myers's remaining 2,000 employees were also laid off, and those retained went to a reduced, four-day work week. Then in 1980, when Liggett's share of the U.S. trade had plummeted to below 3 percent, Grand Metropolitan, Limited, a British hotel, gambling, and liquor conglomerate, bought up all Liggett stock. In 1981, the gates at the remaining Liggett and Myers facilities in Durham might well be closed for good, putting some 1,500 more people out of work. (See chapter 15 for a full corporate profile of Liggett and Myers.)

Even before the Grand Metropolitan takeover, tobacco analysts speculated that Liggett might get out of the cigarette business. By 1969, Liggett and Myers had a higher percentage of its total business in nontobacco lines than any other U.S. cigarette producer. In 1979, the same year it made the Durham layoffs, it reduced its leaf inventory by 33 percent from the 1978 level, from $160 million in inventory to $106 million. And also in 1979, the company cut back its advertising budget for cigarettes. "Now they're letting their marketing and advertising man go," said analyst Jane Gilday in September 1979. "It's no secret they want out of the tobacco business."

In spite of accumulating evidence that Liggett and Myers is moving toward closing its Durham plants, as of May 1981, the company had given no warning of upcoming layoffs. The company keeps up the appearance of continuing indefinitely: smokers who know that their favorite brand will disappear in six months are likely to make the switch to another without waiting. Unless Grand Metropolitan takes a different tact than have past Liggett and Myers officials, the company is unlikely to announce plans to reduce its work force further until the time has come to do so. Information about impending closure is not likely to come voluntarily from Liggett and Myers either, and only six-months notice is required by the union contract. There will be little time for workers or government agencies to plan for new unemployment should Liggett and Myers go out of the tobacco business.

Advance Notice—A Prerequisite to Planning

The major hardships from more layoffs by Liggett and Myers or from a plant closing will fall on the company's remaining 1,500 employees, about 1,100 of whom are in production and make one of the highest hourly wages in the state. (In November 1980, tobacco-manufacturing workers in North Carolina made an average of $9.72 an hour, compared with the overall manufacturing average of $5.59 an hour.)

Sales, clerical, research, and management personnel might find other positions, but Liggett and Myers workers had relatively specialized jobs requiring skills that are not easy to transfer. If the company closes, most of its production workers will have to find lower-paying jobs or move away. Since the 1979 layoffs were based on seniority, none of the production workers let go then had worked at Liggett and Myers for more than eight years; most were in their thirties or younger, an age when looking for a new job is not yet extremely difficult. Not so for the remaining employees: they tend to be older and have worked at Liggett and Myers longer, some for nearly all their working lives. If the plant closes, the costs to these individuals, both financial and psychological, will be high.

Although there are a number of community agencies to aid the unemployed, most of the Liggett and Myers production workers who may lose their jobs will receive little effective relief from the programs currently in place. The Employment Security Commission (ESC), the first line of relief, can provide six months of unemployment benefits once severance pay runs out and can tell individuals about other jobs that are open locally and around the state. The ESC can also undertake "job development"—that is, when a good applicant comes in, the staff can call an employer who uses similar skills and try to develop a job.

Job development would be much easier with advance notice of major layoffs, for then the ESC could let companies know when workers would become available and what their skills are. The Research Triangle is one of North Carolina's fastest growing areas, and although manufacturing is no longer as important in the area as government and research sectors, new manufacturing companies are moving in, especially in electronics and electrical machinery. But the possibility of matching the employment needs of these new industries with the skills of cigarette-manufacturing workers who lose their jobs has not yet been explored by ESC personnel. With advance notice of layoffs, not only could companies be informed about the upcoming availability of individual workers, but group retraining programs for the employees would be possible if a new company needed particular skills. If such a match between a prospective employer and those to be laid off were made, Durham Technical Institute (DTI), the area technical college, could do the training.

Unfortunately, without that sort of match the technical institute can do little. When the 410 Liggett and Myers workers lost their jobs in 1979, DTI put together a four-day workshop on skills in seeking employment, one of the first programs of its kind in the state. The sixty-five workers who attended learned how to use the ESC, were shown the possibilities of "retooling" at

DTI for a new career, and practiced writing job résumés. All left with a résumé in hand—but little else. Since Liggett and Myers workers are listed by the ESC in a variety of occupational classifications, there is no way to track the laid-off workers as a group and no information is available on how many have found jobs. The ESC estimated one-fourth had gone to work as of May 1980. The effect of the DTI workshop on workers seeking employment is not known.

Besides this limited aid, technical schools have no mechanism for responding to large-scale layoffs. At DTI and other technical institutes, the basic curriculum enables individuals to acquire training for a variety of broadly defined occupations. The continuing-education division is designed to respond to the community's need for particular skills; through this division, DTI can offer almost any kind of short-term training—provided the need is clear. For example, if a new employer came to the area and notified DTI that it would need fifty plumbers, the institute could set up a special program to train them. Similarly, if it were clear that twelve to twenty-five plumbers would be needed in the broad Durham area over the next year, the school could institute a special course. But special courses are set up in response to new employment, not designed for groups of unemployed workers. As a community-college curriculum planner in the North Carolina Department of Education explains it, technical institutes throughout the state are geared to the needs of new companies, not to the needs of persons displaced by declining industries.

Federal public-works programs designed for sudden and severe economic dislocation caused by large-scale layoffs, plant closings, and relocation have been used in such cities as Youngstown, Ohio. But Durham's unemployment rate is below the guidelines necessary for such an Economic Development Administration (EDA) grant. Another more flexible federal grant for technical assistance in economic development might be available, however. According to Robert Slade, Durham's assistant director for finance and program development, the city could use such a grant to explore two possible options for laid-off tobacco workers: develop a profile of the skills represented at Liggett and Myers and then plan a public-works program to use those skills; or seek ways to convert the Liggett and Myers facilities to other types of operations and provide retraining. Presumably, the kind of broad survey required to identify skills needed in the area could be done also. Yet, again, all of these require considerable planning time and thus are impossible without advance notice of large-scale layoffs. Even getting such a grant is impossible without advance notice that would establish the need for it. The city could perhaps make a prima facie case that additional layoffs will occur, but city planners are reluctant to do so since that would appear almost to wish for Liggett and Myers's demise—and no one in Durham wants to give that impression.

State and Federal Options

At Liggett and Myers or at other companies that are not held responsible for their employees' future security, suddenly displaced workers may fall between the cracks of the various government unemployment aid programs in this country. Some state laws require advance notice of plant closings; for example, companies in Wisconsin must give a sixty-day notice to state officials there. This notice allows the state some time to plan, through the ESC and other programs, for the soon-to-be unemployed.

National-level policy can help workers, too. In Great Britain, West Germany, Sweden, and Canada, all of which are coping with economic dislocations of the kind the United States is just beginning to face on a large scale, companies must give advance notice of impending mass layoffs, plant closings, or relocations. In Great Britain, the minimum notice is ninety days if a hundred or more workers are affected. During that period, the workers are entitled to time off, with pay, to look for new jobs, and the Department of Employment uses the period to arrange appropriate retraining programs. In West Germany, an employer is required to notify the regional labor department of planned mass dismissals, and the labor department then has two months to stave off or cushion the layoffs with a variety of programs: short-work-week benefits, training, or public-works jobs. (Recent legislation in West Germany, which requires companies to give their supervisory boards a full year's notice of plans, is expected to result in even earlier warnings to the labor departments.) In Sweden, which has the most comprehensive system of programs to cope with economic dislocation, mandatory advance notice of impending dismissals is used to evaluate the appropriateness of employment preservation programs, arrange retraining, promote voluntary labor mobility, and create new jobs for affected workers in their own communities. The requirements for advance notice of layoffs in Canada aid that country's government in coordinating labor-market programs.

A 1979 report, *Economic Dislocation: Plant Closings, Plant Relocations and Plant Conversion*,[4] concluded that the assistance and protections provided European workers could be implemented within the U.S. economic system. Among the report's recommendations for the United States was one-year advance notice of impending layoffs and plant shutdowns, and the creation of labor-market bodies to coordinate a variety of programs aimed at reducing the social costs of economic dislocation to both individuals and communities. The National Employment Priorities Act of 1979, introduced by Representative Ford, contains provisions for advance notice, adjustment assistance for workers, and aid to companies that give advance notice. Such aid could include loan assistance similar to that which Chrysler has received, or technical assistance to undertake manufacturing of new products, especially if the product is one the government could buy.

House and Senate committees have held hearings on the bill but it has not yet faced a vote in Congress; its prospects in the 1981-1982 congressional session appear slim.

Conclusion

The problems caused by large- and small-scale economic dislocations are complex—witness the uncertain futures of Liggett and Myers workers in Durham—and solutions will require special cooperative consideration by policymakers from every level of government. But creative options exist, ranging from requiring industry to give advance notice of layoffs to carefully studying the role of technical schools' training programs. If state and local government officials approach labor displacement with innovation and initiative, they might accommodate the needs of expanding companies while also responding to the hardships of displaced workers. The advance notice of impending dismissals, while important in its own right, takes on far greater significance, as the economic-dislocation report explains, when "it triggers a targeted effort to create jobs to replace those which will be lost, as part of a planning effort which matches the capabilities of affected workers and facilities with the emerging needs of the economy."

Notes

1. *North Carolina Labor Force Estimates, 1980,* Bureau of Employment Security Research, Employment Security Commission of North Carolina.

2. "Reynolds to Put $1 Billion Into Expanding Plants," *Winston-Salem* (North Carolina) *Journal,* September 20, 1980, p. 1.

3. "Plant Closure: A Case History," testimony presented by Carroll H. Teague, vice-president for personnel and labor relations, Brown and Williamson Tobacco Corporation, before the U.S. Senate Committee on Labor and Human Resources, September 17, 1980.

4. *Economic Dislocation: Plant Closings, Plant Relocations and Plant Conversion,* Joint Report of Labor Union Study Tour Participants, May 1, 1979. Representatives of the United Auto Workers, International Association of Machinists, and United Steelworkers toured Sweden, West Germany, and the United Kingdom, and studied plant closings.

20

Valuable Vehicles for Long-Term Gains

John Maxwell

The tobacco industry has been attacked regularly since its inception several hundred years ago, and the Cassandras are once again predicting hard times for tobacco sales. Despite such prophecies, the high-profit cigarette trade continues to make tobacco companies attractive investment vehicles. Tobacco stocks, which usually sell in line with the Dow and the Standard and Poor's stock-exchange averages, are widely utilized by individual as well as institutional investors. Almost 40 percent of Philip Morris stock and more than 30 percent of R.J. Reynolds stock are owned by major institutional investors, a strong indication of long-term investor confidence.

Since 1950, the cigarette industry has continued to grow well, increasing overall unit sales by some 74 percent. In America, those who want to smoke can pretty much afford to do so. Hence, as the population has increased over the last thirty years and as women have moved into the work force in record numbers, overall consumption has increased. More than 51 percent of women are now at work, where both job and social pressures have tended to increase cigarette use as a relaxant.

In the coming years, however, growth in domestic cigarette sales may be more difficult, because of demographics, lifestyles, and publicity concerning smoking and health. The average person starts a lasting smoking habit in his early twenties and begins to cut down in the early forties. Psychologists consider that twenty-year period the pressure years and believe smoking is a response to pressure. Although much has been written about teenage and younger smokers, their consumption is usually in the range of only a few cigarettes a day. Smokers in their early twenties, however, consume an average of a couple of packs a day. The so-called war babies are now in their early-to-mid-thirties, and their demographic impact in terms of entering the critical twenty-year period has already spent itself to some extent. By the time the typical smoker reaches his forties, he knows what he is going to be and do, and pressure decreases; with that change comes a decrease in smoking.

In the changing American lifestyle, people are moving away from items such as alcohol and cigarettes that some feel may be adverse to health. A recent survey indicates that 93 percent of the population think there is a correlation between cancer and smoking, a figure that surely has an effect on cigarette consumption. The problem is exacerbated by aggressive pricing within the industry. If the average person thinks smoking is harmful, he may use the excuse that the price has jumped a nickel a pack in order to reduce or give up the habit. Moreover, government agencies at the federal, state, and local levels, as well as private-sector groups, continue to promote anti-smoking programs and legislation restricting where one can smoke.

For these reasons, the domestic industry may grow little and may even decline slightly in the next few years. There are some 60 to 80 million smokers in the United States, but most of the people who are going to give up smoking for health reasons may have already done so.

There is a direct correlation between per capita income and cigarette consumption, and per capita income is rising worldwide. Therefore, even though the industry is coming under more frequent attacks from anti-smoking groups throughout the world, cigarette sales are rising. Last year, almost four trillion cigarettes were sold outside the United States, six times the number sold within the country. The annual growth rate for the industry outside the United States has averaged 2 to 4 percent in recent years and will probably continue to grow at that rate. This market represents a great potential for Reynolds and Philip Morris, companies particularly well positioned to take full advantage of it.

Exports of cigarettes from American companies have increased substantially in recent years (see table 20-1). Between 1975 and 1979, Philip Morris more than doubled its overseas sales, from 18.13 billion to 39.10 billion cigarettes. During the same period, Reynolds increased its exports by about 60 percent, from 20.50 to 32.50 billion units.

Largely because of this growth in cigarette exports, Philip Morris and Reynolds are now numbers sixteen and twenty-one, respectively, in the *Fortune* magazine listing of the fifty leading exporters. And if one considers consumer products alone, these cigarette industry leaders would probably

Table 20-1
Cigarette Export, by Company
(in billions of units)

Company	1975	1976	1977	1978	1979
R.J. Reynolds	20.50	23.50	26.50	28.90	32.50
Philip Morris[a]	18.13	21.70	29.00	33.53	39.10
Brown and Williamson	6.70	6.60	11.50	16.86	18.40
American Brands	4.00	4.00	1.60	1.60	1.30
Lorillard[b]	10.50	10.53	3.77		
Liggett Group[c]	4.40	5.00	5.10	3.45	

[a]Includes export volume of Liggett since June 26, 1978.

[b]As of June 22, 1977, Lorillard sold its export brands to Moorgate Tobacco, Limited, an affiliate of British-American Tobacco Company.

[c]As of June 26, 1978, Liggett sold its export brands to Philip Morris.

rank one and two among all domestic exporters. As foreign populations become more familiar with American cigarettes and as worldwide per capita income rises, American cigarette exports will continue to grow.

In addition to international growth within the cigarette industry, the tobacco companies in the last decade have been able to branch out into other product areas, primarily because of their high cash flow. This diversification has taken many forms, including shiplines and oil (Reynolds), beer (Philip Morris), department stores (Brown and Williamson), pet food and whiskey (Liggett Group), and insurance and gold products (American Brands). For tobacco companies, diversification is more of an offensive move into larger corporate arenas than a defensive one against declining investor confidence. If these moves had not been made, the companies would have found themselves with a very high cash ratio.

Because many of the investments that the tobacco companies have made are for the longer-term payoff rather than quick profits, and because there is nothing more lucrative than the little white tubes, a preponderant share of the earnings of these companies still comes from tobacco—a situation that will not change in the immediate future.

The likelihood of continued international growth in the high-return cigarette trade appears to have given added confidence to industry leaders concerning their future as cigarette companies. In the closing months of 1980, Reynolds announced an expansion and upgrading of its principal American manufacturing facilities in Winston-Salem, North Carolina. And in 1983, Philip Morris plans to open a new $300-million plant, now under construction, in North Carolina.

The tobacco industry is here to stay. It will grow and remain a viable industry for the foreseeable future. But in some quarters, the industry has its work cut out for it. It will continue to be under attack by both government agencies and private-sector groups on a worldwide basis. Obviously, the controversies surrounding the tobacco industry are well known on the investment market. Yet both individual and major institutional investors continue to regard the tobacco industry, particularly its leaders, as valuable vehicles for long-term capital gains.

Part V
The Risks of Smoking: Rights and Ramifications

21 Tobacco and Health: An Introduction

Harriet Kestenbaum

Since the introduction of tobacco into Europe in the sixteenth century, government leaders have both extolled and decried the use of the golden weed. In 1604, for example, King James I of England wrote *Counter Blast to Tobacco* in which he characterized tobacco as harshly as today's most virulent anti-smoking activist: "A custom lothsome to the eye, hateful to the nose, harmful to the braine, dangerous to the Lungs, and in the blacke stinking fume thereof, nearest resembling the horrible Stigian smoke of the pit that is bottomless." But other royalty considered tobacco to be their saving grace—Catherine de Medici of France used it for migraine headaches. And doctors prescribed tobacco as a remedy for colds, fevers, and even as a preventive to the plague.

As tobacco consumption grew over the centuries, many doctors became more dubious about the medicinal merits; some, in fact, began to suspect a link between tobacco and certain diseases. By the early eighteenth century, case studies that described suspected relationships between tobacco use and certain cancers began appearing in the European and American medical journals. Not until the twentieth century, however, did scientists begin to study the problem seriously. Before the turn of the century, few incidences of lung cancer had been reported, but in the early 1900s American statisticians observed a precipitous increase in deaths resulting from lung cancer. Scientists hypothesized that this pattern was related to a sharp rise in tobacco consumption.

Not until the 1950s, however, did major studies appear that identified a strong correlation between smoking and disease. Sir Richard Doll, a British pioneer in the field, studied the smoking habits and characteristics of more than 34,000 physicians, recording all sicknesses and deaths that occurred between an initial and follow-up contact. By collecting characteristic data from a healthy population at two points several years apart, and by recording whether those persons with a certain characteristic in question (that is, smoking) had a significantly greater incidence of a disease than those without the characteristic, Doll employed a relatively new research methodology—the prospective study. And by using correlation techniques in analyzing the data, he was plowing new ground for the emerging field of epidemiology—the study of patterns of disease.

Doll's findings showed that smokers were fourteen times more likely to develop cancer than nonsmokers. Doll also observed a dose-response relationship between smoking and lung cancer: that is, with increasing levels of exposure to tobacco, he found a corresponding rise in occurrence of the disease; smokers who smoked two packs of cigarettes a day were more likely to develop lung cancer than those who smoked only one. At about the same time, independent but similar studies were being conducted in Sweden and in the United States; and the findings in both were similar to the Doll conclusions.

Throughout the 1950s, research data on the effects of tobacco on human health began to accumulate, prompting the release of two landmark reports—one in Great Britain and one in the United States. In 1962, the Royal College of Physicians of London released a document that appraised the state of tobacco-and-health research. The report concluded that "cigarette smoking is a cause of lung cancer and bronchitis and probably contributes to the development of coronary heart disease." Two years later, the Advisory Committee to the U.S. surgeon general released a report entitled *Smoking and Health* in which more than 6,000 studies in the field were reviewed. Concluding that "cigarette smoking is a health hazard of sufficient importance in the United States to warrant appropriate remedial action," the Advisory Committee reported these findings:

1. Cigarette smoking is associated with a 70-percent increase in the age-specific death rates of males, and to a lesser degree with increased death rates of females.
2. Cigarette smoking is causally related to lung cancer in men.
3. Cigarette smoking is the most important of the causes of chronic bronchitis in the United States and increases the risk of dying from chronic bronchitis and emphysema.
4. Male cigarette smokers have a higher death rate from coronary artery diseases than nonsmoking males.

The 1964 surgeon general's report stimulated thousands of studies around the world and eventually led to the publication of a sequel in 1979. This time, the Advisory Committee reviewed some 30,000 studies covering topics included in the 1964 report and new areas, such as the effects of smoking on women and on workers in hazardous occupations. Many of the earlier findings were repeated, but in a stronger tone. The committee concluded that "cigarette smoking is the largest preventable cause of death in the United States."

The "Causal" Debate

The Advisory Committee has determined that smoking is causally related to lung cancer and heart disease. Most scientists tend to agree that a causal relationship exists if clinical observations and animal experiments have repeatedly shown a relationship between the disease and the agent, and if the evidence from the epidemiological studies meets the following criteria: (1) the disease rate must be much higher among the exposed group and a dose-response relationship must exist; (2) the findings of such an association must be repeated and in different study populations; and (3) removal from the exposure must reduce the risk of the disease. The Advisory Committee used these criteria in making its determination.

Establishing a causal relationship between a suspected agent and a disease is a long and cautious process. Because it is unethical to test the effect of a suspected hazardous substance on human beings, researchers must base their conclusions on a combination of alternative methods: (1) clinical observations and autopsy reports of diseased persons who have been exposed to the agent; (2) animal experiments; and (3) observational population studies that compare the incidence of the disease between those who have willfully exposed themselves to the risk factor in question and those who have not. But each of these methods has limitations. Clinical studies of diseased individuals cannot determine whether exposure to the hazard actually preceded the onset of the disease. Animal studies can never exactly duplicate the form and dosage by which humans absorb the hazard. And epidemiological studies, being statistical associations, cannot explain with scientific certainty why a disease is more prevalent in the exposed group than in the unexposed group.

Consequently, some widely respected scientists disagree with the findings of the Advisory Committee. They argue that although smoking has been statistically associated with various diseases, the conclusion that cigarettes are causally linked to the disease does not necessarily follow. They maintain that medical research has yet to discover the causes of cancer or heart disease, that no specific agent has ever been identified in tobacco that can cause tumors to grow or arteries to clog. If smoking were a cause of lung cancer, for example, they contend that all smokers would eventually contract the disease. However, only some smokers develop lung cancer. In addition, some scientists also reject statistical smoking studies, contending that they overlook genetic factors that may predispose some persons to diseases more than others and, as a consequence, falsely attribute the disease to smoking. "The enigma of cancer and chronic diseases will yield only to the steady advance of scientific knowledge . . . ," wrote Tobacco

Institute president Harold Kornegay in the Institute's *Smoking and Health, 1964-1979: The Continuing Controversy.* "Many scientists are becoming concerned that preoccupation with smoking may be both unfounded and dangerous—unfounded because evidence on many critical points is conflicting, dangerous because it diverts attention from other suspected hazards."

The Debates of the Eighties

While the causal debate continues, three important new areas of concern have emerged: (1) the less hazardous cigarette (LHC); (2) the potential hazards of cigarette smoke on the nonsmoker, often referred to as the "passive" smoker; and (3) smoking among workers in hazardous occupations.

Several of the original researchers who concluded that smoking is harmful have since modified their positions, contending now that smoking can be made less hazardous, perhaps even risk-free. They base this position on the LHC, the cigarettes with low tar and nicotine contents (now about 50 percent of those sold in the United States), and on the increasing use of perforated filters which reduce the amount of smoke inhaled. Other scientists have been more cautious in promoting a less hazardous cigarette, maintaining that cigarettes in any dosage or form are still quite harmful. The lack of support for the LHC among some scientists is usually based on three factors: (1) a lack of epidemiological studies on a population that has smoked nothing but LHCs; (2) a suspicion that LHCs may contain additives and other substances such as carbon monoxide which may be as harmful as high concentrations of tar and nicotine; and (3) a belief that the LHC smoker may be "compensating"—smoking more cigarettes, inhaling more deeply, and covering the holes on the filter tip.

In 1979, in the *New England Journal of Medicine*, Drs. James White and Herman Froeb reported that tobacco can be hazardous to passive smokers. Anti-smoking activists hailed the study as a landmark, yet some in the scientific community have criticized it for flaws in research design. The study reported that prolonged passive smoking—in the specific population studied, nonsmokers worked in an environment with smokers—produced lung-function impairment comparable to that found in people who had smoked one to twenty cigarettes a day for twenty years.

In the 1980s, debates between interests and industries in which workers have had a high incidence of cancer may also receive wide attention. In 1980, for example, an asbestos company filed suit in the California state courts asking the judge to determine if the tobacco industry should help pay damage claims for asbestos workers with chronic lung problems. Health studies of such populations are still in the early stages, and any attempt to determine a proportionate causative responsibility among several possible factors (such as asbestos dust and tobacco smoke) will be difficult. Although a complex area, some governments have already addressed it: Sweden now restricts smoker participation in certain occupations.

Although the debates within the medical community concerning smoking-and-health issues obviously affect policy decisions made at all levels of government, philosophical questions also influence such decisions. For example, does the government have the right to protect an individual from engaging in practices that may be damaging to health, or to help consumers make informed decisions concerning tobacco products and health hazards? Do smokers alone have the right to choose when and where to smoke, or does the nonsmoker have a competitive right to a smoke-free environment? The smoking prohibitions and regulations that have so far emerged in more than thirty countries stem from both the medical debates and the philosophical questions raised in this chapter. Legislative, judicial, and administrative actions have addressed four primary areas: (1) prohibitions on cigarette advertising; (2) mandatory health warnings on cigarette packages; (3) restrictions on smoking in public places; and (4) public funds for anti-smoking education.

See chapter 27 for a comparative listing of regulations on smoking and health in thirty-two countries, an annotated listing of landmark events in the smoking-and-health controversies, and a selected and annotated resource listing for pursuing the medical aspects of tobacco policies.

22 Warning Citizens about the Hazards of Smoking: Where We Are in 1981

John M. Pinney

The Office on Smoking and Health was established in March 1978 as part of the Office of the Assistant Secretary for Health and Surgeon General. The office serves as the focal point for all Department of Health and Human Services smoking-and-health activities. Its responsibilities include the planning, coordination, and development of public information and educational initiatives and maintenance of a Technical Information Center which collects, organizes, and disseminates research information on smoking and health to a worldwide audience. The long-range goal of the office is to reduce deaths, disabilities, and health-care costs associated with cigarette smoking.

The office prepares an annual report to Congress on the health consequences of smoking. The most recent report, which was issued in January 1981, focused on the health consequences of smoking the changing cigarette product. This chapter discusses the changes that have occurred on smoking habits, smoking programs, and the cigarette itself, and the significance of these changes for the cigarette industry and the public health.

It has been sixteen years since the surgeon general issued his report on smoking and health that showed cigarettes to be the chief cause of lung cancer and a contributor to heart disease, lung disease, and other causes of illness and early death. So far, surprisingly little harm has come to America's tobacco growers. In 1965, they grew 977 million pounds of cigarette tobacco and the average price was 65 cents. Last year, growers produced 1.8 billion pounds and received $1.40 a pound for it. Costs have gone up in sixteen years, and the value of the dollar has gone down, but the tobacco economy still appears sound and relatively prosperous. No harm at all has come to the industry that manufactures cigarettes. Cigarettes gave the companies $1.6 billion in profits in 1977.

But two changes have taken place that will have enormous significance for the tobacco economy in the future. The first change is that the market for cigarettes in the United States is getting smaller and smaller. More people are quitting every year and fewer young people are taking up the habit. Tobacco-growing in this country is being supported more and more

This chapter summarizes the material presented in the 1981 surgeon general's report.

241

by its exports to foreign countries. The second change is the new, low-yield cigarette. Almost half the cigarettes sold in the United States today are those yielding 15 milligrams of tar or less, whereas sixteen years ago such cigarettes commanded almost no share of the market.

It is difficult to believe that the market for cigarettes will not continue to shrink. A survey made by the Roper Organization for the Tobacco Institute in 1979 revealed that 58 percent of adults (40 percent of smokers, 69 percent of nonsmokers) believed that cigarette smoking is hazardous to health. Another survey, conducted in North Carolina by the *Charlotte Observer*, showed that 63 percent of adult Carolinians believe so, too. A University of Michigan survey of high-school seniors, also in 1979, showed that 63 percent of high-school seniors think that smoking a pack of cigarettes per day is a great risk to health. Sixty-six percent said this of drinking four or five drinks nearly every day and 42 percent said this of using marijuana regularly.

The move to lower and lower yield cigarettes is likely to continue Nothing in the history of marketing has involved more advertising dollars or represented a greater shift in buying preferences than this, not even the current shift from large to small cars. The new cigarettes appear to satisfy smokers, and the advertising has been very strong, based as it is on the fear-arousing theme that big numbers are bad and small numbers are good.

As these changes continue, what role should the government play, particularly the federal government?

Role of Government Health Agencies

So far, there has been relatively little government intervention. In 1969, Congress passed a law that barred cigarette advertising on radio and television and required that warning labels be placed on cigarette packages. A relatively small amount of money (albeit a great deal of effort) has been expended on efforts to warn people against smoking. But the federal tax on cigarettes remains where it was set in 1952, at eight cents a pack, and there is no significant movement anywhere in the federal establishment to end tobacco price-supports.

Nor has there been significant action by state or local governments. For a time in the late 1960s and early 1970s, state legislatures were busy raising cigarette taxes, but this trend appears to have slowed. There have also been steps taken by state governments, and even more by local governments, to set up regulations governing smoking in public places. Cigarette interests have tried to stir up great excitement about these regulations, and reportedly have spent considerable amounts of money in trying to resist them, but it is doubtful that the regulations have much influence on cigarette consumption. They are the result of, not the cause of, public concern.

The worry that smokers and nonsmokers alike have about cigarette smoking is reasonable and sensible, as reasonable and sensible a worry as any other serious threat to health. In our society today, cigarette smokers are statistically twice as likely as nonsmokers to suffer heart attacks, and ten times as likely to die from lung cancer. The word about these risks has been getting around. I believe it is the clear responsibility of the public- and private-health establishment, and of the educational establishment—notably the U.S. Department of Health and Human Services, the American Medical Association, the American Cancer Society, other voluntary and professional health agencies, and all our schools—to pass this word around in every way possible. But it is not these messengers which are changing the tobacco outlook, it is the message.

It is the responsibility of a government health agency to continue to warn citizens about the hazards of smoking. Congress has recognized this in its appropriations, and it has also given the Public Health Service responsibility for research into the causes and effects of the smoking habit. Approximately $32.6 million in research funds are being used this year (1980-1981) to carry on this research, look into the question of less hazardous smoking, monitor smoking trends, and investigate smoking behavior.

The Public Health Service shares responsibility for research with other agencies. Much of the early work in identifying cigarette hazards was done by private agencies such as the American Cancer Society, other federal agencies such as the Veterans Administration, and foreign groups such as England's Royal College of Physicians. This research continues. Some of it, and some very good research, is also being funded by the tobacco industry.

Public Health Service Research Priorities

Of all the research issues, the most important at present concern low-yield cigarettes. Some observers see this new product as a final solution to the problem, one that will reduce cigarette-caused illnesses and deaths to "tolerable" levels. Others see them as something that can only delude smokers by giving them false hope.

During 1980, the Public Health Service reviewed the health consequences of low-yield cigarettes and the health effects of tobacco additives (such as flavor enhancers, which are used extensively in low-yield cigarettes) under two congressional directives: (1) the Public Health Cigarette Smoking Act of 1971, which requires annual reports on the health consequences of smoking; and (2) the Health Services and Centers Amendments of 1978, which specifically call for an investigation of the risks of additives and low-yield products. We concentrated our research on four types of questions.

First, what is the relevance today of past information on the nature and hazards of smoking? The cigarettes that are being smoked today are very different from those smoked in the 1940s and 1950s and new kinds of cigarettes are continuing to appear. Recently, manufacturers have introduced cigarettes that are advertised as yielding less than one milligram of tar. Our researchers are, obviously, looking at a moving target.

Second, how do the tar and nicotine levels, which are measured by machines and do not necessarily represent the smoker's actual intake of smoke, correspond to the actual hazards a smoker faces? Individuals who switch to lower-yield cigarettes may negate whatever advantage there may be, in whole or in part, by inhaling more deeply, smoking more, and smoking greater proportions of their cigarettes. Even how a person holds his cigarette can affect his intake of smoke, by blocking the movement of air that passes through the filter into the smoke stream.

Third, are tar and nicotine by themselves adequate indicators of hazard? There are some 4,000 known compounds in cigarette smoke; the amounts of these compounds are not reduced equally when tar and nicotine are reduced. Carbon monoxide is a case in point. Some conventional filter cigarettes may, in fact, deliver more carbon monoxide than nonfilter cigarettes.

Finally, and perhaps most important, how can we assess the overall benefits of switching from higher- to lower-yield cigarettes? From present evidence, it appears low-yield cigarettes may have significant advantages in reducing the risk of lung cancer. But they may not be reducing the risks of some other diseases. There is apparently no evidence, for example, that switching has any effect in reducing the risks to the fetus that are incurred when a mother smokes during her pregnancy.

At the present time, the Public Health Service has this advice to give to the smoker:

1. Switching from high-yield to low-yield cigarettes is a good thing. The Public Health Service's formal position is that, "the preponderance of scientific evidence continues to suggest that cigarettes with lower 'tar' and nicotine are less hazardous."
2. However, shifting to a less hazardous cigarette may in fact increase the hazard if more cigarettes are smoked or are inhaled more deeply.
3. And, most important, even the lowest-yield cigarettes present health hazards very much greater than would be encountered if no cigarettes were smoked at all.

The Public Health Service is publicizing this information and is asking others in the health and educational communities to do the same. But at the same time, the Public Health Service is subjecting these recommendations to the most careful scientific scrutiny and will continue to do so. The health of some 55 million citizens is at risk because they smoke cigarettes. They are entitled to learn what science has to tell them about the nature and extent of this risk.

23 Tobacco and Health: A Societal Challenge

E.L. Wynder and
D. Hoffman

For more than a quarter of a century, a wealth of epidemiologic evidence has causatively linked tobacco smoking with lung cancer.[1] Decades ago, smoking was shown to increase the risk of premature heart attack and was recognized as a major factor in chronic obstructive pulmonary disease.[2] Cancers of the mouth, larynx, esophagus, pancreas, kidney, and bladder have also been linked with excessive use of tobacco.[3] Furthermore, the incidence of lung cancer is rising among women[4]—a development that we predicted on the basis of data published in the *Journal* in 1956.[5]

In view of the epidemiologic, biochemical, and purely logical evidence, it seems clear that some action by society is warranted to address the issue of smoking and health. As long as members of a society continue to smoke cigarettes, young people will continue to experiment with tobacco and, for many, casual experimentation may lead to acquisition of a habit that persists for most of their lives.

However, the obvious question is: what, if anything, can be done to ameliorate this important societal problem? In our view, a three-pronged approach is necessary: youth anti-smoking programs to prevent the acquisition of the smoking habit, smoking-cessation programs to help current smokers quit, and a less harmful cigarette for those who cannot or will not quit smoking. In this chapter, we briefly review some of the more important work in each of these areas and, based on the current state of the art, draw conclusions and make recommendations for the future.

Youth Anti-Smoking Programs

Adolescence and the Smoking Problem

As a result of various normative developmental needs, students approaching adolescence face a rapid rise in pressure to conform and a corresponding increase in dependence on their peer group. The peer group serves as an environment in which experimentation with a variety of social

This article is adapted from "Tobacco and Health: A Societal Challenge," *New England Journal of Medicine*, April 19, 1979, by permission. The authors are indebted to Drs. Gilbert Botvin and Linbania Jacobson of the American Health Foundation for their contributions.

behaviors is both permitted and reinforced and where independence and separateness from parents can be freely expressed.[6] Not surprisingly, the acquisition of the smoking habit typically occurs during adolescence, and early experimentation with tobacco occurs within the context of the peer group.[7]

Although the general public has become aware of the hazards of cigarette smoking and millions of smokers have attempted to "kick" the habit,[8] recent surveys have indicated that smoking continues to be common among teenagers.[9] Clearly, past programs have not been sensitive to the needs of adolescents now making a decision about smoking. These special needs, together with societal sanction of the symbolic value of cigarettes, weigh heavily against a young person's decision not to smoke.

For the most part, youth anti-smoking programs can be grouped into two broad categories. The first category includes the more traditional smoking-education programs, which have primarily provided students with information concerning the hazards of smoking. The second category includes more recent approaches to smoking prevention, which have focused on the social and psychologic determinants of the onset of smoking behavior.

Informational Approaches

The major premise of most youth anti-smoking programs has been that students provided with adequate information concerning the hazards of cigarette smoking will simply choose not to smoke. These programs have been conducted in elementary schools and junior-high schools, generally within the framework of health education. For example, one such program included a series of modules designed to teach good health concepts to elementary-school students,[10] and another used a special health-education curriculum with a strong anti-smoking component for junior-high-school students.[11]

A more extensive health-education model is the Berkeley Project, designed for fifth, sixth, and seventh graders.[12] This program provides information on prevention of heart and lung diseases, nutrition functions of the human body, alcohol and drug abuse, cigarette smoking, environmental health hazards, community health programs and resources, persuasive advertising, understanding the handicapped, and many other contemporary issues pertinent to personal and community health behavior.

A multimedia presentation designed to generate the students' interest and curiosity introduces the program. An intense review of the normal functioning of selected body systems focuses first on the lungs and respiratory system, then on the heart and circulatory system, and finally on the brain and nervous system. The next phase considers diseases and disorders of the aforementioned systems and ways in which they are affected by personal behavioral choices, such as smoking and food selections, and by environmental conditions, such as air pollution.

Although these and similar programs seem to succeed in improving students' knowledge about smoking, they have generally had only a minimal impact on actual smoking behavior. Thus, the assumption that students will not become cigarette smokers if they are fully cognizant of the dangers of smoking is not supported by existing data.

Several writers have suggested that increasing prospective smokers' awareness of the immediate physiologic effects of smoking would be more effective than focusing on the long-term effects.[13] To date, only one study has included this component,[14] but because this strategy was combined with another, it was unclear to what extent this approach alone was capable of deterring students from becoming smokers.

Some anti-smoking programs have adopted a less didactic approach and have attempted to give students an active role in both the organization and administration of the programs. In a program reported by Grigson,[15] students organized anti-smoking activities in the form of movies, poster and essay contests, assemblies, and nonsmokers' dances.

Other programs have been led by peers and older students, on the assumption that students would be more receptive to anti-smoking messages from fellow students than to similar messages from teachers or other authority figures. Harnett[16] and Rosner[17] recruited older students (generally from high school) to talk with elementary-school students in an attempt to dissuade them from becoming smokers. Unfortunately, many of these programs failed to include an evaluation component—making it difficult to compare the relative effectiveness of teacher and peer-led approaches.

However, since changes in attitudes, knowledge, and beliefs about cigarette smoking do not necessarily precipitate corresponding changes in smoking behavior, it seems to matter little whether the students are approached by teachers or peer groups. Although attitudinal and informational changes may be a necessary component of any smoking-prevention program, they are clearly not sufficient.

Social and Psychological Approaches

With the realization that anti-smoking programs affecting attitudinal and informational changes have had little, if any, impact on pre-adolescent and adolescent smoking behavior, researchers have begun to focus their programs on the social and psychologic factors that appear to influence a student's decision to smoke. One of the best known of these programs was conducted by Evans[18] and his colleagues, who presented children with videotapes depicting social situations in which they might be pressured or encouraged to smoke. Their aim was to familiarize the students with the nature of the major social pressures to smoke and to teach them ways of effectively coping with these influences. In the intervening ten weeks, 10 percent of the students who had viewed the tapes became smokers, as compared to 18.3 percent of those in a single, no-contact, post-test control group.

Another innovative program designed to combat smoking among California school children is Project CLASP (Counseling Leadership About Smoking Pressures)[19]—a junior and senior high-school program in which youth counsels youth about situations that lead to smoking and how to cope with them. To encourage young people to remain nonsmokers throughout their lives, tenth-grade students aid in the development and implementation of a peer-counseling program for seventh and eighth graders.

Thus, this project attempts to discourage smoking by providing specific behavioral training about possible smoking situations and how to cope with such pressures, rather than teaching about the effects of smoking on health. The project is unique in combining the efforts of young people from many age groups, public-service agencies, school personnel, and experts from the field of social and behavioral sciences. After three years, 5.2 percent of the students in Project CLASP were smokers, whereas a peer group without counseling had 15.1 percent smokers.[20]

Whereas the two programs just discussed attempt to deal with the social factors that influence smoking behavior among students, a recently developed program called Life Skills Training focuses on the psychologic, as well as social, factors that promote cigarette smoking. This program is conducted within the context of a health-education program, called Know Your Body (KYB), for junior-high-school students.[21]

The ten-session program is conducted by the regular classroom teacher and uses a combination of group discussion, modeling, and behavior rehearsal to teach students the kind of basic life skills that will enable them to resist direct social pressure to smoke, decrease their susceptibility to indirect social influences (by promoting greater autonomy, self-esteem, and self-confidence), and decrease the anxiety that may occur in social situations. The program includes sessions on self-image, decision making, advertising techniques, coping with anxiety, social skills, and assertiveness. Thus, the problem of cigarette smoking is addressed indirectly within the context of self-development. Results of the KYB program in 1979 have shown that there is a 75-percent decrease in new smokers among the students in grades eight through ten.[22]

Conclusion

Unfortunately, many smoking-prevention programs have not included evaluation components, so it is difficult to determine the relative effectiveness of the various approaches. However, the existing evidence clearly indicates that smoking programs that merely provide information about the consequences of smoking are not capable of appreciably decreasing the proportion of students who become smokers. On the other hand, approaches that take into account the underlying causes of the acquisition of the smoking habit and teach students to cope with the various social and psychologic factors that promote smoking do seem to be capable of producing behavioral change and, thus, seem to be the most promising.

Anti-Smoking Programs for Adults

In general, anti-smoking campaigns directed toward adults have been somewhat more successful than those directed toward children and teenagers.[23] In a recent national survey, 33 percent of the men and 15 percent of the women included were former smokers.[24] Similarly, in a study conducted by the American Health Foundation, 27 percent of the men and 11 percent of the women were former smokers who had been off cigarettes for a year or more.[25]

The extent to which anti-smoking messages are effective in promoting behavioral change appears to be at least partially a function of education.[26] For example, among male ex-smokers, there is a positive correlation between increased level of education and smoking cessation (figure 23-1). Moreover, a greater proportion of men in the highest educational category smoke low-tar filter cigarettes than do men with less education. Among women, education is also positively related to smoking cessation, but the effect of education on filter-cigarette usage is less pronounced (figure 23-2).

Although many adult smokers give up the smoking habit without help, many others desire to quit but require help.[27] At present, several options are available for smokers who would like assistance.

Clinical Approaches

Traditional approaches to smoking cessation include hypnosis, individual and group counseling, and strategies derived from learning theory.[28] Although most of these efforts have moderately high initial success rates (40 to 89 percent), long-term success rates are less impressive:[29] only about

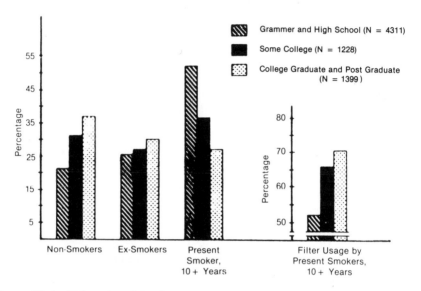

Figure 23-1. Educational Background and Distribution of Smoking Habits among Males

20 to 25 percent of those who quit smoking are still abstinent one year after seeking treatment. It appears, however, that prolonged follow-up activities can improve long-term success rates up to 50 percent.[30]

Unfortunately, comparison of the various approaches to smoking cessation is somewhat problematic. Differences in the criteria used to determine short-term and long-term success rates and dissimilar definitions of an ex-smoker and a participant obfuscate the issue of program effectiveness and may, to some extent, account for reported differences in success rates.

In designing a smoking-cessation program, one must consider several principles: scientific character (the method has been developed and evaluated on an experimental basis, using a statistical method of assessment); efficacy (the method has been demonstrated and compared with other therapies); permanence (reliable data exist on recidivism and cure for at least one year); economic viability (the cost is low relative to the results obtained; the program makes maximum use of nonprofessional staff and time); and broad range of application (it can reach as many smokers as possible).

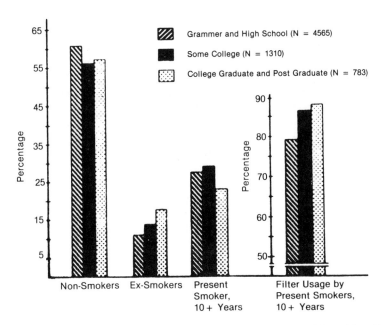

Figure 23-2. Educational Background and Distribution of Smoking Habits among Females

Recognizing the difficulty of determining the relative effectiveness of the various approaches reported in the literature, the American Health Foundation conducted a study that directly compared the effectiveness of hypnosis, individual, and group therapies in more than 2,000 persons who smoked an average of over thirty cigarettes per day.[31] In this study, the group-therapy approach appeared to have the best long-term results. Only about one of nine persons treated by means of hypnosis or individual counseling was abstinent a year later, compared with about one of five treated by means of group therapy. Although the group approach involved a greater number of treatment sessions, it appeared to be well worth the additional time.

Need for Wider Effort

According to a recent Gallup Poll, 33 percent of smokers who want to quit say that they are willing to attend a clinic for help.[32] Moreover, at least 75 percent of current smokers were reported as wanting to quit. Thus, as many as 15 million smokers could be served by organized cessation programs, which should become an integral part of our medical-care delivery system and should be conducted largely by trained allied health professionals. Financial support should be provided, at least in part, by health insurance and also by employers or unions.

A number of less formal and less intensive approaches than those just described may be effective in reaching large numbers of current smokers with a minimum of expense. Self-help kits and other techniques that involve minimal intervention may provide a sensible approach to those who would like to quit but will not seek professional help. Another possible minimal-intervention technique is to deliver a structured daily quitting plan on television and radio to large numbers of smokers in the public.

Conclusions

Smoking-cessation programs can and should take many different approaches, even though some may be less effective than others (table 23-1). We are sometimes asked whether a one-year success rate of 20 or 25 percent indicates a worthwhile and cost-effective effort. Such a question is astonishing when one considers that the five-year survival rate among people with lung cancer is less than 10 percent and the hospital cost alone for those with lung cancer is several thousand dollars; we estimate the cost per person for a year-long smoking-cessation program to be about $80. (In January, 1981, the cost of the smoking-cessation program per person per year was $125. The less expensive program in earlier years was less sophisticated and was held during a less inflationary economy.)

Health economists recognize the cost effectiveness of smoking-cessation programs.[33] It is time for the medical-care establishment to come to grips with the purely economic, as well as the medical and humanitarian, aspects of the smoking-and-health issue. Smoking-cessation programs must receive more support from the media, the scientific community, employers, the health-insurance industry, the health-care delivery system, and, indeed, from every physician.

The Less Harmful Cigarette

Since there are about 54 million smokers in the United States alone,[34] an all-inclusive preventive strategy requires additional efforts beyond smoking-prevention and smoking-cessation programs. Such additional efforts involve "managerial preventive medicine," in which a product or an envi-

Table 23-1
Smoking Cessation Programs

Approach	Advantages	Limitations
Rapid smoking	Very high initial quit rate (100 percent) Follow-up quit rate 60 percent at six months	Very limited appeal, aversive technic Not indicated for those with existing or potential cardio-vascular problems
Multicomponent intervention packages	Success rate of 65 to 100 percent at end of treatment Slightly lower long-term quit rate. Provides smoker with readily available technics for dealing with recurrent smoking urges	Must use social learning technics as a packet No durable results when one component used alone Skilled, experienced, profes-sional therapist necessary
Sensory deprivation	Initial success rate of 100 percent Brief and concentrated	Long-term success rate lower than that of first or second approaches Not practical for use by a large population
Gradual reduction versus abrupt quitting	Sign of "progress" for smoker who cannot quit or go "cold turkey"	Delays or prolongs quitting effort
Contingency contracting	Reduces rate of attrition and increases rate of compliance	"Gimicky" or childish to some participants
Group counseling	Very economical, 1 group leader per 10-15 smokers	Attendance directly related to success
Individual counseling	Focuses on problems with quitting	Costly, time consuming Skilled and experienced therapist required
Counseling with self-hypnosis	Additional skill available to ex-smoker to reinforce nonsmoking behavior	Same as limitations of indi-vidual counseling

ronment is modified by industry or by society's action. In the smoking-and-health issue, the program centers around a less harmful cigarette.

During the last two decades, product modification has led to a con-siderable reduction in the amount of known harmful agents delivered from tobacco smoke, and the epidemiologic results are encouraging.[35]

Research on the identification of the constituents of tobacco smoke and the precursors (risk factors) that specifically relate to disease was a pre-requisite for a definition of the less harmful cigarette. Because of the demonstrated dose response (increase in disease as exposure to tobacco smoke increases), an overall reduction in smoke yield was also considered desirable.[36]

Chemistry and Biology

Animal studies have shown that cigarette smoke, and especially its particulate matter (tar), is carcinogenic (cancer producing).[37] Tobacco smoke contains established tumor initiators as well as cocarcinogens, and the combination of both factors accounts for the major tumorigenic potential of the total tar. The acidic portion contains major cocarcinogens, whereas the neutral fraction mainly harbors tumor initiators, such as polynuclear aromatic hydrocarbons. The quantities of these hydrocarbons present in the most active subfractions have not been shown to elicit tumors by themselves, but, in conjunction with the cocarcinogens that reside in the same neutral subfraction, they produce most of its carcinogenic activity.[38]

Numerous known and suspected tumorigenic agents have been identified in the gaseous and particulate phases of tobacco smoke. Although the gaseous phase contains traces of carcinogens, its tumorigenic effect escapes detection in most current bioassay systems (testing procedures).[39] Tobacco smoke also contains organ-specific carcinogens (for example, nitrosamines), which may contribute to the increased risk of cancer of the upper digestive and respiratory tracts, the pancreas, and the lower urinary system.

The induction of bronchogenic cancer in smokers is usually preceded by an inhibition of the natural clearance mechanisms of the respiratory tract. Toxic agents in the gaseous and particulate phases desynchronize the movements of the cilia and at the same time cause mucus stagnation within the trachea and bronchi. These smoke compounds and the particulate phase as a whole are also considered to be major contributing factors to chronic respiratory diseases in long-term cigarette smokers.[40]

The chemical nature of compounds associated with early induction of cardiovascular disease has not been substantiated by appropriate animal studies. Both nicotine and carbon monoxide have been implicated in the induction of cardiovascular disease, whose major underlying cause is related to hyperlipidemia. The assumption that smoke components such as nitrogen oxides, hydrogen cyanide, and polonium-210 also contribute to the progression of cardiovascular disease is, at present, unconfirmed.[41]

Reduction of undesirable compounds in the smoke can be achieved through elimination of certain constituents of tobacco prior to cigarette manufacture. Other effective means of reducing harmful smoke constituents are selection of specific tobacco varieties and plant components and selective removal of toxic constituents by smoke filtration.[42] Dose reduction, that is, less tar and nicotine delivery in the smoke, can also be brought about by dilution of the mainstream smoke with air (vented filter tips, porous paper).[43] Several smoke modifications have reduced the biologic activity of cigarette smoke. New concepts continue to emerge and, together with presently available techniques, they should further reduce the harmful effects of tobacco products.

The tobacco industry has provided numerous brands of cigarettes with less than 10 milligrams of tar and correspondingly lower levels of nicotine.[44] Increasing consumer acceptance of such brands may be anticipated, but it is likely to depend on increased use of flavoring agents derived from tobacco, and in some cases, from synthetic compounds or mixtures of plant extracts. The biologic activities of such nontobacco flavor additives and their combustion products will then require testing.

Reductions in the tar and nicotine yields of cigarette smoke have been observed in many other countries.[45] During the last twenty years, levels of benzo(a)pyrene, an indicator of the concentration of tumorigenic polynuclear aromatic hydrocarbons in the smoke, have also generally declined in cigarette smoke. This decline suggests that the tumor-initiating activity of tars of American cigarettes is steadily decreasing.[46]

Assuming that all available safety techniques are incorporated into cigarette manufacturing and that none of the flavor additives induces additional toxic effects, some maximal levels for certain smoke constituents in a less harmful cigarette can be proposed (table 23-2). Although giving up smoking is the only safe solution, less harmful cigarettes should be available to those who cannot or do not want to give up smoking.

Epidemiology (The Study of Occurrence of Disease among People)

Although tobacco-related cancers, cardiovascular disease, and chronic obstructive pulmonary disease are effected by different agents in tobacco

Table 23-2
Maximum Concentrations of Some Selected Toxic Agents in the Smoke of Less Harmful Cigarettes

Toxic Component	Maximal Proposed Concentration	
Tar[a]	8	mg
Nicotine	0.6	mg
Carbon monoxide	8	mg
Hydrogen cyanide	100	μg
Benzo(a)pyrene[b]	8	ng
Dimethylnitrosamine[c]	5	ng
N-Nitrosonornicotine	60	ng
Catechol	90	μg
Phenol	20	μg
Acrolein[d]	30	μg

[a]Tar = total—particulate matter, water and nicotine.

[b]Serves as indicator for tumorigenic polynuclear aromatic hydrocarbons.

[c]Serves as indicator for volatile nitrosamines.

[d]Serves as indicator for organic agents toxic to cilia.

smoke, their epidemiologic association with tobacco smoking is dose-related.[47] The data show that the risk of lung and larynx cancer is reduced by about 25 percent in long-term smokers of filter cigarettes (ten years), as compared with smokers of nonfilter cigarettes.[48] Since the 1950s, the particulate (tar) yield of American cigarettes has been repeatedly reduced.[49] The observed reductions in risk suggest that it is primarily the particulate matter that is carcinogenic to the lungs and larynx. Determination of the relative risks for smokers of nonfilter and filter cigarettes must take into account the declining tar and nicotine levels of both types of cigarettes.

A reduction in lung-cancer risk among smokers of filter cigarettes has been shown in a prospective study (selecting a healthy population and observing these persons at several points over a span of time) by Hammond and his colleagues[50] and in our studies.[51] In addition, Hammond and others have noted that the risk of heart attacks is reduced,[52] and Koch has reported a reduction in peripheral vascular disease[53]—suggesting that these cardiovascular events are also effected by components in the particulate matter, probably nicotine. From this evidence, one would infer that carbon monoxide, a major gaseous-phase smoke constituent, does not have a major role in causing lung cancer or heart attacks, since carbon monoxide was not substantially reduced in filter cigarettes until products with perforated filter tips were introduced.[54]

Studies of patterns of chronic obstructive pulmonary disease (COPD) in relation to filter-cigarette smoking have not yet been completed. Studies of the impact of using filter cigarettes versus nonfilter cigarettes on the risk of COPD remain incomplete because of the small number of persons in higher age categories who actually smoked nothing but filter cigarettes. But one would expect with some certainty that the risk is lowered for persons who smoke low-yield cigarettes only.[55] There is some evidence that chronic coughing is reduced by a change to filter cigarettes, especially when certain volatile components are reduced by charcoal filtration.[56]

Even after total cessation of smoking, a reduction in the risk of lung cancer will follow only gradually—a decline dependent on the amount and duration of smoking.[57] Obviously, the reduced risk of lung cancer in the smoker of a low-tar cigarette cannot be greater or faster than that in the ex-smoker.

A quick reduction in the risk of myocardial infarction (heart attacks) has been reported for ex-smokers.[58] Indeed, Kannel has suggestd that some reduction in the risk of heart attack occurs almost immediately after smoking cessation. Thus, one might expect a rapid reduction in risk of heart attacks concomitant with a reduction in nicotine.[59] A reduction of carbon monoxide in smoke would be more apt to bring about a reduction in the incidence of sudden deaths.[60] The reported decline in death from myocardial infarction in the United States may reflect, in part, reduced nicotine levels, as well as increased cessation of smoking.[61] Chronic obstructive pulmonary disease appears to be a nonreversible process, so reductions in smoke-particulate exposures can be expected only to inhibit its progression, not to cause its amelioration.

Most patients who now have tobacco-related diseases began to smoke in the days of the old high-tar, high-nicotine, nonfilter cigarette. Therefore, one cannot fully measure the risk among those who smoked filter cigarettes only, or determine the risk in smokers of cigarettes with tar yields of less than 10 milligrams.

Cigar and pipe smoking are associated with a lower risk of most tobacco-related diseases than cigarette smoking, probably because cigar and pipe smoke are less often inhaled.[62]

Epidemiologic studies indicate that disease patterns in women will be similar to those in men.[63] However, since most women began by smoking the lower-tar, lower-nicotine cigarettes, their tobacco-related disease rates, although increasing, will probably not reach the levels recorded for men.

Future Efforts

If tobacco-related diseases are to be eliminated, more large-scale preventive programs are required. School health programs need to be coordinated on a national scale. Education on smoking and health should be just one facet of a comprehensive, integrated and activist-promoted health-sciences program.

Greater use and availability of smoking-cessation techniques and therapies are in order. More attention should be paid to those who want to stop smoking but do not seek help. Assistance from medical and allied health professionals should be funded, at least in part, by third-party carriers, as are other medical treatments.

Increased support from government sources should be forthcoming for these activities. Studies on development of a less harmful cigarette that is acceptable to the majority of smokers should be continued. A completely "safe" cigarette that is smoked by 1 percent of the smoking public has less preventive value than a low-tar cigarette with some adverse effects that is smoked by 90 percent of that public. These recommendations reflect the comprehensive policy objectives drawn up by the International Union Against Cancer, in their Special Project on Smoking and Lung Cancer.[64]

Smoking-and-health remains one of the great challenges to the field of public health. Successful measures will have a major impact, not only on tobacco-related disease, but also on the entire health-care delivery and health-economics system. It is incumbent upon all those directly or indirectly involved with smoking and disease to become more involved, not just in the "preaching" but also in the "practice" of this vital and challenging aspect of current health care. After all, the true art of medical practice lies not so much in the therapy as in the prevention of disease.

Notes

1. E.L. Wynder and E.A. Graham, "Tobacco Smoking as a Possible Etiological Factor in Bronchiogenic Carcinoma: A Study of Six Hundred and Eighty-Four Cases," *Journal of the American Medical Association* 143 (1950):329-336; R. Doll and A.B. Hill, "Smoking and Carcinoma of the Lung: Preliminary Report," *British Medical Journal* 2 (1950):739-748; E.C. Hammond, "Smoking in Relation to the Death Rates of One Million Men and Women," *National Cancer Institute Monograph* 19 (1966):127-204; *Smoking and Health,* Report of the Advisory Committee to the Surgeon General of the Public Health Service, United States Department of Health, Education, and Welfare, Public Health Service Publication No. 1103 (Washington, D.C.: Government Printing Office, 1964); *The Health Consequences of Smoking: A Report of the Surgeon General: 1971,* DHEW Publication No. (HSM) 71-7513 (Washington, D.C.: Government Printing Office, 1971).

2. E.C. Hammond and D. Horn, "Smoking and Death Rates—Report on Forty-Four Months of Follow-Up of 187,783 Men. I. Total Mortality. II. Death Rates by Cause," *Journal of the American Medical Association* 166 (1958):1159-1172, 1294-1308; R. Doll and A.B. Hill, "Mortality in Relation to Smoking: Ten Years' Observations of British Doctors," *British Medical Journal* 1 (1964):1399-1440, 1460-1467; J.T. Doyle et al., "The Relationship of Cigarette Smoking to Coronary Heart Disease: The Second Report of the Combined Experience of the Albany, New York and Framingham, Massachusetts Studies," *Journal of the American Medical Association* 190 (1964):886-890; H.A. Kahn, "The Dorn Study of Smoking and Mortality among U.S. Veterans: Report on Eight and One-Half Years of Observation," *National Cancer Institute Monograph* 19 (1966):1-25; E.W.R. Best, *A Canadian Study of Smoking and Health* (Ottawa: Department of National Health and Welfare, 1966).

3. E.L. Wynder, I.J. Bross, and R.M. Feldman, "A Study of the Etiological Factors in Cancer of the Mouth," *Cancer* 10 (1957):1300-1323; E.L. Wynder et al. "Environmental Factors in Cancer of the Larynx: A Second Look," *Cancer* 38 (1976):1591-1601; E.L. Wynder and R. Goldsmith, "The Epidemiology of Bladder Cancer: A Second Look," *Cancer* 40 (1977):1246-1268; E.L. Wynder et al. "Epidemiology of Cancer of the Pancreas," *Journal of the National Cancer Institute* 50 (1973):645-667; J.M. Weir and J.E. Dunn, Jr., "Smoking and Mortality: A Prospective Study," *Cancer* 25 (1970):105-112; T. Hirayama, "Smoking in

Relation to the Death Rates of 265,118 Men and Women in Japan." A report on five years' follow-up, American Cancer Society's 14th Science Writers' Seminar, Clearwater Beach, Florida, March 24-29, 1972, pp. 1-4.

4. United States Department of Health, Education, and Welfare, *Cancer Incidence and Mortality in the United States*, DHEW Publication No. (NIH) 78-1837 (Washington, D.C.: Government Printing Office, 1978).

5. E.L. Wynder et al., "Lung Cancer in Women: A Study of Environmental Factors," *New England Journal of Medicine* 255 (1956):1111-1121.

6. B. Sutton-Smith, *Child Psychology* (Englewood Cliffs, New Jersey: Appleton-Century-Crofts, 1973); P. Wohlford, "Initiation of Cigarette Smoking: Is It Related to Parent Smoking Behavior?" *Journal of Consulting and Clinical Psychology* 34 (1970):148-151.

7. A. McKennell, "Implications for Health Education of Social Influences on Smoking," *American Journal of Public Health* 59 (1969):1998-2004; A.B. Palmer, "Some Variables Contributing to the Onset of Cigarette Smoking among Junior High School Students," *Social Science and Medicine* 4 (1970):359-366.

8. "Gallup Opinion Index Report No. 108," Princeton, New Jersey, June 20-21, 1974.

9. S. Kelson, J. Pullela, and A. Otterland, "The Growing Epidemic: A Survey of Smoking Habits and Attitudes towards Smoking among Students of Grades 7 through 12 in Toledo and Lucas County (Ohio) Public Schools—1964 and 1971," *American Journal of Public Health* 65 (1975):923-936.

10. J. Albino and R.L. Davis, "A Health Education Program That Works," *Phi Delta Kappa* 57 (1975):256-259.

11. H.S. Rabinowitz and W.H. Zimmerli, "Effects of a Health Education Program on Junior High School Students' Knowledge, Attitudes, and Behavior concerning Tobacco Use," *Journal of School Health* 44 (1974):324-330.

12. R.L. Davis, "Making Health Education Relevant and Exciting in Elementary School and Junior High School," *Health Service Report* 88 (1973):99-108.

13. W. James, "Where Did We Go Wrong?" *Journal of Health, Physical Education, Recreation* 43 (1972):21-22; J.M. Bynner, *The Young Smoker: A Study of Smoking among Schoolboys Carried Out for the Ministry of Health* (London: Her Majesty Stationery Office, 1969); R.I. Evans, et al., "Deterring the Onset of Smoking in Children: Knowledge of Immediate Physiological Effects and Coping with Peer Pressure, Media Pressure and Parent Modeling," *Journal of Applied Social Psychology* 8 (1978):126-135.

14. Evans, et al., "Deterring the Onset."

15. W.H. Grigson, "Smoking: The Problem and a Solution," *Physical Education* 27 (1970):11-13.

16. A.L. Harnett, "Suggested Guidelines for a High School Smoking Intervention Clinic," *Journal of School Health* 43 (1973):221-224.

17. A. Rosner, "Modifying Attitudes of Upper Elementary Students towards Smoking," *Journal of School Health* 44 (1974):97-98.

18. R.I. Evans, "Smoking in Children: Developing a Social Psychological Strategy of Deterrence," *Preventive Medicine* 5 (1976):122-127.

19. A.C. McAlister and C. Perry, "Project CLASP," presented at a National Interagency Council on Smoking and Health conference on Teenage Cigarette Smoking: A National Health Problem, Washington, D.C., January 10, 1978.

20. C.L. Perry, N. Maccoby, and A.C. McAlister, "Adolescent Smoking Prevention—A Third Year Follow-up," *World Smoking and Health* 5, no. 3 (1980):40-45.

21. C.L. Williams, C.A. Arnold, and E.L. Wynder, "Primary Prevention of Chronic Disease Beginning in Childhood: The 'Know Your Body' Program Design of Study," *Preventive Medicine* 6 (1977):344-357; C.L. Williams, B.J. Carter, and A. Eng, "The 'Know Your Body' Program: A Developmental Approach to Health Education and Disease Prevention," *Preventive Medicine* 9 (1980):371-383.

22. G.J. Botvin, A. Eng, and C.L. Williams, "Preventing the Onset of Cigarette Smoking through Life Skills Training," *Preventive Medicine* 9 (1980):135-143.

23. L.M. Ramstrom, "Public Education: Its Role in Smoking Cessation," *Proceedings of the Third World Conference on Smoking and Health*, DHEW, Publication No. (NIH) 77-1413, vol. 2 (Washington, D.C.: Government Printing Office, 1977), pp. 525-532.

24. *National Clearinghouse for Smoking and Health: Adult Use of Tobacco 1970, and Adult Use of Tobacco 1975* (Atlanta, Georgia: Center for Disease Control, 1971 and 1976).

25. R. Dubren, *Study of Smoking Intervention Techniques*, Project Report HSM-21-72-557 to the National Clearinghouse for Smoking and Health (Atlanta, Georgia: Center for Disease Control, 1977).

26. Ibid.

27. "Gallup Opinion" (see note 8); L.A. Shewchuk, "Guidelines for Organizing Smoking Withdrawal Clinics," *Proceedings of the Third World Conference on Smoking and Health*, DHEW Publication No. (NIH) 77-1413, vol. 2 (Washington, D.C.: Government Printing Office, 1977), pp. 665-668.

28. Shewchuk, "Guidelines for Organizing"; L.A. Shewchuk and E.L. Wynder, "Guidelines on Smoking Cessation Clinics," *Preventive Medicine* 6 (1977):130-133.

29. D.A. Bernstein, "Modification of Smoking Behavior: An Evaluative Review," *Psychological Bulletin* 71 (1969):418-440; J.L. Schwartz, "Research Methodology in Smoking Cessation: A Critique." *Proceedings of the Third World Conference on Smoking and Health*, DHEW Publication No. (NIH) 77-1413, vol. 2 (Washington, D.C.: Government Printing Office, 1977), pp. 649-653.

30. Shewchuk and Wynder, "Guidelines on Smoking."

31. Dubren, *Study of Smoking* (see note 25).

32. "Gallup Opinion" (see note 8).

33. M.M. Kristen, "Economic Issues in Prevention," *Preventive Medicine* 6 (1977):252-264.

34. National Commission on Smoking and Public Policy, *A National Dilemma: Cigarette Smoking or the Health of Americans*, Report to the Board of Directors of the American Cancer Society (New York: National Commission on Smoking and Public Policy, 1978).

35. E.C. Hammond et al., "Some Recent Findings concerning Cigarette Smoking," in *Origins of Human Cancer*, ed. H.H. Hiatt, J.D. Watson, and J.A. Winsten (Cold Spring Harbor, New York: Cold Spring Harbor Laboratory, 1977), pp. 101-112; E.L. Wynder and S.D. Stellman, "Comparative Epidemiology of Tobacco-Related Cancers," *Cancer Research* 37 (1977):4608-4622; United States Department of Health, Education, and Welfare, *The Health Consequences of Smoking, A Reference Edition* (Atlanta, Georgia: Center for Disease Control, 1976).

36. Hammond and Horn, "Smoking and Death Rates" (see note 2); W.B. Kannel, W.P. Castelli, and P.M. McNamara, "Cigarette Smoking and Risk of Coronary Heart Disease: Epidemiologic Clues to Pathogenesis: The Framingham Study," *National Cancer Institute Monograph* 28 (1968): 9-20; C.M. Fletcher, "Consequences of Smoking: Pulmonary Disease," *Proceedings of the Third World Conference on Smoking and Health*, DHEW Publication No. (NIH) 77-1413, vol. 2 (Washington, D.C.: Government Printing Office, 1977), pp. 35-42.

37. E.L. Wynder and D. Hoffman, *Tobacco and Tobacco Smoke: Studies in Experimental Carcinogenesis* (New York: Academic Press, 1967); D. Hoffman et al., "Chemical Studies on Tobacco Smoke, p. XXXIX: On the Identification of Carcinogens, Tumor Promoters, and Cocarcinogens in Tobacco Smoke," *Proceedings of the Third World Conference on Smoking and Health*, DHEW Publication No. (NIH) 76-1221, vol. 1 (Washington, D.C.: Government Printing Office, 1976), pp. 125-145; "Lung Cancer Workshops on the Biology of Human Cancer," in *UICC Technical Report Series*, vol. 25, report 3, ed. E.L. Wynder and S.S. Hecht (Geneva, Switzerland: L'Union Internationale Contre le Cancer, 1976); D. Hoffman et al., "Model Studies in Tobacco Carcinogenesis with the Syrian Golden

Hamster," *Progress in Experimental Tumor Research* (Karger, Basel) 24 (1979):370-390; T.D. Day, "Carcinogenic Action of Cigarette Smoke Condensate on Mouse Skin. An Attempt at a Quantitative Study," *British Journal of Cancer* 21 (1967):56-81; W. Dontenwill et al., "Experimentelle Untersuchungen über die tumorerzeugende Wirkung von Zigarettenrauch Kondensaten an der Mäusehaut," *Zeitschrift fuer Krebsforschung* 73 (1972):264-274; W. Dontenwill et al., "Experimentelle Untersuchungen über die tumorerzeugende Wirkung von Zigarettenrauch Kondensaten an der Mäusehaut," *Zeitschrift fuer Krebsforschung* 73 (1972):236-264; P. Lazar et al., "Bioassays of Carcinogenicity after Fractionation of Cigarette Smoke Condensate," *Biomedicine* 20 (1974):214-222.

38. Wynder and Hoffman, *Tobacco and Tobacco Smoke*; "Lung Cancer Workshops."

39. "Lung Cancer Workshops."

40. T. Abelin, "Types of Tobacco Usage and Chronic Respiratory Disease," *Proceedings of the Third World Conference on Smoking and Health*, DHEW Publication No. (NIH) 76-1221, vol. 1 (Washington, D.C.: Government Printing Office, 1976), pp. 407-413; G.M. Green, et al., "Defense Mechanisms of the Respiratory Membrane," *American Review of Respiratory Diseases* 115 (1979):479-514.

41. P. Hill and E.L. Wynder, "Smoking and Cardiovascular Disease: Effect of Nicotine on the Serum Epinephrine and Corticoids," *American Heart Journal* 87 (1974):491-496; N.J. Wald, "Carbon Monoxide as an Aetiological Agent in Arterial Disease: Some Human Evidence," *Proceedings of the Third World Conference on Smoking and Health*, DHEW Publication No. (NIH) 76-1221, vol. 1 (Washington, D.C.: Government Printing Office, 1976), pp. 349-361; W.S. Aronow, "Carbon Monoxide and Cardiovascular Disease," *Proceedings of the Third World Conference on Smoking and Health*, DHEW Publication No. (NIH) 76-1221, vol. 1 (Washington, D.C.: Government Printing Office, 1976), pp. 321-330; Aronow, "Effect of Cigarette Smoking and of Carbon Monoxide on Coronary Heart Disease," *Chest* 70 (1976):514-518; P. Hill, "Nicotine: An Etiological Factor for Coronary Disease," *Proceedings of the Third World Conference on Smoking and Health*, DHEW Publication No. (NIH) 76-1221, vol. 1 (Washington, D.C.: Government Printing Office, 1976), pp. 313-319; G.C. McMillan, "Evidence for Components Other Than Carbon Monoxide and Nicotine as Etiological Factors in Cardiovascular Disease," *Proceedings of the Third World Conference on Smoking and Health*, DHEW Publication No. (NIH) 76-1221, vol. 1 (Washington, D.C.: Government Printing Office, 1976), pp. 363-367; "Carbon Monoxide and Cardiovascular Disease," Workshop at Berlin, October 11-12, 1978 SozEP Berichte 1/1979, ed. H. Hoffmeister (Berlin: Dietrich Reimer Verlag, 1979).

42. G.B. Gori, "Approaches to the Reduction of Total Particulate Matter in Cigarette Smoke," *Proceedings of the Third World Conference on Smoking and Health*, DHEW Publication No. (NIH) 76-1221, vol. 1 (Washington, D.C.: Government Printing Office, 1976), pp. 451-461; D. Hoffman and E.L. Wynder, "Selective Reduction of Tumorigenicity of Tobacco Smoke. III. The Reduction of Polynuclear Aromatic Hydrocarbons in Cigarette Smoke," *Proceedings of the Third World Conference on Smoking and Health*, DHEW Publication No. (NIH) 76-1221, vol. 1 (Washington, D.C.: Government Printing Office, 1976), pp. 495-504.

43. Gori, "Approaches to the Reduction."

44. K.H. Weber, "Recent Changes in Tobacco Products and Their Acceptance by the Consumer," *Proceedings of the Sixth International Tobacco Scientific Congress*, Tokyo, 1976 (Tokyo: Coresta and the Japan Tobacco and Salt Public Corporation, 1976), pp. 47-63; *U.S. Federal Trade Commission: Report of "Tar" and Nicotine Content of the Smoke of 166 Varieties of Cigarettes* (Washington, D.C.: Government Printing Office, 1977).

45. Ibid.

46. D. Hoffman et al., "Tobacco Carcinogens, Polycyclic Hydrocarbons and Cancer," in *Environment, Chemistry, Metabolism*, vol. 1, ed. H. Gelboin and P.O. Ts'o (New York: Academic Press, 1978), pp. 119-130.

47. Hammond and Horn, "Smoking and Death" (see note 2); Hammond et al., "Recent Findings" (see note 35); Fletcher, "Consequences of Smoking" (see note 36).

48. E.L. Wynder and S.D. Stellman, "The Impact of Long Term Filter Cigarette Usage on Lung and Larynx Cancer Risk: A Case Control Study," *Journal of the National Cancer Institute* 62 (1979):471-477.

49. Weber, "Recent Changes"; *U.S. Federal Trade Commission Report*; G.B. Gori, "Low-Risk Cigarettes: A Prescription," *Science* 194 (1976):1243-1246.

50. Hammond et al., "Recent Findings."

51. Wynder and Stellman, "Comparative Epidemiology" (see note 35); Wynder and Stellman, "Impact of Long-Term Filter Cigarette."

52. Hammond et al., "Recent Findings."

53. A. Koch, "Smoking and Peripheral Arterial Disease," *Proceedings of the Third World Conference on Smoking and Health*, DHEW Publication No. (NIH) 77-1221, vol. 1 (Washington, D.C.: Government Printing Office, 1977), pp. 281-284.

54. "Carbon Monoxide" (see note 41—Berlin Workshop); D. Hoffmann, J.D. Adams, and E.L. Wynder, "Formation and Analysis of Carbon Monoxide in Cigarette Mainstream and Sidestream Smoke," *Preventive Medicine* 8 (1979):344-350; N. Wald et al., "Carboxyhemoglobin Levels in Smokers of Filter and Plain Cigarettes," *Lancet* 1 (1977):110-112.

55. E.L. Wynder, "Some Concepts of the Less Harmful Cigarette," in *A Safe Cigarette—Banbury Report Number 3*, ed. G.B. Gori and F.G. Bock (Cold Spring Harbor, New York: Cold Spring Harbor Laboratory, 1980), pp. 3-12.

56. J. Remington, "Phlegm and Filters," *British Medical Journal*, 2 (1972):262-264; S. Freedman, C.M. Fletcher, and G.B. Field, "Effects of Smoking Modified Cigarettes on Respiratory Symptoms and Ventilatory Capacity," *Journal of the National Cancer Institute* 48 (1972):1805-1810; G.W. Comstock et al., "Cigarette Smoking and Changes in Respiratory Findings," *Archives of Environmental Health* 21 (1970):50-57.

57. Hammond et al., "Recent Findings"; Wynder and Stellman, "Comparative Epidemiology"; Wynder and Stellman, "Impact of Long-Term Filter Cigarette."

58. W.B. Kannel, "Coronary Risk Factors. I. Recent Highlights from the Framingham Study," *Australian and New Zealand Journal of Medicine* 6 (1976):373-386; Kannel, "Some Lessons in Cardiovascular Epidemiology from Framingham," *American Journal of Cardiology* 37 (1976):269-282.

59. Kannel, "Coronary Risk."

60. Kannel, "Some Lessons"; W.S. Aronow, "Effect of Carbon Monoxide on Cardiovascular Disease," *Preventive Medicine* 8 (1979):271-278.

61. Hammond et al., "Recent Findings."

62. *Smoking and Health* report (see note 1).

63. Wynder and Stellman, "Comparative Epidemiology."

64. Union International Contre le Cancer Executive Committee: Endorsement of Policy Objectives of Special Project on Smoking and Lung Cancer, *UICC Bulletin on Cancer* 15(4), December 1977.

24

Cigarette Smoking and Coronary Heart Disease: A Questionable Connection

Carl C. Seltzer

More Americans die from heart disease than from any other single disease. It is the leading cause of death and disability in the western world. Thus, of all the diseases reportedly associated with cigarette smoking, coronary heart disease (CHD) has the potential of affecting the greatest number of people. Consequently, it is necessary to evaluate the available scientific data to determine whether they support claims about smoking and CHD. This chapter examines certain portions of the data, including cessation-of-smoking studies, to show why I believe there is no convincing proof that cigarette smoking is causally related to CHD.

Development of Causal Claims

Few remember or even refer to the fact that the "blue-ribbon" surgeon general's Advisory Committee on Smoking and Health of 1964 did *not* find a causal connection between smoking and CHD. Specifically, the Advisory Committee concluded that "it is not clear that the association has causal significance."[1] On January 29, 1964, the then surgeon general, Dr. Luther Terry, stated "the committee was unable to reach a firm conclusion as to the role smoking plays in causing or precipitating a death from this disease. We need to find out for sure whether smoking is a factor in this disease or whether it should be exonerated . . . we have no real clues as to what it is in tobacco that influences coronary heart disease, if indeed it does."[2]

Within months of the report's publication, however, statements began to be made about the relationship between cigarette smoking and CHD that went far beyond the limited conclusions of the Advisory Committee and Dr. Terry. These statements—from the American Heart Association,[3] persons in medicine and science, numerous medical societies,[4] and others—either claimed or implied that the connection between smoking and CHD was causal.

Having been a consultant to the Advisory Committee, I became curious about this sudden escalation of the conclusions of the 1964 report and reviewed subsequent publications dealing with the epidemiological evidence.

In this review, which appeared in the *Journal of the American Medical Association* in 1968,[5] I determined that the later data did not provide sufficient justification for causally linking cigarette smoking and excess CHD deaths. In 1970, I reviewed the pathological and experimental data and again found that the data did not support the new claims and that the conclusion of the surgeon general's Advisory Committee was still valid.[6]

Since that time, subsequent reports by the surgeon general and by the Department of Health and Human Services have purported to summarize the available information relative to smoking and CHD. For the most part, however, these reports have broken little new ground. Essentially, they have summarized the same type of research that was covered by the 1964 report, provided updates of ongoing epidemiological studies, noted duplicative studies covering the same areas as previous investigations, and proposed mechanisms that might explain the reported association between smoking and heart disease.

Unfortunately, these reports can be characterized as unbalanced, selective, and biased because they ignore or criticize material that conflicts with the causal hypothesis. The net result has been a creeping escalation of the claims of the U.S. Public Health Service, from the conclusion in 1964 that "it is not clear that the association has causal significance,"[7] to "strongly *suggests* that cigarette smoking *can* cause death from coronary heart disease" in 1967[8] (emphasis added), to the flat conclusion in 1979 that "smoking is causally related to coronary heart disease for both men and women in the United States."[9]

It is important to note in considering these statements that the 1964 report was prepared by independent scientists selected by the government and approved by the tobacco industry, but that subsequent reports have been prepared solely by government bureaucrats.

Basis for the Causal Hypothesis

The evidence supporting the causal hypothesis is neither consistent, definitive, nor conclusive. Proponents of this hypothesis rest their case primarily on the following arguments: (1) that there is "overwhelming evidence" of an association between cigarette smoking and heart disease; (2) that there is a raising gradient of CHD with increasing amounts and duration of cigarette smoking; and (3) that cessation of smoking reduces the risk of the disease.

In an annotation to the *American Heart Journal* in 1975,[10] I discussed several findings that do not support these arguments. First, multinational studies have found little or no association between smoking and coronary heart disease, including the Seven Countries Study by Keys[11] which was recently updated.[12] In his first report, Keys found no association between cigarette smoking and CHD in Finland, the Netherlands, Yugoslavia, Italy, Greece, and Japan. This was confirmed in his update, in which Keys stated that the "differences among the cohorts [groups of people in the same age group] in the incidence rates of coronary heart disease and of death from all causes are not explained by, or related to, the differences among the cohorts in their smoking habits." Even advocates of the causal hypothesis have agreed, as late as 1980, that the Keys findings are an example of "inconsistencies in the smoking-CHD evidence."[13] A second finding that I reported in the *American Heart Journal* is that angina pectoris (chest pains), an important manifestation of CHD, "is probably unrelated to cigarette smoking."[14] And third, the "alleged rising gradient of CHD mortality with the amount and duration of cigarette smoking is not consistent and is, in some instances, actually reversed."[15] In another study published in 1975, I demonstrated that death and disability from CHD show little, if any, association with continued cigarette smoking in people sixty-five years and older—a section of the population that accounts for two-thirds of all CHD deaths.[16]

Moreover, arguments based on epidemiological research designs are not substantiated by any proven scientific mechanisms. That is, it has not been demonstrated that some component of tobacco smoke, such as nicotine or carbon monoxide (CO), adversely affects coronary vessels. In addition, some studies have not taken into account the "constitutional" or "genetic" hypothesis. According to this hypothesis, persons who choose to smoke may be more vulnerable to heart disease than nonsmokers, *not* because of their smoking but because of their basic characteristics and health histories. This suggests that the smok*er*—not the smok*ing*—is responsible for the CHD association because of an inherent tendency toward heart trouble.

Proven Mechanisms Needed

Studies that claim there is a causal relationship between smoking and CHD must prove there is some mechanism by which tobacco smoke, or some component of tobacco smoke, causes CHD. After many years of studies, however, researchers have been unable to establish these mechanisms satisfactorily. The 1964 surgeon general's report, for example, stated that "no additional or unique cardiovascular effects" of smoking and of nicotine had been demonstrated that would "seem likely to account for the observed association of cigarette smoking with an increased incidence of coronary disease."[17]

The authors of the 1967 report, apparently dissatisfied with the 1964 conclusion, discussed hypothetical mechanisms by which nicotine and/or CO could affect coronary blood flow, particularly in subjects with preexisting heart disease. The key studies cited to explain the process by which

CO supposedly augmented atherogenesis (clogging) of the coronary vessels were Astrup's animal experiments.[18] But in 1978, Astrup recanted and reported that he had been unable to duplicate the results of those experiments because he discovered flaws in his experimental design.[19] "Irrespective of duration or level of exposure [to CO]," Astrup subsequently stated, "no significant morphological changes were present to discriminate between experimental and control animals."[20]

The 1979 surgeon general's report appraised the hypothetical mechanisms in a more realistic fashion than the 1967 report.[21] With regard to so-called clogging of the blood vessels, the 1979 report stated: "Animal experiments on atherogenesis and CO have provided conflicting data and must be regarded as unsatisfactory, . . . the mechanisms by which smoking enhances atherogenesis require elucidation, . . . nicotine does not affect atherogenesis in animals." The 1979 report also addressed the action of nicotine: "The acute and transient effect of smoking in man is to increase heart rate and blood pressure to a *minor* degree" (emphasis added). A statement in the 1980 American Heart Association *Heartbook* underscored the conclusions of the 1979 report: "The mechanisms by which cigarette smoking is associated with higher rates of coronary heart disease are not yet fully understood."[22] Apparently, experimental and clinical reports to support the epidemiological data have failed to provide the necessary evidence for the causal hypothesis.

Although many scientists and researchers do not acknowledge the inconsistencies in the smoking-CHD evidence, some advocates of the causal hypothesis do. Writing for the *American Heart Journal* in 1980, Dr. Gary D. Friedman of the Kaiser-Permanente Medical Care Program stated:

> The relation between smoking and CHD has not generally been strong. . . . Relatively weak associations are often attributable to some underlying characteristic. Thus, it has been proposed that some constitutional or genetic factors are present in the smoker that both lead him or her to smoke and predispose to CHD. This "counterhypothesis" has had some distinguished support, going back, at least, to the noted statistician, R.A. Fisher. . . . Another problem with the evidence concerning smoking and CHD is that the relationship is not found in all study populations. For example, in the seven-country collaborative study of Keys and associates, U.S. railroad workers showed the smoking-CHD relationship, but using similar data collection methods, men in Finland, the Netherlands, Italy, Greece, Yugoslavia, and Japan did not, and these countries range from low to high CHD incidence. Another troublesome finding is that cigarette smoking tends to be a weaker predictor of CHD in older persons than in young and middle-aged adults. While this is true of other risk factors, too, it does not seem consistent with the generally held notion that smoking acts to induce clinical CHD largely by precipitating acute events such as myocardial infarction and sudden cardiac death. Older persons with advanced atherosclerosis should be especially susceptible to this effect. Then again, the mechanism by which smoking promotes CHD has not been well

established. . . . Finally, data from studies of smoking-discordant identical twins where the smokers and nonsmokers are genetically the same have not shown the degree of association between smoking and CHD as has been found in the general population, where there is obviously no such genetic matching. . . . Similar considerations apply to the association of smoking with total mortality, of which deaths from CHD . . . constitute a major component.[23]

Friedman openly addresses many of the questions concerning the smoking-CHD evidence. He views the "constitutional" hypothesis in its proper historical context and recognizes the research on identical twins that tends to support this hypothesis,[24] research that the U.S. Public Health Service cavalierly dismisses. Despite this frank assessment of the evidence, however, even Friedman curiously omits any reference to inconsistencies in smoking-cessation data, including a recent study on this subject in which he participated.[25]

Cessation of Smoking

A number of studies of ex-smokers show that the CHD mortality rates for persons who stopped smoking are substantially lower than for those who continue the habit. Many consider that such data provide the strongest support for the causal hypothesis. The American Heart Association's ad hoc committee on cigarette smoking and cardiovascular diseases has interpreted these data as forging "the final link in the chain of evidence incriminating cigarette smoking as a causal factor in cardiovascular disease."[26]

However, ex-smoker studies may be flawed because they are based on the questionable assumption that ex-smokers are representative of continuing smokers in regard to all relevant characteristics except for their change in smoking habits. Virtually no attempt has been made by epidemiologists to determine whether this assumption is valid. And if it is not, then differences in mortality outcomes of ex-smokers and smokers are biased, because the test groups did not start from the same baseline. The epidemiologists have compared the health of nonsmokers with continuing smokers even though these two groups did not have the same health-risk characteristics at the baseline point, the point when both groups were smoking.

For the first time, results from a large-scale study are available to test the validity of this assumption. The Kaiser-Permanente group recently concluded investigations which show decisively that, for white and black men and women, this assumption is not valid.[27] When a proper baseline was observed for the comparison of CHD-related characteristics of smokers and ex-smokers, *at a point in time when ex-smokers were still smokers*, it was found that ex-smokers cannot be assumed to be representative of all smokers, thereby making comparisons between the two groups biased as to CHD outcomes. These findings indicate that the ex-smokers were healthier and at lower CHD risk at the baseline point (when still smokers) than were those persons who continued to smoke. When epidemiologists mismanage their ex-smoker studies, it is small wonder that ex-smokers end up with lower CHD rates than continuing smokers.

A 1978 report in the *Journal of Epidemiology and Community Health* supports this conclusion.[28] The researchers, Drs. Rose and Hamilton, took a random sample of middle-aged men who were assumed to be at risk of cardiovascular disease because they smoked and had high scores on tests for such variables as cholesterol levels and blood pressure. The researchers urged one group, the "intervention" group, to stop smoking; they did not urge the "control" group to stop smoking. After almost eight years of surveillance, the intervention group showed *no* improvement in rate of mortality over the control group. Approximately the same percentage of men from both groups died during the study period. Hence, smokers urged to stop smoking during the study did not improve their chances of living longer than smokers who were not urged to stop smoking.

To summarize, it is reasonable to believe at this time that stopping smoking does not reduce the risk of CHD, and that there is no convincing scientific proof that cigarette smoking is causally related to CHD.[29]

The Issue of Public Smoking

The controversy with regard to smoking and coronary heart disease has led to unsubstantiated claims about the effects of smoking on the *non*smoker as well as the smoker. Claims about "passive smoking" have been stimulated by the research of Dr. W.S. Aronow, who reportedly found that heart pain developed sooner after exercise in patients who had angina pectoris and evidence of severe coronary-artery disease when they were exposed to tobacco smoke.[30] Even though his study design and results have been criticized,[31] the attention paid to this issue has continued to increase. Many claims about ambient tobacco smoke have focused on individual constituents, such as carbon monoxide or nicotine. Others have identified special situations, such as parents who smoke around their children and nonsmokers who are exposed to cigarette smoke in some work environments.

Carbon monoxide from tobacco smoke is often singled out as the greatest threat to nonsmokers. But a review by Dr. H.R.R. Wakeham of the claimed hazards of CO generated by burning cigarettes did not find that it was hazardous to nonsmokers in "real-life" situations.[32] Moreover, these findings appeared in *Preventive Medicine*, a journal of the American Health Foundation edited by Dr. Ernst Wynder, well-known for his anti-smoking views. Wakeham considered the sources of CO, its concentrations in enclosed spaces, the amount inhaled, the observed carboxyhemoglobin (COHb) concentrations, and the response of healthy individuals to increased COHb levels. Pointing out that the American Conference of Government Industrial Hygienists has established a threshold limit of 50 parts per million as the maximum for daily eight-hour exposures, Wakeham cited studies which suggest that it is almost impossible to attain this concentration in a closed room or house by smoking alone. Because of ventilation, there appears to be an upper limit to the possible buildup of CO concentrations from smoking in "real-life" situations.

Nicotine is also alleged to have harmful effects on nonsmokers, but this claim has not been proved. Two Harvard University scientists, who tested for the effects of tobacco smoke in public places by measuring nicotine, determined that a nonsmoker could potentially absorb only the equivalent of 1/100 to 1/1,000 of a filter cigarette per hour.[33] With regard to the claim that smoking by parents adversely affects their children, Yale University investigators studied the respiratory symptoms, disease, and lung function of families in three U.S. towns and concluded that "parental smoking had no effect on children's symptoms and lung function."[34]

In 1980, White and Froeb implied in a *New England Journal of Medicine* article that nonsmokers can develop chronic lung disease by inhaling cigarette smoke in working environments.[35] These researchers measured the small-airways function of smokers and nonsmokers who were enrolled in a physical-fitness course sponsored by the University of California at San Diego. They concluded that nonsmokers who were exposed to smoking at work for more than twenty years had reduced function of small airways compared with nonsmokers who reported working in smoke-free offices. In the same issue of this journal, however, scientists from the National Heart, Lung, and Blood Institute noted that the findings of White and Froeb have not been shown to have "any physiological or clinical consequences."[36]

Since the publication of that article, a number of letters to the editor have appeared in the journal raising serious questions about the meaning of White and Froeb's findings.[37] A medical doctor, for example, not only expressed concern about possible "technical problems" in the study but also suggested that "its experimental premise may be questionable."[38] As a consequence, he argued that much of the study "needs verification from an epidemiologic point of view." This conclusion was generally shared by the researchers themselves who conceded that "we agree that our data are new and should be verified."[39] Another possibly serious defect in the White and Froeb paper is the absence of the effect of racial differentiation among the study population. The authors have agreed to examine this problem, but as yet no such analysis has appeared.

The 1979 surgeon general's report, after reviewing the scientific literature, concluded that "healthy nonsmokers exposed to cigarette smoke have little or no physiologic response to the smoke, and what response does occur may be due to psychological factors."[40] A *New England Journal of Medicine* editorial accompanying the White/Froeb study echoed this finding: "Generally speaking, the evidence that passive smoking in a general environment has health effects remains sparse, incomplete, and sometimes unconvincing."[41] Nonetheless, there are persistent demands to restrict smoking in public places on the basis of health claims, despite views of many scientists whose anti-smoking views are well known. Dr. Wynder is quoted as saying that "passive smoking can provoke tears, or can be otherwise disagreeable but it has no influence on the health."[42] Dr. Gio Gori, formerly with the National Cancer Institute, has stated: "The fact remains that we really do not have conclusive scientific evidence about the adverse health effects of passive smoking on the bystander."[43]

Conclusion

The history of medicine throughout the centuries contains many examples of evangelical fervor for both etiologic and therapeutic theories that were later shown to be wrong. Seldom has any target evoked so many strident voices and so much mindless emotion as tobacco smoking. This has made the sober unraveling of the problem more difficult. But a prime responsibility of the investigator is to maintain the skepticism of science amid the passions of evangelism. The health of the public and the welfare of science demand a dispassionate and balanced consideration of all the available evidence if we are to learn the truth.

It seems imperative that well-designed and scientifically sound research in this area should be undertaken. For, if the conventional view that cigarette smoking causes or contributes to CHD is not supported by the scientific data, as I believe it is not, a large number of people no longer will be considered at risk, which would have a profound effect on the preventive strategies presently being employed by numerous organizations and governments.

Notes

1. *Smoking and Health*, Report of the Advisory Committee to the Surgeon General of the Public Health Service, United States Department of Health, Education, and Welfare, Public Health Service Publication No. 1103 (Washington, D.C.: Government Printing Office, 1964).

2. L. Terry, Hearings before the Subcommittee on Tobacco of the Committee on Agriculture, House of Representatives, series 2, p. 5, January 29, 1964.

3. Hearings before the Committee on Commerce, U.S. Senate, part 1, serial no. 89-5, March 22, 1965.

4. J. Stamler, "Nutrition, Metabolism and Atherosclerosis," in *Controversy in Internal Medicine*, ed. F.J. Ingelfinger, A.S. Relman, and M. Finland (Philadelphia: W.B. Saunders, 1966), pp. 27-59; D. Horn, "An Analysis of the Educational Problems of Controlling Cigarette Smoking," read before the International Cancer Congress, Tokyo, October 26, 1966.

5. C.C. Seltzer, "An Evaluation of the Effect of Smoking on Coronary Heart Disease. I. Epidemiological Evidence," *Journal of the American Medical Association* 203, no. 3 (1968):193-200.

6. C.C. Seltzer, "The Effects of Cigarette Smoking on Coronary Heart Disease. Where Do We Stand Now?" *Archives of Environmental Health* 20 (1970):418-423.

7. *Smoking and Health*, 1964.

8. *The Health Consequences of Smoking, A Public Health Service Review: 1967*, United States Department of Health, Education, and Welfare, Public Health Service Publication No. 1696, revised 1968.

9. *Smoking and Health*, A Report of the Surgeon General, United States Department of Health, Education, and Welfare, DHEW Publication No. 79-50066 (Washington, D.C.: Government Printing Office, 1979).

10. C.C. Seltzer, "Smoking and Cardiovascular Disease," *American Heart Journal* 90 (1975):125-126.

11. A. Keys, ed., "Coronary Heart Disease in Seven Countries," American Heart Association Monograph no. 29, 1970.

12. A. Keys, *Seven Countries: A Multivariate Analysis of Death and Coronary Heart Disease* (Cambridge: Harvard University Press, 1980).

13. G.D. Friedman, "Cigarette Smoking and Coronary Heart Disease: New Evidence and Old Reactions," *American Heart Journal* 99, no. 3 (1980):398-399.

14. Seltzer, "Smoking and Cardiovascular Disease."

15. Ibid.

16. C.C. Seltzer, "Smoking and Coronary Heart Disease in the Elderly," *American Journal of the Medical Sciences* 269, no. 3 (1975):309-315.

17. *Smoking and Health*, 1964.

18. P. Astrup, K. Kjeldsen, and J. Wanstrup, "Enhancing Influence of Carbon Monoxide on the Development of Atheromatosis in Cholesterol-Fed Rabbits," *Journal of Atherosclerosis Research* 7 (1967):343-354.

19. C. Hugod, L. Hawkins, K. Kjeldsen, H. Thomsen, and P. Astrup, "Effect of Carbon Monoxide Exposure on Aortic and Coronary Intimal Morphology in the Rabbit," *Atherosclerosis* 30 (1978):333-342.

20. C. Hugod and P. Astrup, "Morphological Investigations on Histotoxicity of Gas Phase Constituents of Tobacco Smoke in the Rabbit," Fourth World Conference on Smoking and Health, Stockholm, Sweden, June 18-21, 1979.

21. *Smoking and Health*, 1979.

22. R.I. Evans, J.K. Thwaites, and J.J. Witte, "Hazards of Smoking," in the American Heart Association *Heartbook* (New York: E.P. Dutton, 1980), pp. 22-40.

23. Friedman, "Cigarette Smoking and Coronary Heart Disease."

24. R. Cederlof, L. Friberg, and T. Lundman, "The Interactions of Smoking, Environment, and Heredity and Their Implications for Disease Etiology; A Report of Epidemiological Studies on the Swedish Twin Registries," *Acta Medica Scandinavica*, Supplement 612, 1977.

25. G.D. Friedman, A.B. Siegelaub, L.G. Dales, and C.C. Seltzer, "Characteristics Predictive of Coronary Heart Disease in Ex-smokers before They Stopped Smoking: Comparison with Persistent Smokers and Nonsmokers," *Journal of Chronic Diseases* 32 (1979):175-190.

26. American Heart Association Ad Hoc Committee, Revision of 1971 Statement on Cigarette Smoking and Cardiovascular Diseases, 1977.

27. Friedman et al., "Characteristics Predictive."

28. G. Rose and P.J.S. Hamilton, "A Randomised Controlled Trial of the Effect on Middle-Aged Men of Advice to Stop Smoking," *Journal of Epidemiology and Community Health* 32 (1978):275-281.

29. C.C. Seltzer, "Smoking and Coronary Heart Disease: What Are We to Believe?" Editorial, *American Heart Journal* 100, no. 3 (1980):275-280.

30. W.S. Aronow, "Effect of Passive Smoking on Angina Pectoris," *New England Journal of Medicine* 299, no. 1 (1978):21-24.

31. A. Niden, "No: Environmental Smoke Can Irritate Not Injure Others," *Los Angeles Times*, October 29, 1978; E. Fisher, Hearing before the Subcommittee on Tobacco of the Committee on Agriculture, House of Representatives, serial no. 95-000, pp. 2-20, September 7, 1978.

32. H.R.R. Wakeham, "Environmental Carbon Monoxide from Cigarette Smoking—A Critique." *Preventive Medicine* 6 (1977):526-534.

33. W.C. Hinds and M.W. First, "Concentrations of Nicotine and Tobacco Smoke in Public Places," *New England Journal of Medicine* 292 (1975):844-845; G. Huber, "Smoking and Nonsmokers—What Is the Issue?" *New England Journal of Medicine* 292 (1975):858-859.

34. R.S.F. Schilling et al., "Lung Function, Respiratory Disease, and Smoking in Families," *American Journal of Epidemiology* 106, no. 4 (1977):274-283.

35. J.R. White, and H.F. Froeb, "Small-Airways Dysfunction in Nonsmokers Chronically Exposed to Tobacco Smoke," *New England Journal of Medicine* 302, no. 13 (1980):720-723.

36. C. Lenfant and B.M. Liu, "(Passive) Smokers versus (Voluntary) Smokers," Editorial, *New England Journal of Medicine* 302, no. 13 (1980):742-743.

37. F. Adlkofer, G. Scherer, and H. Weimann, "Small-Airways Dysfunction in Passive Smokers," *New England Journal of Medicine* 303, no. 7 (1980):392; G. Huber, "Small-Airways Dysfunction in Passive Smokers," *New England Journal of Medicine* 30, no. 7 (1980):392; D. Aviado, "Small-Airways Dysfunction in Passive Smokers," *New England Journal of Medicine* 303, no. 7 (1980):393.

38. Aviado, "Small-Airways Dysfunction."

39. J.R. White and H.F. Froeb, "Small-Airways Dysfunction in Passive Smokers," *New England Journal of Medicine* 303, no. 7 (1980): 393-394.

40. *Smoking and Health*, 1979.

41. Lenfant and Liu, "(Passive) Smokers."

42. E. Wynder, cited in *Schweizer Illustrierte*, October 25, 1976.

43. G. Gori, Hearings before the Subcommittee on Oversight and Investigations of the Committee on Interstate and Foreign Commerce, House of Representatives, serial no. 95-172, pp. 52-73, October 6, 1978.

25 Some Legal Aspects of the Smoking-and-Health Controversy

J.C.B. Ehringhaus, Jr.

Tobacco has given pleasure to millions of persons for more than three hundred years. For almost as long, it has also been the subject of controversy. This discussion does not deal with the scientific or medical aspects of the smoking-and-health debate, but instead describes some of the legal questions that have grown out of it in recent years and attempts to predict future trends. The developments discussed here include efforts to ban smoking in public places, government regulation of cigarette advertising and promotional practices, and efforts to regulate cigarettes under the federal food and drug laws.

Smoking in Public Places

By far the greatest controversy in recent years has concerned smoking in public places. Anti-smoking advocates throughout the country have sought to ban or restrict smoking in stores, restaurants, government buildings, sports arenas, and many other places open to the general public.[1] They have even sought to ban smoking in private places of work. The anti-smokers contend that they have a right, assertedly based on the Constitution or statutory provisions, to live in an environment free of tobacco smoke, and that the federal, state, and local governments have an obligation to enforce that right by restricting smokers' behavior.

Whenever these issues have actually been litigated, the courts have rejected the anti-smokers' arguments. When, for example, anti-smokers brought suit to ban smoking in the Louisiana Superdome, a federal district court dismissed their complaint, refusing to create "a legal avenue, heretofore unavailable, through which an individual could attempt to regulate the social habits of his neighbor."[2] In a carefully written decision, which was later upheld by the federal court of appeals and which the Supreme Court declined to review, the district judge went on to say: "to hold that the First, Fifth, Ninth, or Fourteenth Amendments recognize as fundamental the right to be free from cigarette smoke would be to mock the lofty purpose of such amendments and broaden their penumbral protections to unheard-of boundaries."[3] The courts reached similar conclusions in lawsuits that sought to ban smoking in federal or state office buildings.[4]

279

Anti-smokers have also taken their cause to state legislatures and county and city councils. In recent years, numerous statutes and ordinances have been proposed to ban or restrict smoking in public. Some localities have adopted these proposals, but many have wisely rejected them. Smoking bans are for the most part as unenforceable as Prohibition. They serve mainly to embroil restaurant owners, shopkeepers, and private citizens in disputes about the places and manner in which smoking is permitted.

There are, moreover, serious legal questions about the validity of smoking bans. Often, the laws would impose criminal sanctions for offenses that are vaguely defined. One city was asked, for example, to prohibit smoking in government buildings whenever a "meeting" was in progress, but the proposed ordinance did not define what a "meeting" was.

The proposals frequently establish irrational requirements or do not serve any legitimate governmental objective, and may therefore violate the equal-protection requirement of the Fourteenth Amendment. One legislature, for example, considered banning smoking in taxicabs even when the driver and the passengers did not object.

Anti-smoking advocates ordinarily overlook the possibility that smokers may have a constitutionally protected right to smoke, if they do so in a reasonable manner. Reviewing the court decisions concerning the right of privacy and related constitutional guarantees, some legal scholars have discerned a constitutionally protected right to be free from government interference in the choice of a personal lifestyle, including the decision whether to smoke.[5] Citing a variety of constitutional objections, courts have in fact invalidated or refused to enforce smoking bans in a series of cases decided as early as 1911 and as recently as 1979.[6]

Efforts to ban or restrict smoking in public places will almost certainly continue. As a matter of law and public policy, the proposals should be rejected. Although the scientific questions involved in the smoking-and-health controversy are not within the scope of this chapter, it is fair to say that the proposed bans cannot be scientifically justified as public-health measures. Their proponents almost never attempt to justify them as measures to protect smokers against themselves (if they did, they would confront significant constitutional objections). Yet, it has not been proved that smoking causes harm to healthy nonsmokers. Anti-smoking laws can thus be justified only as a means to restrict a practice that some persons find annoying. Life, however, is full of small annoyances; almost anything that gives pleasure to some persons is likely to disturb others. A society that cherishes individual liberty cannot seek to resolve disputes about taste or personal lifestyle by government edict. The answer now, as in the past, lies not in legislation but in the exercise of common sense and courtesy among private citizens.

Smoking Aboard Airplanes

One facet of the public-smoking question deserves special attention because of the extraordinary controversy it has engendered: smoking aboard airplanes. Nearly a decade ago, the major airlines voluntarily established no-smoking sections aboard their flights to accommodate passengers who objected to smoking. In 1973, the Civil Aeronautics Board (CAB) issued regulations requiring that such sections be set aside.

In the years that have followed, anti-smoking advocates have sought increasing restrictions on smoking aboard aircraft, including bans on pipe and cigar smoking, prohibitions against smoking aboard short flights, and a total ban on smoking. Three separate rulemaking proceedings are now underway at the CAB to modify various provisions of the Board's smoking regulations.

Some anti-smokers have asserted an absolute right to a seat in the no-smoking section, no matter what inconvenience they may cause to other passengers. With the assistance of anti-smoking advocacy groups, passengers have filed hundreds of formal complaints against the airlines, seeking money penalties for alleged violations of their rights. Passengers insisting on their asserted right to a no-smoking seat have engaged in acrimonious disputes with cabin attendants and fellow passengers. In one widely publicized incident, the pilot of a Washington-New York shuttle set his airplane down in Baltimore to bring under control a dispute that apparently arose when a passenger who arrived late insisted that persons next to him stop smoking.

The future of this controversy is difficult to predict. There is, however, some indication that the majority of passengers are satisfied with the relatively simple rules agreed to by the airlines years ago, and are beginning to react to the excesses of some anti-smokers. More than a hundred thousand passengers signed a petition to the CAB calling for equal treatment of smokers and nonsmokers. When the Board recently proposed to permit the airlines to deny no-smoking seats to passengers who failed to arrive on time, there was predictable opposition from anti-smokers, but hundreds of other passengers wrote in to support the proposal.

The Board's smoking regulations have always been on shaky legal ground. The Federal Aviation Act of 1958, which defines the CAB's rulemaking powers, guarantees all passengers (including smokers) the right to travel in reasonable comfort, free from discrimination.[7] The act, moreover, specifically prohibits the Board from interfering with managerial decisions by the airlines concerning passenger convenience and comfort,[8] and the courts have struck down efforts by the CAB to dictate seating arrangements aboard aircraft.[9] When Congress enacted the Airline Deregulation Act of 1978 (under which the CAB and its control of air fares and airline routes will eventually be abolished), it expressed a strong preference for reliance on the business decisions of airline managements, rather than government regulations, to assure that the needs of passengers would be met. The choice of methods to accommodate smoking and nonsmoking passengers, like other questions of passenger convenience and comfort, should be made by the airlines in response to competition and the demands of the marketplace.

Advertising and Promotion

One area in which significant pressure for change can be expected is cigarette advertising and promotion. Government agencies—especially the Federal Trade Commission (FTC)—have had a continuing interest in restricting cigarette advertisements or imposing new requirements on cigarette advertisers. Television advertisements for cigarettes were prohibited by Congress more than a decade ago. A consent agreement between cigarette manufacturers and the FTC provides for inclusion of the cigarette warning notice in newspaper and magazine advertisements, billboards, and other printed promotional materials. Through a voluntary action taken in cooperation with the FTC, cigarette manufacturers include tar and nicotine information in their advertisements.

Some persons believe these measures are not enough. They would like to require that manufacturers print tar and nicotine information on cigarette packages (many now do so voluntarily) and to impose further restrictions on cigarette advertising. Some would prefer to ban such advertising entirely. For its part, the tobacco industry believes it has a constitutionally protected right to advertise lawful products in a truthful manner. The industry's position is supported by recent Supreme Court decisions that have accorded broad First Amendment protection to commercial speech.[10] Any effort to ban cigarette advertising or impose further restrictions on it would raise serious constitutional questions.

Some states and localities have also sought to regulate cigarette advertising and promotion, in particular by banning or restricting the distribution of free samples. These efforts raise the same constitutional questions as the federal proposals to ban cigarette advertising, but they also confront another significant legal difficulty—a section of the Public Health Cigarette Smoking Act of 1969 known as the preemption provision.[11] Congress enacted this statute after an extensive review of the entire smoking-and-health controversy. The act's legislative history shows that senators and representatives viewed that controversy as a national problem affecting commerce throughout the country, and thus within the sole purview of

Congress to issue legislation. Section 5(b) of the act best summarizes the preemptive concept; it expressly provides that no state may impose any "requirement or prohibition based on smoking and health . . . with respect to the advertising or promotion" of cigarettes.[12]

Food and Drug Regulations

One final area merits attention, if only as evidence of the persistence and ingenuity of the anti-smoker advocates. Many years ago, the courts decided that cigarettes promoted solely for smoking enjoyment were not "drugs" within the meaning of federal law.[13] Recently, however, an anti-smoking organization has sought to reopen this question by petitioning the Food and Drug Administration (FDA) to declare that cigarettes are drugs or medical devices, or that cigarette filters are medical devices. The FDA denied the request to regulate cigarettes as drugs, and its decision has been upheld in court (appeal is pending).[14] The agency was slow to respond to the medical-device question, in part because it is in the midst of carrying out major new responsibilities imposed on it by medical-device legislation enacted in 1976. The anti-smokers brought suit to force an agency decision, and a federal district court recently ordered the FDA to set a timetable for dealing with the anti-smokers' petition.[15]

The actions that the anti-smokers are urging the FDA to take should be rejected. It is clear that neither Congress nor the FDA has ever regarded ordinary cigarettes as drugs or medical devices within the terms of federal law. The regulatory systems that govern medical products make no sense when they are applied to cigarettes. Congress has repeatedly made clear that the special cigarette legislation it enacted in 1965 and amended in 1969 is to be the exclusive means by which the federal government deals with the smoking-and-health controversy. To carry out this intention, Congress has included an express exemption for tobacco products in every recent regulatory statute that might otherwise have been interpreted as applying to cigarettes.[16] Yet the anti-smokers continue to seek some means of undermining the legislative purpose, and the FDA is forced to expend its limited resources in an activity never contemplated by Congress.

It is difficult to predict where this latest development in the law concerning smoking and health will lead, but experience suggests that there will be more litigation and controversy before the matter is resolved. In this area, as in others, the proper resolution is, however, the middle path chosen by Congress in 1965 and 1969—to accommodate in some respects those persons who are concerned about the alleged health effects of cigarettes while leaving individual citizens free to make their own informed choices about smoking.

Notes

1. The debate about smoking in public has been a relatively recent outgrowth of the smoking-and-health controversy. The argument about the alleged effects of smoking on the smoker is much older. Although numerous personal-injury suits have been brought, no court has ever imposed liability on a cigarette manufacturer for injury allegedly caused by tobacco smoke.

2. Gasper v. Louisiana Stadium and Exposition District, 418 F. Supp. 716, 721 (E.D.La. 1976), aff'd, 577 F.2d 897 (5th Cir. 1978), cert. denied, 439 U.S. 1073 (1979).

3. Ibid.

4. Federal Employees for Non-Smokers' Rights v. United States, 446 F. Supp. 181 (D.D.C. 1978), aff'd, 598 F.2d 310 (D.C. Cir. 1979); GASP v. Mecklenberg County, 42 N.C. App. 225, 256 S.E.2d 477 (1979). Antismoking advocates often cite Shimp v. New Jersey Bell Telephone Co., 145 N.J. Super. 516, 368 A.2d 408 (Ch. Div. 1976), as a case in which an employee with an unusual susceptibility to smoke successfully argued for restrictions on smoking by fellow employees. But the Shimp case involved one small office of a large company, and the defendant made no real effort to contest the suit, presenting no evidence or legal arguments in its behalf. Subsequently, New Jersey Bell chose to defend itself vigorously in a virtually identical lawsuit, and the same judge who decided the Shimp case dismissed the complaint. Mitchell v. New Jersey Bell Telephone Co., No. C-4159-76 (N.J. Super., Ch. Div., dismissed, April 24, 1978).

5. Wilkinson and White, *Constitutional Protection for Personal Lifestyles*, 62 Cornell L. Rev. 563, 620 (1977).

6. Alford v. City of Newport News, 260 S.E.2d 241 (Va. 1979); Greater Rockford Food Service v. Onthoefer, No. 76-2447 (Ill. Cir. Ct. 1976); City of Zion v. Behrens, 262 Ill. 510, 104 N.E. 836 (1914); Hershberg v. City of Barbourville, 142 Ky. 60, 133 S.W. 985 (1911).

7. Interpreting general principles of tort law applicable to common carriers that are similar to the obligations imposed by the Federal Aviation Act, the Iowa Supreme Court recently rejected a nonsmoker's claims that an airline had a duty to prohibit smoking to accommodate persons who are supposedly unusually susceptible to smoke. The court held that an airline "has an obligation to preserve the comfort of its smoking passengers as well as of nonsmokers." Ravreby v. United Airlines, No. 104/63455 (Iowa Sup. Ct. June 18, 1980), slip op. at 9.

8. Section 401(e)(4), 49 U.S.C. § 1371(e)(4).

9. Continental Airlines v. CAB, 522 F.2d 107 (D.C. Cir. 1974).

10. The watershed decision was Virginia State Board of Pharmacy v. Virginia Citizens Consumer Council, Inc., 423 U.S. 748 (1976), in which

the Court repudiated the doctrine of Valentine v. Chrestensen, 316 U.S. 52 (1942), which had held the First Amendment inapplicable to "purely commercial advertising." Subsequent decisions indicate that truthful advertising which promotes a lawful activity can be restricted only when necessary to serve a "substantial" government interest, and that the government must choose the least restrictive means to achieve its purpose. Central Hudson Gas and Elec. Corp. v. Public Service Commission of N.Y., 48 U.S.L.W. 4783 (June 20, 1980).

11. 15 U.S.C. §§ 1331-39.

12. 15 U.S.C. § 1334(b).

13. FTC v. Liggett and Myers Tobacco Co., 108 F. Supp. 573 (S.D.N.Y. 1952), aff'd, 203 F.2d 955 (2d Cir. 1953).

14. Action on Smoking and Health v. Califano, C.A. No. 78-338 (D.D.C. Jan. 16, 1979), appeal pending.

15. Action on Smoking and Health v. Food and Drug Administration, C.A. No. 79-2989 (D.D.C. Aug. 12, 1980).

16. For example, the Controlled Substances Act of 1970, 21 U.S.C. § 802(b), the Consumer Product Safety Act of 1972, 15 U.S.C. § 2052(a)(1)(b), and the Toxic Substances Control Act of 1976, 15 U.S.C. § 2602(2)(B)(iii). When a district court held in 1975 that the Consumer Product Safety Commission could regulate cigarettes under the Federal Hazardous Substances Act, Congress promptly amended the law to eliminate that authority. See American Public Health Association v. CPSC, C.A. No. 74-1222 (D.D.C. April 23, 1975); 15 U.S.C. § 2052(a)(1).

26 Legal and Policy Issues Concerning Smoking and Health to Be Faced in the 1980s

Joel D. Joseph and
Marcy S. Kramer

As scientific studies continue to link tobacco smoke with various health problems, regulations on tobacco use continue to be debated in courts, legislatures, government agencies, and various other public and private forums. The discussions range wide, from sliding rate scales on health-insurance policies for nonsmokers to regulating cigarettes as an "addictive" drug. Representing one segment of the nonsmokers' advocacy community, we work within this vast spectrum of legal issues. We base our litigation on a broad range of statutory language and constitutional principles. The underlying premise for our work has been stated most simply by the World Health Organization: "Smoking should be confined to consenting adults in private."[1]

In August 1980, we reviewed federal legislation relating to cigarette and smoking regulations and a random sampling of state and local legislative activity. We report on that review in the spirit of objectivity and dispassion rather than advocacy and persuasion.

Regulation and Smoking

This section discusses smoking in work places, in public places, and in transportation. Legislation, litigation, local ordinances, and other regulatory actions have all played a role in restricting smoking, but in varying degrees. As of 1980, litigation has been the primary vehicle addressing the problem of smoking in the work place. Regulatory actions and legislation have had a much more limited impact on this area.

In 1976, the first court ruling that restricted smoking in work places was announced in *Shimp* v. *New Jersey Bell Telephone Company*.[2] The Superior Court of New Jersey for Salem County ordered the phone company to prohibit smoking on the job, except in a designated smoking lounge. In 1977, federal employees filed a lawsuit based on the Shimp case asking the federal courts to order the federal government to restrict smoking in government buildings. Serving as counsel for plaintiffs in that case,

I [Joseph] made oral arguments before a three-judge panel of the U.S. Court of Appeals for the District of Columbia. Judge Skelly Wright, a member of the panel, seemed to hold some sympathy for our arguments. He asked, for example, whether nonsmokers were in about the same positions today as civil-rights advocates were twenty years ago. But the court apparently felt that now was not the time for nonsmokers rights and ruled against our request.[3]

The 1980s should see a flurry of litigation by workers against their employers to restrict smoking in common work areas. Employees who smoke may also bring lawsuits if employers prohibit them from smoking or refuse to allow them to take "smoke breaks." Some anti-smoking groups have proposed the establishment of smoking lounges for smokers as a compromise position. This stance recognizes the "need" or "addiction" of smokers and attempts to balance that with the nonsmokers' right not to breathe tobacco smoke. The right to breathe clean air formed the basis for passage of the Clean Air Act by Congress in 1963.

Many worker's compensation cases for persons who are allergic to tobacco smoke are now pending around the country. A typical case is as follows: a worker allergic to tobacco smoke is forced to work in a factory or office where smoking is common. The worker resigns because of a doctor's advice. He or she then files for worker's compensation, claiming a loss of income because of health injury on the job. No major court decisions have yet been handed down in this area. Within the next few years, many courts will be presented with these types of issues.

Although the federal government has not yet begun regulating smoking in the work place, the Occupational Safety and Health Administration (OSHA) may be asked to consider doing so soon. The OSHA regulates carbon-monoxide levels in the work place as well as levels of other potentially hazardous chemicals. Studies have shown that smoking in confined offices can cause carbon-monoxide levels to exceed Environmental Protection Agency (EPA) maximums.[4]

In 1979, then Congressman Robert Drinan (Democrat, Massachusetts) introduced legislation to regulate smoking in federal work places.[5] During this decade, many bills will be introduced to regulate smoking in government and private work environments.

In the 1980s, litigation, and possibly legislation, will decide whether workers have the right to work in a smoke-free office or factory. Courts and state legislatures will start specifying separate areas for smokers and nonsmokers and will also prohibit smoking entirely in some cases. Although the federal and state OSHAs may regulate smoking at the work place to some extent, the courts will most likely be the central arena for defining workers' rights to a smoke-free work environment.

Smoking in Public Places

Efforts to restrict smoking in public places have been most successful with regard to grocery stores and restaurants, and least successful in public arenas. Local ordinances and state legislation have been more useful tools than litigation.

Throughout the nation, restrictions on smoking in shopping areas, such as department stores and supermarkets, are being imposed. But smoking is more widely prohibited in food stores than in general shopping areas because most people recognize that smoke can affect the taste of foods. Since nonsmokers outnumber smokers nearly two to one, pressure from the electorate should influence legislatures, town councils, and county boards to pass more extensive restrictions on smoking for all shopping areas.

Legislation requiring restaurants to have separate sections for smokers and nonsmokers now exists in Connecticut, Michigan, Minnesota, Rhode Island, and Utah. Generally, only large restaurants, seating fifty or more persons, are subject to these requirements. Many local areas have similar laws, including Prince George's County, Maryland; Rockland County, New York; Berkeley, California; and Champaign, Illinois. During the 1980s, many other states and localities will probably pass laws regulating smoking in eating establishments, and more restaurants will probably establish smoker and nonsmoker sections voluntarily, apparently to keep all their customers happy. Restaurant chains with a nationwide policy of separate sections already include: CoCo's Famous Hamburgers, Denny's, Furr's Cafeteria, The Magic Pan Creperie, Red Lobster Inn, Sambo's, Victoria Station, and Hamburger Hamlet.[6]

The first major legal action to attempt to restrict smoking in a public place, the Superdome in New Orleans, failed.[7] The court held that there is no constitutional right to watch sporting or other events in a smoke-free environment. Legislative bodies in counties and cities will be presented with many bills to restrict smoking in particular sports or convention centers. However, it is not likely that Congress will step into this area of regulation.

Problems in Transportation

During the 1970s, federal, state, and local agencies separated smokers and nonsmokers on most trains, buses, and airplanes. Smoking in elevators has generally been prohibited by local law since the 1960s or earlier. Recently, there has been momentum to regulate smoking in taxicabs. In the 1980s, smoking restrictions on interstate and local transportation systems should increase even more. In 1979, Congressman Drinan introduced a bill that would restrict smoking in any "interstate passenger carrier facility."[8] This issue, which Congress may consider again in 1981, would prohibit smoking in any ticket office, waiting line, or boarding area of airports, bus stations, railroad terminals, and port facilities.

The current federal regulation of interstate buses requires smokers to sit in a separate section (in the rear of the bus) that cannot exceed 20 percent of the seats in the bus.[9] The Interstate Commerce Commission (ICC) enacted this regulation in 1971, and in 1974, was sued by the National Association of Motor Bus Owners.[10] The court ruled that the ICC regulation was valid. During the 1980s, there will be increasing pressure on the ICC either to tighten this regulation or to prohibit smoking on interstate buses entirely.

Most local jurisdictions prohibit smoking on intrastate buses, either through state statutes, city ordinances, or prohibitions by municipally-operated bus companies. In those states and cities where smoking on buses is permitted, pressure will be brought to restrict such smoking. The trend toward a nationwide standard prohibiting smoking on buses appears to be irreversible.

Until 1979, the ICC regulated smoking on interstate trains.[11] But a recent congressional trend toward deregulation caused Amtrak (the National Railroad Passenger Corporation) to be removed from most ICC regulation.[12] Even though Amtrak no longer has to require separate cars for smokers and nonsmokers, it continues to apply ICC guidelines stringently. Amtrak requires that at least 50 percent of its cars be nonsmoking areas and prohibits smoking in dining cars and in coach cars for long-distance travel. Although Amtrak now allows smoking in lounges and restrooms, most likely it will come under pressure to restrict smoking in those places as well. Legislation may be introduced in Congress to restrict smoking on interstate trains further, but there will probably be separate cars for smokers for some time.

Regulating the physical separation of smokers and nonsmokers in airplanes is more difficult than in trains because there is one limited area as opposed to a series of individually linked cars. Nonetheless, after receiving many thousands of complaints from nonsmoking airline passengers and from Ralph Nader's Aviation Consumer Action Project, which advocated a total ban on smoking in aircraft, the Civil Aeronautics Board (CAB) issued a regulation in 1973 that required airplanes to have separate sections for smokers and nonsmokers.[13] In 1979, the CAB issued even more stringent regulations that further protected nonsmokers by providing, among other things, "for expansion of no-smoking areas to meet passenger demand."[14]

As a result, some airlines have, either voluntarily or under threat of suit, changed their policy on smoking. For example, United Airlines has adopted on its own initiative a policy that prohibits pipe smoking entirely. Eastern

Airlines, under threat of suit by Action on Smoking and Health (ASH), has consented to reserve at least 65 percent of its seats for nonsmokers.

Yet, in addition to the displeasure associated with smoking on board aircraft, there is still the important question of the safety of any smoking at all. Pure oxygen is used in airplanes when a sudden drop in air pressure occurs inside the craft. When pure oxygen is present, one lit cigarette could cause a fatal explosion. The Federal Aviation Administration (FAA), the federal agency that regulates aircraft safety, will continue to examine this issue. The CAB, the FAA, and Congress will all come under considerable pressure to eliminate entirely smoking on airplanes for the comfort and safety of the consumer-passenger.

Smokers have not put up much of a fight against rules and regulations that ban smoking on elevators. This is because of the confined nature of elevators and the short duration of their use. Momentum will continue until all jurisdictions prohibit smoking on elevators.

Until very recently, there were no regulations regarding smoking in taxis. In 1979, the District of Columbia passed a regulation that allows a taxi driver or a passenger to make the cab a nonsmoking vehicle.[15] There appears to be a nationwide trend toward this District of Columbia policy, which allows the driver of the cab or the fare-paying passenger to protect his health by banning smoking in the vehicle.

Regulation of Cigarettes and Cigarette Advertising

The regulation of interstate sale and advertising of cigarettes is exclusively within the province of Congress. Traditionally, Congress has moved slowly in regulating cigarettes and cigarette advertising. Congress has taken two decisive actions: it has banned cigarette advertising on radio and television,[16] and it has required a health warning on cigarette labels.[17]

In addition, federal taxes have been imposed on tobacco products.[18] However, this tax is not very high and does not currently serve to discourage smoking. Inconsistently, the federal government supports the price of tobacco crops. The policy of taxing cigarettes and supporting tobacco farmers will be subject to recurring scrutiny during the next decade. In the spirit of deregulation, Congress may move in the direction of limiting or removing farm supports, especially those for tobacco.

During the Ninety-Sixth Congress (1979-1980), three bills were introduced to regulate cigarettes in regard to the fire hazards they present. Two bills (H.R. 4944 and 5504) would prohibit cigarette manufacturers from adding any substance to cigarettes that increases the time that they burn or smolder. A later bill, which has a broader base of support, H.R. 6675, would authorize the Consumer Product Safety Commission (CPSC) to establish performance standards for self-extinguishing cigarettes.[19] The CPSC supports the bill as does the chairman of the Consumer Protection and Finance Subcommittee, to which the bill has been referred. The CPSC found that smoldering cigarettes cause some 1,300 deaths per year, which should force some action on this bill.

The Federal Trade Commission (FTC) and the Department of Health and Human Services (formerly Health, Education, and Welfare) have limited grants of authority concerning cigarettes. The FTC regulates cigarette advertising, the warnings in cigarette ads, and promotion of cigarettes. The FTC has been considering requiring larger health warnings on cigarette billboards.[20] The Department of Health and Human Services studies and reports on the health consequences of smoking and distributes educational information on smoking and health. It has no direct role in the regulation of cigarettes or cigarette advertising.

Congress has carefully excluded cigarettes from the jurisdiction of the Food and Drug Administration (FDA) and the CPSC. Under current law, cigarettes are neither food nor drug nor consumer product. Congress—and regulatory agencies—have also been slow to consider mandatory limits on tar and nicotine levels in cigarettes.

In summary, Congress and federal agencies will consider the following major policy issues in this decade: (1) cigarette taxes and tobacco-farm supports; (2) standards for cigarette safety (especially standards regarding self-extinguishing cigarettes); and (3) further regulation of cigarette advertising, promotion, and health warnings.

Conclusion

Strong national trends now lean toward restricting smoking in public places, including shopping areas, transportation vehicles, and government buildings. And efforts to regulate smoking in the work place have recently begun to gain momentum. At the same time, Congress may strengthen its restrictions on cigarette advertising, require more stringent health warnings, and consider establishing safety standards for cigarettes. Although nonsmokers have gained many new protections in the last decade—only some of which are catalogued here—many smoking-and-health concerns remain. Battles between tobacco advocates and nonsmokers' groups will continue throughout the 1980s on a wide range of legislative, judicial, and administrative fronts.

Notes

1. Third World Conference on Smoking and Health (1975).
2. 145 N.J. Super. 516, 368 A.2d 408 (Ch. Div. 1976).

3. Federal Employees for Non-Smokers' Rights v. United States, 446 F. Supp. 181 (D.D.C. 1978), aff'd, 598 F.2d 310 (D.C. Cir. 1979).

4. J.R. White and H.F. Froeb, "Small-Airways Dysfunction in Nonsmokers Chronically Exposed to Tobacco Smoke," *New England Journal of Medicine* 302, no. 13 (1980):720-723.

5. H.R. 300, 96th Cong. 1st Sess., January 15, 1979. "To regulate smoking in Federal facilities and in facilities serving interstate common carrier passengers, and for other purposes."

6. See M. Horowitz, *Guide to Smoke-Free Dining* (Buffalo, N.Y.: Environmental Press, 1980).

7. Gasper v. Louisiana Stadium and Exposition District, 418 F. Supp. 716 (E.D.La. 1976), aff'd, 577 F.2d 897 (1978), cert. denied, 439 U.S. 1073 (1979).

8. H.R. 300, 96th Cong. (1979).

9. 49 C.F.R. § 106.1.

10. National Association of Motor Bus Owners v. ICC., 370 F. Supp. 408 (1974).

11. 49 C.F.R. 1124.22 (1975).

12. P.L. 96-73, September 29, 1979, 45 U.S.C. § 546, 93 Stat. 558.

13. 14 C.F.R. § 252.2 (1978).

14. 14 C.F.R. § 252.1 and § 252.2.

15. Title 14, District of Columbia Rules and Regulations (1979).

16. 15 U.S.C. § 1335.

17. 15 U.S.C. § 1333.

18. 26 U.S.C. § 5701, et. seq.

19. Introduced in the Senate as 2215.

20. See 120 Cong. Rec. No. 22, February 26, 1974. "Cigarette Advertising," remarks of Senator Moss.

27 Resources on Smoking and Health

Harriet Kestenbaum

Selected Bibliography on Smoking and Health

This first section contains an annotated listing of the primary references among the thousands of studies, books, and anthologies concerned with the smoking-and-health controversy.

Research Methodologies

Hockett, Robert C. "The Tobacco Health Issue: An Overview of Medical Research." In *Social and Economic Issues Confronting the Tobacco Industry in the Seventies,* edited by A. Frank Bordeux and Russel Brannon. University of Kentucky, 1971. Although somewhat dated, this chapter points out some of the methodological problems that the Tobacco Institute and others contend invalidate conclusions about tobacco as a causative agent for certain diseases.

Mausner, Judith S., and Bahn, Anita K. *Epidemiology.* W.B. Saunders Company, 1974. An introduction to the field of epidemiology, the text describes the research steps that are used to determine causal relationships between a risk factor and a disease.

Health Studies

Doll, Richard, and Hill, A. Bradford. "Smoking and Carcinoma of the Lung." *British Medical Journal,* September 20, 1950.

Hammond, C. Cryler, and Horn, Daniel. "The Relationship between Human Smoking Habits and Death Rates." *Journal of the American Medical Association,* August 7, 1954.

Ochasner, Alton, and DeBakey, Michael. "Carcinoma of the Lung." *Archives of Surgery,* 1941.

The Tobacco Institute. *Smoking and Health 1964-1979, The Continuing Controversy.* January 10, 1979. This document refutes many of the findings of the surgeon general's report and includes citations and references to studies at the end of each chapter.

The Tobacco Institute. *Women and Smoking 1979*. The Tobacco Institute's summary of findings on women and smoking.

U.S. Department of Health, Education, and Welfare. *Smoking and Health*, Report of the Advisory Committee to the Surgeon General. DHEW Publication No.(PHS)79-50066. Public Health Service, 1979. A comprehensive compendium of 30,000 studies dealing with social, psychological, medical, and biological aspects of smoking. An earlier report with the same title was first released in 1964.

U.S. Department of Health and Human Services. *The Health Consequences of Smoking for Women*, a Report of the Surgeon General. Public Health Service, 1980.

Wynder, Ernst L., and Graham, Edward A. "Tobacco Smoking as a Possible Etiologic Factor in Bronchiogenic Carcinoma." *Journal of the American Medical Association*, May 27, 1950.

Passive Smoking

"Effect of Smoking on Nonsmokers." Hearing before the Subcommittee on Tobacco of the Committee on Agriculture, House of Representatives. September 7, 1978. Statements from eighteen scientists refute the claim that cigarette fumes are harmful to the nonsmoker.

Repace, James L., and Lowrey, Alfred H. "Indoor Air Pollution, Tobacco Smoke and Public Health." *Science* 208 (1980):464-472. Study shows that indoor particulate levels from cigarette smoke exceeded the Environmental Protection Agency (EPA) outdoor-air standard.

White, James, and Froeb, Herman. "Small-Airways Dysfunction in Nonsmokers Chronically Exposed to Tobacco Smoke." *New England Journal of Medicine* 302, no. 13 (1980):720-723. Considered to be a landmark by many nonsmokers' rights groups, it is the first study to demonstrate that nonsmokers who regularly breathe other people's tobacco smoke are subject to long-term harm.

The Less Hazardous Cigarette

Gori, Gio, ed. *The Less Hazardous Cigarette*, Banbury Report No. 3. Cold Springs Harbor, New York: Cold Springs Harbor Laboratory, 1980. A summary of conference proceedings from experts in agriculture, medicine, chemistry, economics, and public policy.

Gori, Gio B., and Lynch, Cornelius J. "Toward Less Hazardous Cigarettes." *Journal of the American Medical Association* 240, no. 12 (1978):1255-1259. This study raised a lot of controversy in medical circles. It suggested that a certain number of cigarettes could be smoked daily with no discernible risk.

U.S. Department of Health and Human Services. *The Health Consequences of Smoking the Less Hazardous Cigarette*, The Surgeon General's Report. Public Health Service, 1981. This is the thirteenth annual surgeon general's report. The report summarizes all of the medical, biochemical, and behavioral studies on the less hazardous cigarette.

Wynder, Ernst; Hoffman, Dietrich; and Gori, Gio B., eds. *Smoking and Health: I. Modifying the Risk for the Smoker*. Proceedings of the Third World Conference on Smoking and Health, 1975. Washington, D.C.: U.S. Department of Health, Education, and Welfare, 1976.

Legislation and Public Policy

Action on Smoking and Health (ASH). "History of the War Against Smoking, 1964-1978." 1978. An annotated chronology of events.

Klebe, Edward R. "Actions of the Congress and the Federal Government on Smoking and Health." Congressional Research Service, September, 1979.

The Tobacco Institute. "Federal Government Involvement in the Smoking and Health Controversy." January, 1980. An annotated chronology of events.

State Legislation

Action on Smoking and Health. *Digest of State Legislation*. A summary of state and local anti-smoking legislation which is periodically updated.

Brody, Alvan and Betty. *The Legal Rights of Non-Smokers*. Avon Books, 1977.

Roper Organization, Incorporated. "A Study of Public Attitudes Toward Cigarette Smoking and the Tobacco Industry in 1978." An opinion poll commissioned by The Tobacco Institute, this is the sixth and most recent report to be conducted over the course of twelve years.

The Tobacco Institute. *Municipal and County Legislative Report*. This is a yearly summary of all anti-smoking legislation at the county and local levels nationwide.

U.S. Department of Health, Education, and Welfare. *State Legislation on Smoking and Health*. Public Health Service. Since 1975, the National Clearinghouse for Smoking and Health has published this yearly summary of anti-smoking legislation at the state level. Copies of this report may be obtained through the Office on Smoking and Health.

International Policy

Eckholm, Erik. *Cutting Tobacco's Toll.* Worldwatch Institute, 1978. A discussion of the policy dilemmas in the trade-offs between an expanding world tobacco trade and international health concerns.

International Digest of Health Legislation. A quarterly journal of the World Health Organization (WHO), it reports on health-related legislation passed in more than a hundred countries. In 1976, it published a comprehensive survey entitled "Legislative Action to Combat Smoking around the World" and has periodically updated this survey.

Ramstrom, Lars M., ed. *The Smoking Epidemic, A Matter of Worldwide Concern.* Proceedings of the Fourth World Conference on Smoking and Health, Stockholm, 1979. Stockholm Almquist and Wiksell International, 1980.

Steinfield, Jesse; Griffiths, William; Ball, Keith; and Taylor, Robert M., eds. *Smoking and Health: II. Health Consequences, Education, Cessation Activities and Governmental Action.* Proceedings of the Third World Conference on Smoking and Health, 1975. Washington, D.C.: Department of Health, Education, and Welfare, 1976.

Selected Organizations and Agencies

ASH (Action on Smoking and Health), 2000 H Street, N.W., Washington, D.C. 20006. Dr. John Banzhaf, director. A national nonprofit tax-exempt organization that serves as the major legal-action arm of the anti-smoking community. ASH gained prominence in the 1960s when it challenged the fairness doctrine of the Federal Communications Commission (FCC) to allow anti-smoking messages equal time on television. ASH publishes a bimonthly newsletter.

Council for Tobacco Research, 110 East 59th Street, New York, New York 10022. Established in 1954 by tobacco manufacturers, growers, and warehousemen, the council is the sponsoring agency of a program of research into questions of tobacco use and health. The council awards research grants to independent scientists and puts out a yearly report that summarizes projects which have been funded for the year.

GASP (Group Against Smokers' Pollution), P.O. Box 632, College Park, Maryland 20740. A national nonsmokers' rights group, GASP has more than a hundred local chapters throughout the country. They have been active in campaigning for bans on smoking in public places and work sites. GASP publishes "The Ventilator," a quarterly newsletter.

National Interagency Council on Smoking and Health, 291 Broadway, New York, New York 10007. A coordinating agency linking numerous public and private health organizations such as the American Cancer Society, the American Lung Association, and the American Public Health Association. The agency seeks to develop and implement plans and programs aimed at combatting smoking.

Office on Smoking and Health, 5600 Fishers Lane, Rockville, Maryland 20857. John Pinney, director. A part of the U.S. Department of Health and Human Services, it is a clearinghouse and information center for research, health education, and anti-smoking information.

The Tobacco Institute, 1875 I Street, N.W., Washington, D.C. 20006. The lobbying arm of the tobacco industry. The Tobacco Institute has published numerous reports on smoking and health which are available on request. It also publishes "The Tobacco Observer," a monthly newsletter.

Chronology of Major Federal Actions and Events on Smoking and Health

November 9, 1962. Advisory Committee to the Surgeon General on Smoking and Health is established and begins its study of tobacco as a possible health problem.

January 11, 1964. The surgeon general releases a report prepared by the Advisory Committee, entitled *Smoking and Health.* The report concludes that cigarette smoking is a health hazard.

June 23, 1964. The Federal Trade Commission (FTC) issues a trade regulation requiring a health warning on cigarette packages and in advertising.

July 27, 1965. President Johnson signs into law PL 89-92, the Federal Cigarette Labeling and Advertising Act of 1965 requiring a health warning on cigarette packages.

October 1965. The Department of Health, Education, and Welfare (DHEW) establishes a National Clearinghouse on Smoking and Health.

June 1967. The Federal Communications Commission (FCC) in sustaining the complaint of *Banzhaf* v. *FCC* requires that broadcast stations carrying cigarette advertising must also carry a significant amount of anti-smoking messages.

Summer 1967. Public Health Service releases its first annual, *The Health Consequences of Smoking,* which presents a review of 2,000 new research studies. It states "the research [reports] published since 1964 have strengthened those conclusions and have extended in some important respects our knowledge of the health consequences of smoking."

November 22, 1967. The FTC issues a report that lists the tar and nicotine content of fifty-four brands.

1968. The FTC recommends to Congress that it ban television and radio cigarette advertising.

April 1, 1970. President Nixon signs into law PL 91-222, the Public Health Cigarette Smoking Act of 1970 which prohibits advertising of cigarettes on radio and television and strengthens the warning label on the cigarette package.

August 8, 1970. The FTC issues a proposed rule requiring cigarette manufacturers to disclose tar and nicotine content of cigarettes in advertising. The proposal is suspended when manufacturers agree voluntarily to make the disclosures.

November 17, 1971. The Interstate Commerce Commission (ICC) issues an order restricting smoking on interstate passenger buses.

March 30, 1972. Major cigarette manufacturers voluntarily agree to include the warning statement in all advertisements.

May 7, 1973. Civil Aeronautic Board approves a regulation requiring that domestic airlines provide designated "no smoking" areas aboard aircraft.

September 30, 1973. President Nixon signs PL 93-109, Little Cigar Act of 1973, which extends broadcast ban to include the little cigar.

May 17, 1974. Consumer Product Safety Commission rules that it lacks authority to ban high-tar cigarettes.

January 1976. Senators Gary Hart and Edward Kennedy introduce a bill to establish a tax on cigarettes on a graduated basis according to the brand's tar and nicotine content. In August, the bill was defeated.

May 1976. President Ford signs legislation exempting tobacco from the regulation of the Consumer Product Safety Commission.

January 1978. DHEW Secretary Joseph Califano announces new government initiatives to combat smoking: the formation of a new Office on Smoking and Health; restrictions on smoking on DHEW premises; and increased attention to warnings about the hazards of smoking to women taking birth-control pills.

September 1978. The Subcommittee on Tobacco of the House Committee on Agriculture holds hearings regarding the effect of smoking on nonsmokers. Eighteen scientists refute the claim that public smoke is hazardous to nonsmokers.

November 1978. President Carter signs into law PL 95-626, the Health Services and Centers Amendments of 1978 which contain provisions for a youth anti-smoking campaign.

January 1979. The surgeon general releases a new report on smoking and health on the fifteenth anniversary of the 1964 report. The report claims that smoking has been shown to be more dangerous than suspected in 1964.

February 1979. The Internal Revenue Service rules that tax credits will not be allowed for enrollment in "stop smoking" clinics.

March 1979. General Services Administration establishes regulations prohibiting smoking in auditoriums, classrooms, and conference rooms in 10,000 government buildings. Government workers can also declare their offices to be no-smoking areas.

International Regulations on Smoking and Health

Government actions addressing health hazards and smoking have been taken in more than thirty-five countries, primarily within the last decade. Legislation has focused primarily on advertising prohibitions, health warning labels, public funds for education, and restrictions on smoking in public places. The intent of most legislation is to prevent youth and young adults from starting to smoke.

Appendix 27A identifies the major actions taken by these countries. Although the citations are brief and necessarily oversimplified in some cases, they do demonstrate the extent of restrictions thus far enacted. For example, some countries prohibit cigarette advertisements only on broadcasts during hours when children might be awake; others restrict ads from using models or any other methods of conveying youthfulness or vitality; and still others prohibit any type of advertising for cigarettes whatsoever. A few countries have enacted comprehensive legislative packages, such as Sweden which declared in its Tobacco Act of 1975 a national goal of having a generation of nonsmokers among people born after 1975.

Data for this table came from numerous sources, some of which provide greater detail than could be included here. The major sources are as follows:

1. *The International Digest of Health Legislation*, a quarterly journal of the World Health Organization. The 1976 edition included a survey on health legislation throughout the world conducted in 1975 by the Expert Committee on Smoking and Health of WHO. Subsequent editions of this publication have updated this survey.

2. *The Smoking Epidemic: A Matter of Worldwide Concern*, the conference proceedings of the Fourth World Conference on Smoking and Health, held in 1979 in Sweden (Stockholm Almquist and Wiksell International, 1980). This book contains addresses made on comparative legislative approaches.

3. The U.S. Office on Smoking and Health completed a survey similar to the WHO effort for the Fourth World Conference on Smoking and Health. Available from the Office on Smoking and Health, 5600 Fishers Lane, Rockville, Maryland 20857.

Other standard references such as *The New York Times Index* and various medical journals provided information on a few countries that have only recently enacted anti-smoking legislation.

**Appendix 27A:
Major Actions Taken by
Countries on Smoking and
Health**

Appendix 27A
Major Actions Taken by Countries on Smoking and Health

Country	Advertising	Health Warnings	Restrictions	Education	Other
Australia	Bans on cigarette advertising in radio and television (1976).	Warning label required on cigarette packages in advertisements.	Smoking prohibited in public transportation; nonsmoker seating in aircraft and restaurants.	State governments carry out periodic anti-smoking projects; Cancer Society and Heart Foundation also conduct smoking education.	
Austria	Bans on cigarette advertising in radio and television (1973).				
Belgium	Bans on cigarette advertising in radio and television (1973); voluntary agreement to restrict size of print advertising.				
Bulgaria	Bans on cigarette advertising in all forms of domestic media (1973).		No smoking in work sites where nonsmoker is present; bans on smoking in public transportation.	Bulgarian National Temperance Committee conducts nationwide program on smoking and health.	
Burma	Bans on cigarette advertising in radio and television.				

	Advertising	Warning labels	Smoking in public places	Education	Legislation
Canada	Voluntary agreement to eliminate cigarette advertising in radio and television (1972); voluntary guidelines on content and tone of print advertising.	Voluntary warning label on cigarette packages.		Canadian Department of Health and Welfare responsible for smoking-and-health education.	
Colombia	Cigarette advertising in television prohibited during children's viewing hours.				
Costa Rica		Warning label required on cigarette packages.		Ministry of Health with Ministry of Education conduct smoking-and-health education.	
Cyprus	Bans on cigarette advertising in radio and television (1978).		Smoking prohibited in some public places.		
Denmark	Bans on cigarette advertising in radio and television.			Government operates extensive anti-smoking education programs.	
Finland	Bans on all forms of cigarette advertising, including the distribution of free samples and sponsorship by tobacco companies of athletic and other events.		Smoking prohibited in all public areas and public transport facilities.	Board of Health responsible for nation-wide smoking-and-health education.	Comprehensive anti-smoking legislation passed in 1975; all tobacco regulation is administered by health authorities; limits on tar, nicotine, and carbon monoxide set by government.

Appendix 27A *(continued)*

Country	Advertising	Health Warnings	Restrictions	Education	Other
France	Bans on cigarette advertising in radio and television; bans on advertising in public places; expenditures on other forms of cigarette advertising cannot exceed 1974 level; restrictions on size and content of print advertising; bans on sponsorship and/or advertising in sports events.	Warning label required on cigarette packages; warning label must display tar and nicotine content of cigarettes.		Most anti-smoking activity is conducted by private organizations.	
Germany	Bans on cigarette advertising in radio and television.				
Greece	Bans on cigarette advertising in radio and television (1976).		Smoking prohibited on buses and trains.	Greek Ministry of Social Services responsible for nationwide anti-smoking campaign.	
Iceland	Bans of all forms of advertising; smoking prohibited in advertisements concerning other goods and services.	Warning label required on cigarette packages.	Smoking prohibited in certain public places.		

Country	Advertising Restrictions	Warning Labels	Smoking Restrictions	Anti-smoking Campaign
Ireland	Bans on all forms of advertising with the exception of newspapers and magazines; sales-promotion gimmicks are prohibited; restrictions on form and content of advertisements; tobacco advertising expenditures limited to a set level.	Warning label required on advertisements.	Nonsmoking areas in aircraft, airport concourses, restaurants, hotels and cinemas.	Health Education Bureau conducts national anti-smoking campaign.
Italy	Bans on all advertising (1962).		Smoking prohibited in practically all public places and transportation facilities. Smoking prohibited in the capital movie theaters.	
Malaysia	Advertising restrictions on content of cigarette ads; bans on cigarette advertising in youth magazines (1978).			Health Ministry conducts anti-smoking campaign.
Mexico	Advertising restrictions on content of cigarette advertising.	Warning label required on cigarette packages.		
Morocco	Bans on cigarette advertising in radio and television.			

Appendix 27A *(continued)*

Country	Advertising	Health Warnings	Restrictions	Education	Other
The Netherlands	Bans on cigarette advertising in radio and television; voluntary agreement to discontinue advertising aimed at teens and in sports events; legislation pending to give government control of tobacco advertising in all media.	Requirement of warning labels on cigarette packages soon to be implemented.	Smoking prohibited in all government-subsidized schools.		
Nicaragua		Warning label required on cigarette packages.			
Norway	Bans on all forms of cigarette advertising, including use of cigarettes in advertising for other goods and services.	Warning label required on cigarette packages; warning label must display tar and nicotine content of cigarettes.	Smoking restricted in public areas.	Ministry of Health conducts extensive anti-smoking campaign.	Comprehensive anti-smoking legislation passed in 1975.
Panama		Warning label required on cigarette packages.			
Peru	Cigarette advertising on television prohibited before 8 p.m.	Warning label required on cigarette packages.			
Saudi Arabia	Bans on all forms of advertising (1979).				
Singapore	Bans on all forms of advertising (1970).		Smoking prohibited in certain public places (1970).		

Country	Advertising	Warning Labels	Smoking Restrictions	Education	Other
Spain	Cigarette advertising on television and radio prohibited before 9:30 p.m.				
Sweden	Bans on cigarette advertising in radio and television; restrictions on cigarette advertising in print media—no people in advertisements, neutral headlines, and no advertising in outdoor or youth publications.	Warning label required on cigarette packages; variety of warning labels used and rotated frequently.	Smoking prohibited in many public places and work sites.	National anti-smoking campaign aimed especially at school-children; national goal to create a generation of non-smokers of all those born after 1975.	Comprehensive anti-smoking legislation passed in 1975; considered to be strongest in the world; life-insurance premiums are lower for non-smokers than for smokers; employers are restricted from engaging smokers for certain jobs.
United Kingdom	Bans on cigarette advertising in radio and television; billboard advertisements must be concealed in television sporting events.	Voluntary agreement to place warning label on cigarette packages and in advertisements.		Ministry of Health and Ministry of Education conduct anti-smoking education.	Extra tax imposed on high tar and nicotine cigarettes.
Soviet Union	Bans on cigarette advertising in all forms of media.		Smoking restricted in public places.	Ministry of Health conducts anti-smoking campaign aimed at youth and medical workers.	
United States	Bans on cigarette advertising in radio and television.	Warning label required on cigarette packages and in advertisements.	Nonsmoking sections required in aircraft and interstate buses; more than thirty states restrict smoking in public places.	Anti-smoking education primarily conducted by private organizations; some states support anti-smoking education in the schools.	

Part VI
Politics of Tobacco:
Policymaking under a Cloud
of Smoke

28 The Politics of Tobacco in North Carolina: "A Load Not Easy to Be Borne"

Ferrel Guillory

In the politics of tobacco, North Carolina is the Atlas of states. Of the tobacco-growing states, none is more powerful than North Carolina. However, as the mythological Atlas was condemned to hold on his back "the cruel strength of the crushing world," so Tarheel politicians are fated with the burden of protecting the people who grow and sell the controversial golden leaf. It is, as the Greek poet Hesiod wrote of Atlas's task, "a load not easy to be borne."

Tobacco's political base is not nearly as strong as it was a decade ago. The scientific evidence connecting cigarette smoking to lung cancer and heart disease makes defending tobacco more difficult for a politician, and the influence of anti-smoking forces has increased. At the same time, Congress is less dominated by veteran, powerful southerners sympathetic to tobacco-growing.

In response to anti-smoking pressures, North Carolina politicians are groping for new strategies, shifting the tone and emphasis of their arguments in defense of tobacco. For example, they contend less frequently that the link between cigarette smoking and disease has not been proved conclusively. "We have absolutely withdrawn from that fight of defending cigarette smoking," says Congressman Walter Jones (Democrat, North Carolina), member of the Tobacco and Peanut Subcommittee of the U.S. House Agriculture Committee. At the national and at the state level, North Carolina's politicians are in a transition.

In Washington, they are focusing their attention more exclusively on the price-support system, defending it as a social program that can preserve the family farm and rural culture. "I no more want to tie my defense of tobacco farmers to health than a Detroit automobile manufacturer wants to tie his defense of automobiles to emission controls or accidents," former U.S. Senator Robert Morgan (Democrat, North Carolina) said in a May 1980 speech. "If there are those who want to drive a knife into the heart of one of the last islands of traditional rural life and threaten numerous rural communities, then cut out this program."

In Raleigh, Governor James B. Hunt has sought expanded industrialization in rural areas, and state Agriculture Commissioner James A. Graham has promoted agricultural diversification. Both strategies suggest

313

a recognition that tobacco may not always dominate North Carolina as it has in the past. But if politicians have come to such a realization, they do not admit it publicly. "In this state, tobacco is still king," said Hunt in May 1980, "and we intend to keep it king."

Tobacco-state officials retain some important political advantages. Tobacco remains a legal crop, with no serious attempt being mounted to alter that situation. Further, the tobacco price-support system is the only commodity program with a permanent authorization in federal law. Strategically, this puts congressmen from tobacco states in a stronger legislative position than those from corn or wheat states who must appeal regularly for a renewal of the government programs vital to their constituents. Tobacco-state representatives have to do nothing in order for the leaf program to continue, except defend it against challenges.

Within the state, politicians have another kind of advantage by remaining pro-tobacco. Nearly 300,000 North Carolinians are employed in producing and marketing tobacco and making cigarettes. Joseph W. Grimsley, North Carolina Secretary of Administration and former campaign manager to Governor Hunt, calculates that 40 percent of the Democratic party vote in the state is east of a line from Durham to Fayettville, the region most heavily dependent on tobacco production.

Pro-tobacco politicians may have an easier time at the polls in state races, and North Carolina's congressmen may be able to sustain the government's tobacco program. But even working together, they cannot control all the forces affecting demand for their state's major cash crop. Some congressmen concede that the pro-tobacco position, in five or ten years, could suffer some losses. If fewer people smoke, particularly teenagers who may be influenced by federal anti-smoking efforts, cigarette sales will decline. At the same time, low-tar cigarettes, which contain less tobacco than "full-flavor" brands, are gaining a far larger share of the market than in the past. Moreover, high-quality foreign tobacco costing half as much as American leaf to produce may create stiff competition in traditional export markets. All these factors combined could significantly reduce tobacco production in North Carolina.

Should demand for North Carolina tobacco decrease dramatically, profound economic and social changes in the state would follow. However, precious little political leadership is being exercised to prepare North Carolinians for that eventuality. Politicians simply do not perceive the political climate conducive to a frank discussion of a future with less dependence on tobacco.

Shifting Alignments in Washington

North Carolina's congressmen have in effect abandoned the health issue to the cigarette-industry lobbyists, letting the industry fight administrative and regulatory actions, such as the Department of Health and Human Services' anti-smoking campaign and the Federal Trade Commission's limits on cigarette advertising. By focusing on federal legislation, such as the federal cigarette tax and the farm-support program, the state's delegates in Washington are exercising their power where they have the most leverage.

"The tobacco area congressmen as such perhaps had a greater impact back in the days when Harold Cooley was chairman of the [House] Agriculture Committee," says U.S. Representative Charles Whitley (Democrat, North Carolina). Even so, North Carolina members of Congress, as well as those from other tobacco states, still hold key committee positions helpful in defending tobacco. Whitley, Jones, and Congressman Charles G. Rose (Democrat, North Carolina) sit on the House Agriculture Committee. Rose chairs the Tobacco and Peanut Subcommittee, where he can make trade-offs with congressmen from other states. In the Senate, Senator Jesse Helms (Republican, North Carolina) is the chairman of the Agriculture Committee.

From this base, North Carolina congressmen can build broader coalitions as a part of their new strategy for backing tobacco. As a senatorial aide put it, "The politics of tobacco is really the politics of a coalition of agricultural interests." At the conclusion of a pro-tobacco speech on the Senate floor in 1980, then Senator Morgan seemed to be speaking to a broader group of potential allies than tobacco spokesmen have in the past. If the tobacco program is gutted, Morgan warned, "Watch chaos enter into an otherwise stable and tranquil area. Watch the number of family farms decline even more."

Sticking together has become a more visible strategy in recent years. In 1977, for example, the House of Representatives, by a 229-178 vote, made tobacco ineligible for export under the Food for Peace program. The defeat stunned tobacco-state congressmen. Sponsored by a little-known Colorado Republican, the bill showed that Congress, without a vigorous counter-effort by tobacco defenders, was willing to strip away some government-endowed advantages for tobacco. The Food for Peace program, which historically had included tobacco along with foodstuffs, was a vulnerable target in Washington because of the celebrated anti-smoking campaign of Health, Education, and Welfare (HEW) Secretary Joseph Califano.

The Senate eventually restored tobacco as a legal part of the Food for Peace program, largely because of the efforts of the late Senator Hubert H. Humphrey of Minnesota, who supported the tobacco program out of loyalty to farm-support systems. Even with Humphrey's intervention, thirty-seven votes in the one hundred-member Senate were against tobacco.

Later in the 1977 session, legislation to phase out the tobacco price-support program was deflected when tobacco-state congressmen let it be known they would vote against a sugar-support program if sugar-state

congressmen did not back tobacco. And in another effort to broaden political support for tobacco, seven North Carolina congressmen voted in 1978
for federal loan guarantees for New York City. "That was our tobacco
swap," Rose said later. "We'll try to help New York if New York will help
the tobacco area."

As a general strategy, North Carolina congressmen seek to keep
tobacco-related legislation off the House and Senate floors, for fear that a
bill involving tobacco will provide anti-smoking forces an opportunity to
try to change the government's policy toward the commodity. As 1981 approached, when other commodity programs were due for renewal, there
was discussion in Washington about whether to have a section in the Omnibus Farm Bill make some changes in the price-support system, particularly
to help with export sales. A similar issue arose in 1977 and provided an illus-
tration of the political influence of the North Carolina Farm Bureau Feder-
ation. At that time, farm organizations from every other tobacco-growing
state backed some alterations in the price supports, but as a result of the
lone opposition of the North Carolina organization, the idea of tobacco legislation was scuttled.

Although the farm-support program occupies the principal attention of
the congressional delegation, recent efforts to increase the federal cigarette
tax, which has remained at eight cents per pack for about twenty-five years,
have also caused some concern. But in the new spirit of cooperation,
tobacco-state congressmen show a begrudging tolerance for the possibility
of a modest increase. "A slight increase in tobacco taxes might be hard to
defeat," said Jones. "I'm not accepting it, but I don't think a slight increase will cause any great havoc in the retail market."

"It's Perceived as a Sensitive Subject"

While the state's congressmen in Washington have the primary responsibility of maintaining the farm-support program, the Raleigh-based political
leadership has a more narrow responsibility: to promote the concerns of tobacco farmers and cigarette manufacturing already in place in the state. But
such a task is getting more difficult than it was in the past. "Basically, you
have to fight a delaying action," says Grimsley, the Hunt cabinet member.
"In time tobacco will be a much smaller economic factor. That's why we
have to get industrial jobs in the east."

State officials have not yet publicly admitted the possibility that the tobacco economy could be in a decline. Hunt has not linked his search for new
industry with a threatened tobacco economy, and Agriculture Commissioner Graham has not described crop diversification as an alternative to tobacco. Instead, North Carolina officials have fought the most visible and
most easily accepted battles.

For a while, HEW Secretary Califano was an easy target for Tarheel officials to score points with their constituents. Hunt and Morgan met with President Carter about Califano's anti-smoking campaign, and later Carter agreed to come to Wilson, North Carolina, where he reaffirmed his support for the tobacco program. But at the same time, Carter permitted an expanded anti-smoking campaign to proceed. And when Califano left the cabinet, state officials not only were left without their bête noire, but they also faced the reality of a changing tobacco world.

Recently, state officials have begun to confront at least some immediate threats to tobacco. In June 1980, for example, before the annual gathering of the Flue-Cured Tobacco Cooperative Stabilization Corporation, Hunt gave a pro-tobacco political speech, but he also issued a sober warning. He told the farmers that unless they moderated their use of the chemical MH (maleic hydrazide), which controls tobacco suckers, West Germany, one of America's largest foreign tobacco markets, might not buy North Carolina tobacco. Stabilization has since initiated a program to monitor excessive MH residues, a step that might help retain the lucrative West German market.

Although some hard talk on tobacco seems more possible than in the past, a tentative political freedom seems to be emerging as well. There is still no room in North Carolina politics for waffling on the price-support program, but, says Grimsley, "you can talk about it [smoking] as a youth education program." Governor Hunt reportedly told Califano that he would encounter no problems from North Carolina on his program of public-health education on smoking.

State leaders so far have limited their public discussions of tobacco's problems to meeting short-term emergencies like the MH issue or to accepting unpopular federal programs like the anti-smoking campaign. Without shouting about it, however, the Hunt administration apparently understands that industrialization could be needed to pick up the economic slack left by a possible tobacco decline—if not immediately, then in the next generation. And Graham seems to understand that tobacco is going through some profound changes as well.

"In twenty years, ten years, there's definitely going to be some change," explained Graham in a lengthy interview, which he opened by offering his visitor a gold tobacco-leaf lapel pin. "Smokers' tastes are different. This new generation coming on, I'm not sure what they'll be. . . . I don't stand up for tobacco because it will help me politically. I stand up for tobacco because I think it's right. . . . I'm not against tobacco, but tobacco has to make some adjustments."

Then, inadvertently, puffing on a cigar, Graham illustrated the quandary in which North Carolina politicians find themselves. He pointed to pictures of his grandchildren on the shelf behind his desk. "When your own grandchildren, when that pretty young thing up there asks you about smoking—Bam!'' The back of his hand slashed quickly across his desk, signaling how vigorously he would rebuke a youngster wanting to smoke. Even though they know intellectually that the future of tobacco depends heavily on a new generation of smokers, Graham, as well as many other North Carolina politicians, would discourage a teenager from smoking.

Finally Graham turned his attention to the political evolution in his home state. New attitudes are accompanying new industry, he said. With Hunt (who grew up on a farm) as governor, Graham said, there remains a strong advocate for tobacco and other agriculture programs. But beyond 1984, Graham speculated, ''that's when you're going to see a turn, a whole new outlook on how this state is ruled. We are definitely moving out of an agrarian society into a mixture.''

By seeking out new industry, Hunt is stimulating this evolution, which ultimately should diminish further tobacco's importance in the North Carolina economy. Hunt continues to advocate the cause of tobacco growing and manufacturing in the state, but, without publicly articulating it, he is in effect attempting to expand an industrial base that may one day provide an alternative to the economics of tobacco. In that sense, a politician is trying to control events with a bearing on the future of this tobacco-oriented state.

But as they approach the issue of tobacco's future, North Carolina politicians are not so much exercising leadership as they are being controlled by circumstances. By refusing to address frankly tobacco's possible demise, they risk losing the opportunity to regain control over events that will affect the lives of every North Carolinian. If tobacco farming is going to decline, political leaders have a responsibility to address the dilemma head-on—to find ways of preserving rural traditions, to stimulate more intensive research on tobacco as a source of nutrients rather than nicotine, to seek alternatives, and to explore options before the future arrives.

''It's perceived as a sensitive subject,'' says an aide to a North Carolinian in Congress. ''Your average politician thinks in the short term. We're talking about long term.'' And all the while, Atlas's burden is getting heavier.

29 In the Public Interest . . . Not a Constitutional Birthright: An Interview with Former U.S. Secretary of Agriculture Robert Bergland

Blaine Harden

Author: Robert Bergland

On March 31, 1980, Washington Post *staff writer Blaine Harden conducted a taped interview with then U.S. Secretary of Agriculture Robert Bergland concerning federal tobacco policy. A midwesterner, Bergland had to learn tobacco from the top down. His successor, John Block from Illinois, has also had to absorb the nuances of the tobacco program while presiding over its administration.*

Unlike Block, however, Bergland had been a congressman (1970-1976), a product of Minnesota's Democratic-Farmer-Labor party. Bergland was extremely popular in his Minnesota district (he won 73 percent of the vote in 1976) and a prominent member of the U.S. House Agriculture Committee. A nonsmoker from outside the tobacco belt, Bergland had a sympathetic ear for the anti-smoking lobby that became very active in the early 1970s. At the same time, Bergland represented a farm district and knew the importance of crop-support programs. In 1976, Jimmy Carter, a peanut farmer with close ties to the tobacco-producing states, appointed Bergland Secretary of Agriculture.

During his tenure (1977-1981), Secretary Bergland appointed a U.S. Department of Agriculture (USDA) Tobacco Task Force headed by Bobby Smith, a Georgian and a close friend of President Carter. Bergland, as this interview reflects, recognized that the federal program needed some modification and that smoking-and-health controversies would remain a factor in determining agricultural policies. Yet he felt that "it is in the public interest to maintain the price-support program." His remarks provide a valuable yardstick for assessing how the Reagan administration and those which follow will approach the perplexing problems of the federal tobacco-support system.

Have the smoking-and-health controversies made you ambivalent about the federal tobacco program?

More than two years ago, then HEW Secretary Joe Califano was engaged in an enterprise to acquaint the American people with the pitfalls of smoking. In the process, he aroused the ire of the tobacco-producing industry in North Carolina. Joe called me to discuss the issue and we met and agreed on some ground rules. We in USDA [agreed] not to frustrate or complicate—indeed to support—the HEW studies on the effects of smoking. To the extent we can, we have contributed to the ongoing HEW research into smoking and health. Joe Califano in turn agreed he would not get involved in the price-supports side of the industry because [the health and the farm-support system] were really two separate issues. We have conducted our affairs in similar fashion since. Pat Harris (Califano's successor) and I have continued this relationship.

Tinkering with price supports is simply fooling with the lever that has nothing to do with the central question. The smoking issue should be decided on its merit. In our view, reducing the price of tobacco is not going to discourage smoking. And until the general public has decided on the fate of smoking, we believe it is in the public interest to maintain the price-support program.

[The tobacco program] affects about 600,000 families. Tobacco is the sole source of income for, we think, about 100,000 families, the major source of cash income for another 100,000, and an important source of income for the rest. Unfortunately, it is the very small, remote farm that depends most heavily on tobacco, especially in the burley regions of Kentucky and Tennessee. Were it not for tobacco income there would be a wholesale abandonment of the region. Tobacco income runs anywhere from $1,000 to $2,500 an acre. The average operating tobacco farmer grows about ten acres of tobacco—less in the burley regions and more in the flue-cured regions. For the most part, income from tobacco is greater than from any other crop on a per-acre basis.

Does the USDA price-support system, by ensuring tobacco prices above open-market levels, constitute a welfare program?

In some ways, that is true. There isn't any doubt that the tobacco program has had a major impact in the preservation of probably 200,000 of these very small farmers that have absolutely no economic alternative. It keeps those families busy in their hometown. They make a living. If they were forced to leave their communities and go into cities, how many would be tax users through welfare programs? I can't even guess. But I can say they are substantially better off today where they are in a rural setting with a fairly modest income. We are not talking about folks getting rich; we are talking about them staying alive. An objective [of the program] is indeed a sort of social engineering.

But as mechanization moves into the flue-cured tobacco business, we need to examine carefully the role of the government price-support program. We have no intention of subsidizing persons who don't need federal subsidy. We are looking at the impact of price supports on farm size. We know that price supports [nationwide] benefit the very large farm a lot more than the small farm. Indeed, we argue that two-thirds of the farms in the United States benefit very little from price supports. So this business of saving the small family farm by engineering high price supports can be a contradiction in terms.

Older farmers talk of their allotment as though it is a sacred birthright. If the government took away their allotment, they seem to think it would be a crime similar to stealing their property. How do you view the "birthright" issue?

When we examine the tobacco program in 1981, we are going to examine that question. [Many farm-support programs, unlike tobacco, have to be renewed periodically. The 1981 Omnibus Farm Bill will accomplish this. Tobacco-area congressmen have traditionally avoided amending the tobacco program under an omnibus bill for fear of having the entire program abolished. Bergland was apparently considering a review of the tobacco program during the 1981 congressional deliberations.] I know it will be an emotional thing. But we are going to look at it to see whether there is any public benefit derived from a price-support program that grants to an allotment holder a value that is simply a federal license. I have no interest in supporting a program that simply pumps a windfall account. There has got to be some public benefit from all of this—because [the allotment] is not a constitutional birthright.

Do you anticipate any changes in the support program?

We are having some problems with the program, but nothing that is going to sink it. The law does not give the Secretary any discretion for establishing "differentials" [in price-support levels] for the lower grades of tobacco. As a consequence, the poorest quality [grades] tend to accumulate in the inventories of the CCC [Commodity Credit Corporation]. [The unsold leaf actually accumulates in the inventories of the farmers' cooperatives certified to buy tobacco not sold on the open market. The cooperatives use nonrecourse loans from the CCC to finance these purchases; *nonrecourse* means that if the inventories cannot be sold at a profit, the loans do not have to be repaid. See chapter 2 for a full explanation of all the aspects of the price-support system.] This has become something of a problem. The law is written in such a way that if I lower the price of the lower-quality leaves, I have to raise the price of the higher-quality leaves, putting them substantially above the market price. I've discussed the matter with the industry and the leaders of Congress. The general expectation is that in 1981 there will be an amendment to the [federal] tobacco law which would authorize the widening of differentials. [This would] bring the price supports on the poorest qualities of tobacco down in the market range so those tobaccos clear the market. At some price they will sell, but at the moment, they are priced too high. This amendment would allow me to reduce [rates for] the lower-quality leaves without changing [rates for] the upper quality. I expect the amendment will be carried in the Omnibus Farm Bill of 1981. [As this book goes to press, this amendment was not included in the Omnibus Farm Bill.]

What would abolishing the support program do?

It would have major economic impact and result in some pretty substantial dislocation. It isn't like deciding upon the choice between corn and soybeans, a viable choice. It's a matter of farming or quitting.

In a competitive marketplace, without a price-support program, the price would drop substantially in the beginning because there are more growers than buyers. The smaller, at least the weaker growers, would be driven out of business. As things settled down, prices would come back up again, but fewer people would be left. How many fewer, I don't think we know. But it would be substantially fewer.

Can states like North Carolina diversify their economy and absorb the great economic losses of what many predict will be a dwindling tobacco industry?

Yes. The growth in job opportunities in rural areas is the one bright spot in our whole economy. We target our rural development efforts in those kinds of places where we know that there is pressure on the agricultural base brought on by mechanization and now more recently by this smoking [and health] business. We are looking at economic alternatives, some of which are agriculturally oriented. We expect that in time the [health concerns] will reduce the demand for tobacco and that those farmers have to have an alternative. The government should provide an alternative. We are all better off if [the farmers] can stay at home and get a good job rather than [being] forced into a migrant camp some place.

Can people look past the seeming contradiction of the government spending about $53 million a year on anti-smoking efforts and over $300 million a year through USDA on the tobacco-growing industry?

Strictly from a taxpayer's viewpoint, the program is a money-maker— tobacco generates $6 billion a year in tax revenues and only costs $300 million. But this is not a justification for maintaining the tobacco program. Nor should the health issue be decided on tax policy. The two must be separated. We should take the smoking issue head-on and decide if we are going to ban smoking and restrict its use. Then we have to consider not only the production of tobacco, but its importation. We haven't done anything about the health issue if we simply eliminate price supports.

It's the health issue that has everyone excited. I'd like to see a vote in Congress on whether the production, sale, and importation of cigarettes should be banned or not. I know how I'd vote. I'd vote to ban.

30 The Weed
William F. Buckley, Jr.

Smoking. What do we want the government to do about it? Suppose we argue by analogy and ask: What ought the government to do about alcohol? I
can, without even trying, whip up a sentence or two about alcohol that
would earn me honorary membership in the Anti-Saloon League. Watch:
There are (the figures are improvised, because I do not have the stomach to
ring up Alcoholics Anonymous to have them cross my statistical *t*'s or dot
the *i*'s) 5,000,000 American alcoholics; several thousand deaths per year
from biological failures whose proximate cause is alcoholism; 100,000 di-
vorces and 200,000 broken homes per year that result from alcoholic excess;
several hundred thousand children traumatized by a childhood spent with
alcoholic parents; $50 billion per year lost to the economy as the result of
the diminished productivity of men and women who drink too much;
75,000 serious crimes per year committed under the licentious influence of
alcohol . . . enough? But it all is true, and the government does practically
nothing about the sale or distribution of liquor.

Once upon a time it tried to do something, and we know all about the
miserable failure of the experiment and the damage it did to the prestige of
the law. Granted there is a minority opinion that continues to believe the
contrary—and not all who hold it are teetotalers by any means. Henry
Mencken used to say that a sizable number of Kansans would continue to
vote dry every election day so long as they could stagger to the polls and lo-
cate the right lever.

While we are at it, we know as an established fact that obesity is a great
killer. The doctor who cured Dwight Eisenhower after his awesome heart
attack and whose word on the subject has, I am told, influenced Lyndon
Johnson—who also came to the brink because of an unsteady heart—has
said flatly that there are three basic rules for longevity. One must not smoke
cigarettes, one must exercise one's body, and one must not gain weight after
the age of twenty-five. The latter is the most important of the three, according to settled medical testimony.

What then should the government do? Have the census takers weigh us
in, like prizefighters, and commit offenders to Main Chance, until the
avoirdupois melts away? Along, of course, with extra subsidies for farmers,

This chapter, reprinted by permission from William F. Buckley, Jr., appeared in *The Jeweler's
Eye* by William F. Buckley, Jr. (G.P. Putnams, 1968).

325

to compensate them for those of their products which go unconsumed as the result of the program?

We speak nonsense, of course. Yes. Of course. Yes. . . . But we are left feeling a great void, because we are nowadays trained to believe that the government is charged with all matters that deal with the common health. With the common everything, let's face it, and I for one do not doubt that except for the fact that the majority of us are sinners, as regards smoking, as regards alcohol, as regards cholesterol, as regards layer cakes, and apostles of central authority would be calling on the government to do just that—tell us how much, or whether, we can smoke, drink, eat. But let's face it, a political party that takes on all the smokers in this country or all the drinkers will die, if not a more hideous death than those of us who will succumb to lung cancer or cirrhosis of the liver, a much speedier one. We would be entitled to look such a political party in the eye and say to it what one of Rabelais's besotted characters said to his censorious physician: "Forsooth, sir, I do believe I know more old drunkards than I do old doctors."

I do not mean to make light of the subject. My wife is an inveterate cigarette smoker. Need I say more? I suggest only that the government cannot, for reasons that go to the womb of freedom, do anything, anything at all, about smoking. I would not endorse a law requiring the cigarette companies to advertise the dangers of smoking. But I would consider it consistent with the laws of a free society to hold that any company that declined to specify the known dangers of the use of its product become liable to damage actions by victims. But the courts should then hold immune from prosecution those tobacco companies which emblazon, on every pack of cigarettes, the warning: SMOKING CAN CAUSE LUNG CANCER. SMOKE AT YOUR OWN RISK. From there on, it's up to the individual. It pays to remind ourselves that the most important things of all are up to the individual, who can opt, after all, for heaven or hell. That is the way the rules were written well before the surgeon general's report.

Index

Grand Marnier liqueur, 191
Grand Metropolitan Limited, 191, 192, 224
Great Britain, 121, 123, 138, 140, 145,
    146, 149, 151, 160, 167, 168, 180, 185,
    206, 210, 216, 227, 235-236, 309
Greece, 120, 175, 269, 270, 306
Green County, N.C., 50-55
Grigson, W.H., 249
Grimsley, Joseph W., 314, 316, 317
Grimstead, Sidney, 192
Grise, Verner, 68-69, 70
Group therapy, 253
Gulf and Western, 203, 209-210, 214

Hammon, E.C., 258
Harnett, A.L., 249
Harrington Manufacturing Company, 42,
    48
Harrington, Milton E., 190
Harris, Patricia, 320
Harvesting machine, 41, 42, 48-49, 65-
    66, 97
Haus Neuerberg (Germany), 207
Hawaiian Punch company, 172
Hazardous occupations, and smoking, 238-
    239
Health agencies (federal/state), regulatory
    role of, 242-243
Health-education models, 247-254
Health hazards. See Smoking and health
Health Services and Centers Amendments
    (1978), 243, 300
Heart disease, 236, 237, 241, 243, 256, 258,
    267-274
Heartbook (AHA), 270
Heimann, Robert, 182-183, 184-185
Helms, Jesse, 315
Hobbs, William, 171
Hockett, Robert, 295
Hodges, Luther, 104
Holding company, defined, 216
Home Run cigarettes, 190
Homogenized leaf-curing, 113
Honduras, 214, 218
Horrigan, Edward, Jr., 222
Howard Johnson, 210
Humphrey, Hubert H., 315
Hunt, James B., 104-105, 313, 314, 316,
    317, 318
Hypnosis, 253

IBM, 106, 107
Iceland, 306
Imasco, 207, 210
Imperial Tobacco Company, 145-146, 149,
    160, 180, 203, 206, 207, 210, 212
Income, per capita, 53, 230, 320. See also
    Wage rates

Income-transfer programs, 50, 52, 53-54,
    56, 58
India, 120, 121, 140, 147
Infant formulas, 156
International Digest of Health Legislation,
    298, 301
International Union Against Cancer: Special
    Project on Smoking and Lung Cancer,
    259
Interstate Commerce Commission, 290, 300
Iran, 174; Iranian consortium, 172, 208
Ireland, 185, 307
Irrigation, 97
Italy, 120, 121, 140, 154, 179, 203, 208,
    269, 270, 307

J&B Scotch, 191
James I, 235
James B. Beam Distilling Company, 182,
    184
Jamestown, Va., 120
Japan, 120, 121, 122, 127, 138, 139, 151,
    203, 206, 208, 269, 270
Jelliffe, Derrick, 156
"Job development," 225
Jones, Walter, 313, 315, 316
Journal of the American Medical Associa-
    tion, 268
Journal of Epidemiology and Community
    Health, 272
J.P. Morgan and Company, 214
Judge, Curtis, 187-188

Kaiser-Permanente Medical Care Program,
    270, 271
Kannel, W.B., 258
Katz, Arnie, 101
Kent cigarettes, 163, 184, 187, 188
Kenya, 153
Kerr Tobacco Act (1934), 31
Keys, A., 268-269, 270
Koch, A., 258
Koch Label Company, 209
Kohl Corporation, 182
Kool cigarettes, 168, 181, 182
Kornegay, Harold, 237-238
Kuwait, 153, 174

Labor displacement, 40, 45, 47-48, 49-
    57, 69-72, 212, 213, 223, 225, 227
Land development, 178, 199, 209
Lark cigarettes, 190
Latin America, 121, 152, 156, 168, 208,
    214, 215
Leaf Tobacco Exporters Association, 87-88
Lease-and-transfer program, 16, 24, 34,
    38, 40-41, 42-43, 49, 52-53, 56, 66-69,
    137

About the Contributors

Frank Adams is a writer and community educator who has worked extensively with farmer cooperatives.

Anthony J. Badger attended Cambridge University and Hull University where he received the Ph.D. in American history in 1974. Dr. Badger began researching the roots of the American tobacco program during a year of study at North Carolina State University (1969-1970).

Gigi Berardi received the Ph.D. in resources, policy, and planning from Cornell University in 1979. An assistant professor in the Department of Geography, University of Maryland Baltimore County, Dr. Berardi received a Fulbright-Hays Award for advanced research in Italy for the 1980-1981 year where she studied the energy efficiency and environmental impact of agricultural production systems.

William F. Buckley, Jr., is a journalist, author, and commentator.

John Campbell was vice-president of the American Leaf Organization of Imperial Tobacco Limited from 1966-1980. He now directs his own consulting company, which specializes in tobacco and tropical agriculture in North Carolina. From 1978 to 1980, he served on the U.S. Chamber of Commerce Food and Agriculture Committee.

Frederick F. Clairmonte is a senior economics affairs officer with the United Nations Conference on Trade and Development (UNCTAD) and an analyst of transnational corporations. He studied at McGill and Geneva Universities, received the D.Sc. in economics, and has taught at King's College, Dalhousie University, the Indian Institute of Science in Bangalore, and the Stockholm School of Economics. He is the author of *Economic Liberalism and Underdevelopment* and coauthor of *The Web They Weave: The Dynamics of Transnational Oligopolies in Fibres and Textiles* (forthcoming). He is a regular contributor to *Le Monde Diplomatique*.

Robert Dalton, a former staff member at the North Carolina Center for Public Policy Research, is completing graduate work in political science at the University of North Carolina at Chapel Hill.

J.C.B. Ehringhaus, Jr., is general counsel to The Tobacco Institute.

Ferrel Guillory has been a political reporter for *The News and Observer* of Raleigh, North Carolina, since 1972, as chief capitol correspondent and head of the Washington Bureau. Now associate editor, he is responsible for the editorial page.

Blaine Harden is a staff writer for *The Washington Post.*

J. Barlow Herget, formerly an editorial writer for *The News and Observer* of Raleigh, North Carolina, served as special assistant to North Carolina Secretary of Commerce D.M. (Lauch) Faircloth from January 1977 to May 1979. He now works for Data General Corporation in Clayton, North Carolina.

D. Hoffmann is associate director of the American Health Foundation's Naylor Dana Institute for Disease Prevention and chief of its Division of Environmental Carcinogenesis. Dr. Hoffmann has written, lectured, and taught widely in the public-health field and has conducted a number of primary research projects concerning tobacco.

Albert Huebner teaches physics at West Coast University and does documentary programming on science and health for radio station KPFK in Los Angeles.

Joel D. Joseph, general counsel to Federal Employees for Non-Smokers' Rights, is an attorney in private practice in Washington, D.C. After receiving the J.D. at Georgetown University Law School, he became assistant general counsel to Action on Smoking and Health.

Harriet Kestenbaum received the M.P.H. in health planning from the University of North Carolina at Chapel Hill. She is currently a research analyst for the North Carolina Department of Human Resources.

Hugh C. Kiger received the Ph.D. in agricultural economics from North Carolina State University in 1949. He is executive vice-president of the Leaf Tobacco Exporters Association. Prior to taking that position in 1975, Dr. Kiger completed thirty years of government service, primarily with the U.S. Department of Agriculture (USDA). From 1961-1975, Dr. Kiger was director of the Tobacco Division of the Foreign Agriculture Service of the USDA. He has received many honors within the tobacco and international trade community. He was a member of the official U.S. agricultural advisory committee at the 1979 Tokyo Round of the General Agreement on

Trade and Tariffs, and he served as a tobacco consultant to North Carolina Governor James Hunt on the governor's trade trip to China.

Joseph A. Kinney is staff director for the Committee on Agriculture, National Governors' Association. He has been the chief agricultural aide to former U.S. Senators Hubert Humphrey (Democrat, Minnesota) and Robert Morgan (Democrat, North Carolina).

Marcy S. Kramer, a graduate of Mount Holyoke College, is a former assistant to Joel D. Joseph, a contributor to this book.

Charles K. Mann received the Ph.D. in economics from Harvard University in 1971. He received the award for "Professional Excellence" from the American Agricultural Economics Association for his analysis of the tobacco industry, which was expanded into the book, *Tobacco: The Ants and the Elephants*. He is associate director for Agricultural and Social Sciences at the Rockefeller Foundation where he and his colleagues are developing a food and agricultural policy program.

John Maxwell is the chief tobacco analyst for Lehman Brothers Kuhn Loeb brokerage firm. For the last twenty years, Mr. Maxwell has prepared a yearly outlook of the tobacco industry for *Advertising Age* and other publications.

James Overton is research director of the Institute for Southern Studies. He has studied a number of southern industries, particularly textiles, tobacco, and power companies.

John M. Pinney is director of the Office on Smoking and Health, Public Health Service, U.S. Department of Health and Human Services.

Charles Pugh, an extension economist at North Carolina State University, received the Ph.D. from Purdue University in 1961. He has written extensively concerning tobacco issues and conducts educational programs through the Extension Service regarding the economics of tobacco.

Carl C. Seltzer is currently an honorary senior research associate, Harvard University; professor of nutrition, Tufts University; and Fellow, Council on Epidemiology, American Heart Association. He has published widely and conducted extensive research on heart disease.

Bruce Siceloff has been a staff writer for *The News and Observer* of Raleigh, North Carolina, since 1976, frequently reporting on the North Carolina tobacco industry.

J. Paul Sticht is chairman of the board and chief executive officer of R.J. Reynolds Industries.

Elizabeth Tornquist, a free-lance writer and a longtime analyst of the North Carolina economy, currently teaches communications at the University of North Carolina School of Nursing.

George Weissman is chairman of the board and chief executive officer of Philip Morris, Incorporated.

E.L. Wynder is founder and president of the American Health Foundation in New York. He has written, lectured, and taught widely in the public-health field, and has conducted a number of primary research projects concerning tobacco.

About the Editor

William R. Finger is a free-lance writer with training in economics (Duke University) and southern history (University of North Carolina). His articles have appeared in *The New York Times*, *The Washington Post*, *Christian Century*, *Southern Exposure*, and other publications. He is currently editor of *N.C. Insight*, the magazine of the North Carolina Center for Public Policy Research.